The Lottery of Life:
Scholes Family 1814–2016

The Lottery of Life: Scholes Family 1814–2016

Four Generations from Lancashire and Wisconsin

by Harold A. Henderson, CG

Harold A. Henderson

2021

The Lottery of Life: Scholes Family 1814–2016

Creative Commons Attribution-NonCommercial-ShareAlike (CC-BY-NC-SA)

https://creativecommons.org/share-your-work/licensing-types-examples/#by-nc-sa

2021 by Harold A. Henderson, CG, La Porte, Indiana
librarytraveler@gmail.com

Subjects: Genealogy, Family History, England, Wisconsin, Scholes, Stocks, Mills, Sherwin, Hume, Smith, Dixon, Audiss, Hull, Heames, Boren, Russell, Ellison

First Printing: 2021

ISBN: 978-1-7343752-2-0

Printed in the United States

Dedication

To Sandy, *sine qua non*

Table of Contents

PEOPLE FINDER BY DESCENT AND CHAPTER..0

INTRODUCTION...1

PREQUEL ESCAPE FROM THE COTTON FACTORY..5

ENGLISH GENERATION

CHAPTER 1. SAMUEL[4] MILLS–ALICE STOCKS FAMILY...9

FIRST GENERATION
(1814-1875, presidents Madison to Grant)

CHAPTER 2.. ANN MILLS[1]–WILLIAM SCHOLES FAMILY...11

SECOND GENERATION
(1835-1941, presidents Jackson to Franklin Roosevelt)

CHAPTER 3. MARY SCHOLES[2]–BISSELL SHERWIN FAMILY...23

CHAPTER 4. SARAH ANN SCHOLES[2]–ROBERT WALKER HUME SR. FAMILY 29

CHAPTER 5. ELIZABETH SCHOLES[2] FAMILY 37

CHAPTER 6. ALICE SCHOLES[2]–JOSEPH COCKROFT SMITH FAMILY 41

CHAPTER 7. ROBERT[2] SCHOLES–CAROLINE CORNELIA PARKES + ELLISON FAMILY 45

TABLE 1. SCHOLES-ELLISON FAMILIES: SEVEN SOMEWHAT RELATED CHILDREN 54

CHAPTER 8. SAMUEL MILLS[2] SCHOLES–HARRIET NEWELL MOZLEY FAMILY 55

    STORY 1. TRAVELING IN MINNESOTA IN 1879 57

CHAPTER 9. WILLIAM[2] SCHOLES–MARY ELLEN DIXON FAMILY 61

CHAPTER 10. GEORGE WALKER[2] SCHOLES–SUSANNA REBECCA AUDISS FAMILY 65

CHAPTER 11. JAMES MILLS[2] SCHOLES–EMMA MARIA HULL FAMILY 69

THIRD GENERATION (& FOURTH GENERATION THROUGH 2016)
(1856-1995, presidents Pierce to Clinton)

CHAPTER 12. CHARLES TRUMAN[3] SHERWIN–JANE THRESSA YOUNG FAMILY 73

CHAPTER 13. FRANCIS RODERICK "FRANK"[3] SHERWIN–ANNIE HENRY FAMILY 85

CHAPTER 14. WILLIAM ORLANDO[3] SHERWIN–HARRIET M. MANLEY–LOTTIE MAZIE TAYLOR FAMILY 95

CHAPTER 15. FLORA ANN[3] SHERWIN–JOHN JAMES BELL FAMILY 105

CHAPTER 16. MARGARET ALICE[3] "MAGGIE" HUME–JUDSON STILES BERRY FAMILY 111

    STORY 2. THE BERRY PATCH AND ITS HOUSE (ON THE EVE OF WW2) 119

CHAPTER 17. ROBERT WALKER[3] HUME, JR.–ALICE SARAH SMITH FAMILY 123

CHAPTER 18. WILLIAM SCHOLES³ HUME–ELIZA MAY "LIDA" SUTCLIFF FAMILY..................................133

    STORY 3. ENDEAVOR CHRISTIAN ACADEMY (1890–1926)..145

CHAPTER 19. SARAH ANN JANET "NETTIE"³ HUME–HENRY EDEN JONES FAMILY.....................149

CHAPTER 20. JAMES SAMUEL³ HUME–LYDIA ALBERTA "BIRDIE" SAWYER FAMILY 163

    STORY 4. SHOWDOWN IN NORTH DAKOTA, 1918 169

CHAPTER 21. GEORGE WALKER³ HUME–LOIS/LOUISE DEMOTT FAMILY 179

CHAPTER 22. WILLIAM HENRY³ SMITH–RUTH ROSIE HAINES FAMILY................................185

CHAPTER 23. EVA FLORENCE³ SMITH–RICHARD ALBERT BEICHL FAMILY.............................193

CHAPTER 24. MARY IRENE³ SMITH FAMILY 199

CHAPTER 25. ROBERT JOSEPH³ SMITH–MYRTLE M. PAGE FAMILY...201

CHAPTER 26. NETTIE A.³ SCHOLES–THOMAS CLARENCE MORAN FAMILY 205

CHAPTER 27. MARY H.³ SCHOLES–WILLIAM ROBERT HEAMES FAMILY....................................215

CHAPTER 28. HATTIE C.³ SCHOLES–JOHN RODNEY SCHWEMERLEIN FAMILY 229

CHAPTER 29. ELEANOR "NELLIE" ELIZABETH³ SCHOLES FAMILY 233

CHAPTER 30. BONNIE ELIZABETH³ SCHOLES......235

CHAPTER 31. SAMUEL RAY^3 SCHOLES–LOIS E. BOREN FAMILY 239

CHAPTER 32. MARION EDITH^3 SCHOLES FAMILY 255

CHAPTER 33. LILLIAN ESTELLE^3 SCHOLES–FRED GAYLORD RUSSELL FAMILY 259

    TABLE 2. SCHOLES AND RUSSELL, ALLIED FAMILIES 263

CHAPTER 34. ELMER ROY^3 SCHOLES–MARY ELSIE ROOD FAMILY 265

CHAPTER 35. SAMUEL EUGENE^3 SCHOLES–EDNA PEAKE FAMILY 273

CHAPTER 36. ROBERT HENRY^3 SCHOLES–PEARL ALIDA EDWARDS FAMILY 279

CHAPTER 37. RUTH EMMA^3 SCHOLES–LEO ROBLESKE–GEORGE REDMAN FAMILY 289

INDEX 295

People Finder by Descent and Chapter

Name & Spouse	Life & Places	Descendant Chapters
Gen. A		
1. Samuel Mills m. Alice Stocks	married 4 Jan 1810 Lancashire, ENG	Chapter 2
Gen. 1 1814-1875		**Presidents Madison-Grant**
2. Ann Mills m. William Scholes	1814 ENG–1875 WI 1814 ENG–1864 MS	Chapters 3–11
Gen. 2 1835-1941		**Presidents Jackson-FDR**
3. Mary Scholes m. Bissell Sherwin	1835 ENG–1910 WI 1823 NY–1864 VA	Chapters 12–15
4. Sarah Ann Scholes m. Robt. W. Hume Sr.	1837 ENG–1874 WI 1833 SCOT–1915 WI	Chapters 16–21
5. Elizabeth Scholes	1842 ENG–1929 WI	–
6. Alice Scholes m. Joseph C. Smith	1845 ENG–1923 WI 1840 ENG–1908 WI	Chapters 22–25
7. Robert Scholes m. Caroline C. Parkes	1847 ENG–1885 WI 1848 WI–1936 WI	Chapters 26–28
8. Saml. Mills Scholes m. Harriet N. Mozley	1849 WI–1914 WI 1855 WI–1950 CA	Chapters 29–31
9. William Scholes m. Mary Ellen Dixon	1854 WI–1929 WI 1856 ENG–1920 WI	Chapter 32
10. Geo. W. Scholes m. Susanna R. Audiss	1857 WI–1941 WI 1861 ENG–1931 WI	Chapters 33–35
11. James M. Scholes m. Emma Maria Hull	1859 WI–1936 WI 1858 WI–1942 WI	Chapters 36–37
Gen. 3 1856-1995		**Presidents Pierce-Clinton**
12. Charles Sherwin m. Jane T. Young	1856 WI–1910 WI 1856 OH–1914 MT	
13. Frank R. Sherwin m. Annie Henry	1858 WI–1929 WI 1861 WI–1935 IA	
14. Wm. O. Sherwin m1. Harriet Manley m2. Lottie M. Taylor	1860 WI–1953 WI 1868 WI–1938 WI 1877 WI–1924 WI	
15. Flora A. Sherwin m. John James Bell	1862 WI–1925 WI 1853 WI–1917 WI	
16. Margaret Hume m. Judson Berry	1861 WI–1938 SD 1859 NY–1918 SD	
17. Robt. W. Hume Jr. m. Alice Sarah Smith	1863 WI–1940 WI 1867 WI–1951 WI	
18. William S. Hume m. Alida Sutcliffe	1866 WI–1948 WI 1870 IA–1968 WI	

19. Sarah Ann Hume m. Henry Eden Jones	1868 WI–1936 WI 1864 WI–1957 CA	
20. James S. Hume m. "Birdie" Sawyer	1871 WI–1936 CA 1877 MI–1964 CA	
21. Geo. W. Hume m. Lois DeMott	1874 WI–1952 WI 1876 WI–1962 WI	
22. Wm. Henry Smith m. Ruth Rosie Haines	1866 WI–1936 WI 1861 WI–1948 WI	
23. Florence E. Smith m. Richard Beichl	1876 WI–1962 WI 1859 WI–1927 WI	
24. Mary Irene Smith	1877 WI–1955 WI	–
25. Robert J. Smith m. Myrtle M. Page	1892 WI–1976 WI 1895 WI–1984 WI	
26. Nettie Scholes m. Thomas C. Moran	1869 WI–1952 WI 1862 WI–1923 WI	
27. Mary E. Scholes m. William Heames	1871 WI–1948 WI 1859 NJ–1924 WI	
28. Hattie Scholes m. J. R. Schwemerlein	1877 WI–1956 WI 1865 WI–1948 WI	–
29. Nellie E. Scholes	1878 WI–1948 CA	–
30. Bonnie E. Scholes	1882 WI–1957 CA	–
31. Samuel R. Scholes m. Lois E. Boren	1884 WI–1974 NY 1894 PA–1979 NY	
32. Marion E. Scholes	1890 WI–1962 WI	–
33. Lillian E. Scholes m. Fred G. Russell	1885 WI–1970 WI 1885 WI–1951 WI	
34. Elmer Scholes m. Elsie Rood	1891 WI–1955 WI 1893 WI–1988 WI	
35. Samuel E. Scholes m. Edna Peake	1895 WI–1983 WI 1900 WI–1989 WI	
36. Robert Scholes m. Pearl A. Edwards	1891 WI–1934 WI 1893 WI–1967 WI	
37. Ruth E. Scholes m1. Leo E. Robleske m2. George Redman	1897 WI–1995 PA 1903 WI–1941 WI 1878 PA–1948 PA	–

Introduction

William and Ann (Mills) Scholes and their descendants had good luck and worked hard, including the women. Ann bore eleven children in 23 years; her daughter Sarah Ann Scholes bore six in twelve years and died at 36. Most of William and Ann's children and grandchildren (and spouses) stayed in Wisconsin and were buried there.

This book follows those of William and Ann's descendants, spouses, and adoptive children who were no longer living at the end of 2016. Due to unanticipated difficulties at the time of writing, some footnotes refer to index entries rather than original records, and are so identified. For the reader's convenience, the book includes:

- a table of contents,
- a two-page "people finder,"
- a thorough index,
- footnotes (which can be ignored or perused at leisure), and
- as few abbreviations and acronyms as possible. The exceptions are "p." (page), "col." (column), "ED" (enumeration district, in US censuses from 1880 through 1940), and FHL and DGS numbers identifying particular microfilms or digitized images at familysearch.org.

No family history is ever complete or perfect, but something is better than nothing. Comments, additions, and corrections backed by evidence are welcome.[1] The great unsolved puzzle, not attempted here, is to identify William and Ann's English ancestors.

Family members and archivists have preserved and shared letters, records, and stories, without which there would be little to tell: Bonnie[3] and Nellie[3] Scholes, Ann[4] (Scholes) Colvin, James B.[4] Scholes, Norman[4] and Stella Scholes, and others lost in the mist of time. Special

---

[1] This book supersedes an earlier fragment: Harold Henderson, "From the First Industrial City to the Wisconsin Frontier: William Scholes (1814–1864), Ann Mills Scholes (1814–1871), and their Family," *Annals of Genealogical Research* 1:2 (2005) (genlit.org/agr/viewarticle.php?id-5).

thanks are also due to the "local mention" columns of relevant newspapers over the years; Barbara Voss, Joan Benner, Lois M. Wade, Sheryl Otto, and Darlene Lerum for untiring research back in the day; Roger G. Bentley, for locating and sharing information on the Potters' Emigration Society; and Lisa Alzo, for patiently shepherding this book and its predecessors through design and production.

William and Ann had 26 grandchildren (Generation 3), twenty of whom put down deep roots in Wisconsin and were buried there. William Scholes Hume (1866–1948, chapter 18) stayed in Moundville almost his whole life. Some went west until they ran out of country; a few went east.

Fame and fortune escaped most of William and Ann's descendants. Two family members who were repeatedly and widely honored for their work:

- glass chemist, professor, and writer Samuel Ray[3] Scholes (1884–1974, Chapter 31) of Alfred, New York, and his first cousin once removed,

- inventor, businessman, and philanthropist Horace Delbert[4] Hume (1898–2001, Chapter 20, child ii) of Mendota, Illinois.

Families sometimes commemorated events in their naming practices. Two family members, Hume McKinley Jones (1896–1980, Chapter 19, child iii) and his cousin-in-law Oscar McKinley Jenkins (1896–1946, Chapter 20, child iii) were evidently named for William McKinley of Ohio, the 1896 Republican presidential nominee and winner of that landmark election.

Many family members benefited from and contributed to the Congregational church project of establishing the Christian Endeavor Academy (1890–1926) to fill an educational and religious gap in central Wisconsin. (See story #3 for a probably incomplete list of Scholes descendants who attended there.) A reunion occurred as late as 1968.

Many women in the extended family taught school at various levels—before, during, after, or in lieu of marriage. Among them were
- Harriet Manley Sherwin (Chapter 14),

- Margaret Arnsdorf Sherwin (Chapter 14, child i),
- Elizabeth Rodger Berry (Chapter 16, child i),
- Lelah Moran Dahms (Chapter 26, child ii),
- Bonnie Scholes (Chapter 30),
- Doris Hahn Scholes (Chapter 31, child i),
- Ann Scholes Colvin (Chapter 31, child ii),
- Marion Edith Scholes (Chapter 32), and
- Ruth Scholes Robleske Redman (Chapter 37).

But we're getting ahead of ourselves. **Nothing in this book would ever have happened** if William Scholes had not won the lottery in 1849 and received a one-way trip from factory England to frontier Wisconsin.

Prequel: Escape from the Cotton Factory

At the end of 1848, thirty-four-year-old William Scholes was working at a cotton factory in Oldham, Lancashire, England. As a cotton carder, he operated a machine whose needle-pointed wires removed impurities and straightened the cotton fibers, readying them to be spun into cloth. The air in carding rooms was a haze of dust, and "carder's cough" a common medical complaint.[2]

In 1890 a history of three Wisconsin counties stated that William "learned the trade of a silk-weaver in his youth, but afterward worked in a cotton factory. He rose successively step by step until he became superintendent of the carding-room."[3]

This story, published a quarter-century after his death, may appeal to descendants, but there are three reasons to doubt it:

(1) Before they emigrated, between 1835 and 1847, William and Ann had six children baptized at St. Peter's Chapel in Oldham. In each case the baptismal record included names, dates, the family's residence, and the father's occupation. Over these twelve years the Scholes family lived in three different places, but William's recorded occupation remained exactly the same:

---

[2] Chris Aspin, *The Cotton Industry* (Shire Album 63, Shire Publications, 1981), 6–7. Factory name in 1903 letter from Samuel Mills Scholes to Arthur D. Marsh of New York, as transcribed into Scholes ledger book created by Bonnie and Nellie Scholes, 81, in author's possession. Note, however, that no such mill is named in the "Gazetteer of Mills" in Duncan Gurr and Julian Hunt, editors, *The Cotton Mills of Oldham*, 2nd edition (Oldham, England: Oldham Cultural and Information Services, 1989), 19–57.
[3] *Portrait and Biographical Album of Green Lake, Marquette, and Waushara Counties, Wisconsin* (Chicago: Acme Publishing, 1890), 757. Also, Harold Henderson, "Local Histories: Handle With Care," *Association of Professional Genealogists Quarterly* 31:140–41 (September 2016).

Child	Baptism	Family Residence	Father's Occupation
Mary	6 December 1835	Sugar Meadow	Carder
Sarah Ann	12 November 1837	Moorhey	Carder
Maria	10 May 1840	Moorhey	Carder
Betty	13 November 1842	Sheepwashes	Carder
Alice	11 May 1845	Sheepwashes	Carder
Robert	7 February 1847	Sheepwashes	Carder[4]

(2) US county histories in this era can provide helpful information but they were not scholarly enterprises. They were businesses whose survival depended on selling Horatio Alger myths.

(3) If William had indeed risen to a supervisory position, why would he join a workers' organization, or seek to leave England?

Evidence created in England at the time contradicts the assertions in the 1890 book. In fact, William's job did *not* change, he *did* join the Potters' Emigration Society (whose goal was to reduce the number of workers in England and thus increase the pay of the remainder), and his first ecstatic letter from Wisconsin showed little affection for the country or the job he had left (see Chapter 2).[5]

On New Year's Day 1849 William's long-shot bet came home, changing the family's life forever. He was one of six lottery winners at a

---

[4] Mary Scholes baptism, 6 December 1835, St. Peter's Chapel, Oldham, Lancashire, 1834–38, p. 84, #672; FHL #1,656,068, DGS #4,265,426, image 588 of 650 (familysearch.org). Sarah Ann Scholes baptism, 12 November 1837, St. Peter's Chapel, Oldham, Lancashire, 1834–38, p. 236, #1882; image 23 of 641, FHL #1,656,069, DGS #7,567,077 (familysearch.org). Similarly: Maria Scholes baptism, 10 May 1840, image 114 of 641; Betty [Elizabeth] Scholes baptism, 13 November 1842, image 234 of 641; Alice Scholes baptism 11 May 1845, image 301 of 641; and Robert Scholes baptism, 7 February 1847, image 355 of 641.

[5] Roger G. Bentley (Pierrefonds, Quebec) to Harold Henderson (La Porte, Indiana) letter 22 July 2002, in author's possession.

huge "tea party" held by the Lancashire chapter of the society.[6] Later that year the Scholes family embarked on a new life—learning to farm on the central Wisconsin frontier.

    . . . continued in Chapter 2 . . .

---

[6] Clipping from the *Staffordshire Advertiser*, 13 January 1849, courtesy of Roger G. Bentley.

ENGLISH GENERATION

Chapter 1

English Generation

Samuel Mills–Alice Stocks Family

"My brother-in-law Samuel Mills"

1. SAMUEL⁴ MILLS
Spouse: **ALICE STOCKS,** married 4 January 1810 at St. Mary's, Oldham, Lancashire, England⁷

Children of Samuel and Alice (Stocks) Mills, all baptized at St. Peter's Oldham, Lancashire:

    i. JOHN MILLS (*Samuel⁴*) was baptized 3 February 1811.⁸

2   ii. ANN¹ MILLS (*Samuel⁴*) was baptized 20 November 1814, and died 15 February 1875 in Wisconsin. She married 20 April 1835 at Prestwich, Lancashire, WILLIAM SCHOLES.

    iii. SAMUEL MILLS (*Samuel⁴*) was baptized 3 August 1817.⁹ In September 1849 William Scholes arranged for James Grey's share in the local branch of the Potters' Emigration Society to be transferred to "my brother-in-law," Samuel Mills of Bow Street, Oldham.¹⁰

    iv. SALLY MILLS (*Samuel⁴*) was baptized 4 May 1820.¹¹

---

⁷ Mills–Stocks marriage 4 January 1810; Marriages, St. Mary's, Oldham, Lancashire, 1809–12, p. 905, #1229; FHL #1,656,118, DGS #4,499,411 (familysearch.org).
⁸ John Mills baptism, St. Peter's, Oldham, Lancashire, 1803–1812, p. 83; FHL #1,655,906, DGS #4,265,425 (familysearch.org).
⁹ Samuel Mills baptism, St. Peter's, Oldham, Lancashire, 1813–18, p. 250; FHL #1,655,906, DGS #4,265,425 (familysearch.org).
¹⁰ William Scholes to the Oldham branch, Potters' Emigration Society, letter, 23 September 1849, as published in *Potters' Examiner and Emigrants' Advocate* 9(74):587–88, November 1849; supplied by Roger G. Bentley.
¹¹ Sally Mills baptism, St. Peter's, Oldham, Lancashire, 1820–24, p. 8; FHL #1,656,068, DGS #4,265,426 (familysearch.org).

v. MARIA MILLS (*Samuel*[4]) was baptized 5 October 1823.[12]

vi. ALICE MILLS (*Samuel*[4]) was baptized 11 February 1827.[13]

vii. JOSEPH MILLS (*Samuel*[4]) was baptized 15 February 1829.[14]

viii. HANNAH MILLS (*Samuel*[4]) was baptized 23 September 1832.[15]

ix? SOPHIA MILLS (*Samuel*[4])[16] remains undocumented but is named in family tradition.

---

[12] Similarly, Maria Mills baptism, p. 231.
[13] Alice Mills baptism, St. Peter's, Oldham, Lancashire, 1824–29, p. 145; FHL #1,656,068, DGS #4,265,426 (familysearch.org).
[14] Similarly, Joseph Mills baptism, p. 272.
[15] Hannah Mills baptism, St. Peter's, Oldham, Lancashire, 1829–34, p. 190; FHL 1,656,068, DGS #4,265,426 (familysearch.org).
[16] Scholes ledger book, 73 (an incomplete handwritten list).

FIRST GENERATION

1814-1875, Presidents Madison to Grant

Chapter 2

First Generation

Ann Mills–William Scholes Family
parents at chapter 1

"I only wish I had it in my power to send you a sample of some potatoes"

2. ANN¹ MILLS (*Samuel^A*)
Baptized: 20 November 1814 at St. Peter's Oldham, Lancashire[17]
Died: 15 February 1875 in Wisconsin[18]
Spouse: **WILLIAM SCHOLES,** 20 April 1835 at Prestwich, Lancashire[19]
Spouse's parents: Not known
Spouse's birth: In or near Oldham, 14 December 1814 according to family tradition[20]
Spouse's death: 13 October 1864, at Vicksburg, Mississippi, reportedly of "chronic diarrhea"
Spouse's burial: G4874, Vicksburg National Cemetery[21]

William's parents have yet to be identified. He married 20 April 1835 Ann Mills, daughter of cotton carder Samuel and his wife Alice

---

[17] Ann Mills baptism #724, St. Peter's, Oldham, Lancashire, 1813–18, p. 93; FHL #1,655,906, DGS #4,265,425 (familysearch.org).
[18] Robert Scholes affidavit, Scholes minor's pension application #220,230, certificate #170,286, "Declaration for Pension of Children under Sixteen Years of Age Surviving."
[19] Scholes–Mills marriage, 20 April 1835, parish church of St. Mary, Prestwich, Lancashire; marriages 1813–37, p. 90; FHL #2,113,206, DGS #7,568,814 (familysearch.org).
[20] Oldham: Scholes family list in ledger book, 63. Near Oldham: Samuel Mills Scholes letter to Arthur D. Marsh of New York, 1903, stating that William "was born near Oldham . . . though the exact place of his birth I am unable to give at the present writing."
[21] For death date, *Portrait and Biographical Album of Green Lake, Marquette, and Waushara Counties, Wisconsin* (Chicago: Acme Publishing, 1890), 757. Some records in his widow's pension file give 14 October 1864. For burial, Bonnie Scholes notes in author's possession. Also, burial index (where he is called "Sholes"): interment.net/data/us/ms/warren/vicksnat/vicksburg/s.htm.

(Stocks) Mills,[22] at Prestwich, Lancashire, ten miles from their home town.[23]

Ann Scholes

William's supposed siblings:[24]
  i. James
  ii. John
  iii. George (died young)
  iv. Ellen married a Tetlow; their daughter married a Johnson and came to New Jersey.
  v. Amelia
  vi. Elizabeth married Mr. Greanes (?) and came to Cincinnati, Ohio.
  vii. William was supposedly the last of thirteen children.[25]

A good land?

The Scholes family left Liverpool on the *Marmion* and arrived in New York 30 April 1849.[26] In September William wrote home, extolling the new land and encouraging others to support the Potters' Emigration Society:

> Some people said that [the soil at their Wisconsin settlement] was too sandy to produce anything, but I only wish I had it in my power to send you a sample of some potatoes that have been got up this week, and I think the most prejudiced would admit that finer potatoes were never grown, they have not had one particle of manure, the sets were put under the sod; and

---

[22] Ann Mills baptism #724, St. Peter's, Oldham, Lancashire, 1813–18, p. 93; FHL #1,655,906, DGS #4,265,425, items 3–5 (familysearch.org).
[23] Scholes–Mills marriage, 20 April 1835, parish church of St. Mary, Prestwich, Lancashire, marriages 1813–1837, p. 90; FHL #2,113,206, DGS #7,568,814 (familysearch.org).
[24] If indeed William was the youngest, and if he had twelve older siblings, their birth dates might have ranged roughly from 1788 forward.
[25] Scholes ledger book, 74, in author's possession.
[26] Michael Cassady, transcriber, "Wisconsin-Bound Passengers on Ship *Marmion*," *Wisconsin State Genealogical Society Newsletter* 29(1):25, June 1982, from item 337, microfilm roll 78, National Archives series M237.

that is all they have had, except hoeing up, and the crop is a surprising one. . . .

We are ten miles from the post office, and about 120 miles from Milwaukee, about the same from Galena, but in a few years we shall have a market of our own, and every thing requisite to make man comfortable. I expect next year to have 10 acres of wheat with my yoke of oxen and plough, which, together with my labour for others in a few years will render my work much easier, and my family out of the reach of want. How many of our friends in Oldham can say the same? Not many, I think.

For my part, I would not come back for the best shop and two pounds per week in Oldham, for I think I can do much better here; I am only sorry that I did not come sooner, . . . I assure you that the exchange to the back woods, from the stinking factory is greatly in favour of the former, and I often wish that more of our hard working townsmen would leave their sickly toil and come to one of the healthiest spots on the earth.[27]

In December William was one of 58 signers to a note praising Thomas Twigg, the society's Wisconsin agent, for enabling them "to escape from the vile, grasping, and intolerant domination of the aristocracy of England."[28]

A bad land?

William's initial optimism about the family's new start was not borne out. The Potters' Emigration Society soon collapsed, leaving many members stranded without money or proper title to their land.[29]

William Scholes Hume (1866–1948), grandson and namesake of the emigrant, is said to have written the following in 1940. In old age

---

[27] William Scholes to the Oldham branch of the Potters' Emigration Society, letter, 23 September 1849, as published in *Potters' Examiner and Emigrants' Advocate* 9(74):587–88, November 1849. Supplied by Roger G. Bentley.
[28] *Potters' Examiner*, December 1849, p. 606. Supplied by Roger G. Bentley.
[29] Roger G. Bentley (Pierrefonds, Quebec) to Harold Henderson (La Porte, Indiana) letter 22 July 2002, in author's possession.

himself, he would have been putting on paper stories he heard from his mother (perhaps) and aunts and uncles and neighbors no earlier than the late 1870s.

> Each family paid in one hundred dollars and Mr. Twiggs [the manager] was to have a log house built and some land cleared. But all they found was forests and wilderness. The earliest settlers in the community were Scholes and Watsons. They came in June 1849. My grandfather William Scholes was the first early settler who crossed the Fox River near Port Hope, in a small rowboat. He settled on the farm now owned by his youngest son, James Scholes. Others came soon and during the summer the following families settled here: Cockers, Watsons, Bennetts, Sutcliffs, Mountfords, Humes, Falkners, Hills, Chapmans, Skinners, Hopewoods, Coons, Wades, Wells, Shaws, Cadmans, Keenes, Powells, Stantons, and Ellisons. They knew very little about farming for the most of them had been working in the Pottery. Most of them stayed at the Old Fort, East of Portage a few weeks until they could make their claims and build their log houses.
>
> The first year there were many hardships. Many families had several children and only a few cents left when they arrived here. The Potters Society had to furnish them some provisions the first year until they could grub the land and raise a crop. They had to pay it back.[30]

This second-hand account bears little resemblance to William Scholes's enthusiastic early letters, but they stem from different perspectives and different years, and both could be true as far as they go.

Little of the Scholes family's first decade in the New World can be discerned or confirmed.

- The Scholes name is absent from the 1850 census, but does appear in the 1855 state census. As of 1 June, the William "Sholes" household in Moundville Township, Marquette County, contained four men (presumably father William and sons Robert, Samuel, and William) and four women (most likely Ann, Sarah,

---

[30] W. S. Hume (1866–1948) account of the early settlement, provided by Lois M. Wade via email 10 July 2002.

Elizabeth, and Alice); six of the eight were foreign-born. Daughter Mary, the oldest child, may have been overlooked, or been living and working in another household, as she married Bissell Sherwin that August.[31]

- Dubious is the 1954 assertion that the family promptly "settled on a tract of land purchased from the Federal government." Land records show no Scholes land ownership until 1853, and that acreage was purchased from a neighbor.
- William's death in 1864 is said to have "left his wife and their children entirely alone," but they did have neighbors, including the fellow immigrants of the James Hume family, who came soon after, and into which daughter Sarah Ann Scholes (Chapter 4) married in 1858.

The 1954 account is more celebratory than specific. "With much perseverance and economy they carried on, even to the building of a new frame house. The children's formal education was meager, but their religious training was not neglected." The church window the family dedicated in their memory featured a "white cross rising above the rock of ages with the tempestuous sea about it," intended to reflect "the rock like character of these early pioneers."[32]

On 30 June 1853, William paid neighbor Wilhelm Bartels $50 for forty acres.[33] The following year, William purchased a War of 1812 land warrant that the government had issued to Sarah Henderson, whose husband had served from Delaware. Most likely she took a dim view of undertaking frontier life in old age, and sold the warrant to a broker for

---

[31] William Sholes [Scholes] household, 1855 Wisconsin state census, Moundville Township, Marquette County, p. 112, line 11. Only a bare minimum of information was collected in that year.

[32] "Members of Scholes Family Dedicate Memorial Window," *Portage Daily Register* (Wisconsin), Tuesday 24 August 1954, p. 3, col. 1. The dating of the frame house is not known. Marion Scholes (Chapter 32) told the story at the dedication service; she had the family Bible.

[33] Marquette County, Wisconsin, Deeds 36:128, Bartels to Scholes, 30 June 1853; Register of Deeds, Montello.

cash. The broker sold it to William, who located its 80 acres adjacent to his initial forty.[34]

In 1857 the Scholeses sold 80 of their 120 acres to James Hume for $500, probably on James's return from Tennessee (Chapter 4). This would seem to have left William with 40 acres, but in 1860 the US census agriculture schedule credited him with 80.

The Scholeses had land, but they did not prosper. Between 1852 and 1854 they lost two young children. In 1860, eleven years after their arrival from England, their farm was near the bottom of the heap. Seventy-one of the 80 farms in Moundville Township that year had a higher total value than the Scholeses'.[35] William may have lacked farming experience, and he surely lacked field help: Robert, the couple's first-born son after five daughters, was two years old when the family arrived in Wisconsin.

Nor were the economics working well for them. In 1861 the Scholeses paid the Humes $800 to buy back the same 80 acres they had sold to the Humes a few years earlier for $500. As part of the deal the Scholeses borrowed $100 from the Humes, with the property as security. The debt was paid off in 1869, well after William's death. In 1862 the Sherwins headed west to Monroe County, Wisconsin, and sold 26½ acres to William for $200.[36]

---

[34] For a thorough account of the politics and economics of land warrants, James W. Oberly, *Sixty Million Acres: American Veterans and the Public Lands before the Civil War* (Kent, Ohio: Kent State University Press, 1990). The graph of land warrant prices between 1847 and 1861 (108) suggests that prices were at their peak in 1854. Perhaps William paid a premium.

[35] Scholes farm, 1860 US census, agriculture schedule, Moundville Township, Marquette County, Wisconsin. The 80-acre farm had a cash value of $500. Only eight of the eighty farms in the township had lower valuations, and they were all smaller. Most of the crop and livestock details confirm this picture.

[36] Bissell and Mary Sherwin to William Scholes, 4 April 1862, NE corner of Section 4, Township 13 North, Range 9 East, for $200, Columbia County, Wisconsin, Deed 16:433; FHL #1,630,162, DGS #8,550,278, image 16 of 852 (familysearch.org).

Civil War

In 1864 the Civil War was entering its third year, contrary to early expectations of a Union victory. At various times, various cities and counties sought to counter war-weariness by offering bounties up to $300 to enlistees.[37] The cash may have looked promising to William, aged 49, with six of his nine surviving children still at home and the youngest four years old. In January 1864 he joined the Union Army's Company E, 2nd Wisconsin Cavalry.[38] Two of his sons-in-law also joined: Sarah Ann Scholes's husband Robert W. Hume (Chapter 4) enlisted in February in Company C of the 23rd Wisconsin, and Mary Scholes's husband Bissell Sherwin (Chapter 3) enlisted September 20 in Company D of the 19th.[39] Two of the three never returned.

Bissell Sherwin died in action at the Second Battle of Fair Oaks near Petersburg, Virginia.[40] Ordered to march across an open field into heavy fire from entrenched Confederate artillery, his unit was annihilated (see Chapter 3).

Bissell's father-in-law William Scholes perished as most Civil War soldiers did, not from enemy fire but from disease. He died of "chronic diarrhea" at Vicksburg, Warren County, Mississippi, 13 October 1864,

---

[37] "Civil War Letters Describe Brief Time in the Service," *Monroe County Wisconsin Historical Society Newsletter* 19(1):8, June 1991. For a wider view, Richard N. Current, *The History of Wisconsin, Volume 2: The Civil War Era, 1848–1873* (Madison: State Historical Society of Wisconsin, 1976), 325–30.

[38] Ann Mills Scholes, widow's pension application #79,106, certificate #46,660. For an apparently erroneous March 1864 date of entry, *Portrait and Biographical Album of Green Lake, Marquette, and Waushara Counties, Wisconsin* (Chicago: Acme Publishing, 1890), 757.

[39] Mary Scholes Sherwin, widow's pension application #108,205, certificate #73,064; Adjutant General's Office letter, 27 September 1865 (fold3.com/image/271446993). Also, "Another Veteran Joins Silent Ranks," Robert W. Hume obituary, *Portage Daily Register* (Wisconsin), Thursday 13 May 1915, p. 3, col. 3.

[40] "Civil War Letters Describe Brief Time in the Service," *Monroe County Wisconsin Historical Society Newsletter* 19(1):8, June 1991.

and was buried at grave G 4874, Vicksburg National Cemetery.[41] Widow Ann was granted a pension and lived until 1875.[42]

After the war

In 1870, twenty-year-old Samuel Mills Scholes (Chapter 8) headed a Moundville household that included his mother Ann (56), sister Elizabeth (27), and younger brothers William (16), George (13), and James (10). The three youngest attended school, but only William was called a farmer, so he may have attended less often. Sister Sarah (Scholes) Hume (Chapter 4) and family were next door. The Scholes real estate was valued at $750 and personal estate $538; of fifteen adjoining farms (as enumerated in the population schedule), ten were more prosperous.[43] Brother Robert (Chapter 7) with wife and baby was in the township with $300 in real estate and $300 personal property,[44] as was sister Alice (Chapter 6), wife of Joseph C. Smith, with $1600 in real estate and $670 personal.[45]

Father William left no will. His estate was not settled until after Ann's decease in 1875. Robert Scholes (Chapter 7), the estate administrator and oldest son, held an auction of personal property 31 May 1875. The eleven purchasers, neighbors and relatives, paid a total of $422.90:

> G. Creag—5 "lams" $8.50
> Evan Arthur—wool $30.50
> Hamley—1 sow 7.25

---

[41] For death date, *Portrait and Biographical Album of Green Lake, Marquette, and Waushara Counties, Wisconsin* (Chicago: Acme Publishing, 1890), 757. Some records in his widow's pension file give 14 October 1864. For burial, Bonnie Scholes notes in author's possession. Also, burial index (where he is called "Sholes"), interment.net/data/us/ms/warren/vicksnat/vicksburg/s.htm. For cause of death, Ann Mills Scholes, Widow's Pension Application, Surgeon Gess's report, p. 7.
[42] Scholes minors' pension application #220,230, certificate #170,286, "Declaration for Pension of Children under Sixteen Years of Age Surviving," affidavit by Robert Scholes.
[43] Samuel Scholes household, 1870 US census, Moundville Township, Marquette County, Wisconsin, pp. 7–8, dwelling 49, family 48.
[44] Robert Scolds [Scholes] household, 1870 US census, Moundville Township, Marquette County, Wisconsin, p. 3/579, dwelling/family 16.
[45] Joseph Smith household, 1870 US census, Moundville Township, Marquette County, Wisconsin, pp. 5–6/580, dwelling 35, family 34.

C. W. Falkner—1 sow $5.75, 1 hog $4.50, 2 "heffers" $12
W. Scholes (Chapter 9)—1 hog $5.25
W. Brookns—1 hog $5.10
R. Scholes (Chapter 7)—1 hog $6.15, 1 steer $6.50
J. McKanny—9 sheep $22.50
D. C. Berry—1 yoke steers $38.25, another $27.85
A. Maltby—1 cow $16.75, another $23.75
G. W. Scholes (Chapter 10)—2 horses $110, double hames [attachments to a horse collar] $7, lumber wagon $45, 1 pair Sleighs $10, 1 harrow $6[46]

The minor heirs of Sarah Ann (Scholes) Hume received $130, and the minor heirs of William —George and James—each received $130 in real estate. James Hume was paid $220 for his claim on William's estate.[47] The two youngest (nearly grown) children chose guardians in the spring of 1875; George picking older brother Samuel, and James picking older brother Robert.[48]

Finally, the nine siblings found a complex but apparently agreeable way to bestow the land fairly on the youngest child, James (Chapter 7). Each sibling had received an undivided one-ninth part of their parents' 100 acres, and evidently farming by committee was not on the agenda.

In the spring of 1884:
- Mary Scholes Sherwin sold her $1/9^{th}$ to sister Elizabeth for $1; Alice Scholes Smith sold her $1/9^{th}$ to sister Elizabeth for $10. Together with Elizabeth's own $1/9^{th}$ they made up one-third of the property.
- William Scholes sold his $1/9^{th}$ to brother George for $1; Samuel Mills Scholes sold his 1/9th to George for $1. Together with George's own $1/9^{th}$ they made up a second one-third of the property.

---

[46] Estate of William Scholes, Marquette County, Wisconsin, Box 9, File 482; "Wisconsin, Wills and Probate Records, 1800–1987" > Marquette > Probate Records Box 7 File 420–Box 9 File 5222 > images 1486–1534 of 1775, especially image 1487 (ancestry.com).
[47] Ibid., images 1500 and 1526 of 1775 (ancestry.com).
[48] Ibid., images 1530 and 1532 of 1775 (ancestry.com).

- Robert and Caroline Scholes sold their 1/9th to brother James for $10. Robert W. Hume as guardian of his minor children with Sarah Ann Scholes Hume sold her 1/9th to brother James for $100. Together with James's own 1/9th they made up the third one-third of the property.

Interestingly, different family members valued their one-ninth portions differently. The following year they consolidated the thirds: Elizabeth sold her third to James for $300, and Robert sold his third to James for the same amount.[49] This left the youngest child with a reasonable-size 100-acre farm. A family story says that James figured out how to make money on the land—by raising sheep.

Children of Ann^1 (Mills) and William Scholes:

Of William and Ann's eleven children, nine lived to grow up; eight married and had children of their own; and seven had grandchildren. All eight married spouses of British descent, either recent immigrants or old New Englanders. (William and Ann's 26 grandchildren were somewhat more exogamous.) Of the eight married children, the three earliest-married (daughters Mary, Sarah, and Alice, married in the 1850s and early 1870s) had a total of seventeen children, while the three last-married (sons William, George, and James, married in the 1880s) had just seven.

3   i. MARY^2 SCHOLES (*Ann^1 Mills, Samuel^A*) was born 27 September 1835 in Lancashire and died 27 December 1910 in Sparta, Monroe County, Wisconsin. She married 26 August 1855 in Packwaukee, Marquette County, Wisconsin, BISSELL SHERWIN.

4   ii. SARAH ANN^2 SCHOLES (*Ann^1 Mills, Samuel^A*) was born 7 November 1837 in Lancashire, was baptized 12 November at St. Peter's Oldham there, and died 24 March 1874 in Moundville, Marquette County, Wisconsin. She married 7 November 1858 ROBERT WALKER HUME SR.

---

[49] Marquette County, Wisconsin, Quit Claim Deeds 19:524, Scholes to Scholes, 6 February 1884; Register of Deeds, Montello. Similarly, 19:525, Smith to Scholes, 13 February 1884. Similarly, 19:526, Scholes to Scholes, 16 February 1884. Similarly, 19:527, Scholes to Scholes, 16 February 1884. Similarly, 19:528, Hume to Scholes, 24 April 1884. The following year: 19:617, Scholes to Scholes, 20 February 1885; and 19:618, Scholes to Scholes, 30 October 1885; Register of Deeds, Montello.

iii. MARIA[2] SCHOLES (*Ann[1] Mills, Samuel[A]*) was born 27 February 1840 in Lancashire,[50] baptized 10 May 1840 in St. Peter's Oldham there,[51] and died about 1852 in Wisconsin.[52]

5 iv. ELIZABETH[2] SCHOLES (*Ann[1] Mills, Samuel[A]*) was born 12 November 1842 in Lancashire, was baptized the following day in St. Peter's Oldham there as "Betty," and died 2 January 1929 in Portage, Columbia County, Wisconsin.

6 v. ALICE[2] SCHOLES (*Ann[1] Mills, Samuel[A]*) was born 6 April 1845 in Lancashire, was baptized 11 May 1845 at St. Peter's, Oldham, and died 1923 in Moundville, Marquette County, Wisconsin. She married reportedly 1865 JOSEPH COCKCROFT SMITH.

7 vi. ROBERT[2] SCHOLES (*Ann[1] Mills, Samuel[A]*) was born 22 January 1847 in Lancashire, was baptized 7 February 1847 at St. Peter's Oldham, there, and died 12 March 1885 in Moundville Township, Marquette County, Wisconsin. He married 11 December 1868 in Columbia County, Wisconsin, CAROLINE CORNELIA PARKES.

8 vii. SAMUEL MILLS[2] SCHOLES (*Ann[1] Mills, Samuel[A]*) was born 10 August 1849 in Moundville, Marquette County, Wisconsin, and died 25 May 1914 in Oshkosh, Winnebago County, Wisconsin. He married 28 June 1875 in Marquette, Green Lake County, Wisconsin, HARRIET NEWELL MOZLEY.

viii. HANNAH ELLEN[2] SCHOLES (*Ann[1] Mills, Samuel[A]*) was born 12 January 1852 in Wisconsin, and died there about 1854.[53]

9 ix. WILLIAM[2] SCHOLES (*Ann[1] Mills, Samuel[A]*) was born 11 May 1855 in Wisconsin, and died in Portage, Columbia County, Wisconsin, 2 January 1929. He married 26 November 1885 MARY ELLEN DIXON.

---

[50] Scholes family list, Scholes ledger book, 63.
[51] Maria Scholes baptism, 10 May 1840, St. Peter's Oldham, 1838–42, p. 97, #773, FHL #1,656,069, DGS #7,567,077 (familysearch.org).
[52] "Members of Scholes Family Dedicate Memorial Window," *Portage Daily Register* (Wisconsin), 24 August 1954, p. 3, col. 1. Maria is said to have died at the age of 12 years.
[53] Scholes family list, Scholes ledger book, 63. Also, "Members of Scholes Family Dedicate Memorial Window," *Portage Daily Register* (Wisconsin), Tuesday 24 August 1954, p. 3, col. 1. Hannah Ellen is said to have died at the age of 2 years.

10 x. GEORGE WALKER² SCHOLES (*Ann¹ Mills, Samuel^A*) was born 24 March 1857 in Moundville, Marquette County, Wisconsin, and died 21 January 1941 in Endeavor, Marquette County, Wisconsin, the last of the siblings. He married 24 February 1885 SUSANNA REBECCA AUDISS.

11 xi. JAMES MILLS² SCHOLES (*Ann¹ Mills, Samuel^A*) was born 11 July 1859 in Moundville, Marquette County, Wisconsin, and died 29 December 1936 there. He married 15 December 1886 in Buffalo, Marquette County, Wisconsin, EMMA MARIA HULL.

SECOND GENERATION

CHAPTERS 3–11

1835-1941
Presidents Jackson to Franklin D. Roosevelt

Chapter 3

Second Generation

Mary Scholes–Bissell Sherwin Family
<u>parents at chapter 2</u>

"Keep the money where it will be safe and ready when the year is up. Farewell wife and children."

3. **Mary² Scholes** (*Ann¹ Mills, Samuel^A*)
Birth: 27 September 1835 in Lancashire[54]
Baptism: 6 December 1835 at St. Peter's Oldham[55]
Death: 27 December 1910 in Sparta, Monroe County, Wisconsin[56]
Married: **Bissell Sherwin** 26 August 1855 in Packwaukee, Marquette County, Wisconsin[57]
Spouse's birth: about 1823, Town of Warsaw, then Genesee County, New York
Spouse's parents: Bissell and Experience (Whitney) Sherwin

---

[54] Scholes family list, Scholes ledger book, 63, in author's possession.
[55] Mary Scholes baptism, 6 December 1835, St. Peter's Chapel, Oldham, Lancashire, 1834–38, p. 84, #672; FHL #1,656,068, DGS #4,265,426, image 588 of 650 (familysearch.org).
[56] "Mrs. Mary Sherwin," *Monroe County Democrat* (Sparta, Wisconsin), 29 December 1910, p. 8. Also, *Sparta Herald* (Wisconsin), 2 January 1911, p. 3, col. 2.
[57] Sherwin–Scholes handwritten marriage certificate by Rev. John Wilcox (Presbyterian), in Bissell Sherwin pension file; photocopy provided courtesy of Barbara J. Butler, Howell, Michigan. Also, Scholes family list, Scholes ledger book, 63 (in author's possession), where he is erroneously called "Beryl." Some records call him Bissel Sherman or even Sherman Bissel.

Spouse's death: 27 October 1864 near Fair Oaks, Virginia[58]

At age 19, Mary left her parents' struggling farm to marry New Yorker Bissell Sherwin, a man in his 30s. They lived close enough that mother Ann was midwife at Mary's first four births (1856–62).[59] Then the Sherwins moved 80 miles west to farm in Ridgeville Township, Monroe County, Wisconsin.[60] Bissell's sister Amanda and husband Thomas Jones settled in the same neighborhood.[61] When baby George Sherwin came along in 1864, Amanda was the midwife.[62]

In the fall of 1858, in the course of their move west to Monroe County, the Sherwins sold 52½ acres to Bissell's father for $400, with a $50 mortgage.[63]

---

[58] For place, Andrew W. Young, *History of the Town of Warsaw* (Buffalo, New York: Press of Sage, Sons, & Company, 1869), 331–32. Conflicting evidence on Bissell's birth date arguably converges on 1823. <u>1824–25</u>: Bissell Sherman [Sherwin] household, 1860 US census, Fort Winnebago, Columbia County, Wisconsin, p. 260, dwelling 619, family 608. <u>Early 1822</u>: Aney Cemetery gravestone reportedly gives age at death as 42 years, 8 months, 27 days ("Civil War Letters Describe Brief Time in the Service," *Monroe County Wisconsin Historical Society Newsletter* 19 [June 1991]:10). <u>About 1823</u>: "Muster and Descriptive Roll of a Detachment of US Vols forwarded" 1864, age 41; Mary Sherwin, widow's pension claim #108,205, certificate #73,064, service of Bissell Sherwin (Private, Company D, 19th Wisconsin Infantry, Civil War), Civil War and Later Pension Files; Department of Veterans Affairs, Record Group 15; National Archives, Washington DC. <u>1823</u>: Ralph Hendersin, compiler, "Woodlawn Cemetery," Sparta, Monroe County, Wisconsin (http://files.usgwarchives.net/wi/monroe/cemeteries/Woodlawn-cem.txt).

[59] Affidavit of Mrs. Ann Scholes, 19 July 1867; in Mary Sherwin, widow's pension certificate #73,064, service of Bissell Sherwin (Private, Company D, 19th Wisconsin Infantry, Civil War), Civil War and Later Pension Files; Department of Veterans Affairs, Record Group 15; National Archives, Washington DC.

[60] "Mrs. Mary Sherwin," *Monroe County Democrat* (Wisconsin), 29 December 1910, p. 8.

[61] Mary Sherwin household, 1870 US census, Ridgeville, Monroe County, Wisconsin, p. 126, dwelling 110, family 104. Similarly, Thomas Jones household, dwelling 113, family 107.

[62] Affidavit of Mrs. Amanda Jones, 19 July 1867; Mary Sherwin, widow's pension certificate #73,064, service of Bissell Sherwin (Private, Company D, 19th Wisconsin Infantry, Civil War), Civil War and Later Pension Files; Department of Veterans Affairs, Record Group 15; National Archives, Washington DC.

[63] Bissell Sherwin Jr. and Mary Sherwin to Bissell Sherwin Sr., 2 October 1858, Columbia County deeds 25:80; image 484 of 868, FHL #1,618,058, DGS #8,550,250 (familysearch.org).

Bissell was in his forties when he joined Company D of the 19th Wisconsin Volunteer Infantry 20 September 1864.[64] On the last evening of his life, he wrote from Fair Oaks, Virginia, to Mary:

> You must write about everything——if there is water in the well or not. You must hold up good courage. If I live, one year will slip away. Don't want any more land until I see if I come home. Keep the money where it will be safe and ready when the year is up. Farewell wife and children.[65]

On 27 October, Lt. Colonel Strong watched Company D as its men

> emerged from the pines and came out on a clear open field, about three hundred yards from the works [Confederate fortifications]. As we broke cover the rebels opened on us furiously with artillery, and cut us up badly. Upon seeing the rebel works the boys cheered lustily, and advanced rapidly, closing up the breaks in the ranks made by the artillery, and preserving a splendid line. Thus for about one hundred yards, when we were met by a perfect tornado of shot, shell, cannister, and minie balls directly in our faces, mowing us down by the scores. . . . dead and wounded men covered the ground passed over. . . . We lay down and made as thin as possible. No power to move forward or backward, or to assist in the least our wounded comrades.

---

[64] Bissell Sherwin, volunteer enlistment, La Crosse, Wisconsin, 20 September 1864; Mary Sherwin, widow's pension certificate #73,064, service of Bissell Sherwin (Private, Company D, 19th Wisconsin Infantry, Civil War), Civil War and Later Pension Files; Department of Veterans Affairs, Record Group 15; National Archives, Washington DC.

[65] "Civil War Letters Describe Brief Time in the Service," *Monroe County Wisconsin Historical Society Newsletter* 19(1):10, June 1991.

Of 198 soldiers who emerged from the pines, 44 returned; Bissell was not among them.[66] Mary filed a pension application 20 August 1865.[67]

Mary Sherwin

Half a continent away and two weeks earlier, Mary's father William, a member of the 2nd Wisconsin Cavalry, died in a military hospital at Vicksburg, Mississippi.[68] How and when Ann got the news of the two deaths is unknown, but in her obituary later the family paid tribute to "the courage she showed in taking up the duties of caring for the family and running the farm, doing it all uncomplainingly and well."[69]

Mary Sherwin left the home farm around the turn of the century—she was 65—and settled in Sparta.[70] In her last two months' illness, her sister Elizabeth Scholes nursed her by day and youngest son William O. Sherwin by night. In 1911 Elizabeth penned a letter to the pension bureau "to certify that I nursed Mary Sherwin free of charge." Mary's estate amounted to $20 and "a few household goods"; medical and burial bills were $95.50.[71]

The Sherwin family's migratory impulse skipped a generation. Bissell came from New York, Mary from England; their children stayed in Wisconsin. Seven of their ten adult grandchildren resumed their

---

[66] William DeLoss Love, *Wisconsin in the War of the Rebellion* (Chicago: Church and Goodman, 1866), 953–54.
[67] Widow's Declaration for Pension, Mary Sherwin, 20 August 1865, certificate #73064 (fold3.com/image/271446990).
[68] William is buried at Vicksburg National Cemetery in Mississippi, Section G, Grave 4874, no image, memorial #101,885,919 by Charlene Hall (findagrave.com). He also has a recent grave marker at Moundville Cemetery, Endeavor, Marquette County, Wisconsin, memorial #112,065,537 by Erin Foley (findagrave.com).
[69] "Mrs. Mary Sherwin," *Monroe County Democrat* (Wisconsin), 29 December 1910, p. 8.
[70] Mary's 1910 obituary said that she stayed on the farm until 1902. But in 1900 she was enumerated in the household of son-in-law John Bell and daughter Flora in La Grange Township, Monroe County, Wisconsin, ED 99, sheet 3B, dwelling 51, family 53.
[71] William O. Sherwin, application for reimbursement, 13 January 1911, in Mary Sherwin, widow's pension certificate #73,064, service of Bissell Sherwin (Private, Company D, 19th Wisconsin Infantry, Civil War), Civil War and Later Pension Files; Department of Veterans Affairs, Record Group 15; National Archives, Washington DC. Similarly, Elizabeth Scholes note 30 January 1911, Mary Sherwin, widow's pension, p. 42 (fold3.com/image/271447058).

grandparents' odyssey, spending most of their lives farther west. In 1919, Mary and Bissell's oldest grandson Ira returned from Montana to visit. He said the crops were very poor in his vicinity, and farther west everything had dried out.[72] It wasn't just a freak of weather, but a sign they were running out of frontiers to move to; eastern-style agriculture couldn't last in the arid Great Plains. The last Sherwin grandchildren—Herbert Sherwin (Chapter 14, child i) and Charlotte (Sherwin) Bohlig (Chapter 14, child ii)—died in 1977 near the shores of the Pacific.[73] Over 150 years, three generations of Sherwins had pushed the logic of migration to its limit.

Children of Mary² (Scholes) and Bissell Sherwin:

12   i. CHARLES TRUMAN³ SHERWIN (*Mary² Scholes, Ann¹ Mills, Samuel^A*) was born 16 November 1856, and died at Sparta, Monroe County, Wisconsin, 30 March 1910. He married 12 September 1877 in Monroe County, JANE "JENNIE" THRESSA YOUNG.

13   ii. FRANCIS RODERICK "FRANK"³ SHERWIN (*Mary² Scholes, Ann¹ Mills, Samuel^A*) was born 8 July 1858, and died at Sparta, Monroe County, 23 March 1929. He married 5 April 1888 in Adrian Township ANNIE HENRY.

14   iii. WILLIAM ORLANDO³ SHERWIN (*Mary² Scholes, Ann¹ Mills, Samuel^A*) was born 16 April 1860, and died at Sparta, Monroe County, Wisconsin, 8 November 1953. He married first 9 March 1892 at Sparta, HARRIET M. MANLEY, and second 28 November 1916 at Sparta, LOTTIE M. TAYLOR.

15   iv. FLORA ANN³ SHERWIN (*Mary² Scholes, Ann¹ Mills, Samuel^A*) was born 4 February 1862 at Fort Winnebago, Columbia County, Wisconsin; died in early December 1925; and was buried at Woodland Cemetery, Sparta, Monroe County, Wisconsin. She married 7 January 1886 in Ridgeville, Monroe County, JOHN JAMES BELL.

---

[72] Sheri Stuve, transcriber, "Mr. and Mrs. Ira Sherwin…," Clark County, Wisconsin, ALHN and AHGP Internet Library (http://wvls.lib.wi.us/ClarkCounty/clark/data/1/bbs10/10001.htm), citing *Humbird Enterprise* (Wisconsin), 20 September 1919, no p. or col. no. This URL is no longer accessible.

[73] Herbert Sherwin death index entry, San Diego County; California Death Index, 1940–1997 (ancestry.com). Charlotte M. Bohlig, 11 January 1977, "Washington Death Index, 1940–1996" (ancestry.com). She resided in King County.

v. George Herbert³ Sherwin (*Mary² Scholes, Ann¹ Mills, Samuel⁴*) was born 6 August 1864 and died 30 March 1866.⁷⁴

---

⁷⁴ Affidavit of Mrs. Amanda Jones, 19 July 1867, in Mary Sherwin, widow's pension certificate #73,064, service of Bissell Sherwin (Private, Company D, 19th Wisconsin Infantry, Civil War), Civil War and Later Pension Files; Department of Veterans Affairs, Record Group 15; National Archives, Washington DC. According to sexton's records, "Geo. H. Sherwin, 1864–1867, name on stone, no record of burial" in Block 14, Lot 8, Woodlawn Cemetery; *Woodlawn Cemetery, Sparta, Wisconsin, Record Book Copy* (Sparta, Wisconsin: Angelo Books, n.d.), 1:57.

Chapter 4

Second Generation

Sarah Ann Scholes—Robert Walker Hume Sr. Family
<u>parents at chapter 2</u>

Miner, farmer, and Civil War veteran

4. SARAH ANN² SCHOLES (*Ann¹ Mills, Samuel^A*)
Birth: 7 November 1837 in Lancashire[75]
Baptism: November at St. Peter's Oldham there[76]
Death: 24 March 1874 in Moundville, Marquette County, Wisconsin[77]
Burial: Moundville Cemetery, Endeavor, Wisconsin[78]
Spouse: **ROBERT WALKER HUME SR.,** married November 1858 (probably 7 November)[79]
Spouse's parents: James and Ann/Margaret (Walker) Hume[80]
Spouse's birth: 11 August 1833 in Linlithgowshire, Scotland[81]

---

[75] Scholes ledger book, 63, in author's possession.
[76] Sarah Ann Scholes baptism, 12 November 1837, St. Peter's Chapel, Oldham, Lancashire, 1834–38, p. 236, #1882; image 23 of 641, FHL #1,656,069, DGS #7,567,077 (familysearch.org).
[77] Scholes family list, Scholes ledger book, 63, in author's possession.
[78] Sarah Ann Scholes Hume, no image of grave marker, Moundville Cemetery, Endeavor, Wisconsin, memorial #102,543,259 by Marianne Morrison (findagrave.com).
[79] For November 1858, "Another Veteran Joins Silent Ranks," Robert W. Hume obituary, *Portage Daily Register* (Wisconsin), Thursday 13 May 1915, p. 3, col. 3.
[80] Marriage records for three children give her maiden name: Robert Hume, Marquette County, 2:21, 4 April 1889; James Hume, Columbia County, 4:308, #55, 25 March 1896; and George Hume, Marquette County, 2:206, #4, 16 June 1901 (microfilm at Wisconsin State Historical Society, Madison).
[81] "Children of the Scholes Family," Scholes ledger book, 65, in author's possession. Also, large and relatively recent joint grave marker for Robert W. Hume, Sarah Ann Scholes, and Sarah Ann Eager, images, Moundville Cemetery, Endeavor, Marquette County, Wisconsin, respectively memorials #10,563,485 by Marianne Morrison, #102,543,259 by Joey, and #10,563,494 by Marianne Morrison (findagrave.com).

Spouse's death: 12 May 1915[82]

Spouse's burial: Moundville Cemetery, Endeavor, Wisconsin[83]

Robert "was brought up in the coal fields of Scotland and became a miner; his parents emigrated to this county in 1850, and came direct to Portage. . . . in 1854, Mr. Hume went to Tennessee and worked for three years in the coal mines near Chattanooga. He returned to the farm in Moundville [Township] in 1857 and remained there until he enlisted in the 23d Wisconsin Vol[unteers] in February, 1864," remaining in the service until mustered out 27 July 1865. In Moundville he was a prominent figure: "chairman of the town board three years; assessor, five years; treasurer, two years, and on the town board several years."[84]

Sarah Ann (Scholes) Hume died within a month of the birth of her seventh child and fourth son George 27 February 1874. With six children under age 13, Robert married second 7 July 1875 Sarah Ann Eager. She was born in or near Milwaukee 17 April 1851, outlived her husband, and died 26 May 1917. She was the daughter of James and Ann (-?-) Eager, natives of "Glyade," England. (Mother Ann was called Anna Aeger when she died in 1897).[85] Robert and his second wife had two children, and they also took in niece Carrie Eager when her parents died.[86]

In the fall of 1881 Robert was one of four men in the Port Hope, Columbia County, neighborhood who were slated to help prove that George W. Fay had "continuous residence upon and cultivation" of land in Section 28, Township 14, Range 9 East.[87]

---

[82] "Good Mother Is Called to Rest," *Portage Daily Register* (Wisconsin), Thursday 31 May 1917, p. 2, col. 1.

[83] Robert Walker Hume, no image of grave marker, Moundville Cemetery, Endeavor, Wisconsin, memorial #10,563,485 by Marianne Morrison (findagrave.com).

[84] "Family Festival for Aged Citizen," *Portage Daily Register* (Wisconsin), Thursday 13 August 1914, p. 3, col. 1.

[85] "Good Mother Is Called to Rest," *Portage Daily Register* (Wisconsin), Thursday 31 May 1917, p. 2, col. 1. ("Glyade" might possibly be a typo for Glynde, a village in Sussex.) Also, James Eager (age 52) household for wife Ann (age 44) and apparent daughter Sarah A. (age 9), Wauwatosa Township, Milwaukee County, Wisconsin, p. 143/637, dwelling 1064, family 1054. Also, "Obituary: Anna Aeger," *Portage Daily Democrat* (Wisconsin), Wednesday 29 September 1897, p. 3, col. 2.

[86] "Good Mother Is Called to Rest," *Portage Daily Register* (Wisconsin), Thursday 31 May 1917, p. 2, col. 1.

[87] "Notice for Publication," *Wisconsin State Register* (Portage), Saturday 3 September 1881, p. 4, col. 6.

In the fall of 1891, Robert, then of Moundville Township, was planning retirement. He bought a house and lot at the corner of Adams and Carroll streets in Portage, where "Mr. Hume expects to make this city his home after this winter."[88] The move to town also brought the younger children within reach of better schooling.[89]

Three years later Robert was one of four delegates from Portage's third ward to attend the county Republican convention.[90] In 1896 he was an unopposed Republican candidate for alderman.[91] In 1899 his monthly Civil War pension was raised from $14 to $17.[92] After his death, second wife Sarah Eager received a pension.[93]

Children of Sarah Ann[2] (Scholes) and Robert Walker Hume Sr.:

i. ANNA/MARY[3] HUME (*Sarah Ann[2] Scholes, Mary[2] Scholes, Ann[1] Mills, Samuel[A]*) was called Mary (8 months old at the 1860 census), and later Anna (10 years old in the 1870 census).[94] She was born about 1859 and died "a few months after her mother,"[95] perhaps late 1875. In the 1870 census she was characterized as "idiotic" and unable to read or write.[96]

---

[88] "Home News," *Portage Daily Democrat* (Wisconsin), Monday 5 October 1891, p. 3, col. 1.
[89] "Good Mother Is Called to Rest," *Portage Daily Register* (Wisconsin), Thursday 31 May 1917, p. 2, col. 1.
[90] "No Oles Need Apply," *Portage Daily Democrat* (Wisconsin), Wednesday 29 August 1894, p. 3, col. 1.
[91] "Election Notice," *Portage Daily Register* (Wisconsin), Tuesday 31 March 1896, p. 1, col. 2.
[92] "Gossip of the City," *Portage Daily Democrat* (Wisconsin), Wednesday 12 April 1899, p. 3, col. 1.
[93] Robert W. Hume pension card, widow's application #1,048,396, pension #793,655; Civil War > Civil War Pensions Index > Wisconsin > Infantry > Regiment 23 > Company C > Hume, Robert W. (fold3.com/image/249/23671947).
[94] Robert Hume household for apparent daughter Anna age 10, 1870 US census, Moundville, Marquette County, Wisconsin, p. 581, dwelling 48, family 47.
[95] "Another Veteran Joins Silent Ranks," Robert M. Hume obituary and family account, *Portage Daily Register* (Wisconsin), Thursday 13 May 1915, p. 3, cols. 3–4.
[96] Robert Hume household for daughter Anna age 10, 1870 US census, Moundville, Marquette County, Wisconsin, p. 581, dwelling 48, family 47.

16 ii. MARGARET³ HUME (*Sarah Ann² Scholes, Mary² Scholes, Ann¹ Mills, Samuel⁴*) was born 2 June 1861, and died 29 December 1938 in Sioux Falls, South Dakota. She married 16 February 1887 JUDSON BERRY.

17 iii. ROBERT WALKER³ HUME, JR. (*Sarah Ann² Scholes, Mary² Scholes, Ann¹ Mills, Samuel⁴*) was born 29 July 1863 and died 26 April 1940 in Watertown, Jefferson County, Wisconsin. He married 4 April 1889 ALICE SMITH.

18 iv. WILLIAM SCHOLES³ HUME (*Sarah Ann² Scholes, Mary² Scholes, Ann¹ Mills, Samuel⁴*) was born 22 July 1866 and died 5 March 1948. He married in the spring of 1890 ALIDA SUTCLIFFE.

19 v. SARAH ANN JANE "NETTIE"³ HUME (*Sarah Ann² Scholes, Mary² Scholes, Ann¹ Mills, Samuel⁴*) was born 18 November 1868 and died 1936. She married November 1889 HENRY EDEN JONES.

20 vi. JAMES SAMUEL³ HUME (*Sarah Ann² Scholes, Mary² Scholes, Ann¹ Mills, Samuel⁴*) was born 28 March 1871 and died 18 May 1936 in California. He married 25 March 1896 LYDIA ALBERTA "BIRDIE" SAWYER.

21 vii. GEORGE WALKER³ HUME (*Sarah Ann² Scholes, Mary² Scholes, Ann¹ Mills, Samuel⁴*) was born 27 February 1874 reportedly in Marquette County, and died there 2 February 1952. He married January 1900 LOIS DEMOTT.

Children of Robert Walker and Sarah Ann (Eager) Hume, half-siblings of the above, and one adoptee:

viii. MARTHA HUME was born 25 September 1876,[97] and died 7 November 1933.[98] She married about 1900 HENRY LYMAN RUSSELL.[99]

---

[97] Mary Ann Elizabeth Hume Russell grave marker, image, memorial #102,654,388 by Joey (findagrave.com). Exact dates are unsourced; the origin of the obituary is not given. Also, Henry L. Russell household for wife Martha A. married 0 years, born September 1876, 1900 US census, Moundville, Marquette County, Wisconsin, ED 93, sheet 3B, dwelling/family 68.
[98] "Endeavor Man Passes Away After Extended Illness," *Portage Daily Register* (Wisconsin), Tuesday 15 December 1936, p. 1, col. 7.
[99] Henry L. Russell household for wife Martha A. married 0 years, born September 1876, 1900 US census, Moundville, Marquette County, Wisconsin, ED 93, sheet 3B, dwelling/family 68.

A "well known Endeavor resident,"[100] Henry was born 8 November 1873;[101] died at the home of his son Clayton at Prairie du Sac 15 December 1936; and was buried at Moundville cemetery.[102] As of 12 September 1918, "Mrs. Dorothey Russell" of Moundville was his closest relative. He was of medium height and build, with blue eyes and brown hair.[103] His parents, both born in England, were James and Eliza.[104]

Martha graduated from Portage High School in the class of 1898 (not a common accomplishment in those days). Martha and Henry's children as named in 1933 were Mrs. Clarence Adelberg of Milwaukee; Clayton Russell of Prairie du Sac; Harland Russell of Milwaukee, and Wayne Russell and Roberta Russell at home.[105]

> Henry's childhood was spent at the paternal home in East Moundville and when grown to young manhood he sought a larger sphere, he traveled to the grain fields of Dakota and the prairie farms of Wisconsin. He was employed in a creamery at Poynette and in the Lloyd blacksmith shop at Portage. He was a member of the M.W.A. [Modern Woodmen of America] and the Beaver lodges and served his community as Town Treasurer, assessor, supervisor, marshal and constable. He was a man who could be trusted, kind and considerate to all but to be found loyal to the things that would promote cleaner and better community life. He was a lover of nature, of big trees, green lawns and beautiful flowers as his home indicated and the funeral services were

---

[100] "Endeavor Man Passes Away After Extended Illness," *Portage Daily Register* (Wisconsin), Tuesday 15 December 1936, p. 1, col. 7.
[101] Henry Lyman Russell WWI draft card, serial #989, order #a439, 12 September 1918, Montello local board; "US, World War I Draft Registration Cards, 1917–1918" > Wisconsin > Marquette County > ALL > Draft Card R > image 92 of 95 (ancestry.com).
[102] "Endeavor Man Passes Away After Extended Illness," *Portage Daily Register* (Wisconsin), Tuesday 15 December 1936, p. 1, col. 7.
[103] Henry Lyman Russell WWI draft card, serial #989, order #a439, 12 September 1918, Montello local board; "US, World War I Draft Registration Cards, 1917–1918" > Wisconsin > Marquette County > ALL > Draft Card R > image 92 of 95 (ancestry.com).
[104] James Russell household for wife Eliza and son Henry (age 6), Moundville, Marquette County, Wisconsin, ED 223, no dwelling number, family 68, p. 7/565C. Ancestry trees suggest they were James Lorin Russell and wife Eliza Ann Munn, both born in Kent, England (ancestry.com/family-tree/person/tree/2912444/person/140024722153/facts).
[105] Mary Ann Elizabeth Hume Russell grave marker, image, memorial #102,654,388 by Joey (findagrave.com). Exact dates are unsourced; and the origin of the obituary is not given.

held at that home beside highway 51 and at the M. E. Church, Moundville.[106]

ix. MARTHA ELIZABETH SARAH ANN HUME was born 31 December 1880 in Moundville, Marquette County, Wisconsin, and died 13 March 1941 in Portage, Columbia County, Wisconsin. Like her sister, she was a Portage high School graduate.

> Mrs. Voertman has been a fine Christian character, a devout member of the Portage Methodist Church for forty years and an inspirational leader in many of its departments of activity. Though she had no children of her own, she loved them much; and she gave 22 years of her service as superintendent of the Cradle Roll department of our church School. She was an active member of the Ladies' Aid Society and for 11 years Secretary of Literature in the district organization of this society for a short time. Mrs. Voertman has enjoyed a wide circle of friends in other societies as well and her qualities of leadership have been recognized by her friends in these organizations for she was Past Matron of the Order of the Eastern Star, Bethlehem Chapter, No.100; Past Worthy High Priestess of the Shrine, Fort Winnebago Chapter, No. 12; and Past Noble Grand for the Pansey Rebekah Lodge of Portage. She was a woman who found great delight in plant life and hand work and she served as superintendent of the Art department at the county fair for a number of years.

She married in Portage 17 April 1906 ARTHUR L. VOERTMAN.[107] He was born in Columbia County, Wisconsin, 10 September 1883,[108] and died reportedly September 1964.[109] In 1910 he was a photographer living in Portage with his German-born grandmother Frederika

---

[106] Henry Lyman Russell grave marker, image, Moundville Cemetery, Endeavor, Wisconsin, memorial #102,654,159 by Joey (findagrave.com). Transcribed obituary, no source given.
[107] Eliza A. Voertman grave marker, image, memorial #102,781,298 by Joey (findagrave.com), including two transcribed obituaries, undated and unsourced, likely early March 1941 in Portage. Also, "Obituaries . . . Mrs. A. L. Voertman," *Wisconsin State Journal* (Madison), Friday 14 March 1941, p. 2, col. 7.
[108] Arthur L. Voertman index entry, Wisconsin Birth Index, 1820–1907, reel 33, record 2191 (ancestry.com).
[109] Arthur L. Voertman grave marker, image, Moundville Cemetery, Endeavor, Wisconsin, memorial #102,781,433 by Joey (findagrave.com).

Jergens.[110] In the 1920s he and W. H. Horton had a business—the Portage Novelty, Boat and Storage Company at 103–105 West Mullett Street—where they built boats for fishing, hunting, and recreation.[111] Arthur was instrumental in organizing and expanding Portage's Riverside Park over at least 25 years.[112]

x. CAROLINE "CARRIE" EAGER, orphaned daughter of Edward Eager and niece of Robert Hume Sr.'s second wife, was born reportedly 7 July 1876,[113] and died 1 March 1923.[114] She married FREEMAN DEWSNAP.[115] The son of Enoch and Annis (Ellison) Dewsnap, he was born in 1876 and died in 1966. He reportedly married second as her second husband in 1951 Grace E. (Smith) Hall.[116]

Carrie and Freeman (called "Frank" in a daughter's obituary) had four children: Mary, Arden, Geraldine, and Sheldon.[117]

---

[110] Frederika Jergens household for grandson Arthur Voertman, 1900 US census, Portage, Columbia County, Wisconsin, Ward 4, ED 21, sheet 8, dwelling 176, family 188.
[111] "Local Plant Builds Boats," *Portage Daily Register,* Friday 2 June 1922, p. 1, col. 2.
[112] "New Improvements at the City's Riverside Park Recalls Early Work of Men from the First Ward," *Portage Daily Register* (Wisconsin), Tuesday 16 August 1949, p. 1, cols. 2–5.
[113] Carrie Eager Dewsnap grave marker, no image, Moundville Cemetery, Endeavor, Wisconsin, memorial #10,563,391 by Marianne Morrison (findagrave.com).
[114] "Local Happenings," *Portage Daily Register* (Wisconsin), Monday 5 March 1923, p. 1, cols. 2–3.
[115] "Good Mother Is Called to Rest," *Portage Daily Register* (Wisconsin), Thursday 31 May 1917, p. 2, col. 1.
[116] Freeman Ellison Dewsnap grave marker, image, Moundville Cemetery, Endeavor, Wisconsin, memorial #10,563,387 by Marianne Morrison (findagrave.com).
[117] Mary A. Turner obituary, undated and unidentified clipping, August 1999, Stella Scholes collection, item #2, in author's possession. Also, Caroline H. Dewsnap household, 1920 US census, Moundville Township, Marquette County, Wisconsin, ED 133, sheets 1B-2A, dwelling 24, family 25. Caroline was married, a farmer, and owned the house; her implied husband was absent.

Chapter 5

Second Generation

Elizabeth Scholes Family
parents at chapter 2

"Beautiful character"

5. ELIZABETH² SCHOLES (*Ann¹ Mills, Samuel⁴*)
Birth: 12 November 1842 in Lancashire[118]
Baptism: the following day in St. Peter's Oldham there, as "Betty"[119]
Death: 2 January 1929 in Portage, Columbia County, Wisconsin[120]

Elizabeth did not marry. She nursed many family members through hard times and was remembered by a niece as "a maiden lady, a beautiful character, beloved."[121] She "grew to womanhood under conditions incident to pioneer life—conditions aggravated by the death of the father [William] in the Civil War and that of the mother some years later. . . . Elizabeth aided materially in the rearing of the younger children; in fact, her whole life, a long one, lived practically in Moundville, save for brief periods spent in Sparta and Portage, was a life of loving devotion and service to those who needed the care she was able and willing to give."[122]

Through the years:

---

[118] "Were Brother and Sister," *Portage Daily Register* (Wisconsin), Thursday 10 January 1929, p. 2, col. 3. Scholes family list, Scholes ledger book, 63, in author's possession.
[119] Betty Scholes baptism, St. Peter's Chapel, Oldham, Lancashire, 1842–48, p. 12; image 234 of 641, FHL #1,656,069, DGS #7,567,077 (familysearch.org).
[120] "Were Brother and Sister," *Portage Daily Register* (Wisconsin), Thursday 10 January 1929, p. 2, col. 3. Siblings Elizabeth and William died on the same day.
[121] Scholes family list, Scholes ledger book, 63, in author's possession.
[122] "Were Brother and Sister," *Portage Daily Register* (Wisconsin), Thursday 10 January 1929, p. 2, col. 3.

1889: spent the week with brother, George (Chapter 10).[123]

1890: visited her niece, Mrs. Judson Berry, of Fort Winnebago (Chapter 16).[124]

1897: elected superintendent when the Methodists in Portage decided to organize a "Sunday School home department."[125]

1898: visited by "Mrs. Samuel Scholes of Dartford," that is, Harriet (Mozley) Scholes, wife of Samuel Mills Scholes (Chapter 8).[126]

1899: returned from Rockford, Floyd County, Iowa, "where she has been spending the summer."[127] Likely she was visiting the family of her nephew Francis R. Sherwin (Chapter 13).

1900: a nurse in the Almon Jones household in Moundville Township.[128]

1905: a nurse, age 62, boarding with brother-in-law Joseph C. and sister Alice Smith.[129]

1906: "visited her sister [not identified] at Dividing Ridge."[130] Once a series of Native American mounds and burials, most of this landmark ridge in Madison was destroyed for gravel and home sites.[131]

---

[123] "Moundville," *Portage Daily Register* (Wisconsin), Thursday 20 June 1889, p. 3, col. 4.
[124] Similarly, Wednesday 19 November 1890, p. 3, col. 3.
[125] "City Affairs," *Portage Daily Register* (Wisconsin), Tuesday 24 August 1897, p. 4, col. 2.
[126] "Gossip of the City," *Portage Daily Democrat* (Wisconsin), Monday 11 April 1898, p. 3, col. 1.
[127] "Moundville," *Portage Daily Register* (Wisconsin), Friday 3 November 1899, p. 1, col. 2.
[128] Almon Jones household for Elizabeth Scholes, 1900 US census, Moundville Township, Marquette County, Wisconsin, ED 93, sheet 5A, dwelling/family 100. Elizabeth was recorded as having been in the US 51 years (accurate) and having been naturalized in 1846 (impossible).
[129] Joseph C. Smith household, 1905 Wisconsin state census, Moundville, Marquette County, Wisconsin, p. 110.
[130] "Moundville," *Portage Daily Register* (Wisconsin), Saturday 19 May 1906, p. 4, col. 2. The unnamed sister being visited might be Alice (Scholes) Smith (Chapter 6).
[131] "Dividing Ridge" *Historic Madison, Inc., of Wisconsin* (historicmadison.org/Madison%27s%20Past/connectingwithourpast/dividingridge.html).

1910: in the household of widowed sister Mary Sherwin at 312 North Street, Sparta, Monroe County, Wisconsin.[132]

30 January 1911: wrote to pension bureau from Endeavor, Wisconsin.[133]

> This is to certify that
> I nursed Mary Sherwin
> free of charge
>
> Elizabeth Scholes
> Nurse

1920: in the household of widowed sister Alice Smith. Both reportedly arrived in 1849 and were naturalized in 1857.[134]

1924–29: at brother William's home in Portage.[135]

Six nephews were Elizabeth's pallbearers in January 1929:
Robert Hume (Chapter 17),
Henry Jones (Chapter 19),
Elmer Scholes (Chapter 34),
Robert Scholes (Chapter 36),
William Hume (Chapter 18), and
William "Sherwood" [Sherwin] (Chapter 14).[136]

---

[132] Mary Sherwin household for Elizabeth Scholes, 1910 US census, Sparta, Monroe County, Wisconsin, Ward 2, ED 140, sheet 8A, dwelling 184, family 190.

[133] William O. Sherwin, application for reimbursement, 13 January 1911, in Mary Sherwin, widow's pension #73,064, service of Bissell Sherwin (Private, Company D, 19th Wisconsin Infantry, Civil War), Civil War and Later Pension Files; Department of Veterans Affairs, Record Group 15; National Archives, Washington DC. Similarly, Elizabeth Scholes note 30 January 1911, Mary Sherwin, widow's pension, p. 42 (fold3.com/image/271447058).

[134] Alice Smith household for Elizabeth Scholes, 1920 US census, Moundville Township, Marquette County, Wisconsin, ED 133, sheet 1A, dwelling 5, family 6.

[135] "Brother and Sister Dead," clipping likely from *Portage Daily Register* based on typefaces used, early January 1929, undated clipping in Scholes ledger book, 62.

[136] "Were Brother and Sister," *Portage Daily Register* (Wisconsin), Thursday 10 January 1929, p. 2, col. 3.

Chapter 6

Second Generation

Alice Scholes–Joseph Cockroft Smith Family
parents at chapter 2

90 acres split four ways

6. ALICE² SCHOLES (*Ann¹ Mills, Samuel^A*)
Birth: 6 April 1845 in Lancashire[137]
Baptism: 11 May 1845 at St. Peter's, Oldham, England[138]
Death: 1923 in Moundville, Marquette County, Wisconsin[139]
Burial: Moundville Cemetery, Endeavor, Marquette County[140]
Spouse: **JOSEPH COCKROFT SMITH**[141] married reportedly 1865
Spouse's parents: Henry and Zillah (Cockroft) Smith
Spouse's birth: 18 March 1840 in England
Spouse's death: 30 October 1908 in Marquette County, Wisconsin
Spouse's burial: Moundville Cemetery, Endeavor, Marquette County[142]

---

[137] Scholes family list, Scholes ledger book, 63, in author's possession. Birth date also noted at baptism.
[138] Alice Scholes baptism, St. Peter's Chapel, Oldham, Lancashire, 1842–48, p. 143, #1139; image 301 of 641, FHL #1,656,069, DGS #7,567,077 (familysearch.org).
[139] Scholes family list, Scholes ledger book, 63, gives marriage without date, in author's possession. Also, Joseph Smith household for 36 years married, 1900 US census, Marquette County, Wisconsin, p. 133B, dwelling/family 14.
[140] Alice Smith joint grave marker with Joseph C. Smith and Ella F. Smith, image, Moundville Cemetery, Endeavor, Marquette County, Wisconsin, memorial #102,555,182 by Joey (findagrave.com). Undocumented information on the page includes marriage date.
[141] Scholes family list, Scholes ledger book, 63, in author's possession.
[142] Joseph C. Smith joint grave marker with Alice Smith and Ella F. Smith, image, Moundville Cemetery, Endeavor, Marquette County, Wisconsin, memorial #102,555,260 by Joey (findagrave.com). Undocumented information on the page includes Joseph's middle name, birth location, marriage date, and parents' names.

Joseph C. Smith, Alice's future husband, emigrated from England as a babe in arms in 1840.[143] The family spent a few years in Ohio, roughly 1842–46.

1850: the Smiths had settled in Marcellon Township, Columbia County, Wisconsin, Henry was 40, Zillah 38, with apparent children Betty age 13, Joseph 10, Mary 8, Martha 4, and twins Jane and James age 1. Betty and Joseph were born in England, Mary and Martha in Ohio, Jane and James in Wisconsin. Henry was a "B Smith." He listed no real estate, but a near neighbor and likely in-law Peter Cockroft had $600 in property.[144]

1860: Henry was farming, with $500 in real estate and $344 in personal property. All six children attended school, including 20-year-old Joseph, a "farm laborer."[145] By 1870, Henry's family was doing well and had moved to Buffalo Township in Marquette County.[146]

1870: Joseph, now married to Alice and with young children (William 4 and Ella 2), had $1600 in real estate and $670 in personal property.[147]

1880: William was 14, Eva 4, and Mary 3.[148]

1900: Mary I. was 23 and Robert J. 8.[149]

1908–9: Joseph died without a will, and his estate went through probate, Alice acting as executrix. He left $749.23 in goods, and $1000 in land ($800 for his eight-acre homestead, $100 for 42 acres of "river

---

[143] Joseph C. Smith household, 1900 US census, Moundville Township, Marquette County, Wisconsin, ED 93, sheet 1B, dwelling/family 14.
[144] Henry Smith household, 1850 US census, Marcellon Township, Columbia County, Wisconsin, p. 176, dwelling/family 1404.
[145] Henry Smith household, 1860 US census, Marcellon Township, Columbia County, Wisconsin, p. 443, dwelling 412, family 405.
[146] Harry Smith household, 1870 US census, Buffalo Township, Marquette County, Wisconsin, p. 525, dwelling 86, family 85.
[147] Joseph Smith household, 1870 US census, Moundville Township, Marquette County, Wisconsin, pp. 5–6, dwelling 35, family 34.
[148] Samuel Ellis for Joseph Smith household, 1880 US census, ED 223, Moundville Township, Marquette County, Wisconsin, p. 3 or 563C, no dwelling number, family 28.
[149] Joseph C. Smith household, 1900 US census, Moundville Township, Marquette County, Wisconsin, ED 93, sheet 1B, dwelling/family 14.

marsh," and $100 for 40 acres of swamp). Each of the four heirs received an undivided quarter of the property.[150]

1910: Mary I. (31) and Robert J. (17) were in Alice's household on East Moundville Road, both "farm laborers."[151]

1920, a year of surprises: They were renting. Mary I. was 42 and was reported (probably mistakenly) to be a widow. Also in the household were Elizabeth Scholes (Alice's sister), age 77; and Wm. H. Smith, a "ward," age 69, said to have been born in Capetown, father born in Capetown, and mother born in the Cape Colony. (His relationship to the family is likely but has not been determined!) Alice and Elizabeth were naturalized in 1857, suggesting that their father William Scholes may have been naturalized that year.[152]

Children of Alice[2] (Scholes) and Joseph Cockcroft Smith:

22   i. WILLIAM HENRY[3] SMITH (*Alice[2] Scholes, Ann[1] Mills, Samuel[A]*) was born about 1866 in Wisconsin and died there reportedly 1936. He married probably 11 May 1891 RUTH ROSIE HAINES.

---

[150] Estate of Joseph C. Smith, Marquette County, Wisconsin, Box 10, Case 600; "Wisconsin, Wills and Probate Records, 1800–1987" > Marquette > Probate Records Box 9 File 529–Box 11 File 624 > images 943–978 of 1638, especially images 943 and 956 (ancestry.com).
[151] Alice Smith household, 1910 US census, Moundville Township, Marquette County, Wisconsin, ED 149, dwelling 153, family 157.
[152] Alice Smith household, 1920 US census, Moundville Township, Marquette County, Wisconsin, ED 133, dwelling 5, family 6.

  ii. ELLA FLORANCE³ SMITH (*Alice² Scholes, Ann¹ Mills, Samuel^A*) was born about 1868 in Wisconsin,¹⁵³ died 9 May 1872, and was buried at Moundville Cemetery, Wisconsin.¹⁵⁴

23 iii. FLORENCE EVA³ SMITH (*Alice² Scholes, Ann¹ Mills, Samuel^A*) was born in Wisconsin 1875 or 1876, and died 1962 in Beaver Dam, Dodge County, Wisconsin. She married about September 1900 RICHARD BEICHL.

24 iv. MARY IRENE³ SMITH (*Alice² Scholes, Ann¹ Mills, Samuel^A*) was born 17 March 1877 and died 8 February 1955 in Portage.

25 v. ROBERT JOSEPH³ SMITH (*Alice² Scholes, Ann¹ Mills, Samuel^A*) was born May 1892 in Wisconsin, and died in Portage 25 August 1976. He married 13 January 1914 MYRTLE M. PAGE.

---

[153] Joseph Smith household for daughter Ella age 2, 1870 US census, Moundville, Marquette County, Wisconsin, p. 6, dwelling 35, family 34.
[154] Ella Florance Smith grave marker (clearly older than the one with Joseph, Ella, and Alice together), image, Moundville Cemetery, Endeavor, Marquette County, Wisconsin, memorial #103,168,118 by Joey (findagrave.com).

Chapter 7

Second Generation

Robert Scholes–Caroline Cornelia Parkes Family
parents at chapter 2

Twice-widowed spouse of Civil War veterans

7. ROBERT² SCHOLES (*Ann¹ Mills, Samuel^A*)
Birth: 22 January 1847 in Lancashire[155]
Baptism: 7 February 1847 at St. Peter's Oldham[156]
Death: 12 March 1885, Moundville Township, Marquette County, Wisconsin
Burial: Moundville Cemetery, Endeavor, Marquette County[157]
Spouse: **CAROLINE CORNELIA PARKS** married 11 December 1868 in Columbia County, Wisconsin[158]
Spouse's parents: William Norman and Abigail (Welch?) Parks[159]

---

[155] Scholes family list, Scholes ledger book, 63, in author's possession.
[156] Robert Scholes baptism, St. Peter's Chapel, Oldham, Lancashire, 1842–48, p. 243, #1940; image 355 of 641, FHL #1,656,069, DGS #7,567,077 (familysearch.org).
[157] Robert Scholes grave marker (died 12 March 1885), image, Moundville Cemetery, Endeavor, Marquette County, Wisconsin, memorial #102,785,859 by Joey (findagrave.com).
[158] Robert Scholes–Caroline Parkes marriage, Columbia County, Wisconsin, marriages, 2:2, #0125, Wisconsin State Historical Society, Madison. Scholes ledger book, 63, in author's possession, gives the erroneous "Caroline Parkinson."
[159] "Home News," *Portage Daily Democrat* (Wisconsin), Thursday 18 March 1886, p. 3, col. 3, naming Wm. N. Parks, "one of the old residents of Ft. Winnebago, who died 17 March, about 65 years of age, and was the father of Mrs. J. H. Tibbits, of Ft. Winnebago, Mrs. John T. Jones, of this city, and Mrs. Robert Scholes, of Moundville. He has four sons residing in the west. He was married twice, the second wife surviving him." Also, parental names are given without sourcing at Caroline Cornelia Parks-Ellison, no image of grave marker, Moundville Cemetery, Endeavor, Marquette County, Wisconsin, memorial #102,786,108 by Joey (findagrave.com). Also, in 1860, Caroline was reported 13 years old and born Wisconsin, with apparent parents William N. Parks (age 45) and Abigal (age 49): William N. Parks household, 1860 US census, Chester, Adams County, Wisconsin, p. 17 or 93, dwelling 777, family 696.

Spouse's birth: 2 March 1848 in Elkhorn, Walworth County, Wisconsin
Spouse's death: 19 April 1936 at home in Endeavor, Marquette County, after a 15-month illness
Spouse's burial: Moundville Cemetery[160]

In 1870 Robert was farming in Moundville, with $300 in real estate and $300 in personal property.[161] In 1880 Robert was farming and Caroline and their three children were living in the William Audiss household. William was a minister[162] and likely the father of Susanna Audiss, who later married Robert's younger brother George Scholes (Chapter 10). Caroline was a member of the Moundville Methodist Episcopal church. She and her husband "donated the site for the present church."[163]

Following Robert's 1885 death, on 18 December 1887 Caroline married second as his second wife Christopher Ellison, who thus became stepfather to her and Robert's three children (Family A below),[164] and later the father of two more (Family B below). Christopher had married first Priscilla Walters 8 December 1853. She was reportedly born 10 November 1820 in England and died 15 December 1880 in Moundville,

---

[160] "Aged Endeavor Woman Is Dead," *Portage Daily Register* (Wisconsin), Wednesday 22 April 1936, p. 4, col. 1. Also, Caroline Cornelia Parks-Ellison, no image of grave marker and no sources, Moundville Cemetery, Endeavor, Marquette County, Wisconsin, memorial #102,786,108 by Joey (findagrave.com).

[161] Robert Scolds [Scholes] household, 1870 US census, Moundville Township, Marquette County, Wisconsin, p. 3/579, dwelling/family 16.

[162] William Audiss household for Robert Schales [Scholes] family, 1880 US census, Moundville, Marquette County, Wisconsin, ED 223, p. 4, dwelling 39, no family number.

[163] "Aged Endeavor Woman [Caroline (Parks) (Scholes) Ellison] Is Dead," *Portage Register-Democrat* (Wisconsin), Wednesday 22 April 1936, p. 4, col. 1

[164] Christopher Ellison–Caroline Cornelia Scoles [Scholes] marriage index entry, 18 September 1887, Marquette County, Wisconsin; "Wisconsin Marriages, 1836–1930," citing FHL #1,292,024, DGS #7,615,079, image 01295, record 6 (familysearch.org). Also, "Aged Endeavor Woman [Caroline (Parks) (Scholes) Ellison] Is Dead," *Portage Register-Democrat* (Wisconsin), Wednesday 22 April 1936, p. 4, col. 1, stating that she married Christopher Ellison in 1887 and they had two daughters. Compare Christopher Ellison household, 1900 US census, Moundville Township, Marquette County, Wisconsin, ED 93, sheet 1B, dwelling/family 23, which erroneously states that Christopher and Caroline had been married only two years.

Marquette County. Their children: Mary Elizabeth Ellison born January 1855 and Annie Jane Ellison born 29 September 1857 (Family C below).

Christopher himself was reportedly born 21 January 1829 in Salford, Greater Manchester, England, to Martin G. and Alice (Houlker) Ellison. During the Civil War, Christopher served in Company C of the First Wisconsin Infantry, Company G of the 21st Wisconsin, and the Veterans Reserve Corps.[165]

1895: "Mrs. C. Ellison is enjoying a visit from Mr. and Mrs. Wm. Parks, of Illinois. Mr. Parks is a brother of Mrs. Ellison's."[166]

1898: Robert Scholes's estate was probated, thirteen years after his death. He owned the west half of the northeast quarter of section 28 in Township 14 North, Range 9 East. Each of the three heirs received $311.11, and the widow's dower was $466.66. As of 24 October 1898, Nettie (Scholes) Moran was age 28, Mary E. (Scholes) Heames 26, and Harriet Scholes 21. The following spring, Nettie was in Waukesha, Waukesha County; Mary in Moundville, Marquette County; and Hattie Schwemerlein in Briggsville, Marquette County.[167]

December 1900: Christopher Ellison died.

1901: Caroline was granted an $8/month pension on her second husband Christopher's Civil War service, by way of the "agency of A. Holmes."[168]

---

[165] Christopher Ellison military grave marker, image, Moundville Cemetery, Endeavor, Marquette County, Wisconsin, memorial #102,786,288 by Joey (findagrave.com). The birth date, place, and parents are unsourced. More detail is given in Christopher Ellison's pension index card; "US Civil War Pension Index: General Index to Pension Files, 1861–1934" > Ellis–Emerson > image 1081 of 4354 (ancestry.com).
[166] "Moundville," *Portage Daily Register* (Wisconsin), Friday 18 January 1895, p. 4, col. 3.
[167] Robert Scholes probate, Marquette County, Wisconsin, Box 9, file 481, 1898–99; "Wisconsin, Wills and Probate Records, 1800–1987" > Marquette > Probate Records Box 7 File 420–Box 9 File 522 > Box 9 file 481 Robert Scholes, images 1429–1485, specifically 1443–44, 1446, 1454, and 1457–58 of 1775 (ancestry.com).
[168] "Local Jottings," *Portage Daily Register* (Wisconsin), Tuesday 28 May 1901, p. 4, col. 2.

1910: Caroline's five children were all living; she and 18-year-old daughter Pearl were living on Oak Street in Moundville Township. She owned the house free and clear.[169]

1920: Caroline was living alone in Moundville, next door to Pearl and her husband James.[170]

1930: Caroline, age 82, was living with son-in-law blacksmith James Hollerup, daughter Pearl, and family at Prospect Avenue in Moundville. James owned the house and they had a radio set.[171]

1935: "Just her children and grandchildren and great-grandchildren" were assembled at Campbell's Hall to celebrate Caroline's 87th birthday March 3.[172]

Caroline C. Ellison [signature]

The children of families A and B are half-siblings, as are the children of families B and C. But the children of families A and C are not. Strict chronology would place them in order C, A, B; but here family A is listed first as it is the direct Scholes line. See Table 1 at the end of this chapter for a graphic representation of the families.

Family A. Children of Robert² and Caroline Cornelia (Parkes) Scholes, half-siblings of B, all born in Wisconsin:

26   i. NETTIE³ SCHOLES (*Robert² Scholes, Ann¹ Mills, Samuel^A*) was born reportedly 21 October 1869 in Marathon County, Wisconsin, and died

---

[169] Caroline C. Ellison household, 1910 US census, Moundville, Marquette County, Wisconsin, ED 149, sheet 3A, dwelling 65, family 67.
[170] Caroline Ellison household, 1920 US census, Moundville, Marquette County, Wisconsin, ED 133, sheet 4A, dwelling 63, family 64.
[171] James Hollerup household for mother-in-law Caroline C. Ellison, 1930 US census, Endeavor, Moundville, Marquette County, Wisconsin, ED 8, sheet 3B, dwelling/family 91.
[172] "News from Our Neighbors . . . North Endeavor," *Wisconsin State Register* (Portage), Friday 8 March 1935, p. 3, col. 5. "Those from away were Mrs. Myrtle Moore and sons Stanley and Alden, Milwaukee; Mr. and Mrs. R. Schwemerlein, Portage; Mr. and Mrs. Elmer Pomplum [Pomplin?] and family, Princeton; and Mr. and Mrs. John Williamson of Montello."

12 July 1952 in Wauwatosa, Milwaukee County. She married 1 January 1895 THOMAS CLARENCE MORAN.

27   ii. MARY ELIZABETH³ SCHOLES (*Robert² Scholes, Ann¹ Mills, Samuel^A*) was born 22 October 1871 in Moundville and died in Endeavor 1 August 1948. She married 24 December 1890 WILLIAM ROBERT HEAMES.

28   iii. HATTIE³ SCHOLES (*Robert² Scholes, Ann¹ Mills, Samuel^A*) was born May 1877 in Wisconsin, and died 22 December 1956 in Endeavor, Marquette County, Wisconsin. She married 25 January 1899 RODNEY/ J. RODDY/JOHN C. SCHWEMERLEIN.

Family B. Children of Christopher Ellison and Cornelia (Parks) (Scholes), half-siblings of A:

iv. MYRTLE MAY ELLISON was born July 1887 or 1889 (1900 census)[173] or 2 July 1888 (her grave marker); died, reportedly 80 years old, 15 January 1969 in Waukesha, Wisconsin; and was buried at Moundville Cemetery, Endeavor, Wisconsin.[174] She married first reportedly 19 December 1906 in Marquette County, Wisconsin,[175] ALFRED ANSON MOORE.[176] Alfred was born 31 October 1878 or 1879,[177] died reportedly in Montello 6 October 1951, and was buried reportedly at Douglas Cemetery, Douglas Center, Marquette County, Wisconsin.[178] He was

---

[173] Christopher Ellison household for daughter Mary M. age 10 born 1889, 1900 US census, Moundville Township, Marquette County, Wisconsin, ED 93, sheet 1B, dwelling/family 23.

[174] Myrtle M. Ellison grave marker, image, Moundville Cemetery, Endeavor, Wisconsin, memorial #103,098,490 by Joey (findagrave.com). Also, "Mrs. M. Crawford," *Portage Daily Register* (Wisconsin), Thursday 16 January 1969, p. 5, col. 1. Two surviving sons, Alden and Stanley, were named.

[175] Myrtle M. Ellison–Alfred Anson Moore marriage index entry, Wisconsin, Marriage Index, 1820–1907, Marquette County, volume 2, p. 304 (ancestry.com).

[176] Albert A. Moore household for wife Myrtle M. age 21, 1910 US census, Moundville Township, Marquette County, Wisconsin, ED 149, sheet 3A, dwelling 66, family 68. Adjacent as the census taker traveled was Myrtle's twice-widowed mother Caroline.

[177] For 1879: Alfred Anson Moore WW2 draft card, Waukesha, Wisconsin Local Board #1, 25 April 1942, serial #U287, no order #; "US, World War II Draft Registration Cards, 1942" > Monson–Moriarty > images 623–24 of 2144 (ancestry.com). Alfred was unemployed, living at 610 Maple Avenue in Waukesha. For 1878 (closer to the event): Alfred Anson Moore, WWI draft card, Montello Local Board, 12 September 1918, serial #1122, order #A954; "US World War I Draft Registration Cards, 1917–1918" > Wisconsin > Marquette County > Draft Card M > image 196 of 229 (ancestry.com).

[178] Alfred A. Moore grave marker, no image, Douglas Cemetery, Douglas Center, Marquette County, Wisconsin, memorial #104,164,328 by Joey (findagrave.com).

born in New York to Irish parents, William H. and Betsy M. (-?-) Moore.[179]

1910: Alfred was a laborer doing odd jobs; he and Myrtle had two children.[180]

1920: They were renting half of a duplex at 8022 Cornwall Avenue in West Allis, Milwaukee County, Wisconsin, and he was a house carpenter.[181]

1930: Alfred A. Moore, age 51, was a married carpenter living with his mother Betsey Moore in Moundville Township, with no wife or children in sight.[182]

1940: Alfred was divorced.[183]

1942: He was unemployed, living at 610 Maple Avenue in Waukesha, Waukesha County, Wisconsin; the person who would always know his address was son Alden at 128 Cook Street. Alfred was 5 feet 6 inches tall, weighed 130 pounds, and had gray eyes and brown hair.[184]

Myrtle married second before 1940 WILLIAM CRAWFORD. In 1940 she was a "child nurse" for a private family, earning $624 the previous year. William listed no occupation. Myrtle had completed four years of high school, he completed eight years of school. They were renting a $24-a-month apartment in a seven-unit building at 1720 East Lafayette Place in Milwaukee.[185]

v. PEARL CHRISTI ELLISON was born 22 June 1891 in Moundville Township, Marquette County, Wisconsin, and died 26 July 1954 at the Wisconsin General Hospital "after an extended illness. . . . She will long be remembered as an active member in community affairs and especially for her singing ability."

---

[179] William Moore (age 39) household for wife Betsy M. (age 28) and seventh child Alfred A. (age 2), 1880 US census, Douglas, Marquette County, Wisconsin, ED 219, p. 523A, dwelling 6, family 7.
[180] Albert A. Moore household for wife Myrtle M. age 21, 1910 US census, Moundville Township, Marquette County, Wisconsin, ED 149, sheet 3A, dwelling 66, family 68.
[181] Alfred [Albert?] Moore household, 1920 US census, West Allis, Milwaukee County, Wisconsin, Ward 3, ED 329, sheet 26B, dwelling 500, family 623.
[182] Betsey Moore household for son Alfred A. age 51, 1930 US census, Moundville Township, Marquette County, Wisconsin, ED 8, sheet 3A, dwelling/family 81.
[183] Alfred Moore in Asel Waldo household, 1940 US census, Endeavor, Marquette County, Wisconsin, ED 39-8, sheet 4A, dwelling 93. Alfred was a building carpenter; the dwelling on River Road rented for $5 a month.
[184] Alfred Anson Moore WW2 draft card, serial #U287, no order number, Waukesha local draft board, 25 April 1941; "US, World War II Draft Registration Cards, 1940–1947" > Monson–Moriarty > Marks–Popp > image 623–24 of 2144 (ancestry.com).
[185] William Crawford household, 1940 US census, Milwaukee, Milwaukee County, Wisconsin, Ward 1, ED 72-3, sheet 7A, dwelling 145.

She married first 27 March 1911 at her Schwemerlein half-sister's house ELMER FRANK KRUEGER. He was born 21 June 1891 in the town of Brooklyn, Green Lake County, Wisconsin, to Frank Ferdinand and Mary Ann (Birkholz) Krueger.[186] Pearl and Elmer went to live in Princeton in that county, where he was to join his father in the hotel business.[187] The marriage ended prior to 5 June 1917, when Elmer was single, "paying alimony" for one child, and on those grounds claimed exemption from the draft; he was then working as a machinist at Durant Manufacturing and living at 682 Island Avenue in Milwaukee.[188] The exemption did not come through, and he wound up serving serve 25 months in World War I as a machinist's mate first class in the US Navy.[189] He died in a car crash near Clinton, Lenawee County, Michigan, 25 May 1941,[190] and was buried at Bluffton Cemetery, Town of Brooklyn, Green Lake County, Wisconsin.[191]

Pearl married second about 1918 JAMES HOLLERUP, who survived her.[192] He was a blacksmith, born 17 February 1886 in Söngebäk, Denmark, son of Peter Hollerup; and died 19 May 1962, age 76, at an Oxford, Wisconsin, nursing home, after a long illness.[193] He left Denmark 3 June 1910 and was naturalized 30 October 1917 in Marquette County. In 1922 he obtained a passport to visit relations in

---

[186] "Mrs. James Hollerup," *Portage Daily Register* (Wisconsin), Wednesday 4 August 1954, p. 4, col. 5.

[187] "Married…Ellison–Krueger," *Portage Daily Register* (Wisconsin), Tuesday 28 March 1911, p. 2, col. 3.

[188] Elmer Frank Krueger, WWI draft card, #138, Milwaukee Local Board 6, 5 June 1917; "US, World War I Draft Registration, 1917–1918" > Wisconsin > Milwaukee City > 06 > Draft Card K > image 445 of 509 (ancestry.com).

[189] Elmer Frank Krueger, death record; US, Evangelical Lutheran Church in America Church Records, 1781–1969" > Congregational Records > Wisconsin > Milwaukee > Ascension > image 2127 of 2267 (ancestry.com).

[190] "Accidents," *Lansing State Journal* (Michigan), Monday 26 May 1941, p. 4, col. 4.

[191] Elmer Frank Krueger military grave marker, image, Bluffton Cemetery, Brooklyn Township, Green Lake County, Wisconsin, memorial #76,451,163 by Steve Seim (findagrave.com).

[192] "Mrs. James Hollerup," *Portage Daily Register* (Wisconsin), Wednesday 4 August 1954, p. 4, col. 5. Also, "Aged Endeavor Woman Is Dead," *Portage Register-Democrat* (Wisconsin), Wednesday 22 April 1936, p. 4, col. 1. Mrs. Myrtle Moore was then living in Milwaukee, Mrs. Pearl Hollerup in Endeavor. Marriage dates are estimated from 1930 census: James Hollerup household, 1930 US census, Endeavor Village, Moundville Township, Marquette County, Wisconsin, ED 8, sheet 3B, dwelling/family 91.

[193] "James Hollerup," *Wisconsin State Journal* (Madison), Sunday 20 May 1962, p. 12, col. 3.

Denmark and Sweden.[194] In 1940 Pearl and James lived on Elm Street in Endeavor in a house they owned, valued at $2000, below the state average that year. James had completed eight years of school, Pearl one year of high school.[195]

Family C. Children of Christopher Ellison and Priscilla Walters, half-siblings of Family B:

vi. MARY ELIZABETH ELLISON was born January 1855[196] and married March 1881 ALEXANDER POWELL, son of John and Hannah (Stokes) Powell. Alex was born 25 July 1860 in Moundville and died there 18 November 1943. The homestead where he died "has always been in possession of the Powell family." Alex lived "his entire life in the town of Moundville except for a few years which were spent in Milwaukee and Endeavor." Their only child was son Glendon.[197] In 1930 and 1940 Alex was living with son Glendon and daughter-in-law Blanch on Highway 51, in a house valued at $1000, well below the statewide average of $3232. They did have a radio set in 1930. Alex had completed three years of schooling.[198]

---

[194] James Hollerup, US passport #143652, 12 April 1922, Marquette County, Wisconsin; "US Passport Application, 1795–1925" > Applications 2 January 1906–31 March 1925 > 1922 > roll 1899, certificates 143476–143849, 11–12 April 1922 > images 320–21 of 650 (ancestry.com).

[195] James Hollcrup [Hollerup] household, 1940 US census, Endeavor, Moundville Township, Marquette County, Wisconsin, ED 39-8, sheet 3B, dwelling 77. Wisconsin's statewide average in 1940 was $3232. Statewide figures from US Census Bureau, Census of Housing, Historical Census of Housing Tables, Median Home Values Unadjusted 1940 (https://www2.census.gov/programs-surveys/decennial/tables/time-series/coh-values/values-unadj.txt).

[196] Christopher Ellison household for apparent wife Priscilla (age 40, born England) and daughter Mary E. (age 5, born Wisconsin), 1860 US census, Moundville Township, Marquette County, Wisconsin, p. 113, dwelling 353, family 343. Next door was a potential brother James. Also, Alex and Mary E. Powell (born January 1855) household, 1900 US census, Moundville Township, Marquette County, Wisconsin, ED 93, sheet 5B, dwelling/family 109.

[197] "Obituary…Alexander Powell," *Portage Daily Register* (Wisconsin), Friday 26 November 1943, p. 3, col. 4.

[198] Alec Powell household, 1930 US census, Moundville Township, Marquette County, Wisconsin, ED 8, sheet 6A, dwelling/family 168. Similarly, Orah [Alex] Powell household, 1940 ED 39-8, dwelling 151, sheet 6B. Statewide house value figures from US Census Bureau, Census of Housing, Historical Census of Housing Tables, Median Home Values Unadjusted 1940 (https://www2.census.gov/programs-surveys/decennial/tables/time-series/coh-values/values-unadj.txt).

vii. ANNIS JANE ELLISON was born 29 September 1857 and died 27 January 1937. She married 2 February 1876 ENOCH CHARLES DEWSNAP. Their sons were Freeman Ellison and Vernon Charles. Enoch was born in St. Louis 23 November 1851, and then . . .

> His mother died when he was a few weeks old and his father brought him on a Mississippi River steamer [north] to Prairie du Chien and then up the Wisconsin River to Portage. Mrs. Elizabeth Townley Martin and her sister, Hanna Mountford Quinn, brought the tiny baby in a basket to his Grandmother Nixon's over 14 miles of rough wintry road to a log cabin, east of where Enoch Skinner now lives.

As a pioneer child "he attended school in a little log building that stood near his home. . . . Many of his days were spent in cutting brush for a sheep pasture where the village of Endeavor now stands."[199]

---

[199] Enoch Dewsnap and Annis Jane Ellison Dewsnap grave markers, no image, Hill Crest Cemetery, Endeavor, Marquette County, Wisconsin, memorial #208,290,264 by Janet Marie, including a transcribed obituary from an unidentified local newspaper (findagrave.com).

Table 1. Scholes-Ellison Families: Seven Somewhat Related Children

Details and notes in Chapter 7

Ann Mills[1] & Wm. Scholes

FAMILY A	FAMILY B	FAMILY C
Robert[2] Scholes m1 1868 Caroline Parks	Christopher Ellison m2 1887 Caroline Parks	Christopher Ellison m1 1853 Priscilla Walters
Nettie[3] Scholes *b 1869* *m Moran*	*Myrtle Ellison* *b 1888* *m Moore* *m Crawford*	*Mary Elizabeth Ellison* *b 1855* *m Powell*
Mary[3] Scholes *b 1871* *m Heames*	*Pearl Ellison* *b 1891* *m Krueger* *m Hollerup*	*Annie J. Ellison* *b 1857* *m Dewsnap*
Hattie[3] Scholes *b 1877* *m Schwemerlein*		

In point of time, Family C came first, then Family A, then Family B.

Relationships:
The children in families A and B are half-siblings (different fathers).
The children in families B and C are half-siblings (different mothers).
So the children in family B are half-siblings to both A and C.
But the children in families A and C are not related (both parents different).
Only the children in family A are known to be descended from the immigrants William and Ann.

Chapter 8

Second Generation

Samuel Mills Scholes–Harriet Newell Mozley Family
<u>parents at chapter 2</u>

"Frankness of speech made for him a few enemies, but none who would have made good friends"

8. **SAMUEL MILLS² SCHOLES** (*Ann¹ Mills, Samuel^A*)
Birth: 10 August 1849 in Moundville, Marquette County, Wisconsin[200]
Death: 25 May 1914 at St. Mary's Hospital, 85 Boyd Street, Oshkosh, Winnebago County, Wisconsin, of internal hemorrhage following an operation for gastric ulcer[201]
Burial: Dartford Cemetery, Green Lake, Green Lake County[202]
Spouse: **HARRIET NEWELL MOZLEY**,[203] married 28 June 1875 in Marquette, Green Lake County, Wisconsin[204]
Spouse's parents: Thomas and Elizabeth (Van Natta) Mozley[205]

---

[200] Scholes family list, Scholes ledger book. Also, obituary, "Samuel Scholes," *Green Lake County Reporter* (Wisconsin), 4 June 1914. Ann Mills Scholes, Widow's Pension Application #79,106, certificate #46,660, gives 15 August 1849.

[201] Obituary, "Samuel Scholes," *Green Lake County Reporter* (Wisconsin), 4 June 1914. Also, Samuel Ray Scholes, typescript 1960–61, sometimes called "Pop's Peregrinations," in author's possession. Also, St. Mary's Hospital entry, *Konrad's Directory of Oshkosh, Wisconsin, 1914* (Oshkosh: Konrad, [1914]), p. 14, image 22 of 264 (ancestry.com).

[202] Samuel Scholes grave marker, Dartford Cemetery, Green Lake, Wisconsin, image, memorial #90,858,175 for Samuel Mills Scholes by Janet Milburn (findagrave.com).

[203] Scholes–Mozley marriage, marriage certificate attached to Scholes ledger book, 74, in author's possession. Also, Green Lake County, Wisconsin, marriages 2:220, #35, #02836.

[204] Marriage certificate, completed by Rev. Thomas Mozley. J. A. Inglis witnessed. Scholes ledger book, 76, in author's possession.

[205] "Family Register of Henry and Susanna Mozley," Scholes ledger book, between pages 40–41. For more on Mozley cousins and immigrants, including Harriet's parents and grandparents, Harold A. Henderson, *Mozley Migrations and Memories: Four Generations from Nottinghamshire to Pennsylvania, Ohio, the Midwest, Texas, Montana, and California* (lulu.com: 2020).

Spouse's birth: 6 September 1855 in Marquette, Green Lake County, Wisconsin

Spouse's death: 8 August 1950 in Pasadena, Los Angeles County, California[206]

Spouse's burial: Dartford Cemetery, Green Lake, Green Lake County, Wisconsin[207]

In 1870 Samuel was the head of household that included mother Ann and siblings.

Harriet and Samuel's 1875 marriage day was simple. Two neighbors walked up through the dew to the Mozleys' at 5 a.m. the morning of 28 June and breakfasted with the family. At 6 a.m. Harriet's father Rev. Thomas Mozley "tied the knot," and she and Sam boarded a "buss" (train? or wagon?) to her sister Julia Anna's in Ripon. Nine-month-old baby Jay England was on hand there, as was Julia's mother-in-law Ruth. Harriet and Samuel stayed a week followed by a week at home, and then returned to Ripon to help manage a busy household. Harriet later wrote, "Sam paid his board. I *earned* mine."

In September the couple returned to Marquette.[208] Two years later, in 1877, Samuel bought a town lot from his recently widowed mother-in-law, Elizabeth (Van Natta) Mozley: the south one-sixth of Marquette village lot 44 in block 21, a rectangle 60 feet east-west and 30 feet north-south.[209]

---

[206] Thomas Mosely [Mozley] household, 1860 US census, Town of Marquette, Green Lake County, Wisconsin, p. 1039, dwelling 1957, family 1771. For exact dates, Samuel Scholes family record, Scholes ledger book, 30, in author's possession.

[207] Harriet N. Scholes grave marker, image, Dartford Cemetery, Green Lake, Wisconsin, memorial #90,858,171 by Janet Milburn (findagrave.com).

[208] Harriet Mozley Scholes handwritten reminiscence from 1939, as transcribed by the author circa 2005.

[209] Elizabeth V. Mozley to Samuel Scholes, 28 December 1877, south 1/6 of lot 44, block 21, village of Marquette, Green Lake County, Wisconsin, Deeds 40:448, recorded 11 November 1879; Register of Deeds, Green Lake.

STORY #1: Traveling in Minnesota in 1879—
no room at the inn, and no inn either

Sam and Harriet Scholes were probably still weighing whether to stay in familiar Wisconsin or head west. In 1879 a small party including Sam and his brother-in-law William J. Mozley left Harriet and baby Nellie behind, to make an exploratory trip to far western Minnesota. By then trains ran most of the way, but the young family had to pinch pennies, and Sam chose to travel economy class, riding horseback 430 miles from Port Hope (now Fort Winnebago), Columbia County, Wisconsin, to Ortonville, Big Stone County, Minnesota.

A seven-hour drive in 2020, the trip in 1879 took almost two weeks through jolting rain and "blizzard winds." Caught in a thunderstorm, they sought refuge in a sod barn, only to find that it leaked "as bad as outdoors." They went on, through "the worst storm I was ever out in but we keep right side up."

William stayed in Ortonville for a time; Samuel sent postcards home almost daily and did not stay.[210]

---

[210] Harold Henderson, "Across Wisconsin and Minnesota on Horseback, 1879 [Samuel Mills Scholes]," *Minnesota Genealogist* 2014, 45 (4):7–9, drawn from Sam's postcards en route and his account of the trip after they arrived.

Beginning in 1888, Samuel was four times elected Green Lake County Clerk on the Republican ticket.[211] When William McKinley's election as US president brought Samuel back to office in 1896, son Ray recalled that he still kept up his blacksmithing work:

> The office work was spotty, and his pay of $50 per month was not great, even in those days of low prices. The office was only ten minutes' walk away. Father was also a school board director, and was instrumental in getting a new four-room building and a high school course. That was quite a step for a village of 300 persons!

Years later, his son recalled Sam as "stern and strict"—but "he did teach me to work, to love tools and the doing of a good job with them, and to stay with a tough piece of work until I was finished. In times when the money was hard to get, he saw me through the five years at Ripon." As a blacksmith and wagon maker, "his hammering job gave him neuritis [nerve inflammation] in his arm and shoulder and caused him much suffering."

Ultimately a medical procedure did him in. The funeral service "was held on our front porch because the house was too small for those who would attend. The front yard was full of Masons, villagers, farmers, and political friends from all over."[212]

In early December 1914, widowed sisters Harriet Scholes and Julia England, left Wisconsin, visited their sister Sarah Blackmon in Ottawa, Kansas, and continued west to winter with Harriet's daughters Bonnie and Nellie Scholes in Santa Barbara, California.[213] One or more of Harriet, Nellie, and Bonnie lived there between 1915 and 1921.[214] Among other activities, "Aunt Harriet" helped niece Robey Jones survive

---

[211] "Samuel Scholes," local obituary clipping about May 1914; Mozley binder, item 42, in author's possession.
[212] Samuel Ray Scholes, typescript 1960–61, sometimes called "Pop's Peregrinations," in author's possession.
[213] "In Society…Winter in California," *Ottawa Daily Republic* (Kansas), Saturday 12 December 1914, p. 6, col. 1.
[214] Santa Barbara city directories (ancestry.com): *1915* at 1811 Loma (p. 204, image 110 of 204), *1917* at 1908 Ladera (p. 252, image 133 of 259), *1918* at 908 Madera (p. 261, image 136 of 265), *1920* and *1921* at 908 Grand (p. 274, image 140 of 266; and p. 263, 138 of 273). Directory canvassers may have been confused and inconsistent in choosing who to name in a household consisting of three women.

Midwestern winters by leaving them behind (see Chapter 19, child ii). Around this time Harriet also visited the Grand Canyon and "traveled alone across the continent both East and West."[215] In later years her sight dimmed, a malady that her son and at least one grandson may have inherited.[216] Later, at least from 1930 to 1943 and likely until their deaths, Harriet and her daughters lived in a succession of rentals in Pasadena,[217] in their view "the most beautiful city in America."[218]

Children of Samuel Mills[2] and Harriet Newell (Mozley) Scholes, all born in Wisconsin:

29 i. ELEANOR "NELLIE" ELIZABETH[3] SCHOLES (*Samuel M.[2] Scholes, Ann[1] Mills, Samuel[A]*) was born 15 March 1878 and died 24 August 1948.

30 ii. BONNIE ELIZABETH[3] SCHOLES (*Samuel M.[2] Scholes, Ann[1] Mills, Samuel[A]*) was born 12 June 1882 and died 27 March 1957.

31 iii. SAMUEL RAY[3] SCHOLES (*Samuel M.[2] Scholes, Ann[1] Mills, Samuel[A]*) was born 22 January 1884 and died 16 August 1974. He married 10 April 1914 LOIS ELIZABETH BOREN.

iv. LAURA ANNA[3] SCHOLES (*Samuel M.[2] Scholes, Ann[1] Mills, Samuel[A]*) died in infancy.

---

[215] "A Decade Tale: Our Mother—Mrs. Harriet Newell Mozley Scholes," typescript evidently by Bonnie and Nellie Scholes, about 1935, Mozley binder, item 62, in author's possession.
[216] Personal knowledge of the author, which does not extend to the exact diagnosis.
[217] Pasadena city directories (ancestry.com): *1931* at 583 North Los Robles (p. 626, image 321 of 598); *1932, 1933,* and *1934* at 1664 North El Molino Avenue (p. 585, image 294 of 551; p. 511, image 259 of 489; and p. 524, image 268 of 503); *1935, 1936,* and *1937* at 1147 North Catalina (p. 547, image 277 of 525; p. 574, image 290 of 1614; and p. 570, image 285 of 583); *1938* at 2370 Sherwood Road (p. 561, image 281 of 577); *1939, 1940, 1942,* and *1943* at 1147 North Catalina again, p. 550, image 275 of 517; p. 587, image 293 of 550; p. 587 [1942, not on line], and p. 595, image 303 of 560); *1947,* not listed; *1949* at 562 Buckeye (at least Bonnie and perhaps Harriet), p. 838, image 423 of 831; and *1951, 1953,* and *1954* at 773 North Los Robles (which Bonnie purchased in the early 1950s), Bonnie alone (p. 636, image 315 of 494; p. 624, image 320 of 403; and p. 597, images 318 and 488 of 717). Not found after 1954.
[218] "A Decade Tale: Our Mother—Mrs. Harriet Newell Mozley Scholes," typescript evidently by Bonnie and Nellie Scholes about 1935, Mozley binder, item 62, in author's possession.

Chapter 9

Second Generation

William Scholes–Mary Ellen Dixon Family
parents at chapter 2

Six pallbearers – two brothers, two brothers-in-law, two nephews

9. WILLIAM² SCHOLES (*Ann¹ Mills, Samuel^A*)
Birth: 1854 (grave marker); 10 May 1855 in Wisconsin[219]
Death: Portage, Columbia County, Wisconsin, 2 January 1929[220]
Burial: Moundville Cemetery, Endeavor, Marquette County, Wisconsin[221]
Spouse: **MARY ELLEN DIXON,** married 26 November 1885
Spouse's parents: Favil and Sarah Ann (Fish?) Dixon[222]
Spouse's birth: 5 May 1856, Manchester, England[223]
Spouse's death: 22 June 1920, after a "number of years" of "declining health" aggravated in February
Spouse's burial: Moundville Cemetery, Endeavor, Marquette County, Wisconsin

---

[219] 10 May 1855: Ann Mills Scholes Widow's Pension Application, testimony to determine when William would turn 16 (fold3.com/image/269868378). 12 May 1854: "Were Brother and Sister," *Portage Daily Register* (Wisconsin), Thursday 10 January 1929, p. 2, col. 3. 1854: William Scholes grave marker, image, Moundville Cemetery, Endeavor, Marquette County, Wisconsin, memorial #102,554,832 by Joey (findagrave.com).
[220] "Were Brother and Sister," *Portage Daily Register* (Wisconsin), Thursday 10 January 1929, p. 2, col. 3.
[221] William Scholes grave marker, image, Moundville Cemetery, Endeavor, Marquette County, Wisconsin, memorial #102,554,832 by Joey (findagrave.com).
[222] William Scholes–Mary Ellen Dixon marriage, 26 November 1885, Fort Winnebago, Columbia County, Wisconsin, marriage 3:206, #225, #02520; Wisconsin State Historical Society, Madison.
[223] "Mary Ellen Scholes," *Portage Daily Register* (Wisconsin), Friday 25 June 1920, p. 1, col. 2. A quite different birth place is named, without sourcing, in her memorial: Owston Ferry, North Lincolnshire Unitary Authority, Lincolnshire, England. Mary E. Dixon grave marker, image, memorial #102,554,925 by Joey (findagrave.com).

Mary Ellen emigrated from England with her family when she was about eight years old (about 1864). They first settled near Beaver Dam, Dodge County, Wisconsin, in January 1865; later moved to Kingston, Green Lake County; and in 1882 to Fort Winnebago, Columbia County. There William wasted no time in paying $2800 for 80 acres to John and Margaret Reid, who had gone west to Saline County, Nebraska.[224]

William and Mary Ellen farmed for about 28 years at Fort Winnebago; he was "a well-known and well-to-do farmer." In 1910 they retired, buying the William E. Russell house and one lot at 309 West Marion Street in Portage for $2600 (at least $72,200 in 2019 dollars).[225]

She was an active member of the Methodist churches where they lived. For a week in 1918 the family visited relatives in Sparta, Monroe County, Wisconsin— presumably Sherwins—and also nephew Samuel E. Scholes (Chapter 35), who was stationed at nearby Camp Robinson.[226]

The William Scholes home was made available for funerals at least twice, on the deaths of Thomas Fish in 1912 and cousin Flora (Sherwin) Bell (Chapter 15) in 1923.[227] In June 1920, Mary Ellen's pallbearers were brothers Aaron and William Dixon; brothers-in-law James M. Scholes (Chapter 11) and George W. Scholes (Chapter 10); and nephews Frank and William Sherwin (Chapters 13 and 14). Relatives "from a distance" (all from Wisconsin) for the funeral included Mr. and Mrs. Eph. Dixon of Dalton, Green Lake County; Mrs. G. R. Williams of Randolph, Dodge County; Mrs. Harriet [Mozley] Scholes of Green Lake, Green Lake County (Chapter 8); Mrs. Flora Bell and daughter Amy of Tunnel City,

---

[224] John and Margaret Reid to William Scholes, 28 October 1882, Columbia County, Wisconsin, portions of Sections 9 and 10 of Town 13 North, Range 9 East, Deeds 67:452-53; images 781–82 of 879, FHL 1,630,154, DGS 8,550,265 (familysearch.org).
[225] "Short News Stories of a Day in Portage," *Portage Daily Democrat* (Wisconsin), Thursday 20 January 1910, p. 3, col. 2. Also, "Aunt Ruth & Elizabeth" to Stella and Norman Scholes, letter dated "Feb 16," well after 1962; Stella Scholes collection, item #18. For comparison, *Measuring Worth* (measuringworth.com/calculators/uscompare/relativevalue.php).
[226] "Brief News Notes," *Portage Daily Register* (Wisconsin), Friday 14 June 1918, p. 3, col. 1. Camp Robinson was one of two military camps later consolidated as Camp McCoy, between Sparta and Tomah. The Wikipedia account is sketchy on the WWI time period (https://en.wikipedia.org/wiki/Fort_McCoy,_Wisconsin).
[227] "Funeral of Thomas Fish," *Portage Daily Register* (Wisconsin), Monday 5 February 1912, p. 3, col. 2. Also, "Obituary...Mrs. Flora A. Bell," *Portage Daily Register* (Wisconsin), Thursday 6 December 1923, p. 1, col. 6.

Monroe County (Chapter 15); and Mr. and Mrs. Robert Scholes and family of Mineral Point, Iowa County (Chapter 36).[228]

"Mr. Scholes never united with the church, yet was interested in religion and a faithful attendant upon church services. He was a quiet, unassuming man, reserved, ambitious, a great reader, a nature lover and with a fondness for his home which almost precluded other interests. He was a man of strong conviction and integrity."

Siblings Elizabeth and William died the same day, both from influenza, in William's house, 2 January 1929. She had been living there for the previous five years.[229] Those attending his funeral from away were: William Sherwin and Ray Sherwin of Sparta, Monroe County, Wisconsin (Chapters 13 child i, and 14); Mrs. Nettie Moran of Waukesha, Waukesha County, Wisconsin (Chapter 26); William and Clinton Smith of Pardeeville, Columbia County, Wisconsin (Chapter 22); Mrs. Florence Beichl of Beaver Dam, Dodge County (Chapter 23); and Mr. and Mrs. Robert Scholes of Chicago (Chapter 36).[230]

Children of William^2 and Mary Ellen (Dixon) Scholes:

32   i. MARION EDITH^3 SCHOLES (*William^2 Scholes, Ann^1 Mills^1, Samuel^A*) was born about June 1890 in Wisconsin, and died 13 March 1962 in Portage, Columbia County, Wisconsin.

    ii. UNKNOWN CHILD^3 SCHOLES (*William^2 Scholes, Ann^1 Mills, Samuel^A*) died in infancy, probably born after the 1900 census and died before 1910.[231]

---

[228] "Mary Ellen Scholes," *Portage Daily Register* (Wisconsin), Friday 25 June 1920, p. 1, col. 2.
[229] "Brother and Sister Dead," clipping likely from *Portage Daily Register* based on typefaces used, early January 1929, undated clipping in Scholes ledger book, 62, in author's possession.
[230] "Were Brother and Sister," *Portage Daily Register* (Wisconsin), Thursday 10 January 1929, p. 2, col. 3.
[231] In 1900 Mary Ellen reportedly had one child, one living; in 1910, two children, one living. William Scholes household for wife Mary Ellen, 1900 US census, Fort Winnebago, Columbia County, Wisconsin, ED 8, sheet 6A, dwelling 105, family 113. Similarly, 1910, Portage, Ward 4, ED 29 sheet 4B, dwelling 91, family 92. Also, "Mary Ellen Scholes," *Portage Daily Register* (Wisconsin), Friday 25 June 1920, p. 1, col. 2. It is possible that the short-lived child was born prior to 1900 and the 1900 census was in error.

Chapter 10

Second Generation

George Walker Scholes–Susanna Rebecca Audiss Family
parents at chapter 2

A born farmer

10. GEORGE WALKER² SCHOLES (*Ann¹ Mills, Samuel^A*)
Birth: 23 or 24 March 1857 in Moundville Township, Marquette County, Wisconsin[232]
Death: 21 January 1941 in Endeavor, Marquette County, Wisconsin, after "an illness of several months"[233]
Burial: Moundville Cemetery, Endeavor, Marquette County, Wisconsin
Spouse: **SUSANNA REBECCA "SUSIE" AUDISS,**[234] married 24 February 1885[235]
Spouse's parents: reportedly William and Ann (Codling) Audiss

---

[232] Ann Mills Scholes, Widow's Pension Application, testimony to determine when George would turn 16 (fold3.com/image/269868378). Also, "Scholes Rites," *Wisconsin State Journal,* Thursday 23 January 1941, p. 2, col. 8. Also, obituary, "George W. Scholes," local newspaper clipping, copy in author's possession. Scholes ledger book, 63, gives birth year as 1856.

[233] "Scholes Rites," *Wisconsin State Journal* (Madison), Thursday 23 January 1941, p. 2, col. 8.

[234] Obituary, "George W. Scholes," local newspaper clipping, copy in author's possession.

[235] Scholes–Audiss marriage, Marquette County, Wisconsin, marriages 1:305, #25, #01753; Wisconsin State Historical Society, Madison. Also, George W. Scholes household for wife Susanna married 15 years, 1900 US census, Moundville Township, Marquette County, Wisconsin, ED 93, sheet 2A, dwelling/family 38. Also, "Scholes Rites," *Wisconsin State Journal* (Madison), Thursday 23 January 1941, p. 2, col. 8. Also, nickname from Scholes ledger book, 63. Also, "Wedding Anniversary," undated and unlabeled local newspaper clipping, describing a surprise 40th anniversary gathering, so probably 24 February 1921; Scholes ledger book, 64, in author's possession.

Spouse's birth: 1861 (grave marker), reportedly 23 August in Lincolnshire (unsourced)[236]
Spouse's death: 9 February 1931 after an illness of several months[237]
Spouse's burial: Moundville Cemetery, Endeavor, Marquette County, Wisconsin

1875: Farming was in George's future; he was eighteen years old when he bought more than one-third of the goods on offer at his late father's 1875 estate auction (Chapter 2): two horses for $110, double hames (attachments to horse collars) for $7, a lumber wagon for $45, a pair of sleighs for $10, and a harrow for $6.[238] Five years later, at age 23, he was a single farmer, head of a household including sister Elizabeth ("housekeeper," age 30) and brother James ("farm laborer," age 20).[239]

1880: Susanna Audiss was an 18-year-old in her parents' house; her father William Audiss was a minister. Her future husband's brother, Robert Scholes, and family were living with them, Robert being the farmer.[240]

1895: George was "in town" (Portage) from Merrittville (later renamed Endeavor), a 25-mile round trip.[241]

1900: Susanna was said to have emigrated in 1872, when she would have been about eleven. The couple's farm evidently did well, as it

---

[236] Susanna Scholes 1861–1931 grave marker, image, Moundville Cemetery, Endeavor, Marquette County, Wisconsin, memorial #102,555,560 by Joey (findagrave.com).
[237] "Funeral Services Held for Mrs. Geo. Scholes," *Wisconsin State Journal* (Madison), Sunday 15 February 1931, p. 6, col. 4. Also, "Scholes Rites," *Wisconsin State Journal* (Madison), Thursday 23 January 1941, p. 2, col. 8.
[238] Estate of William Scholes, Marquette County, Wisconsin, Box 9, File 482; "Wisconsin, Wills and Probate Records, 1800–1987" > Marquette > Probate Records Box 7 File 420–Box 9 File 5222 > images 1486–1534 of 1775, especially image 1487 (ancestry.com).
[239] George Schales [Scholes] household, 1880 US census, Moundville Township, Marquette County, ED 223, p. 6, family 65, no dwelling number.
[240] William Audiss household for Robert Schales [Scholes] family, 1880 US census, Moundville, Marquette County, Wisconsin, ED 223, p. 4, dwelling 39, no family number.
[241] "In City and Vicinity," *Portage Daily Democrat* (Wisconsin), Thursday 16 May 1895, p. 3, col. 1.

was mortgaged in 1900 but not in subsequent years. Father-in-law William Audiss's farm was enumerated nearby in 1920.[242]

1930: George was an aged laborer doing "odd jobs." He and Susanna had been married 55 years, and lived on Elm Street in Endeavor, where they owned their home, valued at $2800. They did not own a radio set.[243]

1940: the widower George, the last of his siblings, was living with daughter Lillian and son-in-law Fred Russell.[244]

George W. Scholes

Children of George Walker² and Susanna Rebecca (Audiss) Scholes, all born in Wisconsin:

33 i. LILLIAN ESTELLE³ SCHOLES (*George W.² Scholes, Ann¹ Mills, Samuel^A*) was born 18 December 1885 and died 19 January 1970 in Portage, Wisconsin. She married 18 June 1908 FRED RUSSELL.

34 ii. ELMER³ SCHOLES (*George W.² Scholes, Ann¹ Mills, Samuel^A*) was born 19 November 1891, and died 18 November 1955. He married 24 December 1913 ELSIE ROOD.

35 iii. SAMUEL E.³ SCHOLES (*George W.² Scholes, Ann¹ Mills, Samuel^A*) was born 3 August 1895, and died 6 July 1983. He married 23 October 1920 EDNA PEAKE.

---

[242] George W. Scholes household, 1900 US census, Endeavor Village, Moundville Township, Marquette County, Wisconsin, ED 93, sheet 2A, dwelling/family 38. Similarly, 1905 Wisconsin state census, dwelling 67, p. 110. Similarly, 1910 US census on East Moundville Road, ED 149, dwelling 145, family 151, sheets 6B-7A. Similarly, 1920 US census, ED 133, dwelling 8, family 9, sheet 1A.
[243] George W. Scholes household, 1930 US census, Endeavor Village, Moundville Township, Marquette County, Wisconsin, ED 8, sheet 2A, dwelling/family 48.
[244] Fred Russell household for father-in-law George W. Scales [Scholes], 1940 US census, ED 39-8, sheet 2B, dwelling 55.

Chapter 11

Second Generation

James Mills Scholes–Emma Maria Hull Family
parents at chapter 2

"Many of his happiest hours [were] spent in planning and making improvements on the farm he loved so well"

---

11. JAMES MILLS² SCHOLES (*Ann¹ Mills, Samuel^A*)
Birth: 11 or 12 July 1859 in Moundville, Marquette County, Wisconsin[245]
Death: 29 December 1936 there[246] "following a brief illness from pneumonia"[247]
Burial: Moundville Cemetery, Endeavor, Marquette County, Wisconsin[248]
Spouse: **EMMA MARIA HULL,** married 15 December 1886 in Buffalo Township, Marquette County, Wisconsin[249]
Spouse's parents: Henry (31 July 1822–23 June 1911) and Caroline (Brewster) Hull (1827–1920)[250]

---

[245] 10 or 11 July 1859: Ann Mills Scholes Widow's Pension Application, testimony to determine when James would turn 16 (fold3.com/image/269868378). 12 July 1859: obituary, "Descended from Sturdy English Stock," *Portage Daily Register* (Wisconsin), Tuesday 5 January 1937, p. 2, col. 3.

[246] Obituary, "Descended from Sturdy English Stock," *Portage Daily Register* (Wisconsin), Tuesday 5 January 1937, p. 2, col. 3.

[247] "J. M. Scholes, 77, Farmer, Succumbs," *Wisconsin State Journal* (Madison), Thursday 31 December 1936, p. 9, col. 4.

[248] James M. Scholes, no image of grave marker, Moundville Cemetery, Endeavor, Wisconsin, memorial #102,777,369 by Joey (findagrave.com).

[249] Scholes–Hull marriage, Marquette County, Wisconsin, marriages 1:322, #60(?); Wisconsin State Historical Society, Madison.

[250] Emma C. Brewster Jones, compiler and editor, *Brewster Genealogy 1566–1907* (New York: The Grafton Press, 1908), 537–38; "North America, Family Histories, 1500–2000" > B > Brewster > Brewster Genealogy > images 648–49 of 715 (ancestry.com). Children were said to be William (died young), Charles, Mary, Emily, Nathan, Walter, Lilly, and Henry M. (1871–1897). Also, "Hull Cemetery," read 1982 by Mr. & Mrs. William Marsh, *Wisconsin State Genealogical Society Newsletter* 30(3):29–30, January 1984; item 15, Stella Scholes collection, in author's possession.

Spouse's birth: 4 July 1858 in Buffalo Township
Spouse's death: 13 April 1942 in Moundville, age 83[251]
Spouse's burial: Moundville Cemetery, Endeavor, Marquette County, Wisconsin[252]

Reputedly James was the only family member who figured out how to make money raising sheep on the family homestead.

1880: he was a farm laborer in the same Moundville household as brother George and sister Elizabeth.[253]

1900: He and Emma owned their Moundville farm free and clear.[254]

1905: He was elected a director of the Farmers' Mutual Fire Insurance Company of Marcellon, Fort Winnebago, and Buffalo.[255]

1930: they were on River Road in Moundville, and owned a radio set.[256]

Mr. Scholes was a man of great ambition. He loved the great outdoors and joyed in farm activities and production. Many of his happiest hours being spent in planning and making improvements on the farm he loved so well. In his early manhood he joined the Methodist Episcopal church and remained loyal to it the remainder of his life, his rich bass voice often contributing to musical programs. He was active in community life being a director of the Endeavor bank

---

[251] "Mrs. Scholes," *Wisconsin State Journal* (Madison), Wednesday 15 April 1942, p. 12, col 5.
[252] Emma Scholes, no image of grave marker, Moundville Cemetery, Endeavor, Wisconsin, memorial #102,777,595 by Joey (findagrave.com).
[253] George Schales [Scholes] household, 1880 US census, Moundville Township, Marquette County, Wisconsin, ED 223, p. 6, family 65, no dwelling number.
[254] James M. Scholes household, 1900 US census, Moundville Township, Marquette County, Wisconsin, ED 93, sheet 1A, dwelling/family 2.
[255] "Brief News Notes of a Day in Portage," *Portage Daily Democrat* (Wisconsin), Saturday 4 March 1905, p. 3, col. 2.
[256] James M. Scholes household, 1930 US census, Moundville Township, Marquette County, Wisconsin, ED 8, sheet 4B, dwelling/family 124.

for many years and treasurer of the Marcellon Town Mutual Fire Insurance Company at the time of his death.[257]

James M Scholes

Children of James Mills[2] and Emma Maria (Hull) Scholes:

36   i. ROBERT[3] SCHOLES (*James M.[2] Scholes, Ann[1] Mills, Samuel[A]*) was born 22 September 1891 and died 13 November 1934. He married 24 December 1913 PEARL ALIDA EDWARDS.

37   ii. RUTH[3] SCHOLES (*James M.[2] Scholes, Ann[1] Mills, Samuel[A]*) was born 18 August 1897. She married first July 1938 LEO E. ROBLESKE, and second 12 April 1944 GEORGE MANN REDMAN.

---

[257] James M. Scholes obituary, no date or newspaper named, at James Mills Scholes memorial (no image of grave marker) #107,777,369 by Joey (findagrave.com).

Third Generation

Chapters 12–37

1856-1995
Presidents Pierce to Clinton

Chapter 12

Third Generation

Charles Truman Sherwin–Jane Thressa Young Family
parents at chapter 3

On to North Dakota and Montana

12. CHARLES TRUMAN³ SHERWIN (*Mary Scholes², Ann¹ Mills, Samuel^A*)
Birth: 16 November 1856²⁵⁸ at Fort Winnebago, Columbia County, Wisconsin
Death: Sparta, Monroe County, Wisconsin, 30 March 1910²⁵⁹
Burial: Woodlawn Cemetery, Sparta, Monroe County, Wisconsin²⁶⁰
Spouse: married **JANE "JENNIE" THRESSA YOUNG** 12 September 1877 in Monroe County²⁶¹
Spouse's parents: John and Susan Drusilla (Brown) Young

---

²⁵⁸ Affidavit of Mrs. Amanda Jones, 19 July 1867; Mary Sherwin, widow's pension #73,064, service of Bissell Sherwin (Private, Company D, 19ᵗʰ Wisconsin Infantry, Civil War), Civil War and Later Pension Files; Department of Veterans Affairs, Record Group 15; National Archives, Washington DC. Also, "The Grim Reaper . . . Chas. Sherwin," *Monroe County Democrat* (Sparta, Wisconsin), 7 April 1910, p. 1.
²⁵⁹ "The Grim Reaper . . . Chas. Sherwin," *Monroe County Democrat* (Sparta, Wisconsin), 7 April 1910, p. 1.
²⁶⁰ Charles T. Sherwin, grave marker including parents and infant brother, image [difficult to read], Woodlawn Cemetery, Sparta, Monroe County, Wisconsin, memorial #116,677,533 by Tom Mauer (findagrave.com).
²⁶¹ Charles T. Sherwin–Jennie T. Young marriage index entry 12 September 1877; Monroe County Local History Room Index to Marriages in Monroe County, Wisconsin, FHL #1,292,394, DGS #7,615,248, image 609, 2:73, microfilm 2934.

Spouse's birth: Holmes County, Ohio, about 1856[262]
Spouse's death: 1914 (possibly 2 June)
Spouse's burial: with her second husband in Block 22, Row 4, Lot 5 in Beaver Lodge Cemetery, Ekalaka, Carter County, Montana: "Jennie / Wife of I B Chesley / 1862 [*sic*, 1856]–1914"[263]

Sometime during the 1860s the Youngs moved from Knox Township, Holmes County, Ohio, to Monroe County, Wisconsin.[264] In 1880 newlyweds Charles and Jennie were living with her parents in Sparta.[265]

Just as October 1864 marked mother Mary Sherwin's life forever, November and December 1888 marked Charles and Jennie's. Within three weeks they lost three of their five children to diphtheria.[266]

Charles was a farmer, but what was then called "rheumatism" often prevented him from working.[267] For whatever reason, in 1900 he was listed as single, Jennie as "widowed," and they were living apart. Charles and mother Mary were in the Monroe County household of his

---

[262] John Young household for wife Susan age 52 and daughter Jane age 24, 1880 US census, Sparta, Monroe County, Wisconsin, ED 29, p. 94C, dwelling 155, family 156. Also, John Young–Susan Drusilla Brown marriage, Holmes County, Ohio, p. 12 in book beginning 1 January 1850; "Ohio, County Marriage Records, 1774–1993" > Holmes > 1825–1859 > image 341 of 455 (familysearch.org). Justice of the Peace Matthew Cunningham officiated. (The numeral 5 in this record strongly resembles the numeral 3.) Also, John Young household for apparent daughter Jane age 6, 1860 U.S. census, Knox Township, Holmes County, Ohio, p. 373, dwelling 383, family 858. For Jennie's county of birth, see Chesley–Sherwin marriage, note below. In 1900 Jennie was said to have been born in September 1851, an outlier: Albert Stratton household for boarders Jennie, Flossie, and Elbridge Sherwin, Irving Township, Jackson County, Wisconsin, ED 51, sheet 5A, dwelling 88, family 89.
[263] Jennie wife of I. B. Chesley 1852/1862–1914 grave marker, image (difficult to read), Beaver Lodge Cemetery, Ekalaka, Montana, memorial #133,978,142 for Jane "Jennie" Thressa Young Chesley by Ron Penn (findagrave.com).
[264] John Young household, 1860 US census, Knox Township, Holmes County, Ohio, p. 373, dwelling 838, family 858. Similarly, 1870, Town of Sparta, Monroe County, Wisconsin, p. 141, dwelling 31, family 30.
[265] John Young household for daughter Jane age 24 and son-in-law Charles Sherwin age 23, 1880 US census, Sparta, Monroe County, Wisconsin, ED 29, p. 94C, dwelling 155, family 156.
[266] "A Sad Case," *Sparta Herald* (Wisconsin), 4 December 1888, p. 4, col. 2.
[267] "Mrs. Mary Sherwin," *Monroe County Democrat* (Wisconsin), 29 December 1910. Also, "The Grim Reaper," Charles Sherwin obituary, *Monroe County Democrat* (Wisconsin), 7 April 1910.

sister and brother-in-law, Flora and John J. Bell. Charles spent his last six years unable "to be out of his chair."[268]

In 1900 Jennie and children Elbridge and Florence were "boarders" in the household of widowed farmer Albert Stratton in Irving Township, Jackson County,[269] about 20 miles away. In 1905 Jennie and Flora were still there; Jennie was a "servant."[270]

In 1910 Jennie and daughter Flossie were in son Ira's household in Beach, Billings County, North Dakota (near the southwest corner of the state and immediately east of Golden Valley County, which borders on Montana).[271] In the following years Charles and Jennie's three surviving children took up adjoining parcels of homestead land in Carter County, Montana.[272] Ira eventually returned to western Wisconsin and Elbridge to western North Dakota, but Florence lived out her life in Montana.

The marrying kind

Jennie's second husband, Israel Benjamin Chesley, almost needs a chapter of his own. The son of George and Charlotte (Sovereign) Chesley, he was born either in Toronto or in "Simcole" (perhaps Simcoe, Norfolk County, Ontario), Canada, 22 July 1850; and died of uremia and

---

[268] "The Grim Reaper," Charles Sherwin obituary, *Monroe County Democrat* (Wisconsin), 7 April 1910.
[269] John J. Bell household for Charles and Mary Shuman [Sherwin], 1900 US census, La Grange Township, Monroe County, Wisconsin, ED 99, sheet 3B, dwelling 51, family 53. Also, Albert Stratton household for boarders Jennie, Flossie, and Elbridge Sherwin, Irving Township, Jackson County, Wisconsin, ED 51, sheet 5A, dwelling 88, family 89.
[270] Albert Stratton household for servant Jennie, 1905 Wisconsin state census, Town of Irving, Jackson County, Wisconsin, p. 251, family 158.
[271] Ira T. Sherwin household for Jennie Thressa [Sherwin] and Flossie, 1910 US census, ED 5, Beach, Billings County, North Dakota, sheet 4A, dwelling 72, family 87.
[272] Colin Munro (Florence's husband), homestead patent #384,141, issued 10 February 1914; Ira T. Sherwin, homestead patent #449,969 issued 19 December 1914; and Elbridge Sherwin, homestead patent #487,493, issued 21 August 1915; Bureau of Land Management, Land Patent Search database, General Land Office records (glorecords.blm.gov/PatentSearch). All claims were in Township 2 North, Range 57 East, Carter County, Montana. Colin had portions of sections 22, 27, and 28; Ira half of section 20, and Elbridge portions of section 19. Sections 19 and 20 are adjacent, as are sections 22, 27, and 28.

cystitis in Baker, Fallon County, Montana 13 February 1935.[273] He married four or five times:

(1) Israel married first in Jackson County, Wisconsin, 24 March 1880, Marietta Pauley, the daughter of Ira and Lavina (-?-) Pauley.[274] They reportedly had five children. In 1900 Israel was said to be divorced and living in Clear Lake, Deuel County, South Dakota. His household included no wife and four unmarried daughters: Etta (born in Wisconsin August 1882), Anna (born in Minnesota September 1887), Cora (born in Minnesota March 1890), and Ella (born in Minnesota October 1893).[275]

After a two-year absence, in the spring of 1903 Israel returned to Watertown, Codington County, South Dakota, to find that Marietta had married second William Porter (evidently on the reasonable assumption that she had been abandoned). Israel filed suit for bigamy, result not known.[276]

(2) A widow since March 1910, Jennie Thressa (Young) Sherwin married second Israel as his second wife 22 February 1911 at Glendive, Dawson County, Montana. Jennie was said to be 58 years old and Israel 60.[277]

(3) Following Jennie's 1914 death, Israel married third 12 April 1916 at Baker, Fallon County, Montana, as her third husband, Emeline

---

[273] Israel B. Chesley, death 13 February 1935, Montana death certificate, Fallon, 504; "Montana, State Deaths, 1907–2018" > Montana Death Records > 1935 January—1950 August > image 5 of 530 (ancestry.com).
[274] Israel B. Chesley–Marietta Paulley marriage index entry, 24 March 1880, Jackson County, Wisconsin, p. 251/803, image 472; FHL 1,266,681, DGS 7,727,532 (familysearch.org).
[275] Israel Chesley household, 1900 US census, Clear Lake, Deuel County, South Dakota, ED 129, sheet 1A, dwelling 7, family 6.
[276] "Charge of Bigamy Brought," *Sioux City Journal* (South Dakota), Thursday 30 April 1903, p. 3, col. 3.
[277] Israel B. Chesley–Jemmie T. Sherroin [Jennie T. Sherwin] marriage license #908, 21 February 1911, certificate 22 February, Glendive, Dawson County, Montana; "Montana, County Marriages, 1865–1987" > Dawson > Marriage Records, volume 106, 1884–1914 > image 546 of 738 (familysearch.org). Minister of the Gospel Paul C. Burhans officiated; Henry F. Johnson and Mrs. L. E. Burhans witnessed. Jennie's given age of 58 implies birth 1853, contrary to much other evidence. Also, Israel Chesley 1935 grave marker, image, Beaver Lodge Cemetery, Ekalaka, Montana, memorial #133,976,005 for Israel Benjamin Chesley by Ron Penn (findagrave.com).

Ursula (Sabin) (Newhart) Ridgway, who was born about 1857 in Wisconsin to Meritt and Ursula (Jones) Sabin.[278] Emeline had married first Robert Elwood Newhart (1861–1903)[279] and second about 1905 in Wisconsin George Ridgeway (born in Pennsylvania about 1853),[280] the second marriage evidently being terminated prior to her third. Emeline must have soon divorced Israel, because she married fourth 29 September 1919 in Carter County William H. See of "Calumet, Montana," the son of James and Mary (Parker) See. In 1920 Israel himself was divorced, working as a teamster in Ekalaka, Carter County, Montana.[281]

(4) Israel married fourth 9 December 1923 at Ekalaka, as her second husband, Alice (Naylor) Hutton, who was born about 1865 in Claremont, Dodge County, Minnesota, to John and Betsey (Carpenter) Naylor.[282] In 1930 Israel was living alone in a rental in Ekalaka, reported to be married and working as a laborer.[283] Alice was also reported married that year, enumerated as Alice Chesley, although she was living two states away, with relatives in Minnesota.[284]

---

[278] Israel B. Chesley–Emeline Ridgway marriage certificate 190, 17 April 1916, Baker, Fallon County, Montana; "Montana, County Marriages, 1865–1950" > DGS 4,351,443 > image 94 of 751 (familysearch.org).

[279] Robert Elwood Newhart, illegible grave marker except for his first name, image, Oak Park Cemetery, Mondovi, Buffalo County, Wisconsin, memorial #86,148,991 by Scott Goddard (findagrave.com).

[280] George Ridgeway household for Emeline (age 53, one child, one living), 1910 US census, Waterville Township, Pepin County, Wisconsin, ED 154, sheet 14A, dwelling/family 246. Her one child was evidently Almira Esther "Allie" (Newhart) Stuart (1885–1940), buried at Riverview Cemetery, Hamilton, Ravalli County, Montana, grave marker, no image, memorial #65,340,264 by Scott Goddard (findagrave.com).

[281] Israel B. Chesley household, 1920 US census, Ekalaka, Carter County, Montana, Ward 2, ED 29, sheet 5B, dwelling 110, family 115.

[282] Israel B. Chesley–Alice Hutton marriage license #136 and certificate, 8 and 9 December 1923, Ekalaka, Carter County, Montana; "Montana, County Marriages, 1865–1987" > Carter > marriage records 1–2, 1917–1987 > image 98 of 524 (ancestry.com). This marriage record includes an outlier in Israel's birth date records, almost all of which have him born about 1851; in this instance Israel said he was born 22 July 1858. Perhaps that was what he told Alice.

[283] Israel B. Chesley household, 1930 US census, Ekalaka, Carter County, Montana, ED 6, Ward 2, sheet 2A, dwelling 31, family 32.

[284] Ralph Kirkland household for "Aunt Alice Chesley" (age 66 born Minnesota), 1930 US census, Concord Township, Dodge County, Minnesota, ED 5, sheet 8A, dwelling 161, family 169. Israel and Anna were over 700 miles apart.

(5) Israel may possibly have married fifth "Mrs. Marshall Chesley." No information about her has been found other than her appearance on his death certificate 13 February 1935 in Baker, Fallon County, Montana. Israel was buried with his second wife at Beaver Lodge Cemetery in Ekalaka, Carter County, Montana, block 22, row 4, lot 5.[285]

Children of Charles Truman[3] and Jane "Jennie" Thressa (Young) Sherman:

i. MYRTLE "MIRTY" T.[4] SHERWIN (*Charles[3] Sherwin, Mary[2] Scholes, Ann[1] Mills, Samuel[A]*) was born about 1879 in Sparta, Monroe County, Wisconsin; died of diphtheria there 6 November 1888, age 9; and was buried at Block 14, Lot 8, Woodlawn Cemetery, Sparta.[286]

ii. IRA TRUMAN[4] SHERWIN (*Charles[3] Sherwin, Mary[2] Scholes, Ann[1] Mills, Samuel[A]*) was born 9 or 11 October 1880 in Sparta, Monroe County, Wisconsin; died in Black River Falls, Jackson County, Wisconsin, 20 June 1961 "after a short illness";[287] and was buried at Mentor Cemetery, Humbird, Clark County.[288] He married 5 September 1906 in Humbird ETHEL FERN STALLARD. The daughter of Henry Wallace and Ida May (Stiles) Stallard,[289] she was born 3 June 1890 in Humbird; died 13

---

[285] Israel Chesley (died 1935) grave marker, image, Beaver Lodge Cemetery, Ekalaka, Carter County, Montana, block 22, row 4, lot 5, memorial #133,976,005 by Ron Penn (findagrave.com). The memorial omits his first marriage.

[286] "A Sad Case," *Sparta Herald* (Wisconsin), 4 December 1888, p. 4, col. 2. Myrtle is named as the child that Charles and Jennie had before Ira: Monroe County, Wisconsin, Ira Truman Sherwin Delayed Birth Registration, Wisconsin State Historical Society microfilm 2DB, reel 322, record #429 of second series. Also, *Woodlawn Cemetery, Sparta, Wisconsin, Record Book Copy* (Sparta, Wisconsin: Angelo Books, n.d.), 1:57–58.

[287] 9 October: Ira Truman Sherwin, WWI draft card, Ekalaka, Carter County, Montana, serial #150, order #703, 12 September 1918; "World War I Draft Registration Cards 1917–1918" > Montana > Carter County > ALL > Draft Card S > image 53 of 167 (ancestry.com). 11 October: Ira Truman Sherwin Delayed Birth Registration, Wisconsin State Historical Society microfilm 2DB, reel 322, record #429 of second series. Also, Ira T. Sherwin obituary, *Black River Falls Banner-Journal* (Wisconsin), 28 June 1961, p. 6, col. 5.

[288] Ethel and Ira Sherwin, joint grave marker, image, block 22, lot 232, Mentor Cemetery, Humbird, Clark County, Wisconsin, memorials #121,645,227 and #121,645,228 respectively, by Bob Ottinger (findagrave.com).

[289] Sherwin–Stallard marriage 5 September 1906, Clark County, Wisconsin, Register of Marriages 3:59, #01518; Wisconsin State Historical Society microfilm, Madison.

February 1944 in Black River Falls, Jackson County[290]; and was buried with her husband.[291]

After their second child's birth in 1909, Ira and Ethel left Wisconsin for Beach, Billings County, North Dakota, where they lived with his mother and sister in 1910.[292] Following brother-in-law Colin Munro, Ira filed a homestead claim on 320 acres in Carter County, Montana.[293] In 1920 Ira was working in Ekalaka, Montana, as a barber; their two youngest children were born there.[294] About the mid-1920s they returned to western Wisconsin.[295] Ira worked almost half a century as a barber, first in Ekalaka and later in Black River Falls, Wisconsin.[296]

iii. WAYLAND[4] SHERWIN (*Charles[3] Sherwin, Mary[2] Scholes, Ann[1] Mills, Samuel[A]*) was born about 1882 in Sparta; died of diphtheria there 1 December 1888, age 6; and was buried at Block 14, Lot 8, Woodlawn Cemetery, Sparta.[297]

---

[290] Unnamed daughter of Henry Stallard and (-?-) Stiles, birth 3 June 1890, Clark County, Wisconsin, p. 128, record #02873; Wisconsin State Historical Society Microfilm 17B Clark County, Reel 30. Also, "Mrs. Ira Sherwin," obituary transcript by Sheri Stuve, citing *Humbird Enterprise*, 26 February 1944; the transcription is no longer found on line.

[291] Ethel and Ira Sherwin, joint grave marker, image, block 22, lot 232, Mentor Cemetery, Humbird, Clark County, Wisconsin, memorials #121,645,227 and #121,645,228 respectively, by Bob Ottinger (findagrave.com).

[292] Ira T. Sherwin household, 1910 US census, Billings County, North Dakota, p. 190, dwelling 7, family 87.

[293] Ira T. Sherwin homestead patent #449,969 issued 19 December 1914, Carter County (Miles City land office) south half of Section 20, Township 2 North, Range 57 East.

[294] Ira T. Sherwin household, 1920 US census, Ekalaka, Carter County, Montana, ED 29, sheet 4B, dwelling 92, family 97.

[295] "Mrs. Ira Sherwin," obituary transcribed from *Humbird Enterprise* (Wisconsin), 26 February 1944, stating that they lived 14 years in Ekalaka. As of 1910 they were still in North Dakota: Ira T. Sherwin household, 1910 US census, Billings County, North Dakota, p. 190, dwelling 7, family 87.

[296] "Ira T. Sherwin," *Black River Falls Banner-Journal* (Wisconsin), Wednesday 28 June 1961, p. 6, col. 5.

[297] "A Sad Case," *Sparta Herald* (Wisconsin), 4 December 1888, p. 4, col. 2. Also, *Woodlawn Cemetery, Sparta, Wisconsin, Record Book Copy* (Sparta, Wisconsin: Angelo Books, n.d.), 1:57.

iv. ELBRIDGE JAMES*4* SHERWIN (*Charles³ Sherwin, Mary² Scholes, Ann¹ Mills, Samuel^A*) was born 28 May 1884[298] and died in Golden Valley County, North Dakota, 25 May 1951, having suffered from "a severe form of arthritis" for many years (possibly inherited from his father).[299] Elbridge may have been named for his mother's brother.[300] He completed eight years of schooling.[301]

1900: he was living in the Albert Stratton household along with mother Jennie and younger sister Florence "Flossie."[302]

1915: Following brother Ira and brother-in-law Colin Munro, in August Elbridge patented 315.4 acres of homestead land in eastern Montana,[303] near Ekalaka. He lived there for approximately five years before returning to Golden Valley County, North Dakota, "where he was employed at farm work for many years. He was unmarried."

1918: he was of medium height and slender build, with blue eyes and brown hair; brother Ira was his nearest relative.[304] Elbridge has not been found in 1920 or 1930.

1940: he lodged with the Zielsdorf family in Beach, Golden Valley County, North Dakota, with no occupation listed.[305] About that time "he retired because of ill health, and was confined to his hospital bed

---

[298] Elbridge James Sherwin, WWI draft card, 12 September 1918, Golden Valley County local board, serial 557, order 9589; "US, World War I, Draft Registration Cards, 1917–1918" > North Dakota > Golden Valley County A–Z > image 1294 of 1614 (familysearch.org).

[299] "Elbridge Sherwin Taken By Death," *Golden Valley News* (Beach, North Dakota), 31 May 1951, p. 1, col. 5. Also, Elbridge Sherwin death index entry, 28 May 1951, age 67 years, North Dakota Department of Public Health, Public Death Index (https://apps.nd.gov/doh/certificates/deathCertSearch.htm).

[300] The obituary notice for Jennie's father John Young mentions her brother "Mr. Elbridge Young, of La Crosse": "Deaths the Past Week," *Sparta Herald* (Wisconsin), Tuesday 6 December 1892, p. 4, col. 2.

[301] Eldridge [Elbridge] J. Sherwin, lodger in Ernest G. Zielsdorf household, 1940 US census, Beach, Golden Valley County, North Dakota, ED 17-2, sheet 6A, dwelling 97.

[302] Albert Stratton household for boarders Jennie, Flossie, and Elbridge Sherwin, Irving Township, Jackson County, Wisconsin, ED 51, sheet 5A, dwelling 88, family 89.

[303] Elbridge Sherwin, Carter County, Montana, homestead patent #487,492, Bureau of Land Management, Land Patent Search database, General Land Office Records. This was in Township 2 North, Range 57 East of the Montana Principal Meridian, including the SE quarter (160 acres), the east half of the SW quarter (80 acres adjacent), and two tracts (75.4 acres).

[304] Elbridge James Sherwin, WWI draft card, 12 September 1918, Golden Valley County local board, serial 557, order 9589; "US, World War I, Draft Registration Cards, 1917–1918" > North Dakota > Golden Valley County A–Z > image 1294 of 1614 (familysearch.org).

[305] Eldridge [Elbridge] J. Sherwin, lodger in Ernest G. Zielsdorf household, 1940 U.S. census, Beach, Golden Valley County, North Dakota, ED 17-2, sheet 6A, dwelling 97.

for many months with arthritis, but with constant medical treatment he was able to get up and lead a moderately active life. He was a true friend, leading a quiet, unobtrusive, busy life." Dying in 1951, he was survived by brother Ira, sister Florence ("Mrs. Kreager"), and Orin Stockwell, "a life-long close friend."[306]

v. EUSTICE[4] SHERWIN (*Charles[3] Sherwin, Mary[2] Scholes, Ann[1] Mills, Samuel[A]*) was born about June 1886 in Sparta, Monroe County, Wisconsin; died there of diphtheria 2 December 1888, age 2; and was buried at Block 14, Lot 8, in Woodlawn Cemetery there.[307]

vi. UNKNOWN CHILD[4] SHERWIN (*Charles[3] Sherwin, Mary[2] Scholes, Ann[1] Mills, Samuel[A]*) was born say 1891 and died before 1910.[308]

vii. FLORENCE ANORA "FLOSSIE"[4] SHERWIN (*Charles[3] Sherwin, Mary[2] Scholes, Ann[1] Mills, Samuel[A]*) was born 16 May 1896[309] in "Black River" (perhaps Black River Falls, Jackson County), Wisconsin,[310] and died 12 December 1972 in Custer County, Montana;[311] and was buried with her third husband at Custer County Cemetery, Miles City, Custer County, Montana, Section I, lot 330.[312]

---

[306] "Elbridge Sherwin Taken By Death," *Golden Valley News* (Beach, North Dakota), 31 May 1951, p. 1, col. 5.
[307] "A Sad Case," *Sparta Herald* (Wisconsin), 4 Dec. 1888, p. 4, col. 2. Also, *Woodlawn Cemetery, Sparta, Wisconsin, Record Book Copy* (Sparta, Wisconsin: Angelo Books, n.d.), 1:57.
[308] Jennie was twice reported as having had seven children: Albert Stratton household for boarders Jennie, Flossie, and Elbridge Sherwin, 1900 US census, Irving Township, Jackson County, Wisconsin, ED 51, sheet 5A, dwelling 88, family 89; and Ira T. Sherwin household for Jennie Thressa [Sherwin] and Flossie, 1910 US census, ED 5, Beach, Billings County, North Dakota, sheet 4A, dwelling 72, family 87.
[309] Florence A. Kreager application for Social Security account number (Form SS-5), with birth date and parents Charles Sherwin and Jennie Thressa Young. Also, "Mrs. Kreager," *Billings Gazette* (Montana.), Wednesday 13 December 1972, p. 12, col. 7.
[310] Flossie Sherwin–Colin Munro marriage license #1288, 17 June 1912, certificate 18 June, Ismay, Custer County, Montana, p. 119; "Montana, County Marriages 1865–1987" > Custer > Marriage Records, volumes 3–5, 1910–1916 > image 251 of 847 (ancestry.com). Officiant was Justice of the Peace J. E. Prindle; witnesses were Mina Munro and George R. Smith.
[311] "Obituaries: Mrs. Lee V. Kreager," *Miles City Star* (Montana), 17 December 1972, p. 2, col. 5.
[312] Lee Vern and Florence A. Kreager joint grave marker, image, Custer County Cemetery, Miles City, Custer County, Montana, Section I, lot 330, memorials #92,246,434 and #92,246,360 respectively, by Karen Griswold Stroh (findagrave.com). "Obituaries: Mrs. Lee V. Kreager," *Miles City Star* (Montana), 17 December 1972, p. 2, col. 5.

She married first COLIN MUNRO 18 June 1912 in Ismay, Custer County, Montana, son of "Rodic" (Roderick?) and Mary (McCray) Munro.[313] Colin was born 23 September 1883 in Darwin, Falkland Islands; died in Ekalaka, Carter County, Montana, 29 September 1966[314]; and was buried at Block 4, Row 1, Lot 35 in Beaver Lodge Cemetery there.[315] As of 12 September 1918, Colin Munro was a naturalized US citizen, medium in height, slender in build, with blue eyes and brown hair, a self-employed "sheep raiser" in Carter County, Montana.[316]

Florence married second ROBERT RAY LAMB 10 April 1925 (after first-known child) in Baker, Fallon County, Montana. Both parties said they were divorced; both parties evidently gave fictional names for their parents. Robert Ray was born about 1872 (age 53 at marriage) at Amarillo, Potter County, Texas.[317] His burial place has not been found. Flossie's second husband may well be the Robert R. Lamb who patented ten land parcels in the fall of 1925, totaling 640 acres in adjacent sections 4, 5, and 9 in Township 2 South, Range 56 East, in Carter County, Montana.[318]

Florence married third as his second wife LEE VERN KREAGER, perhaps in 1925 or perhaps a year or so later, at Forsyth, Rosebud

---

[313] Flossie Sherwin–Colin Munro marriage license #1288, 17 June 1912, certificate 18 June, Ismay, Custer County, Montana, p. 119; "Montana, County Marriages 1865–1987" > Custer > Marriage Records, volumes 3–5, 1910–1916 > image 251 of 847 (ancestry.com). Officiant was Justice of the Peace J. E. Prindle; witnesses were Mina Munro and George R. Smith. Also, untitled short local items, including marriage between Colin Munro and "Miss Flossy Sherwin," *Ekalaka Eagle* (Montana), Friday 21 June 1912, p. 9, col. 2. At marriage Colin gave his age as 27 (implying birth about 1885), whereas his grave marker (note below) gives his birth as 1883 (implying an age of 29 at marriage).

[314] "Colin Munro, 83," *Billings Gazette* (Montana), Saturday 1 October 1966, p. 9, col. 7.

[315] Colin Munro (1883–1966) grave marker, image, Beaver Lodge Cemetery, Ekalaka, Montana, memorial #138,494,214 by Ron Penn (findagrave.com).

[316] Colin Munro WWI draft card, 12 September 1918, Carter County Local Board, Ekalaka; "US, World War I Draft Registration Cards, 1917–1918" > Montana > Carter County > Draft Card M > images 140–41 of 147 (ancestry.com).

[317] Robert Lamb–Flossie Munroe marriage 19 April 1925, Baker, Fallon County, Montana, license #778; "Montana, County Marriages, 1865–1987" > Fallon > Marriage Records Volumes 1–3 1913–1935 > image 457 of 851 (ancestry.com).

[318] Robert R. Lamb land patents, US Department of the Interior, Bureau of Land Management, General Land Office Records, accession #967945 approved 14 October 1925 (SW SW Section 4; S ½ SE Section 5; and NW and NW NE Section 9), and 5 November 1925 (SW SE, SE SW, and N ½ SW of Section 4; and N ½ SE, Lot/Tract 9, and Lot/Tract 10 in Section 5), totaling 640 acres. On-site deed research in Carter County may be the most promising avenue to identifying this elusive man.

County, Montana.[319] Lee Vern had married first 16 March 1923 in Baker, Fallon County, Montana, Irma L. Orton, the daughter of William and Isabella (Ayers) Orton.[320] She was born 1902 (possibly 17 March) and died 1924 (possibly 18 July).[321]

In 1927 Florence and Lee Vern were married and living in Billings, Montana, at 322 North 17th.[322] Lee was the son of Fred and Nancy (Stanhope) Kreager, born 15 March 1897 in Leland, Winnebago County, Iowa; and died 8 July 1988, age 91, in Miles City, Custer County, Montana, at the Veterans Administration Medical Center following a stroke.

He is said to have attended rural school near Baker, Fallon County, Montana, but the family was not there until he was about thirteen years old, so some early education may have taken place in Minnesota as well.[323]

In 1900 Fred and Nancy Kreager's family was in Arthur, Traverse County, Minnesota, on a rented farm.[324] The family was in Montana by 1911.[325] Ultimately Lee Vern and Florence both completed eight years of school.[326]

---

[319] "Mrs. Kreager," *Billings Gazette* (Montana), Wednesday 13 December 1972, p. 12, col. 7. The date seems precipitous and the report is far removed from the event. Lee Vern's 1930 census entry may imply that they married about 1927: Le Verne Kreager solo household, 1930 US census, Saugus, Prairie County, Montana, ED 17, sheet 1A, dwelling/family 11.

[320] L. Vern Kreager–Irma/Irena Orton marriage, Baker, Fallon County, Montana, 16 March. 1923, license 652; "Montana, County Marriages, 1865–1987" > Fallon > Marriage Records vol. 1–3, 1913–1935 > image 393 of 851 (ancestry.com).

[321] Irma L. Orton (1902–1924) grave marker, image, Ollie Cemetery, Baker, Montana, memorial #26,376,632 for Irma Lillian Orton Kreager by Mary Phea (findagrave.com). Exact birth and death dates are unsourced.

[322] P. Lavern Kreager and implied wife Flossie, *Polk's Billings City Directory 1927* (Butte, Montana: R.L. Polk of Montana, 1927), p. 172, image 90 of 287 (ancestry.com).

[323] "Lee Vern Kreager," *Billings Gazette* (Montana), Friday 10 July 1988, p. 10A, col. 2. For Nancy's birth surname: Fred Kruger–Nancy Stanhope marriage 16 December 1891, Forest City, Winnebago County, Iowa, p. 95-1466; "Iowa, Marriage Records, 1880–1940" > 1892 > 367 (Pottawattomie–Wright), image 330 of 415. Exact birth date from Vern Kreager WWI draft card, Baker, Montana, local board, 5 June 1918, order #31, registration #26; "US, World War I Draft Registration Cards, 1917–1918" > Montana > Fallon County > ALL > Draft Card K > image 76 of 84 (ancestry.com).

[324] Fred Kruger household for son Levern age 3, 1900 US census, Arthur Township, Traverse County, Minnesota, ED 283, sheet 2A, dwelling/family 25.

[325] Fred Kreager household for children's birth states, 1920 US census, Baker, Fallon County, Montana, ED 57, sheet 16A, dwelling/family 8.

[326] Lavern Kreager household, 1940 US census, Thurlow, Rosebud County, Montana, ED 44-30, sheet 3A, dwelling 45.

As of 5 June 1918 Lee Vern was tall and slender, with blue eyes and light-colored hair, working for Miles J. Lunden on a farm in Fallon County, Montana.[327] Lee served as a private in the US Army in World War I,[328] enlisting 23 July 1918 and being released 12 December the same year.[329] In 1920 he was working on his father's rented farm near Baker.[330] In 1930 he was a railroad section foreman, married but living alone in a house rented for $10 a month; he was said to be 29 years old and first married at age 26.[331]

In 1940 the family lived in a Rosebud County house rented for $5 a month, and Lee was a section laborer on the "steam railroad," where he had earned $1450 for 52 weeks' work the previous year.[332] No doubt this was the Milwaukee Railroad, from which he retired due to ill health in 1953. He has grave markers in two locations: with Florence in Custer County Cemetery, Miles City, Custer County, Montana, Section I, lot 330;[333] and at Eastern Montana State Veterans Cemetery, Miles City, Section A, Site R7-2.[334]

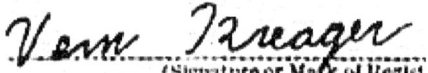

---

[327] Vern Kreager WWI draft card, Baker, Montana, local board, 5 June 1918, order #31, registration #26; "US, World War I Draft Registration Cards, 1917–1918" > Montana > Fallon County > ALL > Draft Card K > image 76 of 84 (ancestry.com).
[328] Lee V. Kreager index entry, "US Veterans' Grave Sites, ca. 1775–2019" (ancestry.com).
[329] Vern Kreager index entry, "US, Department of Veterans Affairs BIRLS Death File, 1850–2010" (ancestry.com).
[330] Fred Kreager household for son "Leevern P." Kreager, 1920 US census, Baker, Fallon County, Montana, ED 57, sheet 16A, dwelling/family 8.
[331] Le Verne Kreager solo household, 1930 US census, Saugus, Prairie County, Montana, ED 17, sheet 1A, dwelling/family 11.
[332] Lavern Kreager household, 1940 US census, Thurlow, Rosebud County, Montana, ED 44-30, sheet 3A, dwelling 45.
[333] Lee Vern and Florence A. Kreager joint grave marker, image, Custer County Cemetery, Miles City, Custer County, Montana, Section I, lot 330, memorials #92,246,434 and #92,246,360 respectively, by Karen Griswold Stroh (findagrave.com).
[334] Lee V. Kreager, military grave marker, image, Eastern Montana State Veterans Cemetery, Miles City, Custer County, Montana, Section A, Site R7-2, memorial #13,332,018 by S. McCoskey ~ Sleuthhound (findagrave.com).

Chapter 13

Third Generation

Francis Roderick "Frank" Sherwin–Annie Henry Family
parents at chapter 3

Wisconsin, Iowa, Minnesota, and back to Wisconsin

13. FRANCIS RODERICK "FRANK"³ SHERWIN (*Mary² Scholes, Ann¹ Mills, Samuel^A*)
Birth: 8 July 1858 in Columbia County, Wisconsin
Death: 23 March 1929 in Sparta, Monroe County, Wisconsin[335]
Burial: Woodlawn Cemetery, Sparta, Monroe County, Wisconsin[336]
Spouse: **ANNIE HENRY**, married 5 April 1888 in Adrian Township, Monroe County
Spouse's parents: George and Esther (Sprit) Henry,[337] Rev. J. P. Galiger officiated[338]
Spouse's birth: 7 April 1861 in Adrian Township
Spouse's death: 22 January 1935 at the home of her daughter Edith (Mrs. Herbert) Burrington at 508 South Jackson Street, Charles City, Floyd

---

[335] *Woodlawn Cemetery, Sparta, Wisconsin, Record Book Copy* (Sparta, Wisconsin: Angelo Books, n.d.), 1:153-54.
[336] Annie and Frank R. Sherwin, joint grave marker, image, Woodlawn Cemetery, Sparta, Monroe County, Wisconsin, memorials #138,431,301 and #138,431,165 respectively, by Joey (findagrave.com).
[337] Frank R. Sherwin–Annie Henry marriage index entry, 5 April 1888, Monroe County, Wisconsin; citing "Wisconsin, County Marriages, 1836–1911," FHL #1,292,395, DGS #7,615,247, image 662 (familysearch.org/ark:/61903/1:1:XRVT-1YH).
[338] "Married . . . Sherwin–Henry," *Tomah Journal* (Wisconsin), 7 April 1888, p. 2, col. 4.

County, Iowa, of "carcinoma of stomach"[339]
Spouse's burial: Woodlawn Cemetery, Sparta, Monroe County, Wisconsin[340]

Annie's father was born in Scotland and her mother in Ireland.[341] Frank Sherwin grew up in Ridgeville, Monroe County, Wisconsin. A year after their marriage, they left the Ridgeville farm for Iowa.[342]

In 1899 Frank's aunt Elizabeth Scholes (Chapter 5) returned from Rockford, Floyd County, Iowa, "where she has been spending the summer."[343] Frank and family were renting the farm in Rockford Township (about 140 miles southwest of Sparta).[344] They moved to Minnesota in March 1904,[345] but evidently returned, as in 1910 they were in Charles City, Floyd County, renting on Grand Avenue, and renting a dairy farm.[346]

In 1914 the Sherwins were again living in Mower County, Minnesota, at Grand Meadow, 55 miles north of Charles City.[347] He reportedly held local offices there.[348] By 1920 they had returned to Sparta, Monroe County, where he worked as a mail carrier. (A map of their travels

---

[339] *Woodlawn Cemetery, Sparta, Wisconsin, Record Book Copy* (Sparta, Wisconsin: Angelo Books, n.d.), 1:153-54. Also, Anna Sherwin, Iowa death certificate, 22 January 1935, Charles City, Floyd County, Iowa, #1922; "Iowa, Death Records, 1920–1967" > 1935 > Clinton–Henry > image 3167 of 5103 (ancestry.com). Daughter Edith did not name Annie's parents.
[340] Annie and Frank R. Sherwin, joint grave marker, image, Woodlawn Cemetery, Sparta, Monroe County, Wisconsin, memorials #138,431,301 and #138,431,165 respectively, by Joey (findagrave.com).
[341] Frank R. Sherwin household for wife Annie, 1900 US census, Rockford Township, Floyd County, Iowa, ED 94, sheet 16A, dwelling 366, family 373.
[342] Frank R. Sherwin grave marker, image, Woodlawn Cemetery, Sparta, Monroe County, Wisconsin, memorial #138,431,165 by Joey, plus obituary as transcribed (findagrave.com).
[343] "Moundville," *Portage Daily Register* (Wisconsin), Friday 3 November 1899, p. 1, col. 2.
[344] Frank R. Sherwin household, 1900 US census, Rockford Township, Floyd County, Iowa, ED 94, sheet 16A, dwelling 366, family 373.
[345] "News of Rockford," *Evening Times-Republican* (Marshalltown, Iowa), Tuesday 8 March 1904, p. 1, col. 4.
[346] Frank R. Sherwin household, 1910 US census, Charles City, Floyd County, Iowa, Ward 1, ED 103, sheet 12B-13A, dwelling 290, family 316.
[347] Untitled local news notes, *Sparta Herald* (Wisconsin), 16 June 1914, p. 3, col. 5.
[348] Frank R. Sherwin obituary, as transcribed at his memorial #138,431,165 by Joey (findagrave.com).

forms a tall triangle lying on its side with the apex at Sparta.) They were renting at 407 East Dall Street, and had four lodgers who worked in the foundry and feed mill.[349]

In April 1928 Frank "was operated upon two weeks ago for the removal of a kidney," and was expected to go home soon.[350] Relatives attending his Sparta funeral in May 1929 included uncles and aunts Mr. and Mrs. George Scholes and Mr. and Mrs. James Scholes, and first cousin Marion Scholes.[351] In 1930 the widow Agnes owned her house in Sparta and was called a farmer.[352]

Children of Francis Roderick[3] and Annie (Henry) Sherwin:

i. RAY FOREST[4] SHERWIN (*Francis[3] Sherwin, Mary[2] Scholes, Ann[1] Mills, Samuel[A]*) was born 3 December 1889 at Rockford, Floyd County, Iowa;[353] died 31 March 1953 in Sparta, Monroe County, Wisconsin,[354] less than a month after his retirement as rural mail carrier;[355] and was buried as Ray E. Sherwin at Woodlawn Cemetery there.[356]
He married as her second husband AGNES OTILIE "TILLIE" POTTS on 25 July 1925 in Cashton, Monroe County, Wisconsin. The daughter of Oluf and Theoline (Torkelson) Hansen, Agnes was born 6 August 1896 in Rockland, La Crosse County, Wisconsin;[357] baptized at Fish

---

[349] Frank R. Shenera [Sherwin], 1920 US census, Sparta, Monroe County, Wisconsin, Ward 3, ED 141, sheet 1A, dwelling/family 3.
[350] Untitled Monroe county short items, *La Crosse Tribune* (Wisconsin), Friday 13 April 1928, p. 6, col. 6.
[351] "Moundville," *Portage Register-Democrat* (Wisconsin), Friday 7 June 1929, p. 5, col. 2.
[352] Annie Sherwin, 1930 US census, Sparta, Monroe County, Wisconsin, ED 32, sheet 1A, dwelling/family 1.
[353] Ray Forrest Sherwin, World War I Draft Registration Card, Angelo Precinct, Monroe County, Wisconsin. Son's birth certificate gives Ray's birthplace: Wisconsin Vital Records Office, Birth Certificates after 1 October 1907, Forrest Douglas Sherwin, Monroe County, 19 May 1926.
[354] "Obituary Ray Sherwin," *Sparta Herald* (Wisconsin), 6 April 1953.
[355] "Tri-State Deaths…Ray Sherwin," *La Crosse Tribune* (Wisconsin), 1 April 1953, p. 21, col. 4.
[356] Ray E. [F.] Sherwin grave marker, image, Woodlawn Cemetery, Sparta, Monroe County, Wisconsin, memorial #141,023,843 by Bob (findagrave.com).
[357] Ray F. Sherwin—Agnes Larson Potts, Wisconsin Vital Records Office, Marriage Certificates after 1 Oct 1907, certificate 1181, Monroe County, 1925. (She had married first Hassen Louis Potts 16 October 1915; he died 11 October 1918.) Gladys and Theodore Torkelson, possibly relatives of Agnes's mother, witnessed.

Creek Lutheran Church in Cashton 20 September;[358] died 2 August 1992 at 219 West Oak in Sparta;[359] and was buried with husband Ray F. at Woodlawn Cemetery in Sparta.[360]

1900: Agnes's mother Theoline/Tillie was a widow, living in a rented house in Leon Township, Monroe County, Wisconsin, with three children under age 10 and a 77-year-old lodger.[361] Tillie married second Thomas Larson about 1901 and they farmed in Leon Township.[362]

1915: Agnes married Hassen Louis Potts. They had three children before his death in 1918.[363]

Ray, a rural mail carrier, married at age 36 and became stepfather to a young family. Prior to the marriage, his new wife, Mrs. Potts, had "held an office in the central telephone at Cashton."[364]

1930: the blended family was living at 207 Rusk Avenue in Sparta—Ray, Agnes, their son, and her three children from her prior marriage to Hassen Louis Potts. The house rented for $25 a month, and they had a radio set.[365]

1940: Ray earned $2080 for 52 weeks' work, and they lived at 219 South K Street in Sparta in a house valued at $5000,[366] well above the

---

[358] Agnes Otilie Hansen baptism, 20 September 1896, #6; "US, Evangelical Lutheran Church in America Church Records, 1781–1969" > Congregational Records > Wisconsin > Cashton > Fish Creek Lutheran Church > image 52 of 74 (ancestry.com). Witnesses were Gunerius [?] and Karoline Pedersen, and Johan and Karoline Torkelsen.

[359] Agnes Ottillia Kress, Wisconsin Vital Records Office, death certificate #20574, Monroe County, 1992. For address, "Agnes O. Kress," *La Crosse Tribune* (Wisconsin), Wednesday 5 August 1992, p. 12, col. 4.

[360] Agnes O. Sherwin (1896–1992) grave marker, image, Woodlawn Cemetery, Sparta, Monroe County, Wisconsin, memorial #210,324,562 by Karen (findagrave.com).

[361] Tillie Hanson household, 1900 US census, Leon Township, Monroe County, Wisconsin, ED 100, sheet 4B, dwelling/family 71.

[362] Thomas Larson household, 1910 US census, Leon Township, Monroe County, Wisconsin, ED 133, sheet 4B, dwelling 86, family 81.

[363] Ray F. Sherwin—Agnes Larson Potts, Wisconsin Vital Records Office, Marriage Certificates after 1 Oct 1907, certificate 1181, Monroe County, 1925. (She had married first Hassen Louis Potts 16 October 1915; he died 11 October 1918.) Gladys and Theodore Torkelson, possibly relatives of Agnes's mother, witnessed.

[364] "Ray Sherwin, Sparta, Weds Cashton Woman," *La Crosse Tribune* (Wisconsin), Monday 3 August 1925, p. 10, col. 6.

[365] Ray F. Therwin [Sherwin] household, 1930 US census, Monroe County, Wisconsin, Sparta, Ward 1, ED 27, sheets 8B–9A, dwelling/family 238.

[366] Ray Sherwin household, 1940 US census, Monroe County, Wisconsin, Sparta, Ward 4, ED 41-32, sheet 4B, dwelling 89.

statewide average of $3232 that year. Agnes completed eight years of schooling, Ray four years of high school.[367]

1950s: At least twice Agnes was visited by Mr. and Mrs. James McGaw of Littleton, Arapahoe County, Colorado.[368] Mrs. McGaw was Ray and Agnes's stepdaughter Lorraine Potts.[369]

1970: Agnes, a widow for 17 years, married third Frederick R. Kress. He was born 20 January 1895 in Tomah, Monroe County, Wisconsin, son of "Mr. and Mrs. Adolph Kress,"[370] and died there Saturday 19 October 1974. He had retired from the Kress Monument Company some years earlier. He was one of the charter members of the board of directors of Farmers and Merchants Bank, Tomah, and served on the state board of real estate appraisers.[371]

ii. EDITH MARY[4] SHERWIN (*Francis[3] Sherwin, Mary[2] Scholes, Ann[1] Mills, Samuel[A]*) was born 22 June 1891 in Iowa; died 2 May 1962 in Mower County, Minnesota;[372] and was buried with her first husband and their

---

[367] Statewide house value figures from US Census Bureau, Census of Housing, Historical Census of Housing Tables, Median Home Values Unadjusted 1940 (https://www2.census.gov/programs-surveys/decennial/tables/time-series/coh-values/values-unadj.txt).

[368] Agnes Sherwin index entries, *Sparta Herald* (Wisconsin), 3 October 1955, p. 3, col. 2, and 3 September 1957, p. 3, col. 3; Monroe County Local History Room and Museum, Sparta.

[369] Lorraine McGaw grave marker, image, Fort Logan National Cemetery, Denver, Denver County, Colorado, Section S, site 3313, memorial #976,072 by US Veterans Affairs Office. The memorial includes a brief informative obituary, "Lorraine McGaw–Townsend," credited to *Rocky Mountain News* (Colorado), 26 June 1996.

[370] Agnes Ottillia Kress, Wisconsin Vital Records Office, death certificate #20574, Monroe County, 1992. Agnes's 1992 obituary ("Agnes O. Kress," *La Crosse Tribune* [Wisconsin], Wednesday 5 August 1992, p. 12, col. 4) placed their marriage in 1968 rather than 1970.

[371] "Frederick R. Kress," *La Crosse Tribune* (Wisconsin), Monday 21 October 1974, p. 7, cols. 3–4.

[372] "Northeast Iowa Deaths…Charles City," Edith Mary Burrington, *Courier* (Waterloo, Iowa), 4 May 1962, p. 5, col. 3.

infant son at Riverside Cemetery, Charles City, Floyd County, Iowa[373] She married first 5 April 1916 WILLIAM O. JOHNSON,[374] the son of Engebret and Olena (Olson) Johnson, both born in Norway. William was born 11 April 1873 in Floyd County, Iowa;[375] died 17 November 1933 at his home, 508 South Jackson Street in Charles City, Iowa, having been ill for several years with stomach cancer; and was buried at Riverside Cemetery there.[376] In 1900 William was farming with his widowed father in Floyd County, Iowa.[377] In later years he worked as a policeman, an oil salesman,[378] and an oil truck driver. In 1925 they owned a $4000 house and were not affiliated with any church.[379] In 1930 the house was valued at $4500, and they had a radio set.[380]

---

[373] "Former Police Officer Dies at Charles City," *Courier* (Waterloo, Iowa), Sunday 19 November 1933, p. 8, col. 7. Also, William O. and Edith M. Johnson, grave marker, image (barely legible), Riverside Cemetery, Charles City, Floyd County, Iowa, Block 12, Section 37, Row 6, Spaces 1 and 2, memorials #13,378,491 and #18,378,496 respectively, both by shawn and Kathy Gerkins (findagrave.com). Also, "Baby Johnson," reportedly born 1917 and interred 18 August 1917, was buried in Space 3, with no stone, memorial #33,597,459 (findagrave.com). Also, William O. Johnson death 17 November 1933 in Charles City, Iowa death certificate; "Iowa Death Records, 1920–1940" > 1933 > Clinton–Henry > image 3228 of 4954 (ancestry.com).
[374] Herbert J. Burrington–Edith Mary [Sherwin] Johnson marriage, 15 December 1934, Charles City, Iowa; "Iowa Marriage Records, 1880–1940" > 1934 > 2 > image 1495 of 5241 (ancestry.com).
[375] William O. Johnson death 17 November 1933 in Charles City, Iowa death certificate; "Iowa Death Records, 1920–1940" > 1933 > Clinton–Henry > image 3228 of 4954 (ancestry.com).
[376] "Former Police Officer Dies at Charles City," *Courier* (Waterloo, Iowa), Sunday 19 November 1933, p. 8, col. 7. He was survived by his widow and one sister, Mrs. O. J. Beyatte, living north of Charles City Also, William O. and Edith M. Johnson, grave marker, image (barely legible), Riverside Cemetery, Charles City, Floyd County, Iowa, Block 12, Section 37, Row 6, Spaces 1 and 2, memorials #13,378,491 and #18,378,496 respectively, both by shawn and Kathy Gerkins (findagrave.com). Also, William O. Johnson death 17 November 1933 in Charles City, Iowa, death certificate; "Iowa Death Records, 1920–1940" > 1933 > Clinton–Henry > image 3228 of 4954 (ancestry.com).
[377] William O. Johnson household, 1900 US census, Floyd Township, Floyd County, Iowa, ED 91, sheet 7B, dwelling 140, family 141.
[378] William O. Johnson death 17 November 1933 in Charles City, Iowa death certificate; "Iowa Death Records, 1920–1940" > 1933 > Clinton–Henry > image 3228 of 4954 (ancestry.com). Also, "Former Police Officer Dies at Charles City," *Courier* (Waterloo, Iowa), Sunday 19 November 1933, p. 8, col. 7.
[379] William O. Johnson household, 1925 Iowa state census, Charles City, Floyd County, unpaginated; "Iowa, State Census Collection, 1836–1925" > 1925 > Floyd > Charles City > images 651–52 of 721 (ancestry.com).
[380] William O. Johnson household, 1930 US census, Charles City, Floyd County, Iowa, Ward 4, ED 5, sheet 9B, dwelling 215, family 241.

Edith married second HERBERT J. BURRINGTON 15 December 1934 in Charles City, the son of Wallace D. and Nettie L. (Ranney) Burrington.[381] Herbert was born 14 August 1887 in Sun Prairie, Dane County, Wisconsin[382]; died 7 February 1965 in Fillmore County, Minnesota[383] and was buried at Grand Meadow Cemetery, Grand Meadow, Mower County, Minnesota[384]

At their 1934 marriage, Herbert was a farmer in New Richmond, St. Croix County, Wisconsin.[385] As of 27 April 1942 he was 5 feet 4 inches tall, weighed 120 pounds, had hazel eyes and black hair, and only half of his right thumb. He was self-employed at Grand Meadow, Mower County, Minnesota.[386] In 1945 they were in Austin, Mower County, where he was a "helper" at the Farmers Produce Company.[387]

iii. ETHEL ESTHER[4] SHERWIN (*Francis[3] Sherwin, Mary[2] Scholes, Ann[1] Mills, Samuel[A]*) was born 22 June 1891 in Rockford, Floyd County,

---

[381] Herbert J. Burrington–Edith Mary [Sherwin] Johnson marriage, 15 December 1934, Charles City, Iowa; "Iowa Marriage Records, 1880–1940" > 1934 > 2 > image 1495 of 5241 (ancestry.com).

[382] Herbert J. Burrington WW2 draft card, Mower County Local Board #2, 27 April 1942, serial #U1670, no order number; "US, World War II Draft Registration Cards, 1942" > Minnesota > Burdick–Burud > images 1684–85 of 2060 (ancestry.com). Also> Herbert J. Burrington–Edith Mary Johnson marriage, 15 December 1934, Charles City, Iowa; "Iowa Marriage Records, 1880–1940" > 1934 > 2 > image 1495 of 5241 (ancestry.com).

[383] Herbert J. Burrington death index entry, Minnesota Death Index, 1908–2017, certificate #5687 (ancestry.com). Original not viewed.

[384] Herbert J. Burrington grave marker, image, Grand Meadow Cemetery, Grand Meadow, Mower County, Minnesota, memorial #11,687,385 by K. Pike (findagrave.com). Exact dates and places are unsourced but corroborated by above notes (Minnesota Death Index and WWII draft card).

[385] Herbert J. Burrington–Edith Mary Johnson marriage, 15 December 1934, Charles City, Iowa; "Iowa Marriage Records, 1880–1940" > 1934 > 2 > image 1495 of 5241 (ancestry.com).

[386] Herbert J. Burrington WW2 draft card, Mower County Local Board #2, 27 April 1942, serial #U1670, no order number; "US, World War II Draft Registration Cards, 1942" > Minnesota > Burdick–Burud > images 1684–85 of 2060 (ancestry.com).

[387] Herb J. Burrington entry, *Austin City and Mower County Minnesota Directory 1945–1946* (Rochester, Minnesota: Keiter Directory Company, 1945), p. 561, image 281 of 399 (ancestry.com). Absent 1950.

Iowa[388]; died 12 July 1964 in Tomah, Monroe County, Wisconsin; and was buried at Oak Grove Cemetery.[389]

She married first LAURENCE B. AUSTIN 5 November 1913 in Grand Valley, Mower County, Minnesota.[390] He was the son of George and Laura (-?-) Austin,[391] born 9 June 1889 in Momence, Kankakee County, Illinois;[392] died reportedly 2 November 1951[393]; and was buried at Oak Grove Cemetery in Tomah, Monroe County, Wisconsin.[394]

---

[388] Ethel Ester [Esther?] Sherwin index entry, "Iowa, Births and Christenings Index, 1800–1999" (ancestry.com), referring to more detailed information although not the original: "Iowa, County Births, 1880–1935," FHL #1,481,724, items 1–3, DGS #4,266,167, image 280, certificate p. 20, cn 350, record 24 (familysearch.org).

[389] "Mrs. William Schrieber," *La Crosse Tribune* (Wisconsin), Monday 13 July 1964, p. 14, col. 2.

[390] Lawrence B. Austin–Ethel Sherwin marriage 5 November 1913, Grand Valley, Mower County, Minnesota; Mower County Marriage Register, H:531; "Minnesota, County Marriages, 1860–1949" > 5,193,206 > image 809 of 847 (familysearch.org).

[391] George Austin household for son Lawrence age 10, 1900 US census, Central Lake Village, Antrim County, Michigan, ED 2, sheet 6B, dwelling 148, family 143. George and Laura married about 1882.

[392] Lawrence B. Austin WWI draft card, West Hoboken, New Jersey, local board, 1 June 1917, serial #1685, order #212; "US, World War I Draft Registration Cards, 1917–1918" > New Jersey > West Hoboken City > Draft Card A > image 339 of 351 (ancestry.com). Lawrence's birthplace varies in different census years.

[393] Lawrence B. Austin index entry, death date, "US, Social Security Applications and Claims Index, 1936–2007."

[394] Laurence B. Austin, no image of grave marker, Oak Grove Cemetery, Tomah, Wisconsin, memorial #79,272,094 by Jim Zingler (findagrave.com).

She married second WILLIAM HENRY SCHRIEBER 10 April 1961 in Winnebago County, Illinois.[395] His family has yet to be identified.[396]

In 1900 Laurence was living with his parents in Central Lake Village, Antrim County, Michigan (near the north end of lower Michigan); father George was a bank clerk. The family owned their home without a mortgage.[397] Laurence completed four years of high school, Ethel four years of college.[398] At marriage, he was of Peoria County, Illinois; she was of Mower County, Minnesota. Ray Sherwin and A. N. Henry witnessed.[399]

Ethel visited her parents in La Crosse during the first half of November 1915, then left to meet her husband in New York City and proceed to Bridgeport, Connecticut, where he had "a responsible position in a munition factory."[400] Their names do not appear in the 1915, 1916, or 1917 Bridgeport city directories, but his job in 1917 was not far off: as of 1 June 1917, he was foreman of the "head and stamp department" at Remington Arms U.M.C. Company in Hoboken, Hudson County, New Jersey.

He claimed an exemption from the World War I draft on grounds that his wife was dependent on him; they were living at 318 Smith Street in

---

[395] William Henry Schrieber–Ethel Austin marriage index entry, 10 April 1961; "Winnebago County, Illinois, Marriages, 1836–1962" (ancestry.com).

[396] The following clues may or may not help: *(1)* Will Schrieber death index entry, US Social Security Death Index, 1935–2014 (ancestry.com). *(2)* "Mrs. William Schrieber," *La Crosse Tribune* (Wisconsin), Monday 13 July 1964, p. 14, col. 2. *(3)* "William Schrieber," *La Crosse Tribune* (Wisconsin), 11 July 1967, p. 4, col. 6. A surviving sister Lena Norris was said to be living in Madison. His Find a Grave memorial names sister Lela S. Schrieber (1892–1960) and brother Fred George Schreiber [*sic*] (1896–1947) and mother Augusta (Albrecht) Schrieber (1860–1919) with an image of a brief obituary: William H. Schrieber grave marker, no image, Oak Grove Cemetery, Tomah, Monroe County, Wisconsin, memorial #100,927,312 by Susanna Parrish (findagrave.com). *(4)* William H. Hely household for hired man William H. Schrieber age 23 (both he and parents all born Wisconsin), 1910 US census, Tomah Township, Monroe County, Wisconsin, ED 145, sheet 4B, dwelling/family 78.

[397] George Austin household for son Lawrence age 10, 1900 US census, Central Lake Village, Antrim County, Michigan, ED 2, sheet 6B, dwelling 148, family 143. George and Laura married about 1882.

[398] Lawrence B. Austin household (wife Ethel informant), 1940 US census, West Allis, Milwaukee County, Wisconsin, Ward 4, ED 40-104, sheet 16B, dwelling 313.

[399] Lawrence B. Austin–Ethel Sherwin marriage 5 November 1913, Grand Valley, Mower County, Minnesota; Mower County Marriage Register, H:531; "Minnesota, County Marriages, 1860–1949" > 5,193,206 > image 809 of 847 (familysearch.org).

[400] "Local and Personal," *La Crosse Tribune* (Wisconsin), Monday 15 November 1915, p. 5, col. 5.

West Hoboken. He was tall and medium stout, with brown eyes and brown hair.[401]

In the next several years they worked their way back toward Wisconsin: in 1920, boarding at 2212 East 73rd Street in Cleveland, where he was a foreman in a machine shop;[402] in 1930, renting half of a duplex for $50 a month at 407 25th Avenue in Milwaukee. They owned a "radio set" and he worked as the "trouble man" in a machine shop.[403] In 1940 they rented at 2000 South 73rd Street in West Allis, Milwaukee County, Wisconsin, for $45 a month. He was employed as a "supervisor of inspection" in farm equipment.[404]

---

[401] Lawrence B. Austin WWI draft card, West Hoboken, New Jersey, local board, 1 June 1917, serial #1685, order #212; "US, World War I Draft Registration Cards, 1917–1918" > New Jersey > West Hoboken City > Draft Card A > image 339 of 351 (ancestry.com).

[402] Lawrence B. and Edith E. Austin, boarders in Clarence A. Shearer household, 1920 US census, Cleveland, Cuyahoga County, Ohio, ED 369, Ward 18, sheet 5B, dwelling 108, family 141.

[403] Lawrence Austin household for wife Ethel, 1930 US census, Milwaukee, Milwaukee County, Wisconsin, Ward 23, ED 305, sheet 9B, dwelling 30, family 43.

[404] Lawrence B. Austin household (wife Ethel informant), 1940 US census, West Allis, Milwaukee County, Wisconsin, Ward 4, ED 40-104, sheet 16B, dwelling 313.

Chapter 14

Third Generation

William Orlando Sherwin–Harriet M. Manley–Lottie Mazie Taylor Family
parents at chapter 3

"Mrs. Sherwin owns a small house in Montana from which she derives a monthly rental of $19"

14. WILLIAM ORLANDO³ SHERWIN (*Mary² Scholes, Ann¹ Mills, Samuel^A*)
Birth: 16 April 1860 in Wisconsin, reportedly Columbia County
Death: 8 November 1953 in Sparta, Monroe County, Wisconsin
Burial: Woodlawn Cemetery, Sparta[405]
Spouse #1: **HARRIET M. MANLEY,** married 9 March 1892 at Sparta,[406] later married second 14 December 1935 in Sparta D. F. Jones
Spouse #1 parents: Jackson and Charlotte (Sawyer) Manley
Spouse #1 birth: 13 June 1868, probably in Greenfield Township, Monroe County, Wisconsin
Spouse #1 death: 15 August 1938[407]

---

[405] William O. Sherwin burial record, as indexed at Monroe County Local History Room (monroecountyhistory.org). Also, William Orlando Sherwin grave marker, image, Woodlawn Cemetery, Sparta, Wisconsin, memorial #138,431,668 by Joey (findagrave.com).
[406] "Wedding," *Sparta Herald* (Wisconsin), Tuesday 15 March 1892, p. 4, col. 3. "At the residence of J. W. Potter." Rev. A. J. Hovey officiated.
[407] "Obituaries . . . Harriet Manley Jones," *Monroe County Democrat* (Wisconsin), Thursday 18 August 1938, p. 4, col. 4. Her first husband's much later obituary erroneously gave her death date as 1937: "William Sherwin," *Monroe County Democrat* (Sparta, Wisconsin), Tuesday 12 November 1953, p. 2, col. 3. Hattie was two years old in 1870: Jackson Monley [Manley], 1870 US census, Greenfield Township, Monroe County, Wisconsin, p. 8, dwelling 61, family 59.

Spouse #2: **LOTTIE MAZIE TAYLOR,** married 28 November 1916 at Sparta,[408] divorced before 1920[409]

Spouse #2's parents: Vine E. and Emma F. Taylor; in 1880 he was a 38-year-old miller and she was 31[410]

Spouse #2's birth: about 1876–1878 in Black River Falls, Jackson County, Wisconsin[411]

Spouse #2's death: 29 April 1924 at her home, 217 East Montgomery Street, Sparta, of "heart trouble" and ill health of about a year[412]

Spouse #2's burial: Woodlawn Cemetery, Sparta, Wisconsin[413]

In the fall of 1908 Harriet was working as secretary of the La Crosse School of Music (headed by Fred Leithold), which advertised for students interested in "instruction in piano, pipe organ, harmony and counterpoint, voice, violin, guitar and mandolin, musical history, and repertoire and interpretation."[414] In 1910 the Sherwins were renting 211 South Fifth Street in La Crosse, La Crosse County, Wisconsin, and had nine lodgers. William was a house carpenter.[415] In 1911 he was at 509 East

---

[408] "Sparta Pair Wed," *La Crosse Tribune* (Wisconsin), Thursday 30 November 1916, p. 4, col. 5.

[409] Emma F. Taylor (widow) household for daughter Lottie M. Taylor (age 35, divorced) on North Benton Street, 1920 US census, Sparta, Monroe County, Wisconsin, Ward 1, ED 139, dwelling 178, family 193.

[410] Vine E. Taylor household for wife Emma F. and daughter Lottie age 4, 1880 US census, Albion, Jackson County, Wisconsin, ED 76, p. 10 B, dwelling 83, family 84.

[411] For birth year 1876: Vine E. Taylor household for wife Emma F. and daughter Lottie age 4, 1880 US census, Albion, Jackson County, Wisconsin, ED 76, p. 10B, dwelling 83, family 84. For birth year 1878: Lottie Taylor grave marker, image, Woodlawn Cemetery, Sparta, Monroe County, Wisconsin, memorial #141,239,326 by Bob (findagrave.com). Her sister Maud and mother Emma share the stone. For birth year 1885 (an outlier): Emma F. Taylor (widow) household for daughter Lottie M. Taylor (age 35, divorced) on North Benton Street, 1920 US census, Sparta, Monroe County, Wisconsin, Ward 1, ED 139, dwelling 178, family 193. All three women in the household were reported several years younger than other evidence suggests.

[412] "Lottie Taylor," *Monroe County Democrat* (Wisconsin), Thursday 1 May 1924, p. 6, col. 1.

[413] Lottie Taylor burial permit, as indexed at Monroe County History Room (monroecountyhistory.org).

[414] "La Crosse School of Music" advertisement, *La Crosse Tribune* (Wisconsin), Saturday 5 September 1908, p. 6, col. 1.

[415] William O. Sherwin household, 1910 US census, La Crosse, La Crosse County, Wisconsin, Ward 2, ED 98, sheet 13B, dwelling 189, family 205.

Franklin in Sparta, Monroe County, Wisconsin, "grower of small fruit and vegetables of all kinds."[416] Harriet divorced him in October 1913.[417]

Harriet M. Sherwin

In the following years Harriet both taught in rural schools and added a degree to her credentials. In 1920 she was school principal in Montpelier, Stutsman County, North Dakota, sharing a duplex with son-in-law Herbert M. Sherwin and daughter Margaret Sherwin, both schoolteachers, son-in-law John "Boaling" [Bohlig], a railroad telegraph operator, and daughter Charlotte.[418] In 1921 she began a twelve-year stint of teaching in North Dakota and Montana, including seventh grade in Linton, Emmons County, North Dakota. (She had previously been in Valley City, Barnes County, 150 miles to the northeast.) In the fall of 1922 she taught eighth grade there.[419] In 1923 she graduated from the La Crosse Business College and received her Bachelor of Arts degree from State Teachers College at Valley City, North Dakota.[420] From the fall of 1924 to the spring of 1929 she taught at Flathead County High School in Kalispell, Montana, where she had various jobs: "assistant normal training teacher" (that is, educating future teachers), one of four debate judges for the two debating teams, history, and normal training. She resigned in the

---

[416] William Sherwin in Sparta to John J. Esch in Washington DC, letter, 1 February 1911, regarding his mother's accrued pension; Mary Sherwin pension WC73064, service of Bissell Sherwin, Civil War, Wisconsin 19th Infantry, Company D, Case Files of Approved Pension Applications of Widows and Other Dependents of Civil War Veterans, 1861–ca.1910 (fold3.com/image/271447043).
[417] *Sparta Herald* (Wisconsin), 14 October 1913, p. 3, col. 2, index, Monroe County Local History Room (monroecountyhistory.org).
[418] Herbert M. Sherwin household, 1920 US census, Montpelier, Stutsman County, North Dakota, ED 233, sheet 10A, dwelling 29, families 30 and 31.
[419] "Linton School Items," *Emmons County Record* (North Dakota), p. 5, col. 5.
[420] Monroe County Newspapers Index, *Sparta Herald* (Wisconsin), 27 December 1921, p. 3, col. 4, and 28 August 1923, p. 5, col. 2; Monroe County Local History Room, Sparta (monroecountyhistory.org). Also, "School Opened Tuesday," *Emmons County Record* (North Dakota), p. 1, col. 3.

spring of 1929, with no public reason given and no stated plans for the next school year.[421]

In 1925 she sold lot 9 in "Hill View Place" in La Crosse County, Wisconsin, to Mrs. Ira H. Hill.[422] In 1927 she visited her son Herbert in Bismarck, Burleigh County, North Dakota.[423]

Returning to Sparta in May 1933,[424] she was no longer able to maintain herself, and came to live with daughter Charlotte and son-in-law John Bohlig in North Dakota. "There were no other relatives who could take care of her," wrote John, explaining to his bosses why his household had just added a new dependent. "In addition to her daughter, who is now my wife, Mrs. Sherwin has a son [Herbert, see child i, below] but this son is married and has been out of work for about two years. He is unable to contribute to her support.

"Mrs. Sherwin owns a small house in Montana from which she derives a monthly rental of $19.00 but this sum hardly more than pays the taxes and other expenses on the property. It is very likely that this dependency will be permanent."[425] However, it was not. Two years later Harriet married second David F. Jones 14 December 1935 in Decorah, Winneshiek County, Iowa—80 miles southwest of their home in Sparta.[426]

William Sherwin's second wife Lottie was the daughter of Vine and Emma Taylor; Vine was a miller, renting a house in Sparta in 1900. Lottie was born in 1878 (grave marker) or April 1876 (1900 census) and

---

[421] "Flathead High School Gets Into Full Swing," *Missoulian* (Montana), Friday 19 September 1924, p. 4, col. 6. "Debate Team Named at Flathead H. S.," *Great Falls Tribune* (Montana), Saturday 12 December 1925, p. 3, col. 6. Also, "Kalispell Has Full Corps of Teachers Now," *Great Falls Tribune* (Montana), Saturday 3 September 1927, p. 4, col. 3. Also, "New Teachers Named by School Trustees," *Montana Standard*, Monday 29 April 1929, p. 15, col. 1.
[422] "Real Estate Transfers," *La Crosse Tribune* (Wisconsin), Friday 30 January 1925, p. 6, col. 3.
[423] "Braddock," *Bismarck Tribune* (North Dakota), p. 2, col. 3.
[424] "Obituaries . . . Harriet Manley Jones," *Monroe County Democrat* (Wisconsin), Thursday 18 August 1938, p. 4, col. 4.
[425] John E. Bohlig railroad company form "submitted to establish dependency of my mother-in-law," about July 1933; "US, Northern Pacific Railway Company Personnel File" > file numbers 1–5406 > file numbers 3357–3851 > image 3882 of 4712 (ancestry.com).
[426] "Sparta," *La Crosse Tribune* (Wisconsin), 18 December 1935, p. 13, col. 8.

was employed as a "retoucher," as was boarder Allie Crossman.[427] In 1910 Lottie was a music teacher,[428] and at the time of her marriage was described as having "a large class of pupils, both in this city and surrounding towns." They were to live at North Benton Street in Sparta after 15 December 1916.[429] Lottie died in 1924 and was buried with mother Emma and sister Maude Hemstock at Woodlawn Cemetery in Sparta.[430]

William completed eight years of schooling. In 1940 he was living at 308 South Court in Sparta, and was said to be "widowed." He had been a member of the Odd Fellows Lodge since 1895 and of the Congregational Church since 1893. His house was valued at $500, less than one-sixth of the statewide average.[431]

Children of William Orlando and Harriet M. (Manley) Sherwin:

i.   HERBERT MANLEY[4] SHERWIN (*William[3] Sherwin, Mary[2] Scholes, Ann[1] Mills, Samuel[A]*) was born 10 May 1894 in Monroe County, Wisconsin, and died 15 August 1977 in San Diego County,

---

[427] Born April 1876: Vine Taylor household for daughter Lottie M., 1900 US census, Sparta, Monroe County, Wisconsin, ED 108, sheet 7B, dwelling 175, family 179. Born 1878: Lottie Taylor grave marker, Woodlawn Cemetery, Sparta, Wisconsin, image, memorial #141,239,326 by Bob (findagrave.com).
[428] Kine [Vine] Taylor household for daughter Lottie M., 1910 US census, Sparta, Monroe County, Wisconsin, Ward 1, ED 140, sheet 13B, dwelling 334, family 342.
[429] "Sparta Pair Wed," *La Crosse Tribune* (Wisconsin), Thursday 30 November 1916, p. 4, col. 5.
[430] Lottie Taylor grave marker, Woodlawn Cemetery, Sparta, Wisconsin, image, memorial #141,239,326 by Bob (findagrave.com).
[431] William O. Sherwin household, 1940 US census, Sparta, Monroe County, Wisconsin, Ward 4, ED 41-32, sheet 64B, dwelling 403. Also, William O. Sherwin grave marker, image, Woodlawn Cemetery, Sparta, Wisconsin, memorial #138,431,668 by Joey (findagrave.com) for transcribed version of his *La Crosse Tribune* obituary, Monday 9 November 1953. Statewide house value figures from US Census Bureau, Census of Housing, Historical Census of Housing Tables, Median Home Values Unadjusted 1940 (https://www2.census.gov/programs-surveys/decennial/tables/time-series/coh-values/values-unadj.txt).

California.[432] He married about 1920[433] MARGARET MATILDA ARNSDORF, the daughter of Henry M. and Mary B. (Stuiber) Arnsdorf. Margaret was born 18 June 1896 in Wisconsin. (Her mother was of Austrian parentage and was born at sea.)[434] She was born 18 June 1896[435] in Eau Claire, Eau Claire County, Wisconsin,[436] and died 24 September 1985 in San Diego County, California.[437]

Herbert enlisted for World War I on 2 March 1918, and was released 24 June 1919,[438] rising from private to sergeant in those fifteen months. After induction at Mandan, Morton County, North Dakota, he was sent to Vancouver Barracks, Washington, where he served in:

- the 601st Aero Supply Squadron to July 8, 1918;
- the 412th Aero Construction Squadron (6th Spruce Squadron, Spruce Production Division) to August 16, 1918; and

---

[432] Herbert Sherwin index entries: For exact dates but not locations, US Department of Veterans Affairs BIRLS Death File, 1850–2010 (ancestry.com). For place of birth, Wisconsin Birth Index, reel 322, DX0316 (ancestry.com). For place of death, California Death Index, 1940–1997.

[433] Herbert Sherwin household, 1930 US census, Fargo, Cass County, North Dakota, ED 33, sheet 7A, dwelling 146, family 161. Both he and Margaret indicated they had been first married ten years earlier.

[434] H. Irnsdorf [Arnsdorf] household for wife Mary and daughter Margaret born June 1896, 1900 US census, Eau Claire, Eau Claire County, Wisconsin, Ward 9, ED 31, sheet 1A, dwelling/family 6. Similarly, Henry Arnsdorf, 1910, ED 57, sheet 23A, dwelling 435, family 496. He was a farmer, with a mortgage. For Margaret's mother's maiden name, California Death Index, 1940–1997, Margaret Matilda Sherwin.

[435] Birth date from California Death Index, 1940–1947, month and year consistent with 1900 US census (note above).

[436] "History of Margaret Arnsdorf Sherwin," in Travois Club (Fargo, North Dakota) scrapbook, "This Is Your Life" (probably late 1930s), Institute Small Collection 1379, Institute for Regional Studies, North Dakota State University Libraries, Fargo; "North Dakota Biography Index" (library.ndsu.edu/db/biography). The last three lines pertaining to her work and location in 1940 and after appear to have been added later than the rest of the material.

[437] Margaret Matilda Sherwin index entry, California Death Index, 1940–1997.

[438] Herbert Sherwin index entry, "US, Department of Veterans Affairs BIRLS Death File, 1850–2020 (ancestry.com).

- the Quartermaster Corps, Vancouver Barracks, until discharge.[439]

The year 1920 saw a sort of family reunion. Herbert and Margaret were teaching school in Montpelier, Stutsman County, North Dakota, sharing a rented duplex there with mother Harriet, the school principal, and sister Charlotte and brother-in-law John Boaling [Bohlig], a railroad telegrapher.[440]

Throughout the 1930s Herbert and Margaret rented an apartment in a six-flat at 1010 12th Avenue North in Fargo, Cass County, North Dakota: over the ten years of the Great Depression its rent fell from $50 a month to $32.50. In 1930 Herbert was a radio equipment manager (but the family possessions did not include a "radio set").[441] According to his brother-in-law John Bohlig (see below), Herbert was out of work for at least two years in the early 1930s.[442] In 1940 Herbert was a "philatelist [stamp collector] in finance;" Margaret was an executive. Both had completed three years of college. In the previous year (1939), he earned $2500 and she earned $1200.[443]

Margaret was a teacher and an executive in Camp Fire. She studied at the State Teachers Colleges in Eau Claire, Wisconsin; Ellendale, North Dakota; and Valley City, North Dakota. She taught at the Girls Department of the State Industrial School in Eau Claire, Wisconsin, and later in North Dakota at Churchs Ferry (Ramsey County), Linton (Emmons County), Braddock (Emmons County), and Sheyenne (Eddy County). She served as executive of Camp Fire's Red River Council, then similar posts in Minneapolis 1940–45, and San Diego 1945–52. In

---

[439] Herbert Sherwin, in *Roster of the Men and Women Who Served in the Army or Naval Service (including the Marine Corps) of the United States or its Allies from the State of North Dakota in the World War, 1917–1918,* in four volumes (Bismarck, North Dakota: Bismarck Tribune Company, 1931) 4:2941; roster image 1484 of 1803 (ancestry.com).
[440] Herbert M. Sherwin household, 1920 US census, Montpelier, Stutsman County, North Dakota, ED 233, sheet 10A, dwelling 29, families 30 and 31.
[441] Herbert Sherwin household, 1930 US census, Fargo, Cass County, North Dakota, ED 33, sheet 7A, dwelling 146, family 161.
[442] John E. Bohlig railroad company form "submitted to establish dependency of my mother-in-law," about July 1933; "US, Northern Pacific Railway Company Personnel File" > file numbers 1–5406 > file numbers 3357–3851 > image 3882 of 4712 (ancestry.com).
[443] Herbert Sherwin household, 1930 US census, Fargo, Cass County, North Dakota, ED 33, sheet 7A, dwelling 146, family 161. Similarly, H. M. Sherwin household, 1940 US census, ED 9-97, sheet 9A, dwelling 182.

1953 she and Herbert resided on five acres at 1001 Capri Road near Encinitas, San Diego County, California.[444]

 ii. CHARLOTTE MAY[4] SHERWIN (*William[3] Sherwin, Mary[2] Scholes, Ann[1] Mills, Samuel[A]*) was born 18 July 1899 in Sparta,[445] and died 11 January 1977 in Tacoma, King County, Washington.[446] She married 1919–20 JOHN ELLSWORTH BOHLIG,[447] the son of John and Mary (Dufner/Tofner) Bohlig.[448] John was born 24 March 1890 in Freeport, Stearns County, Minnesota,[449] and died 6 December 1975 in King County, Washington.[450] Although born in Minnesota, John was in North Dakota as early as 1910, living in a boardinghouse in Corwin Township, Stutsman County (the same county where Charlotte's mother

---

[444] "History of Margaret Arnsdorf Sherwin," in Travois Club (Fargo, North Dakota) scrapbook, "This Is Your Life" (probably late 1930s), Institute Small Collection 1379, Institute for Regional Studies, North Dakota State University Libraries, Fargo; "North Dakota Biography Index" (library.ndsu.edu/db/biography). The last three lines pertaining to her work and location after 1940 appear to have been added later than the rest of the material. Also, "William Sherwin," *Monroe County Democrat* (Sparta, Wisconsin), Thursday 12 November 1953, p. 2, col. 3. Late-life information is scarce: Neither appears in California voter registrations, nor in San Diego County directories in 1963 or 1971 (p. 807, image 995 of 1876; p. 828, 1024 of 1954), nor on findagrave.com as of 21 July 2020.

[445] Charlotte M. Sherwin, Monroe County, Wisconsin, Delayed Birth Registration, 1938; Wisconsin State Historical Society microfilm.

[446] Charlotte M. Bohlig, 11 January 1977, "Washington Death Index, 1940–1996." She resided in King County.

[447] E. John Bohlig household, 1930 US census, Solen Township, Sioux County, North Dakota, p. 221, dwelling/family 45.

[448] John E. Bohlig, (mother Dufner) death certificate #28227 (King County, 1975), Washington Department of Social and Health Services, Bureau of Vital Statistics. Also, John Ellsworth Bohlig (mother Tofner) index entry, US, Social Security Applications and Claims Index, 1936–2007 (ancestry.com).

[449] John Ellsworth Bohlig, WWI draft card, Stutsman County, North Dakota, Local Board, series #46, order #13 or 1412, 5 June 1917; "US, World War I Draft Registration Cards, 1917–1918" > North Dakota > Stutsman County > Draft Card B > image 284 of 496 (ancestry.com). This is closest to the event, but later records differ: John's death certificate (with wife as informant, preceding note) gives 23 February 1889. In 1942 he stated that he was born 24 February 1889: John Ellsworth Bohlig, WW2 draft card, Local Board #2, Oberon, North Dakota, serial #U455, order #18827; "US, WW2, Draft Cards Young Men, 1940–1947" > North Dakota > Aahakke–Eveland > Black–Bohun > images 3254–55 of 3683 (ancestry.com).

[450] John E. Bohlig, death certificate #28227 (King County, 1975), Washington Department of Social and Health Services, Bureau of Vital Statistics.

Harriet was a school principal in 1920).[451] In 1917 he was working as "station agent and [telegraph?] operator" for the Northern Pacific railroad in Ypsilanti, Stutsman County. John was medium in height, slender, with brown eyes, dark brown hair, and a "crippled leg…broken in knee."[452] In 1920 they shared a rented duplex in Montpelier, Stutsman County, with Charlotte's mother Harriet and her brother Herbert and sister-in-law Margaret, who were teaching school there.[453]

Charlotte and John were still in North Dakota in 1953.[454] As a telegrapher, he and the family moved around a lot, residing in at least six North Dakota towns: Solen, Sioux County; Golva, Golden Valley County; Stanton, Mercer County; and Leeds, Oberon, and Minnewaukan, all in Benson County. Charlotte taught school and coached a boys' basketball team in Golva, reputedly the first woman in the state to do so.[455]

The following lists John's starting dates at stations during his half-century with the railroad, usually as agent-operator or telegrapher, all in North Dakota.[456] It shows more stability of location once he had proven skills and increased seniority in the 1930s. Perhaps due to his leg injury, he had frequent time off (not shown here).

22 September 1908 helper at Driscoll @ $35/month
22 May 1909 at Ypsilanti @ $55/month[457]
27 September 1912 at Barlow
16 December 1912 at Ypsilanti[458]
May 1918 at Werner, seeking transfer "to some point west of Paradise" for health reasons[459]
15 September 1918 at various relief posts[460]

---

[451] John E. Bohlig, 1910 US Census, Corwin Township, Stutsman County, North Dakota, ED 214, p. 228, sheet 3B, dwelling/family 33 (ancestry.com).
[452] John Ellsworth Bohlig, WWI draft card, Stutsman County, North Dakota, local board, series #46, order #13 or 1412, 5 June 1917; "US, World War I Draft Registration Cards, 1917–1918" > North Dakota > Stutsman County > Draft Card B > image 284 of 496 (ancestry.com).
[453] Herbert M. Sherwin household, 1920 US census, Montpelier, Stutsman County, North Dakota, ED 233, sheet 10A, dwelling 29, families 30 and 31.
[454] "William Sherwin," *Monroe County Democrat* (Wisconsin), 12 November 1953.
[455] "Jean Christianson," *Bismarck Tribune* (North Dakota), Wednesday 12 March 2008, p. 9, cols. 3–4.
[456] John E. Bohlig, "US, Northern Pacific Railway Company Personnel File" > file numbers 1–5406 > file numbers 3357–3851 > John E. Bohlig file 3849 > images 3862–4047 of 4712 (ancestry.com).
[457] Ibid., images 4025 and 4045 of 4712.
[458] Ibid., image 4025 of 4712.
[459] Ibid., images 3982 and 3983 of 4712.
[460] Ibid., image 3965 of 4712.

27 September 1918 at Stanton[461]
2 May 1919 at Woodworth[462]
10 September 1919 at Ypsilanti[463]
3 October 1919 at various relief posts [464]
14 November 1919 at Montpelier[465]
1 April 1920 at Pingree[466]
11 May 1920 at Wing[467]
4 June 1920 at Denhoff[468]
8 September 1920 at Hazen
20 October 1920 at Dunn Center[469]
10 November 1921 at Solen[470]
19 November 1923 at Timmer[471]
11 July 1924 at Solen[472]
25 September 1930 at Leeds[473]
1 December 1939 at Oberon[474]
24 May 1943 at Carson[475]
11 September 1943 at Minnewaukan[476]
20 May 1958, last working date, at Fargo.[477] As of 24 June 1958, his address was Minnewaukan;[478] probably before 17 September 1958, it was 3040 South 150th Street, Seattle 88, Washington.[479]

---

[461] Ibid., image 3962 of 4712.
[462] Ibid., image 3958 of 4712.
[463] Ibid., image 3956 of 4712.
[464] Ibid., image 3954 of 4712.
[465] Ibid., image 3952 of 4712.
[466] Ibid., image 3949 of 4712.
[467] Ibid., image 3947 of 4712.
[468] Ibid., image 3945 of 4712.
[469] Ibid., image 3937 of 4712.
[470] Ibid., image 3935 of 4712.
[471] Ibid., image 3913 of 4712.
[472] Ibid., image 3907 of 4712.
[473] Ibid., image 3887 of 4712.
[474] Ibid., image 3878 of 4712.
[475] Ibid., image 3876 of 4712.
[476] Ibid., image 3875 of 4712.
[477] Ibid., image 3865 of 4712.
[478] Ibid., image 3863 of 4712.
[479] Ibid., image 3864 of 4712.

Chapter 15

Third Generation

Flora Ann Sherwin–John James Bell Family
parents at chapter 3

"Amy taught school for seven years before marrying"

15. **FLORA ANN³ SHERWIN** (*Mary² Scholes, Ann¹ Mills, Samuel^A*)
Birth: 4 February 1862 at Fort Winnebago, Columbia County, Wisconsin
Death: early December 1925
Burial: at Woodland Cemetery, Sparta, Monroe County, Wisconsin[480]
Spouse: **JOHN JAMES BELL,** married 7 January 1886 in Ridgeville Township, Monroe County, Wisconsin[481]
Spouse's parents: George S. and Jeanett (-?-) Bell[482]
Spouse's birth: 6 August 1853, Racine, Racine County, Wisconsin,[483] or 6 August 1852, Spring Prairie, Walworth County, Wisconsin[484]
Spouse's death: Tomah hospital, Monroe County, 4 January 1917, "after a long illness" involving "kidney trouble"[485]

---

[480] "Mrs. Flora Bell," *Sparta Herald* (Wisconsin), 11 December 1923, p. 1, col. 4. "Obituary…Mrs. Flora A. Bell," *Portage Daily Register* (Wisconsin), Thursday 6 December 1923, p. 1, col. 6.
[481] For marriage date: untitled John James Bell obituary, *Tomah Journal* (Wisconsin), 19 January 1917, p. 5, col. 5. Flora's obituary (above), more distant from the event, gives the marriage date as 1884.
[482] John J. Bell–Flora A Sherwin marriage, 7 January 1886, Monroe County, Wisconsin, Registration of Marriage #01456, #202, 3:202. The Monroe County Marriage Records Index has the same wedding date, but a different volume and page, 2:149, microfilm image 1456 (monroecountyhistory.org).
[483] "John James Bell Dies at Hospital in Tomah Thursday," *La Crosse Tribune* (Wisconsin), Monday 8 January 1917, p. 4, col. 2.
[484] Untitled obituary for John James Bell, *Sparta Herald* (Wisconsin), Tuesday 9 January 1917. Also, Bell grave marker, image, Woodlawn Cemetery, Sparta, Monroe County, Wisconsin, memorial #138,428,374 by Joey (findagrave.com).
[485] "John James Bell Dies at Hospital in Tomah Thursday," *La Crosse Tribune* (Wisconsin), Monday 8 January 1917, p. 4, col. 2.

Spouse's burial: Woodlawn Cemetery in Sparta[486]

The Bell family moved to Ridgeville in 1858, and in 1898 to La Grange Township, Monroe County.[487] In 1900 and 1910 they owned their farm there without a mortgage. In 1900 Flora's mother Mary and brother Charles were in the household.[488] In 1920 daughter Amy was teaching at a country school; she and Flora were living in Greenfield Township, Monroe County; the enumerator did not determine whether they owned the farm.[489] John J. was known as an old settler of Tunnel City, Monroe County.[490]

Children of Flora Ann³ (Sherwin) and John James Bell:

i. WILLIAM ALBERT⁴ BELL (*Flora³ Sherwin, Mary² Scholes, Ann¹ Mills, Samuel^A*) was born 28 January 1888 in Ridgeville, Monroe County, Wisconsin;[491] died 11 April 1923, and was buried at Moundville Cemetery, Endeavor, Marquette County, Wisconsin.[492] He married 15 June 1911 in Moundville EDITH ELIZA RUSSELL,[493] daughter of Lorin

---

[486] J. J. Bell grave marker, image, Woodlawn Cemetery, Sparta, Monroe County, Wisconsin, memorial #138,428,374 by Joey (findagrave.com).

[487] Untitled John James Bell obituary, *Tomah Journal* (Wisconsin), 19 January 1917, p. 5, col. 5.

[488] John J. Bell household for brother-in-law Charley T. Shuman [Sherwin] and mother-in-law Mara Shuman [Mary Sherwin], 1900 US census, La Grange Township, Monroe County, Wisconsin, ED 99, sheet 3B, dwelling 51, family 53. Mary was wrongly reported to have been married for ten years. Similarly, 1910, ED 132, sheet 2B, dwelling 61, family 63.

[489] Flora Bell household, 1920 US census, Greenfield Township, Monroe County, Wisconsin, ED 127, sheet 3B, dwelling 68, family 69.

[490] "John James Bell Dies at Hospital in Tomah Thursday," *La Crosse Tribune* (Wisconsin), Monday 8 January 1917, p. 4, col. 2.

[491] "Mrs. Flora Bell," *Sparta Herald* (Wisconsin), 11 December 1923, p. 1, col. 4. Also, William Albert Bell WWI draft card, series #591, order 14, date 5 June 1917, Local Board, Moundville, Marquette County; "World War I Draft Registration Cards, 1917–1918" > Wisconsin > Marquette County > ALL > Draft Card B > image 48 of 170 (ancestry.com).

[492] William A. and Edith E. Bell, joint grave marker, image, Moundville Cemetery, Endeavor, Wisconsin, memorials #69,931,140 and #69,931,149 respectively (findagrave.com).

[493] Henry and Edith Boettcher, *Rochester City and Olmsted County Directory 1945–1946* (Rochester: Keiter Directory Company, 1945), p. 83, image 38 of 471 (ancestry.com).

J. and Caroline L. (Gaylord) Russell,[494] and sister of Fred G. Russell (Chapter 33). Edith was born 20 March 1892 in Buffalo, Marquette County, Wisconsin;[495] died 26 March 1991 in Olmstead County, Minnesota, at 99 years of age;[496] and was buried with her first husband.[497]

A farmer and asthma sufferer, William died at 35 of influenza and pneumonia.[498] Edith married second mail carrier Harry Colfax Rhodes, 18 December 1926 in Moundville.[499] Harry was born in 1869, died 1957, and was buried at Woodlawn Cemetery, Sparta, Wisconsin.[500]

In 1930 Edith and Harry were living at 205 North Court in Sparta, in a house they owned, valued at $4000; there was no radio set in the household.[501] Edith had completed seven years of schooling; Harry completed one year of high school. Over ten years of the Great Depression, their house lost a quarter of its value, declining to $3000,[502] close to the statewide average that year.[503]

Late in 1943 Edith was divorced and the family moved to Rochester, Olmsted County, Minnesota.[504] She married third by 1945 Henry

---

[494] Bell–Russell marriage, 1911, Monroe County, Wisconsin Vital Records Office, Marriage Certificates after 1 October 1907, Madison.

[495] Edith Eliza Russell, 1892, Marquette County register of births, p. 141, record 71, #01637; Wisconsin Births Before 1907, Wisconsin State Historical Society, microfilm #74B, Madison.

[496] Edith E. Boettcher, death certificate #7221 (1991); Minnesota Department of Health, Section of Vital Statistics.

[497] William A. and Edith E. Bell, joint grave marker, image, Moundville Cemetery, Endeavor, Wisconsin, memorials #69,931,140 and #69,931,149 respectively (findagrave.com).

[498] Obituary, Wm. J. Bell, *Portage Daily Register* (Wisconsin), 16 April 1923.

[499] Harry C. Rhodes—Edith Bell marriage, Monroe County, 1926; Wisconsin Vital Records Office, Marriage Certificates after 1 October 1907.

[500] Harry Rhodes grave marker (1869–1957), image, Woodlawn Cemetery, Sparta, Wisconsin, memorial #98,197,029 by Sunshine and TRISH (findagrave.com).

[501] Harry C. Rhodes household, 1930 US census, Sparta, Monroe County, Wisconsin, Ward 2, ED 29, sheet 5B, dwelling 130, family 133.

[502] Harry C. Rhodes household, 1940 US census, Sparta, Monroe County, Wisconsin, Ward 2, ED 41-30, sheet 15A–B, dwelling 380.

[503] Statewide figures from US Census Bureau, Census of Housing, Historical Census of Housing Tables, Median Home Values Unadjusted 1940 (https://www2.census.gov/programs-surveys/decennial/tables/time-series/coh-values/values-unadj.txt).

[504] Edith E. Rhodes index entries for 1943 divorce: *Sparta Herald* (Wisconsin), 6 December 1943, p. 1, col. 6, in "Monroe County (Wisconsin) Newspapers Index"; also, Monroe County (Wisconsin) Court Records Index 1943, box 95, case #2590 (monroecountyhistory.org).

Boettcher.[505] He was a laborer for the Rochester Dairy Co-op, and they lived at 215 Ninth Avenue SW. In 1950 they were at 619 Sixth Southeast, and Henry was a contract hauler.[506] Sometime in the next two years there was a breakup: in 1952 they were both still in Rochester—but she was at 619 Sixth Southeast, and he was at 528 Fifth Avenue Northwest.[507]

ii. AMY JEANETTE[4] BELL (*Flora*[3] *Sherwin, Mary*[2] *Scholes, Ann*[1] *Mills, Samuel*[A]) was born 17 June 1895 in Ridgeville, Monroe County, Wisconsin;[508] died 16 May 1947 in New Haven Township, Adams County, Wisconsin;[509] and was buried 19 May at Lakeview Cemetery there.[510] She married as his second wife 23 July 1921 at Tunnel City, Monroe County, HARLEY JAMES EVANS JR.,[511] son of George W. and Sarah J. (Shalkop/Schellkopf) Evans.[512] Harley was born 4 April 1898;[513] died 5 October 1964 in Oxford, Marquette County;[514] and was

---

[505] Edith E. Boettcher, Minnesota death certificate #7221 (1991).
[506] Henry A. and Edith E. Boettcher entries, *Polk's Rochester (Olmsted County, Minn.) City Directory 1952* (St. Paul, Minnesota: R. L. Polk & Company, 1952), p. 54, image 27 of 383 (ancestry.com). The directories for 1943 and 1948 appear to have been torn in half and then only one half of each imaged.
[507] Edith E. Boettcher, *Polk's Rochester (Olmsted County, Minn.) City Directory 1952* (St. Paul, Minnesota: R. L. Polk & Company, 1952), p. 57, image 28 of 314 (ancestry.com).
[508] Obituary, Amy Jeanette Evans, *Portage Daily Register* (Wisconsin), 21 May 1947, p. 2, col. 1. Also, US Genweb Archives Project, Wisconsin, Adams County (Jackson Township), Lakeview Cemetery, Tombstone Photos (usgwarchives.net/wi/cemetery/images/adams/lakeview/evansharleyjan.jpg). The 1900 census confirms month and year: John J. Bell household for Emma [Amy] J., 1900 US census, La Grange Township, Monroe County, Wisconsin, ED 99, sheet 3B, dwelling 51, family 53.
[509] "Hold Last Rites for Mrs. Evans," *Portage Daily Register* (Wisconsin), Wednesday 21 May 1947, p. 2, col. 1.
[510] Amy Jeannette Bell and Harley J. Evans, joint grave marker, Lakeview Cemetery, Brooks, Adams County, Wisconsin, memorials #76,466,558 and #76,466,815 respectively, by J.B. (findagrave.com).
[511] "Hold Last Rites for Mrs. Evans," *Portage Daily Register* (Wisconsin), Wednesday 21 May 1947, p. 2, col. 1.
[512] Evans–Bell marriage certificate, Wisconsin Vital Records Office, Marriage Certificates after 1 October 1907. Harley and first wife Emilia Cleary had one son.
[513] Harley James Evans WWI draft card 12 September. 1918; "United States World War I Registration Cards, 1917–1918 > Wisconsin > Marquette County A–Z > image 448 of 2247 (familysearch.org).
[514] US Genweb Archives Project, Wisconsin, Adams County (Jackson Township), Lakeview Cemetery, Tombstone Photos (usgwarchives.net/wi/cemetery/images/adams/lakeview/evansharleyjan.jpg).

buried with his second wife.[515] He was a farmer in the Wisconsin Dells.[516]

Harley married first Emilia or Amelia Cleary; their son Chester was born 25 February 1919 and Amelia died five days later. Chester "Chet" was raised by Uncle Louis and Aunt Carrie (Wagner) Evans and lived to a ripe old age, as his lengthy obituary attests.[517]

In 1918 Harley was tall, of medium build, with brown eyes and brown hair.[518] He completed seven years of schooling; Amy one year of college.[519] Amy taught school for seven years before marrying.[520]

In 1930, they were living and farming in Jackson Township, Adams County. Like about half of their near neighbors, they owned a radio set.[521] In 1940 the family was farming in New Haven, Adams County, Wisconsin. They owned a $1000 house, well below the $3232 Wisconsin statewide average.[522] Amy died in 1947, age 51. "All of her married life was spent in the communities of Oxford and Briggsville where she was well known."[523]

---

[515] Amy Jeannette Bell and Harley J. Evans, joint grave marker, Lakeview Cemetery, Brooks, Adams County, Wisconsin, memorials #76,466,558 and #76,466,815 respectively, by J.B. (findagrave.com). Harley's memorial includes a fine picture of the young couple.

[516] "Harley Evans," *Capital Times* (Wisconsin), Wednesday 7 October 1964, p. 28, col. 2.

[517] "Chester H. "Chet" Evans," *Portage Daily Register* (Wisconsin), Wednesday 8 September 1999, p. 2, col. 3.

[518] Harley James Evans WWI draft card 12 September 1918; "United States World War I Registration Cards, 1917–1918" > Wisconsin > Marquette County A–Z > image 448 of 2247 (familysearch.org).

[519] Hailey [Harley] J. Evans household, 1940 US census, New Haven Town, Adams County, Wisconsin, ED 1-13, sheet 5A, dwelling 89.

[520] "Hold Last Rites for Mrs. Evans," *Portage Daily Register* (Wisconsin), Wednesday 21 May 1947, p. 2, col. 1. Also, Flora Bell household for daughter Amy teaching in a "rural school," 1920 US census, Greenfield Township, Monroe County, Wisconsin, ED 127, sheet 3B, dwelling 68, family 69.

[521] Harley J. Evans household, 1930 US census, Jackson Township, Adams County, Wisconsin, page 44, ED 1-8, sheet 5A, dwelling/family 78.

[522] Hailey [Harley] J. Evans household, 1940 US census, New Haven Town, Adams County, Wisconsin, ED 1-13, sheet 5A, dwelling 89. Statewide figures from US Census Bureau, Census of Housing, Historical Census of Housing Tables, Median Home Values Unadjusted 1940 (https://www2.census.gov/programs-surveys/decennial/tables/time-series/coh-values/values-unadj.txt).

[523] "Hold Last Rites For Mrs. Evans," *Portage Daily Register* (Wisconsin), Wednesday 21 May 1947, p. 2, col. 1.

Chapter 16

Third Generation

Margaret Alice "Maggie" Hume–Judson Stiles Berry Family
parents at chapter 4

Elizabeth "taught six years in rural Wisconsin schools in German-speaking communities."

16. MARGARET ALICE "MAGGIE" [3] **HUME** (*Sarah Ann*[2] *Scholes, Ann*[1] *Mills, Samuel*[A])
Birth: 2 June 1861, Marquette County, Wisconsin
Death: 29 December 1938 in Sioux Falls, Minnehaha County, South Dakota
Burial: Graceland Cemetery, Howard, Miner County, South Dakota, with her husband[524]
Spouse: **JUDSON STILES BERRY,** married 16 February 1887[525]
Spouse's parents: Buel and Lydia A. (–?–) Berry[526]
Spouse's birth: Tompkins County, New York, October 1859[527]
Spouse's death: 19 October 1918 in Davison County, South Dakota[528]

---

[524] "Short Illness Claims Mrs. Margaret Berry," *Argus-Leader* (Sioux Falls, South Dakota), Friday 30 December 1938, p. 14, col. 1.
[525] Judson S. Berry marriage index entry, 16 February 1887, Marquette County, Wisconsin, volume 1, p. 327. Also, "Children of the Scholes Family," Scholes ledger book, 65, in author's possession. The 1938 obituary (above) mistakenly gives 1897. For a list of wedding presents and the giver(s) of each, "Hymeneal: Berry–Hume," *Wisconsin State Register* (Portage), Saturday 26 February 1887, p. 3, col. 7.
[526] Buel Berry household, 1900 US census, Fort Winnebago, Columbia County, Wisconsin, sheet 1A, dwelling 62, family 68, next door to the Judson Berry household.
[527] For county of birth, Buel Berry household for son Judson age 5, 1865 New York state census, Tompkins County, p. 31, dwelling 223, family 261. For month and year of birth, Judson S. Berry household, 1900 US census, Fort Winnebago, Columbia County, Wisconsin, sheet 1A, dwelling 61, family 68.
[528] Judson S. Berry death index entry, South Dakota, p. 683, certificate 59417; "South Dakota, Death Index, 1879–1955" > B > image 67 of 430 (ancestry.com).

Spouse's burial: reportedly at Graceland Cemetery, Howard, Miner County, South Dakota[529]

Maggie resided in Topeka, Shawnee County, Kansas, for two years some time prior to 1902. Judson "sold out" in the spring of 1902;[530] they went west and settled on a farm near Fedora, Miner County, South Dakota, in 1902.[531] In August 1903, Margaret was the one Hume child living too far away to join in father Robert Hume's surprise 70th birthday party.[532] In 1910 they were living on a mortgaged farm in Clinton Township, Miner County, South Dakota.[533]

The widow Margaret and her two youngest children moved into town soon after Judson's death. For most of the next two decades, they lived at 117 North Prairie Avenue in Sioux Falls, Minnehaha County, South Dakota.

1919: Robert was the only one of the three employed, working as a salesman at McKinney–Beveridge Automotive Company at 208 East Tenth Street.[534]

1920: mother Margaret was listed as "retired"; they were renting to three roomers. Son Robert was an auto service salesman, and daughter Mildred was teaching public school.[535]

1921: Mildred was teaching at Lowell School, Robert was in automotive sales.[536]

---

[529] Judson Stiles Berry, no grave marker image, Graceland Cemetery, Howard, South Dakota, memorial #113,979,811 by William Ewing (findagrave.com).
[530] "Fort Winnebago," *Portage Daily Register* (Wisconsin), Friday 11 April 1902, p. 1, col. 2.
[531] "Short Illness Claims Mrs. Margaret Berry," *Argus-Leader* (Sioux Falls, South Dakota), Friday 30 December 1938, p. 14, col. 1.
[532] "Birthday Surprise," *Portage Daily Democrat* (Wisconsin), Wednesday 12 August 1903, p. 2, col. 1. The town of Roswell disincorporated in 2012.
[533] Judson S. Berry household, 1910 US census, Clinton Township, Miner County, South Dakota, ED 314, sheet 9B, dwelling/family 38.
[534] Berry entries, *Sioux Falls City Directory 1919* (Sioux Falls, South Dakota: R. L. Polk & Company, 1919), p. 80, image 41 of 331 (ancestry.com).
[535] Margaret A. Berry household, 1920 US census, Sioux Falls, Minnehaha County, South Dakota, Ward 7, ED 193, sheet 4B, dwelling 72, family 84. The 1920 city directory has not been viewed, if indeed it exists.
[536] Berry entries, *Sioux Falls City Directory 1921*, p. 48, image 25 of 220 (ancestry.com).

1922: Mildred was teaching, Robert was a mechanic with no named employer.[537]

1923: Mildred was teaching, Robert was a garage superintendent at Northern States Power Company. His titles varied over the following decades, but he was usually supervising something at Northern States.[538]

1924: Mildred was not listed, only Robert and Margaret.[539]

1925–27: Mildred was teaching, Robert supervising.[540]

1928: Mildred was not listed, having married and gone west (see iii below). Mother Margaret was teaching at Longfellow School; she did not teach again. Robert and new wife Margaret Gale were in the household at 117 North Prairie.[541]

1929: Mother Margaret was at 117; Robert and wife Margaret Gale at 501 South Minnesota, Apartment 4.[542]

1930: Mother Margaret remained at 117 North Prairie, now valued at $9000, and was renting to three roomers.[543] (There may well have been roomers all along.) Robert and wife Margaret Gale did not appear in the census, but they were at 117 in the city directory.[544]

1931: Mother Margaret remained at 117; Robert and wife Margaret were at 516 South Grange Avenue.[545]

1932–34: Mother Margaret remained at 117; Robert and wife Margaret resided at 1215 West Tenth Street.[546]

---

[537] Berry entries, *Sioux Falls City Directory 1922*, p. 54, image 29 of 241 (ancestry.com).
[538] Berry entries, *Sioux Falls City Directory 1923*, p. 60, image 31 of 268 (ancestry.com).
[539] Berry entries, *Sioux Falls City Directory 1924*, p. 60, image 32 of 263 (ancestry.com).
[540] Berry entries, *Sioux Falls City Directory 1925*, p. 104, image 54 of 278 (ancestry.com). Similarly, *1926*, p. 85, image 45 of 258; *1927*, p. 69, image 39 of 242.
[541] Berry entries, *Sioux Falls City Directory 1928*, p. 74, image 36 of 272 (ancestry.com).
[542] Berry entries, *Sioux Falls City Directory 1929*), p. 82, image 40 of 323 (ancestry.com).
[543] Margaret Berry household, 1930 US census, Sioux Falls, Minnehaha County, South Dakota, Ward 7, ED 36, sheet 12B, dwelling 271, family 297.
[544] Berry entries, *Sioux Falls City Directory 1930*, p. 88, image 45 of 300 (ancestry.com).
[545] Berry entries, *Sioux Falls City Directory 1931*, p. 87, image 43 of 289 (ancestry.com).
[546] Berry entries, *Sioux Falls City Directory 1932*, p. 72, image 37 of 259 (ancestry.com). Similarly, *1933*, p. 60, image 31 of 248; *1934*, p. 60, image 32 of 245.

1935: Mother Margaret was not listed (perhaps directory error); Robert and wife Margaret were back at 117 North Prairie.[547]

1936–38: All three present; mother Margaret died 29 December 1938.[548]

1939: Robert and wife Margaret were at 117.[549]

Children of Margaret Alice[3] (Hume) and Judson S. Berry, all born in Wisconsin[550]:

i. WILLIS HAROLD [4] BERRY (*Margaret A.[3] Hume, Sarah Ann[2] Scholes, Ann[1] Mills, Samuel[A]*) was born 30 November 1893[551]; died reportedly 26 August 1953 in Lake County, South Dakota;[552] and was buried at Graceland Cemetery, Howard, Miner County, South Dakota.[553] He married 8 June 1921 in Roswell, Miner County, ELIZABETH M. RODGER,[554] daughter of David and Lucy (Burwell) Rodger.[555] Elizabeth was born 29 January 1897 in Moundville, Marquette County, Wisconsin; died 25 January 1989 at her home at 2900 South Lake Avenue, Sioux Falls, Minnehaha County, South Dakota; and was

---

[547] Berry entries, *Sioux Falls City Directory 1935*, p. 63, image 32 of 259 (ancestry.com).
[548] Berry entries, *Sioux Falls City Directory 1936*, p. 66, image 35 of 265 (ancestry.com). Similarly, *1937*, p. 45, image 21 of 315; *1938*, p. 47, image 22 of 331.
[549] Berry entries, *Sioux Falls City Directory 1939*, p. 45, image 27 of 321 (ancestry.com).
[550] In both 1900 and 1910 Margaret was reported to have had three children, three living: Judson S. Berry household, 1900 US census, Fort Winnebago, Columbia County, Wisconsin, sheet 1A, dwelling 61, family 68. Similarly, 1910, Clinton Township, Miner County, South Dakota, ED 314, sheet 9B, dwelling/family 38.
[551] Judson S. Berry household, 1900 US census, Fort Winnebago, Columbia County, Wisconsin, sheet 1A, dwelling 61, family 68. Exact date from Scholes ledger book, 67, in author's possession.
[552] Willis H. Berry death index entry, 26 August 1953, Lake County, South Dakota, certificate #273,570, p. 83; "South Dakota, Death Index, 1879–1955" > B > image 399 of 430 (ancestry.com).
[553] Willis H. Berry grave marker, image, Graceland Cemetery, Howard, Miner County, South Dakota, Block G, Lot 34, grave 10, memorial #113,979,896 by William Ewing and Charlene Hall (findagrave.com).
[554] Exact date from Scholes ledger book, 67, in author's possession.
[555] Lucy M. (Burwell) Rodger and David L. Rodger, joint grave marker, image, Hill Crest Cemetery, Endeavor, Marquette County, Wisconsin, memorials #104,306,160 and #104,306,374, respectively, by Joey (findagrave.com).

buried at Graceland Cemetery, Howard, Miner County, South Dakota.[556]

1915: Elizabeth graduated from the Christian Endeavor Academy in Endeavor, Wisconsin (see story 3, following Chapter 18), in 1915, took six weeks of teachers' training in Stevens Point, Wisconsin, and began teaching that fall. She taught six years in rural Wisconsin schools in German-speaking communities.[557]

1930: She and Willis were renting in Clinton Township, Miner County, South Dakota.[558]

1938: in December they were in Roswell, Miner County, South Dakota.[559]

1940: they owned a $700 home there. (The statewide average home value in South Dakota that year was $1,618.) "Cousins" William and "Evangline" Bell, aged 21 and 18 and born in Oregon, were living with them.[560]

1953: After her husband's death she moved to Sioux Falls and worked in "the kitchen and student nurses' dormitory at McKennan Hospital for six years." She was a Methodist and a member of the Royal Neighbors Lodge.[561]

ii. ROBERT BUELL[4] BERRY (*Margaret A.[3] Hume, Sarah Ann[2] Scholes, Ann[1] Mills, Samuel[A]*) was born 17 May 1895 in Portage, Columbia County, Wisconsin, and died 27 August 1966 at his residence, 3011 South Lincoln Avenue, Sioux Falls, Minnehaha County, South Dakota. He married MARGARET GALE 26 December 1927 in Gary, Lake

---

[556] Elizabeth R. Berry grave marker, image, Graceland Cemetery, Howard, Miner County, South Dakota, Block G, Lot 34, grave 9, memorial #113,980,534 by William Ewing and Charlene Hall (findagrave.com).
[557] "Elizabeth Berry" [Elizabeth M. Rodger] obituary, *Argus-Leader* (Sioux Falls, South Dakota), Friday 27 January 1989, p. 18, col. 1.
[558] Willis H. Berry household, 1930 US census, Clinton Township, Miner County, South Dakota, ED 9, sheet 1A, dwelling/family 1.
[559] "Short Illness Claims Mrs. Margaret Berry," *Argus-Leader* (Sioux Falls, South Dakota), Friday 30 December 1938, p. 14, col. 1.
[560] Willis Berry household, 1940 US census, Clinton Township, Miner County, South Dakota, ED 49-9, sheet 1A, dwelling/family 1. Statewide figures from US Census Bureau, Census of Housing, Historical Census of Housing Tables, Median Home Values Unadjusted 1940 (https://www2.census.gov/programs-surveys/decennial/tables/time-series/coh-values/values-unadj.txt).
[561] "Deaths…Sioux Falls…Elizabeth Berry," *Argus-Leader,* Sioux Falls (South Dakota), Friday 27 January 1989, p. 2C, col. 1. Also, Willis H. Berry household, 1930 US census, Clinton Township, Miner County, South Dakota, ED 9, sheet 1A, dwelling/family 1. Both gave their age at first marriage as nine years younger than they were in 1930. The obituary misstates her husband's death as 1956.

County, Indiana.[562] Her parents were Clarence L. and Annie (Hughes) Gale. In 1920 her father Clarence was a locomotive engineer for the "EJ&E" (Elgin, Joliet, and Eastern Railroad, which partially encircled Chicago).[563] Margaret was born 26 July 1904 in Chicago and died 21 January 1967.[564] She and Robert both completed two years of college.[565] As a small child, she moved with her family from Chicago to Gary, Lake County, Indiana, where they were living in 1920.[566] She attended teachers college at Muncie, Delaware County, Indiana (now Ball State University), taught school first at Gary and then at Longfellow School in Sioux Falls when she moved there in 1925.

1917, June 5: Robert was an "automobile mechanic" working for John P. Bleeg in Sioux Falls. He was medium in height and weight, with dark brown eyes and hair.[567]

---

[562] For marriage date, "Robert Berry Dies in S.F.," *Argus-Leader* (Sioux Falls, South Dakota), Saturday 27 August 1966, p. 2, col. 6. Also, for marriage and his birth date, Scholes ledger book, 67, in author's possession.

[563] Clarence L. Gale household for wife Annie age 41 born Canada and daughter Margaret age 15 born Illinois, 1920 US census, Gary, Lake County, Indiana, Ward 2, ED 98, sheet 6A, dwelling 136, family 137. (The enumerator applied dwelling and family numbers wrongly; thus the next household was dwelling 138 and family 139.) For Annie's birth surname: Norma Lorraine Gale birth certificate #2075, 19 January (?) 1920, Indiana State board of Health, naming parents Clarence Gale and Annie Hughes; "Indiana, Birth Certificates, 1907–1940" > 1920 > 001 > image 2071 of 3000 (ancestry.com). For the EJ&E: ejearchive.com.

[564] Robert Buell Berry and Margaret Augusta Gale Berry joint grave marker, Westlawn section, Woodlawn Cemetery, Sioux Falls, South Dakota, image, memorials #57,376,744 and #57,376,810, both by Charlene Hall and Dr. Marie C. Karban DVM ret. (findagrave.com). Also, Judson S. Berry household, 1900 US census, Fort Winnebago, Columbia County, Wisconsin, sheet 1A, dwelling 61, family 68. Also, for Margaret's birth state, Robert B. Berry household, 1930 US census, Sioux Falls, Minnehaha County, South Dakota, Ward 8, ED 37, sheet 12B, dwelling 169, family 313.

[565] Robert Berry household, 1940 US census, Sioux Falls, Minnehaha County, South Dakota, ED 50-39B, sheet 11A, dwelling 226.

[566] Clarence L. Gale household, 1920 US census, Gary, Lake County, Indiana, Ward 2, ED 98, sheet 6A.

[567] Robert B. Berry WWI draft card, 5 June 1917, Sioux Falls, South Dakota, precinct 3, #1335 and #188; "US, World War I Draft Registration Cards, 1917–1918" > South Dakota> Minnehaha County > ALL > Draft Card B > image 352 of 897 (ancestry.com).

1918: Robert was a sergeant in the 13th Company, 4th Motor Mechanic Regiment, poised to leave Hoboken, New Jersey, on the *Themistocles* 15 July.[568]

1920: he was a salesman for an "auto service" in Sioux Falls, living with his mother Margaret and sister Mildred.[569]

1921, January 13: He began his career working for Northern States Power at the Sioux Falls power plant, later in transportation and right-of-way, retiring in 1960. He also spent 23 years in sales and agricultural sales.[570]

1930: they were renting an apartment in a fourplex at 501 Minnesota Avenue South there for $45 a month, with no radio set.[571]

December 1938: they were in Sioux Falls.[572]

1940: Robert was a traveling salesman for Northern States and wife Margaret was a substitute teacher. They owned a $5000 house—well above the South Dakota average that year of $1618, but well below its stated value of $9000 ten years before.[573]

1954–1966: "She was associated with World Book [Encyclopedia] since 1954 and at the time of her retirement [October 1966] she was district manager for Field Enterprises," the encyclopedia's parent company.[574]

1958: Robert was a supervisor at the Sioux Empire Farm Show.

---

[568] Robert B. Berry, "Passenger List of Organizations and Casuals," US, Army Transport Service, Passenger Lists, 1910–1939 > Outgoing > Themistocles > 15 July 1918–18 February 1919 > image 40 of 144 (ancestry.com).

[569] Margaret A. Berry household, 1920 US census, Sioux Falls, Minnehaha County, South Dakota, Ward 7, ED 193, sheet 4B, dwelling 72, family 84, at 117 North Prairie Avenue.

[570] "Robert Berry Dies in S.F.," *Argus-Leader* (Sioux Falls, South Dakota), Saturday 27 August 1966, p. 2, col. 6. The years do not add up; no doubt he was moonlighting some of the time.

[571] Robert B. Berry household, 1930 US census, Sioux Falls, Minnehaha County, South Dakota, Ward 8, ED 37, sheet 12B, dwelling 169, family 313.

[572] "Short Illness Claims Mrs. Margaret Berry," *Argus-Leader* (Sioux Falls, South Dakota), Friday 30 December 1938, p. 14, col. 1.

[573] Robert Berry household, 1940 US census, Sioux Falls, Minnehaha County, South Dakota, ED 50-39B, sheet 11A, dwelling 226. Statewide figures from US Census Bureau, Census of Housing, Historical Census of Housing Tables, Median Home Values Unadjusted 1940 (https://www2.census.gov/programs-surveys/decennial/tables/time-series/coh-values/values-unadj.txt). Also, Margaret Berry household, 1930 US census, Sioux Falls, Minnehaha County, South Dakota, Ward 7, ED 36, sheet 12B, dwelling 271, family 297.

[574] "Deaths Sioux Falls…Mrs. Margaret Berry," *Sioux Falls Argus-Leader* (South Dakota), Sunday 22 January 1967, p. 2, col. 3.

1960: He served on the executive committee for the Soil Conservation Field Days and National Plowing Contest held in South Dakota.[575]

13 February 1961: The plat of Robert and Margaret's "Berry Patch Addition" in the southwest portion of Sioux Falls was approved.[576]

---

[575] "Robert Berry Dies in S.F.," *Argus-Leader* (Sioux Falls, South Dakota), Saturday 27 August 1966, p. 2, col. 6.

[576] "A Resolution Approving the Plan of Berry Patch Addition to the City of Sioux Falls . . . by Robert B. Berry and Margaret Gale Berry," *Argus-Leader* (Sioux Falls, South Dakota), Saturday 25 February 1961, p. 7, col. 6. Also, "Deaths Sioux Falls…Mrs. Margaret Berry," *Sioux Falls Argus-Leader* (South Dakota), Sunday 22 January 1967, p. 2, col. 3.

Story #2: The Berry Patch and Its House (on the eve of WW2)

In 1941, a local newspaperman called the Berrys' new/old house possibly the "last log cabin to be built in the Sioux river valley." Robert salvaged old power poles no longer needed by his employer, the Northern States Power company, and had them cut at a sawmill: "flat on three sides, about eight to ten inches thick. The one curved side becomes the log or exposed side of the cabin. The walls are from six to eight inches thick."

Otherwise the cabin is "to be modern in the extreme, playroom in the basement, attached garage, etc.," but "laid pioneer fashion one on top of another, windows and doors inserted, and a rustic treatment at the corners accentuates the log motif." Inside, a two by four is used as furring, and modern treatment, such as plaster, applied.

The Berrys planned the story-and-a half house as a year-around abode. "Two fireplaces give it a rustic tinge that will last for years." The cabin sits on ten acres of rolling Sioux River valley land which the Berrys and their friends call "The Berry Patch."[577]

---

[577] Ken Robertson, "Maybe You've Heard," *Argus Leader* (Sioux Falls, South Dakota), Wednesday 3 December 1941, p. 2, col. 6.

iii. MILDRED ELIZA[4] BERRY (*Margaret A.[3] Hume, Sarah Ann[2] Scholes, Ann[1] Mills, Samuel[A]*) was born 23 November 1898 in Wisconsin[578] and died 8 February 1989 in Cleveland, Cuyahoga County, Ohio. Mildred married two financiers: first HOWARD JUDD BLAKE 31 March 1927 in Spokane, Spokane County, Washington. He was the son of Louis and Clara Rosetta (Judd) Blake.[579] Howard was born 17 January 1900; died 11 November 1956, possibly in Iowa; and was buried at Blakesburg Cemetery, Blakesburg, Wapello County, Iowa.[580]

Howard completed four years of high school, Mildred one year of college.[581] "Miss Betty [Berry], a graduate of Eastern normal, has been teaching in the primary department at Lowell school. Before the closing of the Sioux Falls National Bank, Mr. Blake was connected with that institution. Two years following he was a state bank examiner and is now with the Halsey-Stewart bond company in Seattle."[582]

"Both participants of the marriage are well known in Sioux Falls [South Dakota]. The bride taught in the city schools for several years and was much feted prior to her departure for Spokane. Mr. Blake was in the banking business in the city until January 1926, when he went into the employ of the Halsey–Stuart company [a Chicago-based investment bank]. He motored to Spokane to meet his bride."[583]

1930: they lived in a large apartment house at 1000 Chemeketa Street in Salem, Marion County, Oregon; Howard was a bond salesman. Like practically all their neighbors, they had a "radio set."[584]

---

[578] Judson S. Berry household, 1900 US census, Fort Winnebago, Columbia County, Wisconsin, sheet 1A, dwelling 61, family 68. Exact date from Scholes ledger book, 67, in author's possession. Also, US Social Security Death Index, 1935–2014.

[579] Mildred Berry–Howard Blake marriage license #39184, Spokane, Spokane County, Washington, 31 March 1927; "Washington, Marriage Records, 1854–2013" > Spokane > Marriages 1927 Jan–Apr > image 261 of 315 (ancestry.com). Rev. Henry A. Van Winkle, Central Christian Church, officiated. Mildred was residing in Sioux Falls, South Dakota, and Howard in Portland, Oregon. Also, Scholes ledger book, 67, in author's possession.

[580] Howard Judd Blake grave marker, Blakesburg Cemetery, Blakesburg, Wapello County, Iowa, image, memorial #95,470,904 by zoey (findagrave.com).

[581] Howard Blake household, 1940 US census, Cleveland, Cuyahoga County, Ohio, ED 92-2, sheet 11B, dwelling 276.

[582] "New Year Wedding," *Argus-Leader* (Sioux Falls, South Dakota), Saturday 18 December 1926, p. 7, col. 5.

[583] "Berry–Blake Nuptials Takes Place in Spokane, Washington," *Argus-Leader* (Sioux Falls, South Dakota), Friday 1 April 1927, p. 7, col. 1.

[584] Howard Blake household, 1930 US census, Salem, Marion County, Oregon, ED 56, sheet 4A, dwelling 86, family 99.

1935: they lived in Mansfield, Richland County, Ohio.[585]
1938: they were in Cleveland.[586]
1940: Howard was a bond salesman in Cleveland; they rented apartment 406 at 9823 Lake Avenue for $65 a month.[587]
1942: as of 15 February, Howard was 5 feet 10 inches tall and weighed 155 pounds, with blue eyes and brown hair. They were living at 9823 Lake Avenue, and he was employed by the Federal Reserve Bank of Cleveland.[588]

After Howard's 1956 death, Mildred married second EDWARD MUSGRAVE BLAIKLOCK. He was born 27 April 1902, possibly in Chiswick, Borough of Honslow, London, England; died 7 March 1973 in Cleveland;[589] and was buried with his wife at Woodlawn Cemetery, Sioux Falls, Minnehaha County, South Dakota.[590] In September 1935 he was appointed chairman of the education committee of the American Institute of Banking. "Mr. Blaiklock has been associated with banking activities for a number of years, having been with the Washington Loan & Trust Co. for the past 10 years. He started working in the A.I.B. in 1926 and received his standard certificate in 1929. Last year he served as chairman of the Entertainment Committee. He was born in England and attended school there."[591] In 1967, at the time of his brother's death in Tampa, Florida, he was in Cleveland.[592]

---

[585] Howard Blake household, 1940 US census, Cleveland, Cuyahoga County, Ohio, ED 92-2, sheet 11B, dwelling 276.
[586] "Short Illness Claims Mrs. Margaret Berry," *Argus-Leader* (Sioux Falls, South Dakota), Friday 30 December 1938, p. 14, col. 1. Daughter "Mrs. Howard Blake" was in Cleveland, Ohio.
[587] Howard Blake household, 1940 US census, Cleveland, Cuyahoga County, Ohio, ED 92-2, sheet 11B, dwelling 276.
[588] Howard Blake WW2 draft card, 15 February 1942, Cuyahoga County Local Board #1, serial #T159, order #T11,531; "US, WWII Draft Cards Young Men, 1940–1947" > Ohio > Berik–Brahler > Blair–Blamer > images 914–15 of 2244 (ancestry.com).
[589] Transcribed obituary, Edward M. Blaiklock, *Cleveland Press*, 9 March 1973; "Cleveland Necrology File and News Index," reel 94, Cleveland Public Library (https://cpl.org/newsindex). Also, Edward M. Blaiklock joint grave marker, Woodlawn Cemetery, Sioux Falls, South Dakota, image, memorial #53,951,832 for Edward Musgrave Blaiklock by Dr. Marie C. Karban DVM ret (findagrave.com).
[590] Mildred B. Blaiklock joint grave marker, Woodlawn Cemetery, Sioux Falls, South Dakota, image, memorial #53,951,887 for Mildred Eliza Hume Berry Blaiklock by Dr. Marie C. Karban DVM ret (findagrave.com).
[591] Edward C. Stone, "Blaiklock New A.I.B. Committee Chairman," *Evening Star* (Washington, DC), Sunday 1 September 1935, p. 20, col. 1.
[592] "Deaths in Tampa and the Bay Area . . . John Blaiklock," *Tampa Tribune* (Florida), Sunday 13 August 1967, p. 19, cols. 4–5.

Chapter 17

Third Generation

Robert Walker Hume, Jr.–Alice Sarah Smith Family
parents at chapter 4

"He has gone—suddenly—and we are sad. But his rugged personality, his hospitable smile, and his kind acts to his fellow travelers will be remembered"

17. ROBERT WALKER³ HUME, JR. (*Sarah Ann² Scholes, Ann¹ Mills, Samuel^A*)
Birth: 29 July 1863[593]
Death: 26 April 1940 in an automobile accident at Watertown, Jefferson County, Wisconsin
Burial: Moundville Cemetery, Endeavor, Marquette County, Wisconsin[594]
Spouse: **ALICE SARAH SMITH**, married 4 April 1888 or 1889[595]
Spouse's parents: Isaac and Mary (Ellison Smith[596]
Spouse's birth: 1867, reportedly 27 July, Marquette County, Wisconsin
Spouse's death: 1951

---

[593] Mrs. A. R., "Obituary, Robert W. Hume," *Portage Register-Democrat* (Wisconsin), Wednesday 8 May 1940, p. 2, col. 2.
[594] "Funerals . . . Robert W. Hume," *Portage Register-Democrat* (Wisconsin), Thursday 2 May 1940, p. 2, cols. 1–2.
[595] 4 April 1889: "Children of the Scholes Family," Scholes ledger book, 65, in author's possession. Or 4 April 1888: Mrs. A. R., "Obituary, Robert W. Hume," *Portage Register-Democrat* (Wisconsin), Wednesday 8 May 1940, p. 2, col. 2.
[596] Isaac Smith (12 January 1846–26 December 1922) and Mary Ellison his wife (13 June 1845–5 January 1914), joint grave marker, Moundville Cemetery, Endeavor, Marquette County, Wisconsin, memorials #10,564,729 and #10,564,730 respectively, by Joey. Also, Alice S. Hume joint grave marker with husband Robert W. Hume, image, Moundville Cemetery, Endeavor, Marquette County, Wisconsin, memorials #102,788,276 and #102,787,909 respectively, by Joey (findagrave.com).

Spouse's burial: Moundville Cemetery, Endeavor, Marquette County, Wisconsin[597]

Alice completed four years of high school, Robert eight years of school.[598] The Humes first farmed in Buffalo Township, then moved to Moundville, and in 1922 to Endeavor, "and soon made many friends by their hospitable attitude."

In 1920 they owned their home with a mortgage.[599] In 1930 they lived on Prospect Street in Endeavor; they owned their house, valued at $3500. In 1940, after ten years of the Great Depression, it was valued at $3300, almost exactly the statewide average.[600] Robert was a salesman of household products.[601] At the Hume family's second reunion in Endeavor in August 1936, Robert was elected president.[602] Robert's death in 1940

> seemed an unusual, sad happening. Mr. Hume appeared young for his age. His figure was erect and youthful, his step quick and active, and he enjoyed good health. His plans were all made for his summer work in his garden and berry field and he was looking forward with interest and anticipation.
>
> He liked to have a part in the affairs of men, was interested in people, and was always ready and pleased to open his home as a meeting place for friends or as a resting place for the weary. He was a man of clean habits, proud of his family, true to his convictions, kind-hearted and a good citizen.

---

[597] Alice S. Hume joint grave marker with husband Robert W. Hume, image, Moundville Cemetery, Endeavor, Marquette County, Wisconsin, memorials #102,788,276 and #102,787,909 respectively, by Joey (findagrave.com).
[598] Robert W. Hume household, 1940 US census, Endeavor, Marquette County, Wisconsin, ED 39-8, sheet 3B, dwelling 78.
[599] Robert W. Hume household, 1920 US census, Moundville Township, Marquette County, Wisconsin, ED 133, sheet 2A, dwelling 39, family 40.
[600] Robert W. Hume household, 1940 US census, Endeavor, Marquette County, Wisconsin, ED 39-8, sheet 3B, dwelling 78. Statewide figures from US Census Bureau, Census of Housing, Historical Census of Housing Tables, Median Home Values Unadjusted 1940 (https://www2.census.gov/programs-surveys/decennial/tables/time-series/coh-values/values-unadj.txt).
[601] Robt. W. Hume household, 1930 US census, Endeavor, Marquette County, Wisconsin, ED 8, sheet 1B, dwelling/family 25.
[602] "Reunion of Hume Family Held Sunday," *Portage Daily Register* (Wisconsin), p. 4, cols. 1–2. Includes an enormous list of attendees and their locations.

He has gone—suddenly—and we are sad. But his rugged personality, his hospitable smile and his kind acts to his fellow travelers will be remembered, and in the hearts of his loved ones he still lives.[603]

Children of Robert Walker[3] Jr. and Alice Sarah (Smith) Hume:

In an unusual pattern for these families, two of the three youngest children left Wisconsin for the east and south, spending time in Indiana, Ohio, and Florida.

    i. EDNA ALICE[4] HUME (*Alice*[3] *Smith, Sarah Ann*[2] *Scholes, Ann*[1] *Mills, Samuel*[A]) was born 22 July 1890, died 29 (November?) 1892, and was buried at Moundville Cemetery, Marquette County, Wisconsin.[604] Grandmother Mrs. Isaac Smith was there to help with the ten-pound baby.[605]

    ii. BABY BOY[4] HUME (*Alice*[3] *Smith, Sarah Ann*[2] *Scholes, Ann*[1] *Mills, Samuel*[A]) was born perhaps 22 April 1891, died possibly 1 May 1891, and was buried with his likely sister Edna at Moundville Cemetery (above). The grave marker is badly worn.[606]

    iii. ROBERT ISAAC[4] HUME (*Alice*[3] *Smith, Sarah Ann*[2] *Scholes, Ann*[1] *Mills, Samuel*[A]) was born 29 March 1896 in Moundville, Marquette County, Wisconsin.[607] He died 3 December 1978 at Divine Savior Hospital in

---

[603] Mrs. A. R., "Obituary, Robert W. Hume," *Portage Register-Democrat* (Wisconsin), Wednesday 8 May 1940, p. 2, col. 2.
[604] Edna A. Hume grave marker, image, Moundville Cemetery, Marquette County, Wisconsin, memorial #179,053,279 for Edna Alice Hume by Diane K (findagrave.com).
[605] "Moundville," *Portage Daily Democrat* (Wisconsin), Thursday 31 July 1890, p. 3, col. 3.
[606] Baby Boy Hume grave marker, image, Moundville Cemetery, Marquette County, Wisconsin, no memorial, same stone as Edna's (findagrave.com). In all likelihood this is the second child the family lost. In 1900 Alice reportedly had four children, two living; in 1900, six children, four living.
[607] Robert I. Hume, grave marker, image, Moundville Cemetery, Endeavor, Wisconsin, memorial #102,787,520 by Joey (findagrave.com). Also, Robert Hume household for Robert I. born March 1896, 1900 US census, Moundville, Marquette County, Wisconsin, ED 93, sheet 1A, dwelling/family 4.

Portage, Columbia County, Wisconsin, and was buried at Moundville Cemetery.[608]

Robert's future wife ELIZABETH MORAN graduated from Portage High School and Story's business college.[609] In 1917 she was a bookkeeper at the *Democrat* (Portage newspaper), living at 628 East Cook with parents and siblings.[610] As of 5 June 1917, Robert was working on his father's farm: tall and of medium build, with light brown eyes and dark brown hair.[611] Robert served as PFC (Private First Class) in World War I,[612] enlisting 3 April 1918 and being released 8 March 1919.[613]

Robert and Elizabeth married about 1919 (first-born child).[614] She was the daughter of Edward C. and Emogene (Jones) Moran,[615] born reportedly 29 July 1896, died 15 November 1936 "after a long illness,"[616] and was buried at Silver Lake Cemetery, Portage, Columbia County.[617]

---

[608] "Obituaries . . . Robert Hume," *Portage Daily Register* (Wisconsin), Monday 4 December 1978, p. 5, col. 4.

[609] "Mrs. Hume, Portage, Dies," *Wisconsin State Journal* (Madison), Tuesday 17 November 1936, p. 5, col. 1. Story's business college was a trade school for office workers such as stenographers and typists. The Portage school advertised in *The Columbian*, a quarterly for Columbia County, Wisconsin, schoolteachers and residents. There appear to have been local branches, as president H. O. Story describes it as "The Great Northern Training School": H. O. Story, "An Open Letter," *The Columbian* 3(1), unpaginated, first page of advertising, November 1912. Also, H. J. Davis, "A Letter for Young Men and Women to Read," *The Columbian* 2(4), unpaginated, first page of advertising, June 1912 (books.google.com).

[610] Miss Elizabeth Moran entry, *Farrell's Portage City Directory 1917–18* (Milwaukee: John T. Farrell, 1917), p. 96, image 51 of 81 (ancestry.com).

[611] Robert Isaac Hume WWI draft card, 5 June 1917, Moundville, series #[three are given], order #8; "US, World War I Draft Registration Cards, 1917–1918" > Marquette County > Draft Card H > image 160 of 162 (ancestry.com).

[612] Robert I. Hume, grave marker, image, Moundville Cemetery, Endeavor, Wisconsin, memorial #102,787,520 by Joey (findagrave.com).

[613] Robert Hume index entry, "US, Department of Veterans Affairs BIRLS Death File, 1850–2010" (ancestry.com).

[614] "Obituaries…Mildred Henke" (31 August 1920–13 December 2018), *Beaver Dam Daily Citizen* (Wisconsin), Monday 17 December 2018, p. A2, col. 1. Also, Mildred E. Hume Henke, no grave marker image, Hillside Cemetery, Columbus, Columbia County, Wisconsin, memorial #195,495,760 by Kathy (findagrave.com).

[615] Edward C. Moran and Emogene (Jones) Moran joint grave marker, image, memorials #106,291,311 and #106,290,961 respectively by Joey (findagrave.com).

[616] "Mrs. Hume, Portage, Dies," *Wisconsin State Journal* (Madison), Tuesday 17 November 1936, p. 5, col. 1.

[617] Elizabeth Moran Hume, no grave marker or sources, memorial #106,291,556 by Joey (findagrave.com). Also, previous note.

Luck was not Robert's friend: in 1925 he used a lighted lantern to find a dropped gas cap near his car, and wound up setting the car afire and badly burning his hand.[618]

As of 1 April 1940, widower Robert was living in Portage with his widowed mother-in-law Emogene Moran at 109 Emmett Street. She owned it and it was valued at $2500. Robert had completed eight years of schooling and was a "shoe worker" at a local shoe factory, earning $710 for 40 weeks' work in 1939.[619]

A few weeks later came a devastating accident: "On the way to Milwaukee Friday, R. I. Hume met with an automobile accident in which his father was killed and his mother seriously injured."[620] It was a head-on collision in which the setting sun and a third car, passing, also played a role, on Route 14 just outside of Watertown.[621]

As of 27 April 1942, Robert was employed at Weyenburg Shoe Manufacturing Company in Portage and living at 109 Emmett there (phone number 352R). He was 5 feet 10 inches tall, weighed 200 pounds, and had brown eyes, gray hair, and a ruddy complexion.[622] That same spring he had debts totaling $2102 and assets of $103, and voluntarily went into bankruptcy.[623]

Robert married second ELIZABETH E. "BETH" (TOPPING) JONES 25 May 1946 in Briggsville, Marquette County, Wisconsin, as his second wife and her second husband.[624] The daughter of James and Edith (Pattee) Topping, she was born 18 December 1894 in Stockton, Portage County, Wisconsin; died 15 March 1991 in Portage, Columbia

---

[618] "Endeavor Man Looks for Tank Cap with Lantern," *Portage Daily Register* (Wisconsin), Saturday 18 April 1925, p. 1, col. 2.

[619] Emogene Moran household for son-in-law Robert I. Hume, 1940 US census, Portage, Columbia County, Wisconsin, Ward 3, ED 11-25, sheet 2A, dwelling 22. Statewide figures from US Census Bureau, Census of Housing, Historical Census of Housing Tables, Median Home Values Unadjusted 1940 (https://www2.census.gov/programs-surveys/decennial/tables/time-series/coh-values/values-unadj.txt).

[620] "Moundville," *Portage Register-Democrat* (Wisconsin), Tuesday 30 April 1940, p. 4, cols. 2–3.

[621] "Endeavor Man Killed in Crash," *Wisconsin State Register* (Portage), Friday 3 May 1940, p. 1, col. 5.

[622] Robert Isaac Hume WW2 draft card, 27 April 1942, Portage local board 1, serial #U3532, no order number; "US, World War II Draft Registration Cards, 1942" > Wisconsin > Hughes–Hussar > Gould–Kantz > images 701–702 of 2028 (ancestry.com).

[623] "Bankruptcy," *Capital Times* (Madison, Wisconsin), Friday 3 April 1942, p. 26, col. 6. Also, "Notice of First Meeting of Creditors," legal advertisement, *Capital Times* (Wisconsin), Monday 6 April 1942, p. 14, col. 4.

[624] "Couple Wed Saturday in Briggsville," *Portage Daily Register* (Wisconsin), Wednesday 29 May 1946, p. 5, col. 2.

County; and was buried with her first husband, Walter F. Jones (1895–1937) at Moundville Cemetery, Marquette County. She graduated from Endeavor Christian Academy and then attended Stevens Point Normal School.[625]

Evidently the bankruptcy process served its purpose in helping him toward a new start; in 1946 he and his second wife purchased a farm in Moundville.[626] In the 1950s he was one of three central Wisconsin dealers in hybrid Pioneer seed corn.[627]

He was a member of Moundville Methodist Church.[628] His widow Beth (Topping) (Jones) Hume, in her early 90s, was the oldest attendee at the 54th annual Hume Reunion in Moundville, 26 July August 1987.[629]

iv. GLENDON ELLISON[4] HUME (*Alice*[3] *Smith, Sarah Ann*[2] *Scholes, Ann*[1] *Mills, Samuel*[A]) was born in Wisconsin[630] 2 December 1898,[631] and died 9 August 1972 in Ravenna, Portage County, Ohio.[632] As of 12 September 1918, he was of medium height and build, with brown eyes and dark hair, and was farming for his father.[633] In 1920 he was in his

---

[625] "Obituaries…Elizabeth 'Beth' Hume," *Portage Daily Register* (Wisconsin), Sunday 17 March 1991, p. 2, col. 5.

[626] "Couple Wed Saturday in Briggsville," *Portage Daily Register* (Wisconsin), Wednesday 29 May 1946, p. 5, col. 2.

[627] "Plant Pioneer," advertisement, *Portage Daily Register* (Wisconsin), Friday 11 May 1951, p. 5, col. 3.

[628] "Obituaries…Robert Hume," *Portage Daily Register* (Wisconsin), Monday 4 December 1978, p. 5, col. 4.

[629] "47 present at 54th annual Hume reunion," *Portage Daily Register* (Wisconsin), Saturday 1 August 1987, p. 12, cols. 1–2.

[630] Robert Hume household for Genden [Glendon] E. born December 1898, 1900 US census, Moundville, Marquette County, Wisconsin, ED 93, sheet 1A, dwelling/family 4.

[631] Glendon Ellison Hume WWI draft card, serial #953, order #a959, Montello, Wisconsin, local board, 12 September 1918; "US, World War I Draft Registration Cards, 1917–1918" > Wisconsin > Marquette County > ALL > Draft Card H > image 157 of 162 (ancestry.com).

[632] Glenn E. Hume death index entry, 9 August 1972, Ravenna, Portage County, Ohio, certificate #064,918; "Ohio, Death Records, 1908–1932, 1938–2018" (ancestry.com). Also, Ruth F. Hume, the James family, and David Hume posted a "card of thanks" 17 August 1972 in the *Akron Beacon Journal*, p. 73, col. 4.

[633] Glendon Ellison Hume WWI draft card, serial #953, order #a959, Montello, Wisconsin, local board, 12 September 1918; "US, World War I Draft Registration Cards, 1917–1918" > Wisconsin > Marquette County > ALL > Draft Card H > image 157 of 162 (ancestry.com).

parents' house.⁶³⁴ In about 1928 he began a 44-year career in barbering on East Market Street in Akron, Summit County, Ohio.⁶³⁵ In 1930 he and younger brother Frank were rooming together in Akron.⁶³⁶ Glen married in Endeavor, Marquette County, Wisconsin, 10 October 1932 RUTH FLORENCE KUNOW of Baraboo, Sauk County, Wisconsin.⁶³⁷ She was born 8 March 1905 in Caledonia Township, Columbia County, Wisconsin, to Hugo Charles and Caroline (Schirmer) Kunow,⁶³⁸ and died in 1978 in Brimfield Township, Portage County, Ohio.⁶³⁹

v. ELDA MARY⁴ HUME (*Alice³ Smith, Sarah Ann² Scholes, Ann¹ Mills, Samuel^A*) was born 10 November 1902 in Marquette County, Wisconsin;⁶⁴⁰ died 10 February 1992 in Waukesha, Waukesha County, Wisconsin; and was buried at Forest Home Cemetery, Milwaukee, with her husband.⁶⁴¹ She married about 1927 FRED CHARLES QUADEN.⁶⁴² The son of Bernhard and Alma Quaden,⁶⁴³ he was born

---

⁶³⁴ Robert W. Hume household for son Glendon E. age 21, 1920 US census, Moundville Township, Marquette County, Wisconsin, ED 133, sheets 1A–2B, dwelling 39, family 40.
⁶³⁵ "Glenn E. Hume, 73, Barber 44 Years," *Akron Beacon Journal* (Ohio), Thursday 10 August 1972, p. 16, cols. 1–2.
⁶³⁶ Gleen H*le [Glen Hume] household for single boarder Frank R., 1930 US census, Akron, Summit County, Ohio, Ward 7, ED 123, sheet 6B, dwelling 68, family 95.
⁶³⁷ "Endeavor," *Portage Daily Register* (Wisconsin), Monday 24 October 1932, p. 4, col. 1.
⁶³⁸ Ruth Florence Kunow birth index entry, birth 8 March 1905 in Caledonia Township, Columbia County, Wisconsin, vols. 2–4, p. 314, #866, record #1869; "Wisconsin Births and Christenings, 1826–1926," FHL #1,302,855, DGS #7,609,643 (familysearch.org).
⁶³⁹ "Ruth F. Hume," *Akron Beacon Journal* (Ohio), Wednesday 13 December 1978, p. H5 or 30, col. 6.
⁶⁴⁰ Month and date for birth and death unsourced: Elda M. Quaden memorial #108,111,350 by Nadine Subottka (findagrave.com). Also, Robert Hume household for Elda M. age 7, 1910 US census, Moundville, Marquette County, Wisconsin, ED 149, sheet 7B, dwelling 162, family 166.
⁶⁴¹ Fred C. and Elda M. Quaden joint grave marker, image, Forest Home Cemetery, Milwaukee, memorials #108,111,300 and #108,111,350 respectively, by Nadine Sobottka (findagrave.com).
⁶⁴² Mrs. A. R., "Obituary, Robert W. Hume," *Portage Register-Democrat* (Wisconsin), Wednesday 8 May 1940, p. 2, col. 2. For approximate marriage date, Fred C. Juodden [Quadden], 1930 US census, Milwaukee, Milwaukee County, Wisconsin, Ward 25, ED 337, sheet 97B, dwelling 16, family 17.
⁶⁴³ Bernhard Quaden household for son Frederick age 16, 1910 US census, Milwaukee, Milwaukee County, Wisconsin, Ward 19, ED 224, sheet 16B, dwelling 245, family 363.

18 April 1903 in Bremen, Germany;[644] died 1977, and was buried with his wife.[645]

Fred's family members were mostly clerks as of 1910; father Bernhard was in the courthouse.[646] Fred completed three years of high school, Elda four.[647] In 1930, they were renting part of a duplex for $50 a month; like almost all their neighbors, they had a radio set. Fred was a bank cashier and Elda was a stenographer for an insurance agency.[648] Quadens who attended Robert W. Hume Jr.'s 1940 funeral were Mrs. Bernard Quaden, Mr. and Mrs. John Quaden, and Miss Ollie Quaden.[649]

In 1940 Fred was a bank cashier earning $4200 a year; they owned a house on Godsell Avenue in Milwaukee, valued at $8500 (the statewide average in Wisconsin that year was $3232).[650] As of 14 February 1942, Fred was 6 feet 1 inch tall, weighed 192 pounds; had blue eyes and brown hair;

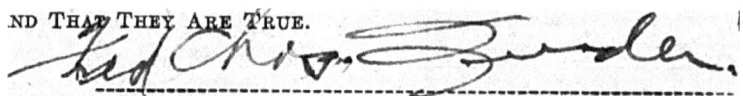

---

[644] Frederick Charles Quaden, WW2 draft card, 14 February 1942, Milwaukee local board 29, serial #T123, order #T10238; "US WWII Draft Cards Young Men, 1940-1947" > Wisconsin > Perkins–Rieseng > Putz–Quick > images 748–49 of 1944 (ancestry.com).

[645] Fred C. and Elda M. Quaden joint grave marker, image, Forest Home Cemetery, Milwaukee, memorials #108,111,300 and #108,111,350 respectively, by Nadine Sobottka (findagrave.com).

[646] Bernhard Quaden household, 1910 US census, Milwaukee, Milwaukee County, Wisconsin, Ward 19, ED 224, sheet 16B, dwelling 245, family 363.

[647] Fred Quaden household, 1940 US census, Hales Corners, Town of Greenfield, Milwaukee County, Wisconsin, ED 40-19, sheet 33B, dwelling 698.

[648] Fred C. Juodden [Quadden], 1930 US census, Milwaukee, Milwaukee County, Wisconsin, Ward 25, ED 337, sheet 97B, dwelling 16, family 17.

[649] "Funerals . . . Robert W. Hume," *Portage Register-Democrat* (Wisconsin), Thursday 2 May 1940, p. 2, cols. 1–2.

[650] Fred Quaden household, 1940 US census, Hales Corners, Town of Greenfield, Milwaukee County, Wisconsin, ED 40-19, sheet 33B, dwelling 698. Statewide figures from US Census Bureau, Census of Housing, Historical Census of Housing Tables, Median Home Values Unadjusted 1940 (https://www2.census.gov/programs-surveys/decennial/tables/time-series/coh-values/values-unadj.txt).

and was living at 11318 West Godsell Avenue, Hales Corners, Milwaukee County, Wisconsin.[651] They were in Milwaukee in August 1972,[652] and in suburban Waukesha in 1976.[653]

vi. FRANK ROLAND[4] HUME (*Alice*[3] *Smith, Sarah Ann*[2] *Scholes, Ann*[1] *Mills, Samuel*[A]) was born 23 April 1905 in Endeavor, Wisconsin;[654] died "very suddenly" Sunday 12 November 1950 in Baltimore, Maryland, where he had been living; and was buried at the family plot in Moundville Cemetery, Wisconsin.[655] He married 28 June 1930, probably in South Bend, St. Joseph County, Indiana, LOIS JOAN MURNER.[656] The daughter of Gideon Wallace and Florence Lucinda (Riffe) Murner,[657] Lois was born 27 October 1902 in Hutchinson County, South Dakota; died 7 August 1976, last residence Huntington Park, Los Angeles County, California; and was buried with her husband in Moundville.[658]

1930: Just prior to his marriage, Frank was rooming with brother Glenn, the barber, in Akron, Ohio, and working in a "rubber shop."[659] That year Lois was teaching school and living with her widowed mother, who

---

[651] Frederick Charles Quaden, WW2 draft card, 14 February 1942, Milwaukee local board 29, serial #T123, order #T10238; "US WWII Draft Cards Young Men, 1940–1947" > Wisconsin > Perkins–Rieseng > Putz–Quick > images 748–49 of 1944 (ancestry.com).

[652] "Glenn E. Hume, 73, Barber 44 years," *Akron Beacon Journal* (Ohio), Thursday 10 August 1972, p. 16 or E14, cols. 1–2. Also, Mrs. A. R., "Robert W. Hume," *Portage Register-Democrat* (Wisconsin), Wednesday 8 May 1940, p. 2, col. 2.

[653] "Personals," *Lake Geneva Regional News* (Wisconsin), Thursday 16 September 1976, p. 9, col. 7.

[654] Robert Hume household for Frank R. age 5, 1910 US census, Moundville, Marquette County, Wisconsin, ED 149, sheet 7B, dwelling 162, family 166.

[655] "Frank R. Hume, 45, Dies at Baltimore," *Portage Daily Register* (Wisconsin), Tuesday 14 November 1950, p. 2, col. 4.

[656] For license: "Cupid Has Business Slump in June Despite Final Rush," *South Bend Tribune* (Indiana), Sunday 29 June 1930, p. 25 or Section 4, p. 1, col. 5: Lois J. Murner (1047 Van Buren, South Bend, Indiana) and Frank R. Hume (Akron, Ohio). For marriage: similarly, p. 10, or Section 2, p. 2, col. 4. Also, Frank R. Hume household for wife Lois, 1940 US census, "other places," Hillsborough County, Florida, Election Precinct 37, ED 29-10, sheet 1A, dwelling 11.

[657] Lois Joan Murner birth index entry, South Dakota, Birth Index, 1856–1917 (ancestry.com). Also, Frank R. Hume household for wife Lois, 1940 US census, "other places," Hillsborough County, Florida, Election Precinct 37, ED 29-10, sheet 1A, dwelling 11. Her year of birth from grave marker (note below).

[658] Lois and Frank R. Hume joint marker, image, Moundville Cemetery, Endeavor, Marquette County, Wisconsin, memorials #102,873,553 and #102,873,397 respectively by Joey (findagrave.com). A transcribed obituary on the site gives death date.

[659] Gleen [Glen] Hume household for single boarder Frank R., 1930 US census, Akron, Summit County, Ohio, Ward 7, ED 123, sheet 6B, dwelling 68, family 95.

ran a small boarding house at 1047 Van Buren Street, South Bend, St. Joseph County, Indiana.[660]

1935: they were renting at 1606 Virginia in Hillsborough County, Florida, evidently an unincorporated development near Tampa called Palma Cela Park.

1940: the rent was $20 a month and he was service manager for a retail tire company, earning $2400 for 52 weeks in 1939.[661]

1940, 16 October: 300 miles southeast, Frank was 5 feet 10½ inches tall, weighed 235 pounds, with blue eyes and brown hair, and they were living at 2413 North Greenway Drive, Coral Gables, Dade County, Florida. He worked for Goodyear Tire and Rubber at 900 Biscayne Boulevard in Miami.[662]

---

[660] Florence L. Murner household for daughter Lois age 26, 1930 US census, South Bend, St. Joseph County, Indiana, Ward 1, ED 13, sheet 6B, dwelling 135, family 145.
[661] Frank R. Hume, 1940 US census, "other places," Hillsborough County, Florida, Election Precinct 37, ED 29-10, sheet 1A, dwelling 11.
[662] Frank Roland Hume WW2 draft card, 16 October 1940, local board 7, Coral Gables, Florida, serial #32, order #1927; "US, WW2 Draft Card Registrations, 1940–1947" > Florida > Howell–Jones > Hughes–Humphreys > images 1657–58 of 2110 (ancestry.com). Also, Mrs. A. R., "Obituary, Robert W. Hume," *Portage Register-Democrat* (Wisconsin), Wednesday 8 May 1940, p. 2, col. 2.

Chapter 18

Third Generation

William Scholes Hume–Eliza May "Lida" Sutcliff Family
<u>parents at chapter 4</u>

"He saw his community change from log houses, ox carts, kerosene lamps and muddy roads"

18. WILLIAM SCHOLES³ HUME (*Sarah Ann² Scholes, Ann¹ Mills, Samuel^A*)
Birth: 22 August 1866 in Moundville Township[663]
Death: 5 March 1948
Burial: Moundville Cemetery, Endeavor, Marquette County, Wisconsin[664]
Spouse: **ELIZA MAY "LIDA" SUTCLIFF,** married 24 May 1893, Bremer, Butler County, Iowa
Spouse's parents: Edward and Mary (Riden) Sutcliff[665]
Spouse's birth: probably March 1870[666] in Fremont Township, Butler County, Iowa[667]

---

[663] "Obituary . . . William Scholes Hume," *Portage Daily Register* (Wisconsin), Tuesday 23 March 1948, p. 5, col. 4.
[664] "William S. Hume Dies Friday in Moundville," *Portage Daily Register* (Wisconsin), Saturday 6 March 1948, p. 3, col. 7.
[665] William S. Hume–Lida M. Sutcliff, license #2460, Return of Marriages, Butler County, Iowa, year ending 1 October 1893, p. 12-176, top two lines; "Iowa, Marriage Records, 1880–1940" > 1893 > 368 (Adair–Dallas) > image 178 of 351 (ancestry.com). A. E. Sutcliff and Susan Sutcliff witnessed; Rev. J. B. Metcalf officiated.
[666] Lida's birth date: <u>March 1870</u> as reported in Will S. Hume household for wife Eliza M., 1900 US census, Moundville Township, Marquette County, Wisconsin, ED 93, sheet 1A, dwelling/family 3. Or <u>18 March 1871</u> as stated without sourcing in 1968 memorial, Eliza May "Lila May" Sutcliffe Hume grave marker, no image, Moundville Cemetery, Endeavor, Marquette County, Wisconsin, memorial #102,779,694 by Joey (findagrave.com).
[667] Lida's birthplace: William S. Hume–Lida M. Sutcliff, license #2460, Return of Marriages, Butler County, Iowa, year ending 1 October 1893, p. 12-176, top two lines; "Iowa, Marriage Records, 1880–1940" > 1893 > 368 (Adair–Dallas) > image 178 of 351 (ancestry.com).

Spouse's death: 25 September 1968 in Portage, Wisconsin[668]
Spouse's burial: with her husband

"Mr. Hume lived all of his life on the old homestead in Moundville except for a few years when as a young man he worked on a farm near Poynette. In 1892 he bought the farm home from his father."[669] In 1930 William and Eliza had a radio set. Uncle James and Emily Scholes were next door as the census taker traveled.[670] In 1940 their home on River Road was valued at $2000, less than the statewide average of $3232. William completed seven years of schooling, Lida four years of high school. Emma, then James's widow, was next door again as the census taker traveled.[671]

Lida "held offices in the Ladies Aid, was school clerk for two terms, and has been active in the Eastern Star."[672]

> Mr. Hume was active in the church, school and civic affairs of his community. Although he led a busy life operating a farm and raising a family he always managed to find time for other activities.
> In 1891 Mr. Hume became a member of the Masonic Lodge at Poynette No. 173 F. and A.M. In 1896 he transferred to Portage to the Fort Winnebago Lodge No. 33 and in 1906 he was a Charter Member and helped organize Endeavor Lodge No. 292.
> He petitioned for and helped organize Rural Free Delivery route No. 2 at Endeavor and helped organize and was a director of the Endeavor State Bank. Mr. Hume was interested in school affairs and held such offices as school clerk of the town of Moundville, District No 2, and was a

---

[668] "Mrs. Lida Hume," *Portage Daily Register* (Wisconsin), Wednesday 25 September 1968, p. 5, col. 1.
[669] "Obituary . . . William Scholes Hume," *Portage Daily Register* (Wisconsin), Tuesday 23 March 1948, p. 5, col. 4.
[670] William S. Hume household, 1930 US census, Moundville Township, Marquette County, Wisconsin, ED 8, sheet 4B, dwelling/family 123.
[671] William Herme [Hume] household, 1940 US census, Moundville Township, Marquette County, Wisconsin, ED 39-8, sheet 6A, dwelling 138. Statewide figures from US Census Bureau, Census of Housing, Historical Census of Housing Tables, Median Home Values Unadjusted 1940 (https://www2.census.gov/programs-surveys/decennial/tables/time-series/coh-values/values-unadj.txt).
[672] "Endeavor Couple Celebrate Their Golden Wedding," *Portage Daily Register* (Wisconsin), Wednesday 2 June 1943, p. 2, col. 2.

trustee of Endeavor Academy. He was a member of the Methodist Church in Moundville and consistently supported its various activities. He was trustee for many years and also the Sunday school superintendent.

. . . He saw his community change from log houses, ox carts, kerosene lamps and muddy roads to our modern farms, electric lights, automobiles and good roads. He adapted himself to those changes and was always one of the first to accept them. He was always ready to help with those things which meant progress to his community and at the same time he did not hesitate to oppose those things which he felt did not contribute to its welfare.

Those attending his funeral included
Mr. and Mrs. Lloyd Hume (Chapter 18, child i) of Milwaukee;
Mr. and Mrs. Ernest Frisch and Mr. Lawrence Tuttle of Madison;
Mrs. Wendell Ingraham, Mr. and Mrs. Ernest Reid, Mrs. Leon Reid, Mr. Earl Reid, and Mr. Harold Reid of Oxford;
Mr. and Mrs. Horace Hume (Chapter 20, child i) of Mendota, Illinois;
Mr. Will Sherwin (Chapter 14) and Mr. Ray Sherwin (Chapter 13, child i) of Sparta; and
Mr. Arthur Voertman (Chapter 4, child ix), Miss Alma Voertman, Miss Marion Scholes (Chapter 32), Mr. and Mrs. Harland Topping, Mrs. John Hume, Mrs. George Bain, Mr. and Mrs. Arthur Jacobson, Charles Hansom, and Fred Swannell of Portage.[673]

Children of William Scholes[3] and Alida (Sutcliffe) Hume, all born in Wisconsin:

---

[673] "Obituary . . . William Scholes Hume," *Portage Daily Register* (Wisconsin), Tuesday 23 March 1948, p. 5, col. 4. The text has been transcribed at William's memorial #102,779,394 by Joey (findagrave.com).

i. ESSIE S.⁴ HUME (*William S.³ Hume, Sarah Ann² Scholes, Ann¹ Mills, Samuel^A*) was born November 1894 ⁶⁷⁴ died 24 September 1979, and was buried at Moundville Cemetery, Wisconsin.⁶⁷⁵ She married WILLIAM H. J. FREDRICK 29 May 1917 in Briggsville, Marquette County, Wisconsin, the son of Julius and Amelia (Leverentz?) Fredrick. William was born 4 December 1894 in Packwaukee Township, Marquette County, Wisconsin; died 26 April 1983 in Baraboo, Sauk County, Wisconsin;⁶⁷⁶ and was buried at Moundville Cemetery.⁶⁷⁷ A lifelong resident and farmer, William was a member of the Moundville United Methodist Church.⁶⁷⁸

ii. LLOYD E.⁴ HUME (*William S.³ Hume, Sarah Ann² Scholes, Ann¹ Mills, Samuel^A*) was born 16 October 1896 in Endeavor, Wisconsin,⁶⁷⁹ and died 2 May 1972 in Milwaukee "after a short illness."⁶⁸⁰ He married about 1932 VERNA MILDRED "LINA" MAAS (oldest-known child),⁶⁸¹ the daughter of Edward and Meta (Gaubatz) Maas. Lina was born 12 May 1905 at 941 Eleventh Street, Milwaukee,⁶⁸² and died in Milwaukee (last residence) December 1984.⁶⁸³ Edward Maas was an engraver in 1905; Verna's older siblings

---

⁶⁷⁴ Will S. Hume household for daughter Essie age 5 born November 1894, 1900 US census, Moundville Township, Marquette County, Wisconsin, ED 93, sheet 1A, dwelling/family 3.
⁶⁷⁵ "Fredrick, Mrs. William (Essie)," *Wisconsin State Journal*, Thursday 27 September 1979, p. 33, col. 2.
⁶⁷⁶ "William H. J. Fredrick," *Portage Daily Register* (Wisconsin), Thursday 28 April 1983, p. 12, cols. 2–3, followed by "Correction," Saturday 30 April 1983, p. 9, col. 3.
⁶⁷⁷ William Herman Julias Fredrick grave marker [mostly illegible], Moundville Cemetery, Endeavor, Marquette County, Wisconsin, memorial #102,779,694 by Joey (findagrave.com).
⁶⁷⁸ "William H. J. Fredrick," *Portage Daily Register* (Wisconsin), Thursday 28 April 1983, p. 12, cols. 1–2.
⁶⁷⁹ Will S. Hume household for son Lloyd age 3, 1900 US census, Moundville, Marquette County, Wisconsin, ED 93, sheet 1A, dwelling/family 3. Also, Lloyd Hume military index entry for birth, death, enlistment, and release; US Department of Veterans Affairs, BIRLS Death File, 1850–2010 (ancestry.com). For birthplace, WWI registration card below.
⁶⁸⁰ Lloyd E. Hume index entry, Wisconsin Death Index, 1959–1997. Also, "Obituaries . . . Lloyd Hume," *Portage Daily Register* (Wisconsin), Thursday 4 May 1972, p. 5, col. 2.
⁶⁸¹ Lloyd Edward Hume household for wife and informant Verna M., 1940 US census, Madison, Dane County, Wisconsin, Ward 19, ED 13-63A, sheet 8B, dwelling 192.
⁶⁸² Verna Mildred Maas, Milwaukee birth certificate 3950, 392:215; "Milwaukee, Wisconsin, Births, 1839–1911" > 1905 > 390–392 > image 592 of 725 (ancestry.com).
⁶⁸³ Verna Hume index entry, US Social Security Death Index, 1935–2014.

were Raymond, Anita, and Harold.[684] Lloyd completed four years of college, Verna four years of high school.[685]

As of 5 June 1918, Lloyd was of medium height and weight, with brown hair and eyes. He listed three occupations—mechanic, farmer, and schoolteacher— and named his employer as Thomas W. Dixon of West Allis, Wisconsin. (Nevertheless, Lloyd's stated residence remained in Endeavor, some 100 miles to the northwest.)[686] Lloyd enlisted for World War I on 14 August 1918, and was released 9 April 1919,[687] having served as a private in the Army Ambulance Service, Section 508.[688]

1920: Lloyd did not stay in the countryside after the war ended; he was "of Milwaukee" when he visited his parents in April.[689]

1930: still single, he was sharing an apartment in an eight-flat at 1110 Oakland Avenue in Shorewood Village, Milwaukee County—and working as a purchasing agent for a department store. The apartment rented for $84 a month; it did have a radio set.[690]

1935: Lloyd, Verna, and child were still in Shorewood.

1940: in Madison, they rented a $60-a-month apartment at 2215 Chadbourne; he earned $1050 as an insurance salesman during 1939.[691]

1942: Lloyd was employed by the Lincoln National Insurance Company of Fort Wayne, Indiana; his place of employment was at 722 Bankers Building in Milwaukee; and his residence was 5840 North

---

[684] Verna Mildred Maas, Milwaukee birth certificate 3950, 392:215; "Milwaukee, Wisconsin, Births, 1839–1911" > 1905 > 390–392 > image 592 of 725 (ancestry.com).
[685] Lloyd Edward Hume household for wife and informant Verna M., 1940 US census, Madison, Dane County, Wisconsin, Ward 19, ED 13-63A, sheet 8B, dwelling 192.
[686] Lloyd Edward Hume, WWI draft card, 5 June 1918, Marquette County local board, serial #20, registration #55; "US, World War I Draft Registration Cards, 1917–1918" > Wisconsin > Marquette County > Draft Card H > image 159 of 162 (ancestry.com).
[687] Lloyd Hume index entry for birth, death, enlistment, and release; US Department of Veterans Affairs, BIRLS Death File, 1850–2010 (ancestry.com).
[688] Lloyd E. Hume, Passenger List of Organization and Casuals, Hoboken, New Jersey; "US, Army Transport Service, Passenger Lists, 1910–1939" > Outgoing > Cedric > 26 May 1918–November 1918 > image 1173 of 1287 (ancestry.com).
[689] "Moundville," *Portage Daily Register* (Wisconsin), Monday 12 April 1920, p. 5, col. 1.
[690] Norman M. Mitchell for Lloyd E. Hume, lodger, 1930 US census, Shorewood Village, Milwaukee County, Wisconsin, ED 361, sheet 8A, dwelling 96, family 232.
[691] Lloyd Edward Hume household for wife and informant Verna M., 1940 US census, Madison, Dane County, Wisconsin, Ward 19, ED 13-63A, sheet 8B, dwelling 192.

Shoreland in Whitefish Bay, Milwaukee County, Wisconsin.⁶⁹²

iii. VELMA E./BEULAH⁴ HUME (*William S.³ Hume, Sarah Ann² Scholes, Ann¹ Mills, Samuel^A*) was born 14 February 1900 in Moundville Township, Marquette County, Wisconsin; died 17 December 1987 in Portage, Columbia County, Wisconsin; and was buried at Hill Crest Cemetery, Endeavor, Wisconsin.⁶⁹³ She married RAYMOND IRA HOPWOOD 26 February 1919.⁶⁹⁴ Raymond was the son of Elijah Hopwood, born 20 March 1898,⁶⁹⁵ died January 1966,⁶⁹⁶ and was buried with his wife.⁶⁹⁷

Velma graduated from the Christian Endeavor Academy and was a member of the Endeavor United Church of Christ.⁶⁹⁸ As of 12 September 1918, Raymond was tall, of medium build, with blue eyes and light hair.⁶⁹⁹ Both Raymond and Velma completed four years of high school.⁷⁰⁰

---

⁶⁹² Lloyd Edward Hume, WW2 draft card, serial #U3924, no order #, Milwaukee local board 32, 27 April 1942; US, World War II Draft Registration Cards, 1942" > Wisconsin > Hughes–Husar > Gould–Kantz > images 697–98 of 2028 (ancestry.com).
⁶⁹³ Raymond and Velma Hopwood, joint grave marker, image, Hill Crest Cemetery, Endeavor, Marquette County, Wisconsin, memorials #102,792,974 and #102,792,815 respectively, by Joey (findagrave.com).
⁶⁹⁴ "Obituaries . . . Velma Hopwood," *Portage Daily Register* (Wisconsin), Saturday 19 December 1987, p. 11, cols. 4–5.
⁶⁹⁵ Raymond Ira Hopwood, WWI draft card, 12 September 1918, Marquette County Local Board, serial #977, order #a28; "US, World War I Draft Registration Cards, 1917–1918" > Wisconsin > Marquette County > Draft Card H > image 146 of 162.
⁶⁹⁶ "Obituaries . . . Velma Hopwood," *Portage Daily Register* (Wisconsin), Saturday 19 December 1987, p. 11, cols. 4–5.
⁶⁹⁷ Raymond and Velma Hopwood, joint grave marker, image, Hill Crest Cemetery, Endeavor, Marquette County, Wisconsin, memorials #102,792,974 and 102,792,815 respectively, by Joey (findagrave.com).
⁶⁹⁸ "Obituaries . . . Velma Hopwood," *Portage Daily Register* (Wisconsin), Saturday 19 December 1987, p. 11, cols. 4–5.
⁶⁹⁹ Raymond Ira Hopwood, WWI draft card, 12 September 1918, Marquette County Local Board, serial #977, order #a28; "US, World War I Draft Registration Cards, 1917–1918" > Wisconsin > Marquette County > Draft Card H > image 146 of 162.
⁷⁰⁰ Raymond Hopwood household, 1940 US census, Moundville Township, Marquette County, Wisconsin, ED 39-8, sheet 8A, dwelling 184.

In 1920 he was farming in Moundville and living in a rented house, where they remained in 1930 (no radio set) and 1940.[701] In 1927 he was a nominee for second supervisor in Moundville.[702]

As of 1942, he was 5 feet 11 inches tall, weighed 190 pounds, with blue eyes and brown hair. He was farming at Endeavor; their phone number was Endeavor 34R2.[703]

At the end of 1950, the Hopwoods left town for Phoenix and California, and were considering making the return trip by way of Florida.[704]

iv. GRACE EDNA[4] HUME (*William S.[3] Hume, Sarah Ann[2] Scholes, Ann[1] Mills, Samuel[A]*) was born 28 July 1902 and died 9 January 1933 of carbon monoxide poisoning. She married 21 June 1924 at her parents' house, Moundville Township, Marquette County, Wisconsin, HENRY GEORGE CHRISTOPHERSON.[705] The son of Carl and Annie C. Christopherson of Buffalo Township, Marquette County,[706] he was born 23 July 1899 in Wisconsin, probably in Portage County,[707] and died 13 July 1991.[708]

---

[701] Raymond Hopwood household, 1920 US census, Moundville Township, Marquette County, Wisconsin, ED 133, sheet 4B, dwelling 81, family 83. Similarly, 1930, ED 8, sheet 4A, dwelling/family 105. Similarly, 1940, ED 39-8, sheet 8A, dwelling 184.

[702] "Moundville," *Portage Register-Democrat* (Wisconsin), Tuesday 29 March 1927, p. 5, col. 2.

[703] Raymond Ira Hopwood WW2 draft card, serial #219, order #T10141, Westfield, Wisconsin, local board 14 February 1942; "US WWII Draft Cards Young Men, 1940–1947" > Wisconsin > Harwell–Jantoa > Hopkins–Horn > image 1157–58 of 1976 (ancestry.com). This is a different person from the 60-year-old of the same name in Nebraska in 1942.

[704] "Endeavor," *Portage Daily Register* (Wisconsin), Thursday 28 December 1950, p. 5, col. 2.

[705] "The Altar . . . Hume–Christopherson," *Journal Times* (Racine, Wisconsin), Tuesday 24 June 1924, p. 9, col. 2. The obituary, eight years later and composed no doubt under stress, gives a different location and date for the marriage: "A Holiday Journal Fatal To 2d Member of Family," Monday 9 January 1933, *Journal Times* (Racine, Wisconsin), p. 1, cols. 6–7.

[706] Carl Christopherson household for son Henry age 10, 1910 US census, Buffalo Township, Marquette County, Wisconsin, ED 143, sheet 5A, dwelling 77, family 78.

[707] Charles Christopher [Carl Christopherson] household for wife Annie C. age 28 and son Henry age 10/12 years, 1900 US census, Portage, Columbia County, Wisconsin, Ward 2, ED 22, sheet 2A, dwelling 19, family 21.

[708] Henry G. Christopherson index entry, US Social Security Applications and Claims Index, 1936-2007 (ancestry.com).

In 1920 Grace, age 17, was teaching school in Westfield, Marquette County.[709] After their 21 June 1924 marriage, they took "a ten days' honeymoon tour of northern Wisconsin" before settling down in Racine.[710]

> She received her early education in the Pleasant View School. After receiving her diploma she entered the Christian Endeavor Academy at Endeavor, Wisconsin and graduated in the class of 1918 and also graduated from the 4 year music course. The following year she attended the Milwaukee Normal and fitted herself as a teacher which profession she followed for four years.
> When a young girl she became a member of the Moundville M. E. Church and later transferred her membership of the Moundville M. E. Church by letter to the First M. E. Church of Racine, Wisconsin. She also was a member of the O. E. S. Endeavor Chapter 233 and three years ago demitted to the O. E. S. Racine Chapter.[711]

In 1930 the family was renting an apartment at 420 La Fayette in Racine. They paid $35 a month and owned a radio set. Henry worked as a repair man in a garage.[712] Three years later a Christmas trip killed Grace and their young daughter, but left Henry alive.

> Dr. Robert Thackeray, attending physician, said that the three apparently had received some monoxide poisoning while making the journey in their closed car. The father and mother complained of severe headaches at the end of the trip, and shortly after they returned to Racine, on Dec. 27, were stricken with

---

[709] William S. Hume household for daughter Grace E., 1920 US census, Moundville Township, Marquette County, Wisconsin, ED 133, sheet 2B, dwelling 45, family 46. Also, "Moundville," *Portage Daily Register* (Wisconsin), Monday 12 April 1920, p. 5, col. 1.
[710] "The Altar . . . Hume–Christopherson," *Journal Times* (Racine, Wisconsin), Tuesday 24 June 1924, p. 9, col. 2.
[711] Obituary from an unnamed newspaper: Grace Edna Hume Christopherson, no image of grave marker, Moundville Cemetery, Endeavor, Marquette County, Wisconsin, memorial #102,792,521 by Joey (findagrave.com).
[712] Henry Christopherson household, 1930 US census, Racine, Racine County, Wisconsin, ED 27, Ward 8, sheet 4A, dwelling 60, family 88.

serious illness, which developed into pneumonia. . . . The father, Henry E. Christopherson, Lincoln auto service mechanic at the Applegate garage, and residing at 420 Lafayette avenue, has been seriously ill, but is expected to recover.[713]

Henry married second on 24 February 1940 Gladys Anna Elizabeth Peterson; both were living at 7935 Parnell in Chicago.[714] She was born 4 May 1911 to Gottfrid and Anna Petterson and baptized 15 October; Conrad and Jennie Lindstrom were sponsors.[715] She died reportedly 23 May 1995 and was buried at Floral Lawn Cemetery, South Beloit, Winnebago County, Illinois.[716]

Following their marriage, Henry and Gladys rented an apartment on West Washington Street in Waukegan, Lake County, Illinois. He completed eight years of schooling and worked as a motor mechanic in a boat yard; she completed four years of high school and was a general office worker in a machine shop. His pay the preceding year was double hers.[717]

As of 14 February 1942, Henry was 5 feet 8½ inches tall and weighed 160 pounds. He had blue eyes, brown hair, and "Scar on Shoulder Blade." He was employed by Fairbanks Morse & Company in Beloit, Rock County, Wisconsin (then a wide-ranging manufacturer of engines and related equipment), where his mailing address was 253 West Grand Avenue. His wife was at 7935 Parnell in Chicago.[718]

---

[713] "A Holiday Journey Fatal To 2d Member of Family," Monday 9 January 1933, *Journal Times* (Racine, Wisconsin), p. 1, cols. 6–7.
[714] Henry G. Christopherson–Gladys O. Peterson marriage 24 February 1940, license #1,627,123, Records of Marriages p. 355; "US, Evangelical Lutheran Church in America, Swedish American Church Records, 1800–1947" > USA > Illinois > Chicago > Gustavus Adolphus Lutheran Church > image 997 of 1394 (ancestry.com).
[715] Gladis Anna Elizabeth Petterson birth and baptism, 1911, Records of Baptisms pp. 50–51; "US, Evangelical Lutheran Church in America, Swedish American Church Records, 1800–1947" > USA > Illinois > Chicago > Gustavus Adolphus Lutheran Church > image 856 of 1394 (ancestry.com).
[716] Gladys Peterson Christopherson, no image of grave marker, Floral Lawn Cemetery, South Beloit, Winnebago County, Illinois, memorial #193,274,974 by Sue (findagrave.com).
[717] Henry Christopherson household, 1940 US census, Waukegan, Lake County, Illinois, ED 49-92, Ward 4, sheet 9B, dwelling 194.
[718] Henry George Christopherson WW2 draft card, 14 February 1942, Local Board 29, Chicago, serial #T214, order #11,421; "US WWII Draft Cards Young Men, 1940–1947" > Brooks–Clanner > Christine–Chubinski > images 1219–20 of 2146 (ancestry.com).

v. VERNE WILLIAM "VERN"*4* HUME (*William S. 3 Hume, Sarah Ann2 Scholes, Ann1 Mills, Samuel1*) was born 27 March 1905 in Marquette County, Wisconsin;[719] died 1 August 1990 in Wyocena, Columbia County, Wisconsin; and was buried at Moundville Cemetery, Endeavor, Wisconsin. He graduated from the Endeavor Christian Academy[720] and soon headed for Milwaukee. In 1930 he was single and lodging at 889 Island Avenue there, working as a department store salesman.[721]

Vern married first OLIVE MAE SLATER on Memorial Day 1931 at Baraboo, Sauk County, Wisconsin. The daughter of Thomas E. and Maebelle (Etkington) Slater, Olive was born 8 June 1909 in Sault St. Marie, Chippewa County, Michigan, and died 13 January 2005 in Stoughton, Dane County, Wisconsin (last residence in Portage), outliving both her husbands. She graduated from Sault Ste. Marie High School in 1927, and later attended Northern State Teachers College at Marquette, Marquette County, Michigan.[722] After marriage, Vern and Olive went back to work at the Schuster Store. In 1940 the family lived in a $3000 house they owned at 216 62nd Street in Milwaukee; he was a department store stock clerk and earned $1560 during 1939. They reportedly lived in Milwaukee until 1942.[723]

---

[719] Vern W. Hume index entry, "Wisconsin, Birth Index, 1820–1907," reel D0008, record 19,785 (ancestry.com).
[720] "Vernon W. Hume" obituary as transcribed at findagrave.com: memorial #102,792,133.
[721] Frederick W. Ludwig household for lodger Vern Hume, 1930 US census, Ward 13, ED 161, sheet 7A, dwelling 17, family 24.
[722] "Obituaries . . . Olive M. Nordness," *Portage Daily Register* (Wisconsin), Saturday 15 January 2005, p. 11, cols. 3–5.
[723] Vern Hume household, 1940 US census, Milwaukee, Milwaukee County, Wisconsin, Ward 23, ED 72-515, sheet 8A, dwelling 142. House value was close to the statewide average in 1940: Statewide figures from US Census Bureau, Census of Housing, Historical Census of Housing Tables, Median Home Values Unadjusted 1940 (https://www2.census.gov/programs-surveys/decennial/tables/time-series/coh-values/values-unadj.txt).

After retiring as superintendent of the American Woodworking Company in Montello, he farmed in Moundville Township.[724]

Olive later worked for the Dane County Social Services Department in Madison, Wisconsin. She married second in 1960 as his third wife Eugene H. "Curley" Nordness. A plumber and World War II veteran, he was born 12 September 1925, the son of Mr. and Mrs. Obert Nordness; died 24 September 1976 in Madison; and was buried in Roselawn Memorial Park.[725] Olive spent her later years in Tucson, Pima County, Arizona, and had both a funeral in Portage, Wisconsin, 17 January 2005, and a memorial service in Tucson 29 January.[726]

Vern married second as her second husband in 1960 MYRTLE GRACE (ANDERSON) LUGER, the daughter of Albert and Maybelle (Ostrander) Anderson.[727] Myrtle was born 24 June 1912 in Tomahawk, Lincoln County, Wisconsin; died 4 December 2000 in Portage; and was buried at Greenwood Cemetery in Tomahawk, Lincoln County, Wisconsin, although the joint memorial at Moundville bears Myrtle's name. (She had married first Freimund Luger, who died in 1952.) Myrtle was a member of the United Methodist Church in Portage. She worked as a secretary at General Indicator in Pardeeville, Columbia County, until she retired in the late 1960s.

General Indicator, a sign manufacturer, was purchased by CompuDyne in 1968. In 1988 General Indicator was sold to Everbrite Electric Signs.[728] Everbrite built a new headquarters in Greenfield, Milwaukee County, Wisconsin, and now bills itself as "a world leader in the visual branding and identity industry."[729] Everbrite's Pardeeville plant remains at 401 South Main.[730]

---

[724] "Vernon W. Hume" obituary as transcribed at findagrave.com: memorial #102,792,133.

[725] "E. Nordness," *Portage Daily Register* (Wisconsin), Wednesday 29 September 1976, p. 5, col. 1.

[726] "Obituaries . . . Olive M. Nordness," *Portage Daily Register* (Wisconsin), Saturday 15 January 2005, p. 11, cols. 3–5.

[727] "Myrtle Grace Hume…Northview Resident of the Month," *Portage Daily Register*, Friday 20 June 1997, p. 5, cols. 2–4.

[728] "Records…Obituaries…Myrtle G. Hume," *Portage Daily Register*, 6 September 2000, p. 2A, cols. 5–6. General Indicator was purchased by Compudyne in 1968 (referenceforbusiness.com/history2/1/CompuDyne-Corporation.html).

[729] See https://www.everbrite.com/our-history. Also, since 2002 Everbrite claims to be the largest Minority/WBE (Women's Business Enterprise) signage company in the US.

[730] See facebook.com/EverbritePardeeville, and Google.com/maps.

vi. MERL GEORGE[4] HUME (*William S.[3] Hume, Sarah Ann[2] Scholes, Ann[1] Mills, Samuel[A]*) was born 31 August 1907 in Marquette County, Wisconsin; died 7 April 1985 in St. Mary's Hospital, Madison (last residence Endeavor, Marquette County), and was buried at Moundville Cemetery.[731] He married LILA EDITH SHAW 29 June 1929.[732] The daughter of Joseph W. and Bertha (Mountford) Shaw, Lila was born 21 July 1906 in Moundville;[733] died 7 May 1993 in Wyocena, Columbia County, Wisconsin, and was buried at Moundville Cemetery. Lila taught elementary school in Portage for several years.[734] Merle completed three years of high school, Lila two years of college.[735]

In 1930, the newlyweds were renting one of 11 apartments at 719 Plankington Avenue in Cudahy, Milwaukee County, Wisconsin, for $44 a month, and they had a radio set. He was a chemist for a drop forge, and she was clerking at a five-and-dime store.[736]

They were back in Moundville by 1935; in 1940 they lived in a house valued at $800,[737] less than one-quarter of the statewide average.[738] He was a member of Moundville United Methodist Church.[739] As of 16 October 1940, Merl was 5 feet 10 inches tall, weighed 155 pounds, and had gray eyes and brown hair.[740]

---

[731] "Hume, Merl G.," *Wisconsin State Journal*, Monday 8 April 1985, p. 25, col. 1.

[732] "Happy Ad," Merl and Lila Hume anniversary, *Portage Daily Register* (Wisconsin), Saturday 28 June 1980, p. 8, col. 7. Also, Scholes ledger book, 68.

[733] "Lila Hume Honored," *Portage Daily Register* (Wisconsin), Monday 14 June 1986, p. 5, col. 1. Similarly, her obituary: "Lila E. Hume," Sunday 9 May 1993, p. 2, cols. 1–2.

[734] "Lila E. Hume," *Portage Daily Register* (Wisconsin), Sunday 9 May 1993, p. 2, cols. 1–2.

[735] Merl Hume household, 1940 US census, Moundville Township, Marquette County, Wisconsin, ED 39-8, sheet 5B, dwelling 124.

[736] Merl Humes [Hume] household, 1930 US census, Cudahy, Milwaukee County, Wisconsin, ED 338, sheet 17A, dwelling 255, family 309.

[737] Merl Hume household, 1940 US census, Moundville Township, Marquette County, Wisconsin, ED 39-8, sheet 5B, dwelling 124.

[738] Statewide figures from US Census Bureau, Census of Housing, Historical Census of Housing Tables, Median Home Values Unadjusted 1940 (https://www2.census.gov/programs-surveys/decennial/tables/time-series/coh-values/values-unadj.txt).

[739] "Death Notices . . . Merl G. Hume," *Wisconsin State Journal* (Madison), Monday 8 April 1985, p. 25, col. 1.

[740] Merl G. Hume WW2 draft card, local board 1, Marquette County, Wisconsin, serial #201, order #822; "US WWII Draft Cards Young Men, 1940–1947" > Wisconsin > Harwell–Jantowa > Hulter–Hunter > images 212–13 of 1937 (ancestry.com).

Story #3: Endeavor Christian Academy (1890–1926)

In the summer of 1890, missionary revival meetings at Merritt's Landing on Buffalo Lake in Marquette County, Wisconsin, helped lead to the founding of the Endeavor Christian Academy by Congregational Church adherents. The impulse was educational as well as religious—at the time the only high schools available to would-be scholars were 13 miles away (in Portage, to the south, and Westfield, to the north). Five students comprised the academy's first graduating class in 1894 (many more took part episodically), and diligent fundraising made some new buildings possible.[741]

As of 1913 the academy offered preparatory, normal, and business classes "as demanded" ("preparatory" being college prep, "normal" for aspiring teachers, and "business" for would-be businessmen, bookkeepers, and secretaries). The preparatory course in 1913 required four years of English—to be accompanied by algebra and history in the first year, by plane geometry and science in the second, by more history in the third, and by "Bible" in the fourth. Optional courses included Latin, German, advanced algebra, agriculture, home economics, bookkeeping, and music. In 1913–14 there were six instructors, four women and two men.[742]

The sixteen Scholes descendants and future spouses currently known to have been affiliated with the academy were mostly members of the fourth generation.

    Eliza Russell (Chapter 15, child i)
    Elizabeth Rodger (Chapter 16, spouse)
    Robert Hume (Chapter 17, child iii)
    Beth Topping (Chapter 17, child iii)
    Elda Hume (Chapter 17, child v)

---

[741] *The Story of Endeavor: Its Founding, Its Struggles, Its Relation to the Churches, Its Product* (no date). Also, "Christian Endeavor Academy: Its Aims, Achievements, and Needs," July 1916. Wisconsin Historical Society, Madison.

[742] *Bulletin of Christian Endeavor Academy, Annual Catalogue* 1:2, July 1913. Wisconsin Historical Society, Madison.

William Scholes Hume, trustee (Chapter 18)
Essie Hume (Chapter 18, child i)
Lloyd Hume (Chapter 18, child ii)
Raymond Hopwood (Chapter 18, child iii)
Velma Hume (Chapter 18, child iii)
Grace E. (Hume) Christopherson (Chapter 18, child iv)
Vern Hume (Chapter 18, child v)
Hume Jones (Chapter 19, child iii)
Jane Heames (Chapter 27, child iv)
Hazel Heames (Chapter 27, child v)
Edna (Peake) Scholes (Chapter 35)

Enrollment at any one time probably peaked around eighty. By no means did all students complete the four-year course. The graduating class of 1912 consisted of sixteen (one from faraway Springfield, Illinois). Those who completed the academy course sometimes went on to college or normal schools, or direct to teaching.

In the early 1920s the academy placed advertisements in local newspapers calling itself a "Christian Home School," and embarked on a fundraising drive to deal with its chronic lack of an adequate endowment.[743] President Walter M. Ellis called 1922–23 the academy's "best year yet."[744]

But it was not to be. Since the 1890 founding, the Wisconsin landscape had changed. Thirty-two years had brought more public high schools, more and better roads, automobiles, and wider employment opportunities. The academy now had to cope with these changes and, ultimately, a "lack of funds." In October 1926 the academy's trustees were transferring any remaining funds to Northland College in Ashland, Ashland County, Wisconsin.[745]

---

[743] Advertisement, *Portage Daily Register* (Wisconsin), Friday 15 July 1921, p. 4, cols. 6–7.
[744] "Best Year in History of Endeavor Academy," *Portage Daily Register* (Wisconsin), Thursday 14 June 1923, p. 3, col. 2.
[745] "Arrange Endowment Fund," *La Crosse Tribune* (Wisconsin), Friday 8 October 1926, p. 3, cols. 5–6.

The building stood empty until 1931, when it was re-established as a public school, combining grade school and the first two years of high school.[746]

---

[746] "Old Academy Building Now Public School," *Portage Daily Register* (Wisconsin), Tuesday 10 March 1931, p. 1, col. 3.

Chapter 19

Third Generation

Sarah Ann Janet "Nettie" Hume–Henry Eden Jones Family
parents at chapter 4

"The doctor told our folks that if they kept her in Wisconsin another winter they would lose her."

19. SARAH ANN JANET "NETTIE"[3] **HUME** (*Sarah Ann*[2] *Scholes, Ann*[1] *Mills, Samuel*[A])
Birth: 18 November 1868
Death: 13 July 1936 in Moundville
Burial: Moundville Cemetery, Marquette County, Wisconsin[747]
Spouse: **HENRY EDEN JONES**,[748] married November 1889 (or 18 December 1889 according to the newspaper obituary)[749]
Spouse's parents: Thomas and Ann (Faulkner) Jones, both born in England
Spouse's birth: 18 September 1864 in Wisconsin
Spouse's death: Sunday 19 May 1957 in Bell, Los Angeles County, California
Spouse's burial: Moundville Cemetery, Marquette County, Wisconsin[750]

Before 1889: "Early in life she joined the M. E. [Methodist Episcopal] church of Moundville, where she was active in all the departments."

---

[747] "Laid to Rest in Moundville," *Portage Daily Dispatch* (Wisconsin), Thursday 23 July 1936, p. 7, col. 3.
[748] "Children of the Scholes Family," Scholes ledger book, 65, in author's possession.
[749] "Laid to Rest in Moundville," *Portage Daily Dispatch* (Wisconsin), Thursday 23 July 1936, p. 7, col. 3.
[750] Henry Eden Jones death certificate #9386, 19 May 1957, Bell, Los Angeles County, California; "California, County Birth and Death Records, 1800–1994" > Los Angeles > Death Certificates 1957, 8200–10299 > image 1504 of 2577 (familysearch.org).

1889: "Immediately following their [1889] marriage, they began home making on the farm where they have resided continuously except for a few years spent in Washington and California."[751]

1900: Henry and Nettie owned their Moundville farm without a mortgage.[752]

1910: Nearby was James M. Scholes's family; next door Arthur M. Jones, possibly Henry's brother.[753]

1920: Still farming.[754]

1930: They owned no radio set; the farm was on Section Line Road.[755]

1936: Henry and "Mrs. Nettie" both registered as Democrats living at 3521 Nevada in Bell City, Los Angeles County, California.[756] In the summer they came back to Moundville, where Nettie unexpectedly died:

> A busy useful life was hers, her strength and inspiration given freely with no thought of reward. Faithfulness, courage, humility, friendliness were her characteristics. . . . Coming back to Moundville for the summer [1936], after three years in California, Mrs. Jones seemed especially happy to visit with relatives. . . . Six nephews acted as pallbearers: Glen and Merl Hume, Clayton and Wayne Russell, and Walter and Willard Jones.
>
> Those from a distance to attend the service were Mrs. W. E. Maltbey and Mrs. Marvin Harvey of Los Angeles, Calif.;

---

[751] "Laid to Rest in Moundville," *Portage Daily Dispatch* (Wisconsin), Thursday 23 July 1936, p. 7, col. 3.
[752] Henry E. Jones household, 1900 US census, Moundville Township, Marquette County, Wisconsin, ED 93, sheet 2A, dwelling/family 26.
[753] Henry E. Jones household, 1910 US census, Moundville Township, Marquette County, Wisconsin, ED 149, sheet 8A, dwelling 178, family 182.
[754] Henry E. Jones household, 1920 US census, Moundville Township, Marquette County, Wisconsin, ED 133, sheet 2A, dwelling 28, family 29.
[755] Henry E. Jones household, 1930 US census, Moundville Township, Marquette County, Wisconsin, ED 8, sheet 6A, dwelling/family 160.
[756] Henry E. and Nettie Jones, Index to Register of Voters, Bell City Precinct 15, Los Angeles County, California, 1936; "California, Voter Registrations, 1900–1968" > Los Angeles County > 1936 > Roll 036 > image 192 of 1257 (ancestry.com).

Harlan Jones of Riverside, Calif.; Mrs. J. S. Barry [Berry] of Sioux Falls, S. D., and Mrs. James Hume of Temple, Calif.; Mr. and Mrs. Ed Miller, Eva Jones and Mr. and Mrs. Lloyd Stewart, Chicago; Will Sherwin, Sparta, Mr. and Mrs. Will Hume, Mr. and Mrs. Gaylord Dahlstrom and Robert Ebert, Neenah; Mr. and Mrs. Clarence Adelberg, Mr. and Mrs. Ray Maltbey and Miss Roberta Russell of Milwaukee; Matt Hume, Plainfield; Mr. and Mrs. Clayton Russell and Marion of Prairie du Sac, Wayne Russell and Mr. and Mrs. Harvey Barron, Madison; Mrs. Ann Hume, Alexandria, Minn.; and the following from Portage: Mr. and Mrs. Arthur L. Voertman, Glen Hume, E. B. Maltbey and daughter Laura, Miss Ada M. Baker, Miss Selena Whitson, Mrs. Mae Dixon, Mr. and Mrs. Wallace Murison, Mrs. B. Morehouse, Frank H. Kaiser; and Fred Turner Sr. and Mrs. Fredrick Turner, Jr., of Marcellon.[757]

1938: Henry (of Pomona) married second as her second husband his widowed sister-in-law Lydia Alberta "Birdie" (Sawyer) Hume 31 March 1938 in Alhambra in a Methodist ceremony; she was age 60, born about 1878 in Michigan.[758] (Chapter 20)

1940: Henry and Birdie were living and farming at 3521 Nevada. The house was valued at $1500, about half the statewide California average. He had completed six years of schooling, Birdie eight. They were enumerated adjacent to son-in-law Willis Maltby and family, who were renting for $35 a month; Willis was working as a monument maker.[759]

1940, 1942, 1944: Henry E. Jones, retired (registered Democrat), and Mrs. Lydia A. Jones, housewife (registered Republican) were at 3521

---

[757] "Laid to Rest in Moundville," *Portage Daily Dispatch* (Wisconsin), Thursday 23 July 1936, p. 7, col. 3.
[758] Henry E. Jones–Lydia Alberta Hume marriage licensed 5 March 1938, married 31 March, by Methodist Episcopal minister Rulufe [?] A. Chase in Alhambra, Los Angeles County, California, book 1503, p. 131; "California, County Marriages, 1850–1952" > DGS #5,698,617 (familysearch.org).
[759] Henry Jones household, 1940 US census, Bell City, San Antonio Township, Los Angeles County, California, ED 19-552, sheet 12B, dwelling 328. Statewide figures from US Census Bureau, Census of Housing, Historical Census of Housing Tables, Median Home Values Unadjusted 1940 (https://www2.census.gov/programs-surveys/decennial/tables/time-series/coh-values/values-unadj.txt).

Nevada Street in the 15th precinct of Bell City.[760] Not found thereafter.

Children of Sarah Ann Janet "Nettie"[3] (Hume) and Henry Eden Jones:

i. PEARL ELIZA[4] JONES (*Sarah Ann*[3] *Hume, Sarah Ann*[2] *Scholes, Ann*[1] *Mills, Samuel*[A]) died in infancy, possibly 21 December 1891–22 December 1896.[761]

ii. ROBEY ISABEL[4] JONES (*Sarah Ann*[3] *Hume, Sarah Ann*[2] *Scholes, Ann*[1] *Mills, Samuel*[A]) was born September 1894[762] and died 25 October 1975 at Inglewood, Los Angeles, County, California. Robey was a graduate of Portage High School.[763] She completed three years of college; her husband-to-be completed two years of high school.[764]
Her life was almost cut short in 1918–1920 when she was slow to recover from an operation for appendicitis and gallstones. "The doctor told our folks that if they kept her in Wisconsin another winter they would lose her." Their minister was able to get her appointed as a Methodist missionary to Utah, where she did well until winter set in there. Mother Nettie then got in touch with her aunt Harriet Scholes (Chapter 8) in southern California, and arranged for Robey to stay with her and her daughters in Santa Barbara. "She gained rapidly and by February 1920 was working as a librarian there."[765]
Robey married 1920 (reportedly 26 June in Santa Barbara, California) WILLIS ELISHA MALTBY, who was born 26 February 1892 in Fort Winnebago Township, Columbia County, Wisconsin and died 19 May

---

[760] Henry E. and Lydia A. Jones, Index to Register of Voters, Bell City Precinct 15, Los Angeles County, California, 1940 and 1942; "California, Voter Registrations, 1900–1968" > Los Angeles County > 1940 > Roll 046 > image 218 of 520 (ancestry.com). Similarly, 1942, Roll 052 > image 236 of 564. Similarly, 1944, Roll 056 > image 234 of 622.
[761] Scholes ledger book, 68.
[762] Henry E. Jones household for daughter Robey I. age 5, 1900 US census, Moundville Township, Marquette County, Wisconsin, ED 93, sheet 2A, dwelling/family 26.
[763] "Rubey Maltbey," *Portage Daily Register* (Wisconsin), 29 October 1975, p. 5, col. 1.
[764] Willis Maltby household, 1940 US census, Bell City, Los Angeles County, California, ED 19-552, sheet 12B, dwelling 328. The Maltbys were at 329.
[765] Lois M. Jones Henry Bennett, "Jones Family Journeys & Happenings," p. 7 of 18, typescript downloaded 19 May 2005 but no longer found on line.

1962 at Inglewood, Los Angeles County, California.⁷⁶⁶ He was the son of Elisha B. and Caroline Adelia (Spicer) Maltby.⁷⁶⁷

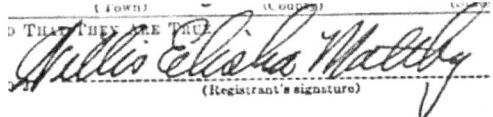

Willis attended "the Spicer school" and Portage High School; on 4 December 1917 he enlisted at Jefferson Barracks, Missouri, as a private in the Air Corps. He was discharged 2 April 1919 at Camp Grant, Illinois.⁷⁶⁸

They settled in southern California where they owned and operated a monument business in Los Angeles.

1926: they were living at 127 North Orchard Drive in Bell Precinct #5, Los Angeles County. She was a housewife and he was a salesman; both registered as Republicans.⁷⁶⁹

1930: they owned a house at 6325 Orchard Avenue in Bell City, valued at $4000; they did own a "radio set."⁷⁷⁰

1932: Willis was admitted to the Pacific Branch of the National Home (near Sawtelle in Los Angeles County) 21 January on account of a "dislocation" of his right hip. His outcome and length of stay were not noted.⁷⁷¹

1935: 1 September, they visited and photographed William Scholes's grave at Vicksburg, Mississippi.⁷⁷²

---

⁷⁶⁶ "Willis E. Maltby, 70," *Portage Daily Register* (Wisconsin), Monday 28 May 1962, p. 3, col. 6.

⁷⁶⁷ Willis Elisha Maltby application to Wisconsin Society of the Sons of the American Revolution #30774, March 1918; "US, Sons of the American Revolution Membership Applications, 1889–1970," images 459–61 of 534.

⁷⁶⁸ "Willis E. Maltby, 70," *Portage Daily Register* (Wisconsin), Monday 28 May 1962, p. 3, col. 6. Also, Willis E. Maltby resident #40465, Sawtelle Branch, National Home; "US National Homes for Disabled Volunteer Soldiers, 1866–1938" > Sawtelle > Registers > W > image 2431 of 2830 (ancestry.com).

⁷⁶⁹ Willis and Robey J. Maltby voter registrations, Bell Precinct, Los Angeles County, California; "California, Voter Registrations, 1900–1968" > Los Angeles County > 1926 > Roll 016 > image 98 of 814 (ancestry.com).

⁷⁷⁰ Willis E. Maltby household, 1930 US census, Bell City, Los Angeles County, California, ED 1308, sheet 3B, dwelling/family 88.

⁷⁷¹ Willis E. Maltby resident #40465, Sawtelle Branch, National Home; "US National Homes for Disabled Volunteer Soldiers, 1866–1938" > Sawtelle > Registers > W > image 2431 of 2830 (ancestry.com).

⁷⁷² Willis and Robey Maltby photo, 1 September 1935, Vicksburg, Mississippi; Stella Scholes collection #10, in author's possession. Unfortunately, the snapshot image is too distant from the stone for it to be read.

1936: July, she and Lois Harvey visited Elsie Scholes (Chapter 34) at Moundville.[773]

1940: they were renting ($35 a month) at 6628 Lucille in Bell City, Los Angeles County, California.[774]

1942: as of 26 April, Willis was 5 feet 10 ½ inches tall and weighed 200 pounds; he had blue eyes, blonde hair, and a "scar, shape of cross, on upper thumb on left hand." They were at 7121 Eighth Avenue in Los Angeles; Willis ran the Maltby Monument Company at 3101 West Florence there.[775]

1948 and 1950: Willis E. and Mrs. Robey J. and children (Elwin B. and Winston E.) lived at 7121 Eighth Avenue (about halfway between LAX and downtown); all four registered Republican.[776]

In retirement they moved to Inglewood, Los Angeles County. Willis was a founder of the Monument Dealers Association of California. In his later years (1950–1962) he was in poor health.[777]

iii. HUME MCKINLEY[4] JONES (*Sarah Ann³ Hume, Sarah Ann² Scholes, Ann¹ Mills, Samuel^A*) was born 17 July 1896 in Moundville Township, Marquette County, Wisconsin, and died 6 July 1980 in Hemet, Riverside County, California, of pneumonia. He married 1919 ADALENE MCGOWAN,[778] who was born 25 January 1897 in Illinois[779] and died 12 April 1989 in Carmichael, Sacramento County,

---

[773] "Moundville," *Portage Daily Register* (Wisconsin), p. 5, col. 6.
[774] Willis Maltby household, 1940 US census, Bell City, Los Angeles County, California, ED 19-552, sheet 12B, dwelling 329.
[775] Willis Elisha Maltby WW2 draft card, Los Angeles Local Board 260, 26 April 1942, serial #U1859; "US, World War II Draft Registration Cards, 1942" > California > Carrington–Roth > images 2613–14 of 3790 (ancestry.com).
[776] Maltby registrants, "Index to Register of Voters," Los Angeles City Precinct #2306, 1948; "California, Voter Registrations, 1900–1968" > Los Angeles County > 1948 > Roll 074 > image 1041 of 1104 (ancestry.com). Similarly, 1950, Roll 081, image 971 of 1234.
[777] "Willis E. Maltby, 70," *Portage Daily Register* (Wisconsin), Monday 28 May 1962, p. 3, col. 6.
[778] "Hume M. Jones," *Portage Daily Register* (Wisconsin), Tuesday 8 July 1980, p. 4, cols. 7–8.
[779] Adalene A. Jones, "California, Death Index, 1940–1997" (ancestry.com). The index gives her mother's maiden name as Vroman. Tentatively confirmed by census entry: Josiah Vroman household for wife Henrietta and daughter Elizabeth age 22, 1880 US census, Jackson, Adams County, Wisconsin, ED 5, p. 28C, dwelling 53, family 54.

California[780], daughter of a father born in Germany, mother Swiss German, and the adopted daughter of Frank A. and Elizabeth W. (Vroman) McGowan.[781]

1917: Adalene was one of two employees in charge of "local work" in journalism at Endeavor for two small local newspapers under one management, *The Westfield Union* and the *Marquette County Epitome*.[782] Hume completed two years of college, Adalene four years of high school.[783]

1920: The newlyweds owned a mortgaged house in Moundville Township, and Hume was farming.[784]

1929: They moved to California.[785]

1930: They rented 3521 Nevada in Bell City, Los Angeles County, for $27 a month; no radio set. For many years Hume worked as a stone cutter.[786]

1940: They rented 636 Columbia Avenue in Pomona, Los Angeles County, for $20 a month. Hume earned $2171 for 52 weeks' work the previous year.[787]

1942: as of 6 April, Hume was 5 feet 10 inches tall and weighed 220 pounds; he had blue eyes, brown hair, and a scar on his right thigh. They lived at 355 Garfield in Pomona, where they remained for at least 20 years; he was working for Pomona Granite Company at 217 North Towne. His brother Everett at 155 Columbia would always know his address.[788]

---

[780] "Jones, Adalene A.," *Sacramento Bee* (California), Saturday 15 April 1989, p. 36, col. 2.
[781] Josiah Vroman household for wife Henrietta and daughter Elizabeth age 22, 1880 US census, Jackson, Adams County, Wisconsin, ED 5, p. 28C, dwelling 53, family 54.
[782] Untitled note, *Portage Daily Register* (Wisconsin), Tuesday 10 April 1917, p. 2, col. 5.
[783] Hume M. Jones household, 1940 US census, Pomona, Los Angeles County, California, Ward 4, ED 19-733B, dwelling 220.
[784] Hume M. Jones household for wife Adeline A., 1920 US census, Moundville Township, Marquette County, Wisconsin, ED 133, sheet 2A, dwelling 37, family 38.
[785] "Hume M. Jones," *Portage Daily Register* (Wisconsin), Tuesday 8 July 1980, p. 4, cols. 7–8.
[786] Hume M. Jones household, 1930 US census, Bell City, Los Angeles County, California, ED 1308, sheet 11B, dwelling 303, family 321.
[787] Hume M. Jones household, 1940 US census, Pomona, Los Angeles County, California, Ward 4, ED 19-733B, dwelling 220.
[788] Hume M. Jones WW2 draft card, serial #U1227, Pomona Local Board 92, 6 April 1942; "US, World War II Draft Registration Cards, 1942" > California > Hamann–Sarafian > images 674–75 of 2675 (ancestry.com).

1949 to 1963 (at least): Adalene served as an election clerk in Pomona.[789]

1952 and 1962: she and Hume registered to vote as residents of 355 Garfield. Hume's middle name notwithstanding, both registered as Democrats.[790]

iv. EVERETT HENRY[4] JONES (*Sarah Ann³ Hume, Sarah Ann² Scholes, Ann¹ Mills, Samuel^A*) was born 8 December 1902 in Everett, Snohomish County, Washington[791] and died 9 October 1975 after a long illness.[792] He married 12 August 1925[793] RUTH MAY DIXON, the daughter of William and May (Watson) Dixon. Ruth was born 28 June 1903 at Fort Winnebago, Columbia County, Wisconsin,[794] and died 31 July 1981 in Sonoma County, California.[795] Everett completed four years of high school and Ruth two years of college.[796]

1930: Everett and Ruth were in Bell City, Los Angeles County, where they owned their house at 6627 California, valued at $3000; they had a radio set.[797]

---

[789] Adalene A. Jones, clerk, precinct 13, *Progress-Bulletin* (Pomona, California), Saturday 19 March 1949, p. 15, col. 2. Similarly, special precinct 29, Sunday 17 February 1963, section 3, p. 4, col. 2. Numerous newspaper notes in between.

[790] Jones registrations, Index to Register of Voters, Pomona City Precinct #13; "California, Voter Registrations, 1900–1968 > Los Angeles County > 1952 > roll 085 (ancestry.com). Similarly, 1962, roll 164.

[791] Everett H (initial only) Jones WW2 draft card, Pomona local board #192, 14 February 1942, serial #T1429, order #T10080; "US WWII Draft Cards Young Men, 1940–1947" > California > Jolley–Kaenel > Jones–Jones > images 1709–10 of 2077 (ancestry.com).

[792] "Obituaries . . . Everett Jones," *Portage Daily Register* (Wisconsin), Friday 10 October 1975, p. 5, col. 1.

[793] "Local Happenings," *Portage Daily Register* (Wisconsin), Wednesday 5 August 1925, p. 3, col. 2. For exact date, see preceding note.

[794] Ruth May Dixon entry, volumes 2–4, p. 230, #354; "Wisconsin Births and Christenings, 1826–1926," FHL #1,302,855, DGS #7,609,643 (familysearch.org). Father William was reported born in Green Lake County, mother May in Moundville, Marquette County.

[795] Ruth May Jones index entry, 29 July 1981, Sonoma County, California; "California, Death Index, 1940–1997" (ancestry.com).

[796] Everett Jones household (Ruth informant), 1940 US census, Pomona, San Jose Township, Los Angeles County, Ward 4, ED 19-733A, sheet 8A, dwelling 219.

[797] Everett H. Jones household, 1930 US census, Bell City, Los Angeles County, California, ED 1308, sheet 11B, dwelling 300, family 318.

1936: Everett was the manager of the Pomona Granite Company at 217 North Town Avenue (telephone 1505), with eleven years in the business.[798]

1940: at a new address; their house was valued at $4000 (above the statewide average).[799]

1942: as of 14 February, Pomona Granite was Everett's company, and they were living at 155 East Columbia in Pomona. He was 5 feet 8 inches tall, weighed 190 pounds, with gray eyes, brown hair, and a scar on his left knee.[800] Two months later he was voted into the Pomona Chamber of Commerce.[801]

1960: Everett flew from Guatemala or Mexico to Los Angeles on 20 April.[802]

1970: Pomona Granite, now at 1433 North Orange, was apparently in Redlands, and did not renew its business license with the city of Pomona.[803] At some point the business had moved half an hour east.

v. MERRILL ROBERT[4] JONES (*Sarah Ann*[3] *Hume, Sarah Ann*[2] *Scholes, Ann*[1] *Mills, Samuel*[A]) was born 29 October 1907 in Moundville, Marquette County, Wisconsin, and died there 3 December 1907 of what was thought to be diphtheria. "Little Merrill was taken sick Tuesday morning . . . . Saturday evening after a hard fight the change came for the better. Sunday and Monday he gained when, almost

---

[798] Pomona Granite advertisement, *Pomona Progress Bulletin* (California), Friday 16 September 1938, p. 14, cols. 5–7. Also, *Chino Champion* (California), item 26 in a descriptive list of businesses, Friday 1 May 1936, p. 7, col. 6.

[799] Everett Jones household (Ruth informant), 1940 US census, Pomona, San Jose Township, Los Angeles County, Ward 4, ED 19-733A, sheet 8A, dwelling 219. Statewide figures from US Census Bureau, Census of Housing, Historical Census of Housing Tables, Median Home Values Unadjusted 1940 (https://www2.census.gov/programs-surveys/decennial/tables/time-series/coh-values/values-unadj.txt).

[800] Everett H (initial only) Jones WW2 draft card, Pomona local board #192, 14 February 1942, serial #T1429, order #T10080; "US WWII Draft Cards Young Men, 1940–1947" > California > Jolley–Kaenel > Jones–Jones > images 1709–10 of 2077 (ancestry.com).

[801] "Big Crowd To Hear Tibbetts," *Pomona Progress Bulletin* (California), Thursday 23 April 1942, p. 8, col. 8.

[802] Everett Henry Jones passenger card 20 April 1960; "California, Passenger and Crew Lists, 1882–1959" > A3619 Los Angeles 1957–1964 > 093 (ancestry.com). Passport #1,069,723; airline and flight number difficult to read.

[803] "11 New Businesses in April," *Redlands Daily Facts* (California), Monday 18 May 1970, p. 3, cols. 1–3.

without any warning, Tuesday morning his little life passed into the other and better world."[804]

vi. LOIS MARGARET[4] JONES (*Sarah Ann*[3] *Hume, Sarah Ann*[2] *Scholes, Ann*[1] *Mills, Samuel*[A]) was born 14 May 1908, in Moundville Township, Marquette County, Wisconsin; died 24 April 2005, St. Mary's Hospital, Madison, Dane County, Wisconsin; and was buried at Moundville Township Cemetery. Lois grew up in rural Wisconsin, moving with her family to California as a teenager, where she graduated from high school in Huntington Park.
She married first in 1928 (reportedly 20 June) DAVID MARVIN HARVEY,[805] who was born 2 August 1904 in Burdett, Washington County, Colorado);[806] died unexpectedly 1 April 1964 "while vacationing in Los Angeles, California";[807] and was buried at Moundville Cemetery, Endeavor, Marquette County, Wisconsin.[808] He was the son of John H. and Corinna (Fletcher) Harvey.[809]
Lois married second 6 April 1981 at Moundville United Methodist Church CLAIRE WATSON BENNETT. It was a second marriage for both. The son of William Carey and Ruth (Watson) Bennett, he was born 18 May 1907 in Endeavor, Wisconsin; died 27 August 1992 in an

---

[804] "Merrill Robert Jones," *Portage Daily Democrat* (Wisconsin), Saturday 7 December 1907, p. 2, cols. 2-3.
[805] "Obituaries…Lois J. Bennett," *Portage Daily Register* (Wisconsin), Thursday 12 May 2005, p. 15, cols. 1–2.
[806] Lois J. and D. Marvin Harvey, joint grave marker, Moundville Cemetery, Endeavor, Wisconsin, memorials #102,874,117 and #102,874,186 respectively, by Joey (findagrave.com). Also, David Martin Harvey, WW2 draft card, 15 February 1942, local board 267, Maywood, California; "US, World War II Draft Cards Young Men, 1940–1947" > California > Hartzke–Helmrich > Hartzke, Edgar–Harvick, William > images 460–61 of 2153 (ancestry.com).
[807] "D. Marvin Harvey," *Capital Times* (Madison, Wisconsin), Saturday 4 April 1964, p. 16, col. 1.
[808] Lois J. and D. Marvin Harvey, joint grave marker, Moundville Cemetery, Endeavor, Wisconsin, memorials #102,874,117 and #102,874,186 respectively, by Joey (findagrave.com). Also, "Obituaries…Lois J. Bennett," *Portage Daily Register* (Wisconsin), Thursday 12 May 2005, p. 15, cols. 1–2.
[809] John H. Harvey household for son David M. Harvey age 5, 1910 US census, Otis precinct 5, Washington County, Colorado, ED 260, sheet 2A, dwelling 34, family 35. For mother Corinna's birth surname, John H. Harvey–Corinna Fletcher marriage certificate, Burdette, Washington County, Colorado, 2 November 1898, p. 154; "Colorado, County Marriage Records and State Index, 1862–2006" > County Marriages > Washington > 1875–1915 > image 251 of 428 (ancestry.com).

automobile accident;[810] and was buried at Moundville Cemetery, Endeavor, Marquette County, Wisconsin, with his first wife.[811] Claire was first married to Mildred Hazel Jones for 43 years. "He farmed all of his working life, and also worked at Badger Ordnance, Portage Plastics, and Bremner Granite in Portage."[812]

1930: Lois and first husband D. Marvin Harvey owned their house at 6525 Orchard Avenue in Bell, Los Angeles County, California, valued at $4500, with a radio set. He was employed as an electrician (possibly with US Water Company).[813] He had completed one year of high school, she completed four.[814]

1936, summer: Lois Harvey and Robey Maltby were visiting at the home of Elsie Scholes in Moundville.[815]

1940: after ten years of the Great Depression, the Harveys' house at 6525 had lost almost half its value (down to $2500, well below the California statewide average of $3,527 that year); he worked as a "motor winder" in a factory, earning $1806 in 1939.[816]

1942, February 15: He was employed at US Electric Manufacturing Company (likely the same place mentioned in 1940) at 200 East Slauson, Los Angeles. He was 6 feet one inch tall, weighed 185 pounds, with blue eyes and brown hair, and "right upper arm underdeveloped."[817]

1944: they moved back to Moundville.

---

[810] "Obituaries...Mr. Claire W. Bennett," *Portage Daily Register* (Wisconsin), Sunday 30 August 1992, p. 2, col. 1. For father's middle name, Claire Watson Bennett index entry, "Wisconsin, Births and Christenings Index, 1801–1928," FHL 1,305,092.

[811] Mildred H. and Claire W. Bennett, joint grave marker, Moundville Cemetery, Endeavor, Wisconsin, image, memorials #102,872,920 and #102,872,550 respectively, by Joey (findagrave.com).

[812] "Obituaries...Mr. Claire W. Bennett," *Portage Daily Register* (Wisconsin), Sunday 30 August 1992, p. 2, col. 1.

[813] D. Marvin Harvey household, 1930 US census, Bell, Los Angeles County, California, ED 1308, sheet 8B, dwelling/family 236.

[814] Danvid [David] Marvin Harvey household, 1940 US census, Bell City, Los Angeles County, California, ED 19-552, dwelling 422, sheet 16B.

[815] "Moundville," *Portage Daily Register* (Wisconsin), p. 5, col. 6.

[816] Danvid [David] Marvin Harvey household, 1940 US census, Bell City, Los Angeles County, California, ED 19-552, dwelling 422, sheet 16B. Also, statewide figures from US Census Bureau, Census of Housing, Historical Census of Housing Tables, Median Home Values Unadjusted 1940 (https://www2.census.gov/programs-surveys/decennial/tables/time-series/coh-values/values-unadj.txt).

[817] David Martin Harvey, WW2 draft card, 15 February 1942, local board 267, Maywood, California; "US, World War II Draft Cards Young Men, 1940–1947" > California > Hartzke–Helmrich > Hartzke, Edgar–Harvick, William > images 460–61 of 2153 (ancestry.com).

1964: after her first husband's death, she moved back to California for ten years.
1974: she re-returned to Moundville, having been a lifelong member of Moundville's United Methodist Church.[818]

vii. GEORGE WALKER[4] JONES (*Sarah Ann[3] Hume, Sarah Ann[2] Scholes, Ann[1] Mills, Samuel[A]*) was born probably 1910 and died 6 March 1912,[819] "at 14 months."[820]

viii. HARLAN EDMOND[4] JONES (*Sarah Ann[3] Hume, Sarah Ann[2] Scholes, Ann[1] Mills, Samuel[A]*) was born 28 June 1913 in Moundville Township, Marquette County, Wisconsin;[821] died 29 August 1978 in San Bernardino County, California;[822] and was buried at Olivewood Cemetery, Riverside, Riverside County, California.[823]

He married first 10 January 1934 in Huntington Park, Los Angeles County, California,[824] ETHEL LOUISE CORRIGAN, who was born reportedly 5 February 1914 in San Diego County, California, and whose death date has not been ascertained.[825] She is likely the Louise Corrigan, daughter of James C. and Grace (Courtis) Corrigan, who was 16 years old in 1930, living with her parents in Maywood, Los Angeles County,

---

[818] "Obituaries…Lois J. Bennett," *Portage Daily Register* (Wisconsin), Thursday 12 May 2005, p. 15, cols. 1–2.
[819] "Obituary…George Walker Jones," *Portage Daily Democrat* (Wisconsin), Saturday 9 March 1912, p. 3, col. 3.
[820] "Laid to Rest in Moundville," *Portage Daily Register* (Wisconsin), Thursday 23 July 1936, p. 7, col. 3.
[821] Harlan Edmond Jones WWII draft card, local board 154, Riverside, California, 16 October 1940, serial #1392, order #892; "US WWII Draft Cards Young Men, 1940–1947" > California > Jolley–Kaenel > Jones–Jones > images 1220–21 of 2074 (ancestry.com).
[822] Harlan Edmund Jones index entry, "California Death Index, 1940–1997" (familysearch.org).
[823] Harlan Edmund Jones grave marker (1913–1978), image, Olivewood Cemetery, Riverside, Riverside County, California, memorial #142,374,750 by CRob (findagrave.com).
[824] Harlan Edmond Jones–Ethel Louise Corrigan marriage 10 January 1934, Huntington Park, Los Angeles County, 1197:244; "California, County Marriages, 1850–1952" > 5,698,549 > images 2521–22 of 2537. Rev. S. S. Sampson of the Methodist Episcopal Church officiated. Witnesses were J. C. Corrigan and Henry E. Jones. Also, "Intention to Marry" by Harlan E. Jones age 20 and Ethel L. Corrigan age 19; *Los Angeles Times*, Wednesday 3 January 1934, p. 16, col. 5.
[825] Ethel L. Corrigan entry, California Birth Index, 1905–1995 (ancestry.com). Also, Harlan E. Jones household, 1940 US census, Riverside, Riverside County, California, ED 33-60, Ward 7, sheet 8B, dwelling 215.

California. James was a salesman in a lumber yard. They owned the house, valued at $4500, and had a radio set.[826]

Ethel Louise was in the Girls' Glee Club at Bell High School in 1928.[827] At their 1934 marriage, she was a stenographer in bankruptcy court.[828] The following year they were living in Bell, Los Angeles County, California.[829] As of 16 October 1940, Harlan was 6 feet one inch tall, weighed 199 pounds, with blue eyes and brown hair. They were living at 4375 Linwood Place, Riverside, Riverside County, California, and he was employed by Everett H. Jones of Pomona Granite Company at 217 North Towne Avenue there.[830] They owned their home, valued at $3100, just under the statewide average that year. He and Louise both completed four years of high school; he was a salesman of retail monuments and markers, for which he earned $2160 in 1939.[831]

During World War II, he enlisted at "Fort Macarthur San Pedro" 4 April 1944.[832] He might be the infantryman of this name who took a bullet in the shoulder in combat, received penicillin, and was discharged probably in December 1944.[833]

---

[826] James C. Corrigan household for daughter Louise age 16, 1930 US census, Maywood, Los Angeles County, California, ED 1342, sheet 2B, dwelling 50, family 54. For Ethel Louise's mother's maiden name, California Birth Index, 1905–1995 (familysearch.org).

[827] Louise Corrigan, Bell High School Yearbook 1928, p. 35; "US, School Yearbooks, 1900–1999" > California > Bell > Bell High School > 1928 > image 39 of 70 (ancestry.com).

[828] Harlan Edmond Jones–Ethel Louise Corrigan marriage 10 January 1934, Huntington Park, Los Angeles County, 1197:244; "California, County Marriages, 1850–1952" > 5,698,549 > images 2521–22 of 2537.

[829] Harlan E. Jones household, 1940 US census, Riverside, Riverside County, California, ED 33-60, Ward 7, sheet 8B, dwelling 215.

[830] Harlan Edmond Jones WWII draft card, local board 154, Riverside, California, 16 October 1940, serial #1392, order #892; "US WWII Draft Cards Young Men, 1940–1947" > California > Jolley–Kaenel > Jones–Jones > images 1220–21 of 2074 (ancestry.com).

[831] Harlan E. Jones household, 1940 US census, Riverside, Riverside County, California, ED 33-60, Ward 7, sheet 8B, dwelling 215. Statewide figures from US Census Bureau, Census of Housing, Historical Census of Housing Tables, Median Home Values Unadjusted 1940 (https://www2.census.gov/programs-surveys/decennial/tables/time-series/coh-values/values-unadj.txt).

[832] Harlan E. Jones, enlistment 4 April 1944; "US, World War II Army Enlistment Records, 1938–1946" (ancestry.com).

[833] Harlan E. Jones entry, "US WWII Hospital Admission Card Files, 1942–1954" (ancestry.com).

In 1950 Harlan and Louise lived and registered together as Democrats at 4375 Linwood Place, Riverside, Riverside County, California.[834] But in 1952 she remained at the Linwood address, while he voted from 5551 Brockton in Riverside.[835]

Identifications beyond that year in these records are difficult, but two additional clues may fuel further research:

- In 1954 the couple registering to vote from 4190 Sequoia in Arlington, Riverside County, were Harlan E. and MRS. GEORGIA W. JONES.[836] Georgia's identity and status have not been determined; she does not appear in Nevada or California marriage indexes.

- Harlan married second or third 7 June 1964 in San Bernardino County BEATRICE LEWIS WHITE, who was born 1916;[837] died 1995; and was buried with her husband at Olivewood Cemetery, Riverside, Riverside County, California.[838] Her parents may well be Harry J. and Louise (-?-) White, in which case she was about ten years old when her father died, and at that time she had an older sister Jessica Hampton. Harry J. would have been born about 1870.[839]

---

[834] Harlan E. and Mrs. Ethel L. Jones, 1950 voter registration, Riverside, Precinct 38; "California, Voter Registrations, 1900–1968" > Riverside County > 1950 > 422 > image 874 of 1036 (ancestry.com).

[835] Harlan E. and Mrs. Ethel L. Jones, 1952 voter registration, Riverside, Precinct 38; "California, Voter Registrations, 1900–1968" > Riverside County > 1952 > 423 > image 760 of 920 (ancestry.com).

[836] Harlan E. and Mrs. Georgia W. Jones, 1954 voter registration, Riverside, Precinct 73; "California, Voter Registrations, 1900–1968" > Riverside County > 1954 > 424 > image 868 of 948 (ancestry.com).

[837] Harlan E. Jones–Beatrice L. White marriage index entry, "California Marriage Index 1960–1985" (familysearch.org).

[838] "Beatrice Lewis Jones" grave marker (1916–1995) adjacent to Harlan's, image, Olivewood Cemetery, Riverside, Riverside County, California, memorial #139,640,070 by CRob (findagrave.com).

[839] "Deaths . . . White," *Los Angeles Times,* Thursday 8 April 1926, p. 16, col. 8.

Chapter 20

Third Generation

James Samuel Hume–Lydia Alberta "Birdie" Sawyer Family
parents at chapter 4

"A good organizer, active and aggressive for everything to benefit the place where he lived"

20. JAMES SAMUEL³ HUME (*Sarah Ann² Scholes, Ann¹ Mills, Samuel^A*)
Birth: 27 March 1871[840] in Wisconsin[841]
Death: 18 May 1936 in California[842]
Burial: Moundville Cemetery, Endeavor, Marquette County, Wisconsin[843]
Spouse: **LYDIA ALBERTA "BIRDIE" SAWYER,**[844] married 25 March 1896[845]
Spouse's parents: Noah D. and Lizzie Sarah (Carson) Sawyer
Spouse's birth: 6 September 1877 or about 1879 in Michigan (perhaps

---

[840] "Service Held at M. E. Church in Moundville," *Portage Daily Register* (Wisconsin), Saturday 6 June 1936, p. 3, col. 5.
[841] Robert Hume household for son James age 9 born Wisconsin, 1880 US census, Moundville Township, Marquette County, Wisconsin, ED 223, p. 7, no dwelling number, family 71.
[842] "Service Held at M. E. Church in Moundville," *Portage Daily Register* (Wisconsin), Saturday 6 June 1936, p. 3, col. 5. Also, James S. Hume death index entry, age 65, Los Angeles County; "California, Death Index, 1905–1939" > image 110 of 1018 (ancestry.com). Also, Family Tree, Horace D. Hume of Mendota, Illinois, handwritten, unsourced; Stella Scholes collection, item #8, in author's possession.
[843] Lydia A. and James S. Hume, joint grave marker, image, Moundville Cemetery, Endeavor, Moundville Township, Marquette County, Wisconsin, memorials #103,102,008 and #103,101,725 respectively, by Joey (findagrave.com).
[844] "Children of the Scholes Family," Scholes ledger book, 65, in author's possession.
[845] "Service Held at M. E. Church in Moundville," *Portage Daily Register* (Wisconsin), Saturday 6 June 1936, p. 3, col. 5.

Sanilac County)[846]
Spouse's death: 30 March 1964 in Los Angeles[847]
Spouse's burial: with her first husband in Moundville Cemetery, Endeavor, Marquette County, Wisconsin[848]

James reportedly built the first telephone line between Endeavor and Portage in about 1906 (roughly twelve miles as the crow flies), but he was badgered by quarrels about where the line should run and how many circuits it should have. Having visited relatives in North Dakota, he decided a move was in order. Soon the family was in southwestern North Dakota; although he maintained ties to central Wisconsin, he did not return there to live.[849]

Every relative should have such a thorough remembrance:

> James resided in Moundville until 1906 when he went to North Dakota. There he took great interest in public matters. He was postmaster of Hume for eight years, the township being named in his honor. He established a telephone exchange and operated a store. His place of business was called the 'Halfway House' between Scranton and Bellfield, N. D.; also the 'Travelers Home.' He was county auditor at Amidon in 1915 and 1916. . . . He was a good organizer, active and aggressive for everything to benefit the place where he lived. He has left monuments to his memory in many industrial establishments he helped to promote and locate.
>
> In 1920 he went to Garfield, Wash., where he ran a large hotel for several years. From Garfield he went to Monterey

---

[846] Born 6 September 1877: Lydia A. Hume death index entry, California Death Index, 1940–1977. Born 1879: Noah D. Sawyer household (in same building as William Carson family) for daughter Alberta age 1, 1880 US census, Marion Township, Sanilac County, Michigan, ED 339, p. 6, dwelling 48, family 56. Born 1877: Family tree below.
[847] Family Tree, Horace D. Hume of Mendota, Illinois, handwritten, unsourced; Stella Scholes collection, item #8, in author's possession. For exact date and place, California Death Index, 1940–1997 (ancestry.com).
[848] Lydia A. and James S. Hume, joint grave marker, image, Moundville Cemetery, Endeavor, Moundville Township, Marquette County, Wisconsin, memorials #103,102,008 and #103,101,725 respectively, by Joey (findagrave.com).
[849] Horace D. Hume, Rosalie McLaughlin, and Kelly Meils Poremba, *Cowboy to Industrialist: The Story of Horace D. Hume, A Midwestern Centenarian* (Bushnell, Illinois: Spoon River Press, 1999), 10, 13–15.

Park, Calif., and later he purchased a home in Temple City, Cal. Here he acted as hydraulic engineer for the Graham Rock company for several years.

He suffered a stroke on January 25, 1936, and never fully recovered. On April 28, he was taken worse and passed away May 18. During his illness he showed the same uncomplaining spirit of courage, patience, and fortitude that characterized his life. He realized the end was near and requested his body be brought to the home of his childhood and to the church he joined when young. . . .

He was a loving husband, a kind and thoughtful father, truest and most faithful friend. He so lived that the common level of humanity was lifted by his having lived.[850]

James Hume

Year by year . . .

1926: James and Lydia were settled in southern California; newlyweds Horace and Minnie visited them.[851]

1930: James and Lydia were renting 127 North Rowland in Pasadena, Los Angeles County, California, for $27 a month. They had no radio set; he worked as a "hoist man" for a rock and gravel company. Youngest son George, age 15 (child iv below) was in the household.[852]

1935: They were at 119 North Rowland in Temple City, Los Angeles County, and James was a stationary engineer.[853] James and sister

---

[850] "Service Held at M. E. Church in Moundville," *Portage Daily Register* (Wisconsin), Saturday 6 June 1936, p. 3, col. 5.
[851] Horace D. Hume, Rosalie McLaughlin, and Kelly Meils Poremba, *Cowboy to Industrialist: The Story of Horace D. Hume, A Midwestern Centenarian* (Bushnell, Illinois: Spoon River Press, 1999), 54.
[852] James Hume household, 1930 US census, Pasadena, Los Angeles County, California, ED 1283, sheet 5B, dwelling 139, family 140.
[853] Jas. S. Hume entry, *Los Angeles Directory Co.'s Alhambra (California) City Directory 1935 Including El Monte, Monterey Park, Rosemead, San Gabriel, Temple City, and Wilmar*, p. 665, image 348 of 463 (ancestry.com). The 1937 directory as filmed is incomplete and does not include all the suburbs.

Nettie both died the following year. Two years later James's widow "Birdie" married second as her second husband her widowed brother-in-law Henry Jones (Chapter 19).[854]

1940: Henry and Birdie were living and farming at 3521 Nevada in Bell City. The house was valued at $1500, less than half the California average. He had completed six years of schooling, Birdie eight. They were enumerated adjacent to son-in-law Willis Maltby and family, who were renting for $35 a month; Willis was working as a monument maker.[855]

1940s: In the first three elections of the 1940s (1940, 1942, 1944), retiree Henry E. Jones (registered Democrat), and housewife Mrs. Lydia A. Jones (registered Republican) were at 3521 Nevada Street in Bell City Precinct 15.[856]

Children of James Samuel^3 and Lydia Alberta "Birdie" (Sawyer) Hume:

i. HORACE DELBERT^4 HUME *(James S.^{3} Hume, Sarah Ann^2 Scholes, Ann^1 Mills, Samuel^A)* was born 15 August 1898 in Endeavor, Marquette County, Wisconsin;[857] died 20 September 2001 in Mendota, La Salle

---

[854] Henry E. Jones–Lydia Alberta Hume marriage licensed 5 March 1938, married 31 March, by Methodist Episcopal minister Rulufe [?] A. Chase in Alhambra, Los Angeles County, California, book 1503, p. 131; "California, County Marriages, 1850–1952," DGS #5,698,617 (familysearch.org).

[855] Henry Jones household, 1940 US census, Bell City, San Antonio Township, Los Angeles County, California, ED 19-552, sheet 12B, dwelling 328. Statewide figures from US Census Bureau, Census of Housing, Historical Census of Housing Tables, Median Home Values Unadjusted 1940 (https://www2.census.gov/programs-surveys/decennial/tables/time-series/coh-values/values-unadj.txt).

[856] Henry E. and Lydia A. Jones, Index to Register of Voters, Bell City Precinct No. 15, Los Angeles County, California, 1940 and 1942; "California, Voter Registrations, 1900–1968" > Los Angeles County > 1940 > Roll 046 > image 218 of 520 (ancestry.com). Similarly, 1942, Roll 052 > image 236 of 564. Similarly, 1944, Roll 056 > image 234 of 622.

[857] Horace Delbert Hume WWI Draft Card, Bowman, Bowman County, North Dakota, 12 September 1918, serial #400, order #866; "US, World War I Draft Card Registrations, 1917–1918" > North Dakota > Bowman County > Draft Card H > image 133 of 144 (ancestry.com). For birth place, see WW2 draft card registration below.

County, Illinois;[858] and was buried with his first wife at Restland Cemetery, Mendota, La Salle County, Illinois.[859]

He married first 2 June 1926, Moscow, Latah County, Idaho,[860] MINNIE LUVENIA HARLAN, the daughter of James Franklin and Mary Elizabeth (Hale) Harlan. Minnie was born in Whitman County, Washington, 8 September 1899,[861] and died 1972.[862] At marriage both lived in Garfield, Whitman County.[863]

Horace married second in 1973 SARAH "SALLY" LYLE ROOD, who was born about 1897–98 in Wisconsin, died of "heart problems" in 1988,[864] and was buried as Sarah D. Rood-Hume at Graceland Cemetery, Racine, Racine County, Wisconsin. She was reportedly the daughter of Morris and Susanna (-?-) Rood.[865]

Horace was past 90 when he was licensed to marry third as her third husband 15 November 1989 DOROTHY LOUISE (BOHAN) (GREENWOOD) JASPER.[866] The daughter of William P. and Anna C. (Rogers) Bohan, she was born 18 November 1901, died 7 May 1994 at home in Mendota, and was buried at St. Mary's Cemetery, Alexis, Warren County, in western Illinois. She attended schools in Alexis; the Villa in Rock Island, Rock Island County, Illinois; and St. Mary's of

---

[858] Horace D. Hume entry, US Social Security Death Index.

[859] Horace Delbert Hume grave marker, image, Restland Cemetery, Mendota, La Salle County, Illinois, memorial #137,202,304 by Tyler James McCane (findagrave.com).

[860] Horace D. Hume–Minnie L. Harlan marriage license #103240 and certificate, 2 June 1926, Moscow, Latah County, Idaho, p. 123; "Idaho, County Marriages, 1864–1950" > 4533534 > image 784 of 811. Witnesses were Frank and Mary Harlan; Baptist pastor E. Burton officiated (ancestry.com).

[861] Minnie Luvenia Harlan birth index entry, "9-8-99" Whitman County, Washington; "Washington, Birth Records, 1870–1935" > Washington State Department of Health > Washington State Department of Health Birth Index > Reel 1 1930 > image 471 of 776 (ancestry.com).

[862] Minnie L. Harlan Hume (1899–1972), grave marker, image, Restland Cemetery, Mendota, La Salle County, Illinois, memorial #137,202,330 by Tyler James McCane (findagrave.com).

[863] Horace D. Hume–Minnie L. Harlan marriage license #103,240 and certificate, 2 June 1926, Moscow, Latah County, Idaho, p. 123; "Idaho, County Marriages, 1864–1950" > 4533534 > image 784 of 811 (ancestry.com). Garfield and Latah are some 20 miles apart.

[864] Horace D. Hume, Rosalie McLaughlin, and Kelly Meils Poremba, *Cowboy to Industrialist: The Story of Horace D. Hume, A Midwestern Centenarian* (Bushnell, Illinois: Spoon River Press, 1999), 100, 173.

[865] Sarah D. Rood-Hume, "Mother," grave marker, image, section 1, Graceland Cemetery, Racine, Racine County, Wisconsin, memorial #179,436,238 by Nadeen Sobottka (findagrave.com).

[866] "Marriage Licenses," *Times* (Streator, Illinois), Monday 15 November 1989, p. 9, col. 1. Both resided in Mendota, no ages given.

the Woods College in Terre Haute, Vigo County, Indiana. "An accomplished pianist and horsewoman," she was survived by a dozen grandchildren. Her first two husbands were C. H. "Bill" Greenwood, married 11 April 1923 in Alexis, died 26 November 1960; and Edmund Jasper, married 19 October 1964, died 30 September 1987.[867] After completing eighth grade in North Dakota, Horace attended the Endeavor Academy back in Wisconsin during the 1914–15 school year.[868] The following year he stayed home with a severe case of double pneumonia. There was no treatment other than constant nursing care, but he survived. The ordeal left him a semester behind his high-school classmates, and he decided to leave school and work with his father, who sought to build a ranching empire and was counting his older sons to help.[869] Meanwhile Horace and Clarence rekindled their interest in automobiles, and Horace agreed to work for the local Ford auto agency. When father James heard of this malfeasance, "without a word he promptly paid a visit to the agency, canceled the job, leased a 160-acre farm not far from the Hume homestead, and set his eldest son to work planting a crop of wheat."[870] As of 12 September 1918, Horace was short, of medium build, with blue eyes and light hair.[871] Having just turned twenty, he probably had no idea that he would live through the entire twentieth century and into the twenty-first.

---

[867] "Obituaries…Area…Dorothy Hume," *Dispatch and Rock Island Argus* (Illinois), Thursday 12 May 1994, p. 33 or E1, col. 6.
[868] Horace D. Hume, Rosalie McLaughlin, and Kelly Meils Poremba, *Cowboy to Industrialist: The Story of Horace D. Hume, A Midwestern Centenarian* (Bushnell, Illinois: Spoon River Press, 1999), 22–24.
[869] Ibid., 24–25.
[870] Ibid., 29.
[871] Horace Delbert Hume WWI draft card, Bowman, Bowman County, North Dakota, 12 September 1918, serial #400, order #866; "US, World War I Draft Card Registrations, 1917–1918" > North Dakota > Bowman County > Draft Card H > image 133 of 144 (ancestry.com).

Story #4: Showdown in North Dakota, 1918

As had been the case for generations, the Hume family took for granted that a father owned his son's labor until the son turned 21. But in the fall of 1918 father James was once more infuriated when he found that twenty-year-old Horace had not accumulated enough buffalo grass to tide the cattle over the winter.

James laid down the law and did not listen to Horace's explanation (that there was no grass to be had). "When James's anger was spent, he glared at Horace, waiting for a response. Horace met his eyes and informed his father that he was quitting."

James stood in silence as his son climbed on his horse and took off down the road toward the Livingston ranch, a few miles north of Bowman, where he was taken up as a hired hand.[872] Some years later in eastern Washington the family lived and worked together and reconciled.

---

[872] Horace D. Hume, Rosalie McLaughlin, and Kelly Meils Poremba, *Cowboy to Industrialist: The Story of Horace D. Hume, A Midwestern Centenarian* (Bushnell, Illinois: Spoon River Press, 1999), 34. The book, especially the earlier part, is based on Horace's memories taken down years after the fact. His father James's obituary (above, Chapter 20) paints a friendlier picture; probably there is some truth in both.

In 1930 Horace and Minnie were running a garage in Garfield; he was the owner and she kept the books. They were renting for $12.50 a month and owned a "radio set."[873] In the late 1930s he served as mayor.[874]

Meanwhile Horace and friend Ed Love (a college graduate in mechanical engineering) got interested in an ongoing problem for eastern Washington farmers: how to harvest the peas they grew without losing half or more of the crop as the vines shattered, scattering the vegetables on the ground. Their interest led to a series of inventions and patents beginning in 1932 that enabled farmers to combine three laborious and inefficient harvest operations—mowing, windrowing, and threshing—into one. Before, harvesting would lose over 50 percent of the crop; with the new equipment, losses dropped below 10 percent.[875]

1940: they owned their home in Garfield, Washington (valued at $1000, less than half the statewide average of $2359) and Horace's business was now manufacturing agricultural equipment. He had completed two years of high school, Minnie four.[876]

1942: Horace was in partnership with J. E. Love in the Hume–Love Company there.[877] But Horace saw potential in the Midwest; at the center of the prime marketing areas was the small city of Mendota, Illinois. Hume and Love settled up and parted ways, and the Humes went east to where more farmers needed more efficient machinery.

1949: Horace was serving his third term as president of the Mendota Chamber of Commerce.[878]

---

[873] Horace D. Hume household, 1930 US census, Garfield, Whitman County, Washington, ED 47, sheet 3B, dwelling 39, family 45.

[874] "More than 200 Attend Banquet of Chamber," *Spokesman-Review* (Spokane, Washington), Sunday 12 November 1939, p. 18, col. 5.

[875] Horace D. Hume, Rosalie McLaughlin, and Kelly Meils Poremba, *Cowboy to Industrialist: The Story of Horace D. Hume, A Midwestern Centenarian* (Bushnell, Illinois: Spoon River Press, 1999), 66.

[876] Horace D. Hume household, 1940 US census, Garfield, Whitman County, Washington, ED 38-85, sheet 2B, dwelling 49. Statewide figures from US Census Bureau, Census of Housing, Historical Census of Housing Tables, Median Home Values Unadjusted 1940 (https://www2.census.gov/programs-surveys/decennial/tables/time-series/coh-values/values-unadj.txt).

[877] Horace Delbert Hume, WW2 draft card, 16 February 1942, Whitman County, Washington, local board; "US, World War II Draft Cards Young Men 1940–1947" > Washington > Hill–Mathews > Hughes–Huston > images 1483–84 of 5061 (ancestry.com).

[878] "Personal Notes," *Alton Telegraph* (Illinois), Tuesday 20 September 1949, p. 9, col. 5. The Humes were visiting a former Mendota resident.

1957: He was the Mendota agent for the United Republican Fund in La Salle County; Illinois Governor William G. Stratton had just been elected to a second term.[879]

1959: Horace was elected president of the Hume family association (descendants of James and Ann [Walker] Hume) at its annual meeting at Pauquette Park in Portage, Wisconsin.[880]

1987: Horace was the oldest direct descendant present at family's 54th annual meeting, held in Moundville.[881]

1993: Horace was honored four times in less than four months across the country:

- 24 June near Rosalie, Washington, the American Society of Agricultural Engineers celebrated the invention of the flexible floating cutterbar and the tined pickup reel by Hume and partner James E. Love, said to have saved the equivalent of 2.75 million acres of soybeans annually.
- 4 August in the *Congressional Record*, then House Speaker Dennis Hastert called him "one of a rare breed of geniuses of invention."
- 15 August, Mendota recognized for his 95th birthday his recent donation of $750,000 for construction of a new 10,000-square-foot library.
- 27 September at the Chicago-based Equipment Manufacturers Institute (EMI), Horace was described as "one of the most significant contributors to the mechanization of agriculture and construction in the past century."[882]

1995: Horace was inducted into the Senior Illinoisans Hall of Fame. "He holds over 100 patents for inventions, notably two (the floating cutter bar and the pickup reel) that helped simplify harvesting of soybeans and other low-lying crops. He has served his community by holding public office and striving to bring new business to the area. He helped build a new hospital, a public swimming pool and donated a building to the city for a new public library. Hume plans to turn the old library building into a museum to preserve the history of Mendota and surrounding area."[883]

---

[879] "GOP To Start Fund-Raising Campaign October 1," *Times-Press* (Streator, Illinois), Thursday 12 September 1957, p. 21, col. 1.

[880] "Hume Family Gathers Here," *Portage Daily Register* (Wisconsin), Thursday 30 July 1959, p. 3, col. 2.

[881] "47 present at 54th annual Hume reunion," *Portage Daily Register* (Wisconsin), Saturday 1 August 1987, p. 12, cols. 1–2.

[882] "Southwest Talk . . . Honors keep on coming," *Chicago Tribune,* Sunday 14 November 1993, Section 18 (Tempo Southwest section, p. 1), p. 191, col. 1.

[883] "Area man inducted in Hall of Fame," *Times* (Streator, Illinois), Tuesday 22 August 1995, p. 6, col. 1.

ii. CLARENCE[4] O. HUME *(James S.[3] Hume, Sarah Ann[2] Scholes, Ann[1] Mills, Samuel[A])* was born 2 May 1901 in Wisconsin;[884] died in Bowman, Bowman County, North Dakota, 27 July 1917, after about three weeks' illness described as an "infection" or "typhoid fever";[885] and was buried at Moundville Cemetery, Marquette County, Wisconsin. Clarence and Horace were close, sharing a fascination with the newly developed automobile.[886]

iii. ESTHER LYDIA[4] HUME *(James S.[3] Hume, Sarah Ann[2] Scholes, Ann[1] Mills, Samuel[A])*, was reportedly born 15 September 1907 in Moundville Township, Marquette County, Wisconsin;[887] died 14 December 1982 "after a lengthy illness" in St. Mary's Hospital, Grand Junction, Mesa County, Colorado; and was buried at Traer Cemetery, Traer, Decatur County, Kansas.[888] Esther "spent her childhood in Wisconsin and

---

[884] Exact dates from grave marker photo: Horace D. Hume, Rosalie McLaughlin, and Kelly Meils Poremba, *Cowboy to Industrialist: The Story of Horace D. Hume, A Midwestern Centenarian* (Bushnell, Illinois: Spoon River Press, 1999), 35. Clarence was called four years old in 1905 (when the family was still in Moundville Township, Marquette County, Wisconsin), Wisconsin state census, Moundville Township, Marquette County, Wisconsin, family 3, p. 105. He was eight years old in 1910, when the family was in Billings County, North Dakota, ED 6, sheet 2A, dwelling/family 38. He was said to be age 16 in July 1917 at the time of his death there: "Brief News Notes," *Portage Daily Register* (Wisconsin), Friday 27 July 1917, p. 3, col. 3—but giving his death at the nonexistent "Bowman, Montana" rather than Bowman, North Dakota.

[885] Typhoid fever: "Brief News Notes," *Portage Daily Register* (Wisconsin), Friday 27 July 1917, p. 3, col. 3. Infection: Horace D. Hume, Rosalie McLaughlin, and Kelly Meils Poremba, *Cowboy to Industrialist: The Story of Horace D. Hume, A Midwestern Centenarian* (Bushnell, Illinois: Spoon River Press, 1999), 34.

[886] Horace D. Hume, Rosalie McLaughlin, and Kelly Meils Poremba, *Cowboy to Industrialist: The Story of Horace D. Hume, A Midwestern Centenarian* (Bushnell, Illinois: Spoon River Press, 1999), 19, 31–33.

[887] Esther L. Hume index entry, "Wisconsin Birth Index 1820–1907," reel 138, record 383 (ancestry.com). Similarly, "Wisconsin Births and Christenings, 1826–1926," FHL #1,305,092, DGS #7,615,064, item 383, specifying Moundville (familysearch.org). Film not digitized. She was said to be age 75 at death in 1982: "Obituaries…Esther Walton," *Daily Sentinel* (Grand Junction, Colorado), p. 14, cols. 3–4. The obituary also states that she was born 26 September 1907 at Portage, Wisconsin.

[888] Esther L. Walton and Hilbert E. Walton joint grave marker, image, Traer Cemetery, Traer, Decatur County, Kansas, memorials #69,904,521 and #69,911,095 respectively by Allison and Dusting Trails (findagrave.com). Hilbert's and Esther's exact birth and death dates are engraved on the marker; other information is not sourced.

North Dakota and attended schools in North Dakota and Washington."[889]

She married first OSCAR MCKINLEY JENKINS 14 October 1922 in Colfax, Whitman County, Washington, the son of Grant and Anna (Bagley) Jenkins. Oscar was born 13 December 1896 (age 24 in 1922) in either Peola or Pomeroy, Garfield County, Washington;[890] died 19 January 1946 (said to be age 50) at 917 Fifth Street in Clarkston, Asotin County, Washington; and was buried at Vineland Cemetery there.[891]

The first marriage evidently did not last. Esther married second as his second wife 20 June 1928 in Josephine County, Oregon, ORITIS ELMER "READY" SMITH,[892] the son of George Walter (1870–1935) and Mattie Cardlie (Sisk) Smith (1881–1969).[893] He was born 30 April 1902 in Latah County, Idaho[894]; and died 4 December 1951, "when his car plunged 200 feet over Winchester grade," 30 miles southeast of Lewiston. State police said Smith's car missed a turn and went over the bluff[895] two miles west of Potlatch on Highway 14 between 1 and 1:30 am, December 4–5.[896] He was buried at Freeze Cemetery, Freeze,

---

[889] "Obituaries…Esther Walton," *Daily Sentinel* (Grand Junction, Colorado), p. 14, cols. 3-4.

[890] Oscar Jenkins–Esther L. Hume marriage return, 14 October 1922, #7011; "Washington, Marriage Records, 1854–2013" > Whitman > Marriage Returns 1922 September–December > image 5 of 60 (ancestry.com). B. F. Shoemaker of the Christian Church officiated. Witnesses were Mrs. Lydia A. Hume and Horace D. Hume, the bride's mother and brother.

[891] Oscar McKinley Jenkins death certificate, 19 January 1946, Washington State, 917 Fifth Street, Clarkston, Asotin County, Washington, of influenza and heart problems; image 492 of 2611, FHL #2,032,474, DGS #4,223,013, items 2–6 (familysearch.org).

[892] Ready Smith–Esther L. Hume, 20 June 1928, Josephine County, Oregon; "Oregon, Marriage Indexes, 1906–2009" (ancestry.com). Also, Ready E. Smith age 27 household for wife Esther L. age 22, 1930 US census, Clatskanie Election Precinct 1, Columbia County, Oregon, ED 5, sheet 6A, dwelling 145, family 146. For marriage, Scholes ledger book, 68.

[893] Antis Elmer Smith (born 30 April 1902) entry, birth certificate #344829, "Idaho, Birth Index, 1861–1917, Stillbirth Index 1905–1967" (ancestry.com).

[894] Ready Elmer Smith WW2 draft card, serial #T10464, order #T10336, Latah County Local Board, 16 February 1942; "US WWII Draft Cards Young Men, 1940–1947" > Idaho > Smith–Sorenson > images 2–3 of 2219 (ancestry.com). Mrs. Mattie Smith of Potlatch, Idaho, (likely his mother) would always know his address.

[895] "Idahoan Killed," *Idaho State Journal* (Pocatello), Wednesday 5 December 1951, p. 1, col. 1.

[896] Oritis Elmer Smith death certificate, Nez Perce County, Idaho, 4–5 December 1951; "Idaho, Death Records, 1890–1967" > 1951 > image 4845 of 4953 (ancestry.com).

Latah County, Idaho.[897] (Ready had married first Marie E. Olson 29 April 1921 in Moscow, Latah County, Idaho. Both were residents of Potlatch.[898] His marriage to Esther was the second for both of them.) The second marriage evidently did not last, as Esther married third, as his second wife, HILBERT EUGENE WALTON 29 June 1942 in California.[899] He was reportedly the son of Oscar Hilbert and Ruby (Thomas) Walton. He was born 27 March 1910, Atwood, Rawlins County, Kansas; died 28 December 1999; and was buried with his wife; the inscription reads "tried to leave this world a better place."[900] As of 16 October 1940, Hilbert was 6 feet one inch tall and weighed 168 pounds, with brown eyes and brown hair. He was living at 338 South Pomelo Avenue in Monterey Park, Los Angeles (where his landlady, Mrs. Nellie Naylor, would always know his address) and employed by the Alhambra School District at 601 North Garfield Avenue.[901] Hilbert had already married once, 20 July 1936 in Salt Lake City, to Grace Fay Watson.[902]

---

[897] Oritis E. Smith grave marker, image, Freeze Cemetery, Latah County, Idaho, memorial #25,190,000, by jbc and Kathleen Peck Probasco Ketchum (findagrave.com). Walter and Mattie are named as parents without sourcing.

[898] Ready Elmer Smith—Marie E. Olson, marriage license and certificate #87906, Moscow, Latah County, Idaho; "Idaho, County Marriages, 1864–1950" > image 372 of 811, FHL #1,535,102, DGS #4,533,534 (familysearch.org). Probate judge Adrian Nelson officiated; witnesses were Mrs. Mattie Smith and Guy W. Wolfe. The Western States Marriage Index locates the record at volume 6, page 601 (abish.byui.edu/specialCollections/westernStates/westernStatesRecordDetail.cfm?recordID=128706).

[899] Hilbert E. Walton—Esther L. Smith marriage index entry 29 January 1942, citing volume 1781:148 but giving no jurisdiction; "California, County Birth, Marriage, and Death Records, 1849–1980" > Unknown > Marriage > 1942 > image 662 of 798 (ancestry.com).

[900] Esther L. and Hilbert E. Walton joint grave marker, image, Traer Cemetery, Traer, Decatur County, Kansas, memorials #69,904,521 and #69,911,095 respectively by Allison and Dusting Trails (findagrave.com). Hilbert's and Esther's birth and death dates are on the grave marker; other information is not sourced. Also, for birth place, Hilbert Eugene Walton WW2 draft card, serial #3287, order #1195, 16 October 1940, Local Board 202, Montebello, California; "US WWII Draft Cards Young Men, 1940–1947" > California > Wackerman—Ware > Walters—Wapack > images 828–29 of 2121 (ancestry.com).

[901] Hilbert Eugene Walton WW2 draft card, serial #3287, order #1195, 16 October 1940, Local Board 202, Montebello, California; "US WWII Draft Cards Young Men, 1940–1947" > California > Wackerman—Ware > Walters—Wapack > images 828–29 of 2121 (ancestry.com).

[902] Hilbert Eugene Walton—Grace Fay Watson marriage index entry, 20 July 1936, Salt Lake City, certificate A074032, FHL #429,154, DGS #4,706,033, image 706.

1930: Esther and Ready and young Vernon were living in a rented house in lumbering country in the northwest corner of Oregon; Ready was employed as "fireman" on a steam donkey engine in a logging camp. They did not own a "radio set,"[903] but in 1931–32 Ready did own a 1924 Dodge.[904]

1935: Esther and Vernon were in Potlatch, Latah County, Idaho.

1940: They were living with her younger brother George Hume (below) at 127 North Rowland in Monrovia, Los Angeles County, California; Esther was working as a maid in a "rest home." She was reportedly married, but Ready was not in the household.[905] In fact, he was still logging, this time in Fernwood, Benewah County, Idaho, lodging with a farmer in a rented house—exactly where he was in 1935.[906] They may have been living separately for at least five years.

16 February 1942: Ready's mother was the person who would always know his address. He was 5 feet 11 inches tall, weighed 180 pounds, with hazel eyes, brown hair, and "scars on head."[907]

1945: Esther and Hilbert Walton were at 1730 Ogden Street in Denver.[908]

1957: Hilbert was vice-president and she was secretary-treasurer of Local 23 of the West Orchard Mesa chapter of the Farmers Union.[909]

---

[903] Ready E. Smith household, 1930 US census, Clatskanie Election Precinct #1, Columbia County, Oregon, ED 5, sheet 6A, dwelling 145, family 146.

[904] Registration #73378 Ready E. Smith, Clatskanie, Columbia County, Oregon; "Oregon, Motor Vehicle Registrations, 1911–1946" > 1931–1932 > Volume 3 > image 38 of 158 (ancestry.com).

[905] George W. Hume household for sister Ester L. Smith, 1940 US census, Monrovia, Los Angeles County, California, ED 19-386, sheet 26B, dwelling 127.

[906] William Tucker or Herder household for lodger Ready E. Smith, age 37, born in Idaho, 1940 US Census, Fernwood, Benewah County, Idaho, ED 5-9, sheet 3A, dwelling 66.

[907] Ready Elmer Smith WW2 draft card, serial #T10464, order #T10336, Latah County Local Board, 16 February 1942; "US WWII Draft Cards Young Men, 1940–1947" > Idaho > Smith–Sorenson > images 2–3 of 2219 (ancestry.com). Mrs. Mattie Smith of Potlatch, Idaho, (likely his mother) would always know his address.

[908] Vernon Hume Smith WW2 draft card, serial #W226A, order #12748-A, 11 June 1945, Local Board 7, Denver County, Colorado; "US WWII Draft Cards Young Men, 1940–1947" > Colorado > Smith–Smith > Smith–Smith > images 2087–88 of 2149 (ancestry.com). His mother was Mrs. Esther L. Walton.

[909] "Carroll President of Farmers Union Local," *Daily Sentinel* (Grand Junction, Colorado), Sunday 22 December 1957, p. 8, col. 7.

1965: He was employed at the State Home and president of the Western Slope Local of the American Federation of State, County, and Municipal Employees (AFSCME).[910]

Esther lived in Denver about 1942–1957, and for her last 25 years in Grand Junction, Mesa County, Colorado. "She was interested in bowling and was secretary of three bowling leagues."[911]

iv. GEORGE[4] HUME (*James S.[3] Hume, Sarah Ann[2] Scholes, Ann Mills[1], Samuel[A]*) was born 2 April 1914 or 1915[912] in Hume Township, Slope County, North Dakota; and died 6 February 1989 in Los Angeles.[913] He married 30 June 1934 in Colfax, Whitman County, Washington, FREEDA JANE EMERT,[914] the daughter of R. West and Lily (Sharp) Emert. Freeda was born 10 January 1911 (age 23 at marriage) in St. John, Whitman County, Washington,[915] and died 1 January 2004 in Ukiah, Mendocino County, California.[916]

Evidently George was age 20 at their marriage, not 22 as he claimed. The couple soon left the Pacific Northwest for the Pacific Southwest. Both completed four years of high school. They moved around quite a bit in the 1930s to 1950s, and always registered as Republicans. Their residences over 40 years ranged within an area south of Pasadena, east of downtown LA, north of Lakewood, and west of Hacienda Heights and the City of Industry.

---

[910] "Union Problems Studied at Meet," *Daily Sentinel* (Grand Junction, Colorado), Saturday 22 May 1965, p. 6, col. 7.

[911] "Obituaries…Esther Walton," *Daily Sentinel* (Grand Junction, Colorado), p. 14, cols. 3–4.

[912] <u>1914:</u> George Walker Hume WW2 draft card, local board 207, Temple City, California, 16 October 1940, serial #1267, order #1053; "US, WWII Draft Cards Young Men, 1940–1947" > California > Houfek–Iglehard > Hultsch–Humphreys > images 435–36 of 2105 (ancestry.com). <u>1915:</u> Scholes ledger book, 68, in author's possession. George's draft card date is more likely accurate.

[913] George Walker Hume index entry, California Death Index 1940–1997 (ancestry.com).

[914] For wife's name, Scholes ledger book, 68, in author's possession.

[915] George W. Hume–Frieda J. Emert marriage 30 June 1934, license #9675 and return, Whitman County, Washington; "Washington, Marriage, Records, 1854–2013" > Whitman > Marriage Returns 1934 May–Aug > image 3 of 65 (ancestry.com). George claimed to be age 22 (implying birth 1912). Rev. Brown officiated in Colfax; witnesses were Mrs. Esther L. Smith of Potlatch, Idaho, and John G. Lortz [?]. Frieda's parents were said to be born at Knoxville, Tennessee, and Asheville, North Carolina. Frieda's birth date from her entry in the US Social Security Death Index, 1935–2014.

[916] Freeda J. Hume index entry, US Social Security Death Index, 1935–2014.

1936 & 1938: 309 North Nicholson, Monterey Park, Los Angeles County, city precinct 8; George was a laborer.[917]

1940: 127 North Rowland (rented, $25 a month), Monrovia Township, Los Angeles County; George was an electrical welder in steel manufacturing, earning $1400/year.[918] As of 16 October 1940, he was 5 feet 10 inches tall and 170 pounds, with gray eyes and brown hair, working for American Pipe and Steel, 320 South Date Street, Alhambra.[919]

1942: 127 North Rowland, Santa Ana precinct 7; George was a welder.[920]

1944: 125 North Rowland, Santa Ana precinct 9, George was a superintendent (no occupations were given after this date).

1946: 125 North Rowland, Santa Ana precinct 9.[921]

1948: 1740 North Santa Fe Avenue, Compton City Precinct 35.[922]

1950 & 1952: 15130 Amantha Avenue, Compton City, precincts 8 and 47 respectively.[923]

1954: 10610 Roseton Avenue, Norwalk, precinct 76.[924]

1956 & 1958: 2114 West Rincon Drive, Whittier, precinct 37.[925]

---

[917] George W. and Freeda Hume, 309 North Nicholson, Monterey Park City, Precinct 8; "California, Voter Registrations, 1900–1968" > Los Angeles County > 1936 > Roll 37 > image 106 of 768 (ancestry.com); similarly, 1938 > Roll 42 > image 520 of 815.

[918] George W. Hume household, 1940 US census, Monrovia Township (in 1942, Temple City), Los Angeles County, ED 19-386, sheet 26B, dwelling 640.

[919] George Walker Hume WW2 draft card, local board 207, Temple City, California, 16 October 1940, serial #1267, order #1053; "US, WWII Draft Cards Young Men, 1940–1947" > California > Houfek–Iglehard > Hultsch–Humphreys > images 435–36 of 2105 (ancestry.com).

[920] George W. and Freeda Hume, 127 North Rowland, Monterey Park City, Precinct 7; "California, Voter Registrations, 1900–1968" > Los Angeles County > 1942 > Roll 54 > image 811 of 931 (ancestry.com)

[921] George W. Hume, 125 North Rowland, Santa Ana, Precinct 9; "California, Voter Registrations, 1900–1968" > Los Angeles County > 1944 > roll 60 > image 571 of 979 (ancestry.com). Similarly, George and Freeda, 1946 > roll 66 > image 126 of 971.

[922] George W. and Freeda Hume, 1740 North Santa Fe Avenue, Compton City, Precinct 35; "California, Voter Registrations, 1900–1968" > Los Angeles County > 1948 > roll 70 > image 627 of 1427 (ancestry.com).

[923] George W. Hume, 15130 Amantha Avenue, Compton City, Precinct 68; "California, Voter Registrations, 1900–1968" > Los Angeles County > 1950 > roll 76 > image 736 of 792 (ancestry.com). Similarly, George and Freeda, 1952 > roll 83 > image 829 of 1247.

[924] George W. and Freeda Hume, 10610 Roseton Avenue, Norwalk Precinct 76; "California, Voter Registrations, 1900–1968" > Los Angeles County > 1954 > roll 92 > image 1104 of 1137 (ancestry.com).

[925] George W. and Freeda Hume, 2114 West Rincon Drive, Whittier, Precinct 37; "California, Voter Registrations, 1900–1968" > Los Angeles County > 1956 > roll 106 > image 666 of 803 (ancestry.com). Similarly, 1958 > roll 125 > image 498 of 2065.

1969: in Whittier; he was president of the California Tank & Manufacturing Corporation, located at 5674 Cherry Avenue in Long Beach.[926]

1974, 1976, 1977: at 11038 East Rincon Drive in Whittier, still president.[927]

---

[926] Geo. W. & Freeda Hume, *Polk's Long Beach Directory 1969*, p. 485, image 687 of 2216, and for the business, p. 149, image 351 of 2216 (ancestry.com).

[927] Geo. W. and Freeda J. Hume, *Polk's Whittier (Los Angeles County, Calif.), City Directory 1974* (South El Monte, California: R. L. Polk & Co., 1974), p. 216, image 350 of 990 (ancestry.com). Similarly, *1976*, p. 211, image 339 of 1002; *1977*, p. 222, image 356 of 1040.

Chapter 21

Third Generation

George Walker Hume–Lois/Louise DeMott Family
<u>parents at chapter 4</u>

"Ask Vera; she never forgets anything."

21. GEORGE WALKER³ HUME (*Sarah Ann² Scholes, Ann¹ Mills, Samuel^A*)
Birth: 27 February 1874[928] reportedly in Marquette County, Wisconsin
Death: "very suddenly Saturday evening" 2 February 1952 in Marquette County[929]
Burial: Moundville Cemetery, Endeavor, Marquette County, Wisconsin[930]
Spouse: **LOIS/LOUISE DEMOTT**,[931] married 16 January 1901 at the Presbyterian Church in Westfield, Marquette County, Wisconsin[932]
Spouse's parents: Isaac and Esther (-?-) DeMott[933]
Spouse's birth: 1876, reportedly 24 June[934]

---

[928] George Walker Hume WWI draft card, Montello, Wisconsin, local board, 12 September 1918, serial #990, order #a887; US, World War I Draft Registration Cards, 1917–1918 > Wisconsin > Marquette County > Draft Card H > image 156 of 162 (ancestry.com).
[929] "George W. Hume Dies at Westfield," *Portage Daily Register* (Wisconsin), Monday 4 February 1952, p. 3, col. 3.
[930] George W. and Lois D. Hume, joint grave marker, image, Moundville Cemetery, Endeavor, Marquette County, Wisconsin, memorials #103,102,232 and #103,102,488 respectively, by Joey (findagrave.com).
[931] "Children of the Scholes Family," Scholes ledger book, 65, in author's possession.
[932] "Married...DeMott–Hume," *Portage Daily Register* (Wisconsin), Thursday 17 January 1901, p. 4, col. 3.
[933] Isaac DeMott household for daughter Louise age 4, 1880 US census, Westfield, Marquette County, Wisconsin, ED 228, p. 5, dwelling 38, family 39.
[934] George W. and Lois D. Hume, joint grave marker, image, Moundville Cemetery, Endeavor, Marquette County, Wisconsin, memorials #103,102,232 and #103,102,488 respectively, by Joey (findagrave.com).

Spouse's death: 2 March 1962, age 85[935]

Spouse's burial: Moundville Cemetery, Endeavor, Marquette County, Wisconsin[936]

In 1910 the Humes were living on West Moundville Road with an eleven-year old "lodger" (possibly a cousin?) Verda or Virla Conger, born in Wisconsin of Wisconsin-born parents.[937] (See child ii below.) George completed eight years of school, Lois one year of high school.[938]

As of 12 September 1918, George was a farmer of medium height and medium build, with blue eyes and brown hair.[939] For many years he served as tax assessor of Moundville Township.[940]

In 1920 the Hume household included a Wisconsin-born baby Vera Jones (surname crossed out), a "ward" aged one year and eight months.[941] In 1930 ten-year-old Vera was their daughter; they owned a "radio set."[942] In 1940 they remained in Moundville and Vera was gone.[943]

---

[935] "Hume Funeral Rites Will Be on Monday," *Portage Daily Register* (Wisconsin), Saturday 3 March 1962, p. 3, col. 6.

[936] George W. and Lois D. Hume, joint grave marker, image, Moundville Cemetery, Endeavor, Marquette County, Wisconsin, memorials #103,102,232 and #103,102,488 respectively, by Joey (findagrave.com).

[937] George W. Hume household for wife Lois age 33 and lodger Verda age 11, 1910 US census, Moundville Township, Marquette County, Wisconsin, ED 149, sheet 6B, dwelling 136, family 138. The enumerator apparently omitted asking the question of how many children had been born and how many were living.

[938] George Hume household, 1940 US census, Moundville Township, Marquette County, Wisconsin, sheet 7B, dwelling 176.

[939] George Walker Hume WWI draft card, Montello, Wisconsin, local board, 12 September 1918, serial #990, order #a887; "US, World War I Draft Registration Cards, 1917–1918" > Wisconsin > Marquette County > Draft Card H > image 156 of 162 (ancestry.com).

[940] "'Off to Dover...'" clipping from *Portage Daily Register,* labeled January 1951, Stella Scholes collection, item #2, in author's possession.

[941] George W. Hume household for "ward" Vera Jones (surname crossed out), age 1 year 8 months, 1920 US census, Moundville Township, Marquette County, Wisconsin, ED 133, sheet 2A, dwelling 26, family 27.

[942] George Hume household, 1930 US census, Moundville Township, Marquette County, Wisconsin, ED 8, sheet 5B, dwelling/family 140.

[943] George Hume household, 1940 US census, Moundville Township, Marquette County, Wisconsin, sheet 7B, dwelling 176.

In 1951 the Humes observed their Golden Wedding anniversary "by taking a ride in a sleigh similar to the one they used on their honeymoon."[944]

Children of George and Lois (DeMott) Hume:

i. GERALD A. HUME (*George W.³ Hume, Sarah Ann² Scholes, Ann¹ Mills, Samuel^A*). "One infant died one week after birth (boy)."[945]

ii. VERA LOIS⁴ JONES/HUME (*George W.³ Hume* [adoptive father], *Sarah Ann² Scholes, Ann¹ Mills, Samuel^A*) was born 12 May 1918; died 7 April 2017 in Portage, Columbia County, Wisconsin; and was buried at Moundville Cemetery, Marquette County.

> Vera was born on May 12, 1918, the daughter of Merlin and Verda Conger Jones. Her mother passed away 9 days after giving birth to Vera and her father was in the military service, so Vera was adopted by cousins George and Lois Hume.[946]

In 1937–38 Vera attended Central State Teachers College in Stevens Point, Portage County, Wisconsin, where on 29 July 1938 she was one of thirty receiving diplomas in the "two-year-rural-state graded course." (Twenty-four others received bachelor's degrees in science or education.)[947] In the fall of 1938 she was teaching near Pardeeville and boarding at home in Moundville Township.[948] Early in

---

[944] "'Off to Dover…'" clipping from *Portage Daily Register*, labeled January 1951, Stella Scholes collection, item #2, in author's possession.
[945] Gerald A. Hume (1911–1911) grave marker, image, Moundville Cemetery, Endeavor, Marquette County, Wisconsin, memorial #103,179,795 by Joey (findagrave.com). Also, Scholes ledger book, 68, in author's possession.
[946] Vera Lois Thornton Banks obituary, Pflanz Mantey Mendrala Funeral Home in Portage (pmmfh.com/obits2017/aaobitBanksVera.html). Excerpts on Vera's memorial #178,413,831 by TRISH (findagrave.com). The obituary states that Vera (born in 1918) graduated from Endeavor Academy at age 17 (1935), which is nine years after its doors closed. The informant may have given the academy's name to the public school that later occupied its buildings.
[947] "54 Graduate on Friday at Central State," *Stevens Point Journal* (Wisconsin), Thursday 28 July 1938, p. 1, col. 6.
[948] "West Moundville," *Portage Daily Register* (Wisconsin), Thursday 15 September 1938, p. 3, col. 2. Neither point is clearly defined but the distance appears to be roughly 20 miles.

1940 she obtained a job teaching at Stenker (later described as a school near Wisconsin Rapids).[949]

Vera married first as his second wife CHARLES ROSCOE THORNTON 31 March 1940.[950] He was born 28 August 1902 in Sac County, Iowa,[951] died 10 May 1968,[952] and was buried at Moundville Cemetery, Marquette County.[953] His parents were William P. and Mamie B. Thornton.[954]

In 1930 an Iowa-born 27-year-old Charles R. and 24-year-old Thelma (-?-) Thornton were married and renting part of one of four apartments at 521 Fifth Street in Nevada, Story County, Iowa, for $25 a month. Charles was a produce buyer and Thelma a telephone operator. They were married in 1929 or 1930.[955] On 19 March 1940 Mrs. Thelma Thornton of Green Bay, Wisconsin, was granted a divorce from Charles R. Thornton of the same, charging cruel and inhuman treatment.[956] That year Thelma was enumerated as a widow in Green Bay, living in the household of her probable parents Thomas and Angeline (-?-) Reinhart.[957]

Vera married second ALVIN/ALLEN BANKS 4 June 1992[958] in Lake Mills, Jefferson County, Wisconsin, the son of Allie and Elizabeth

---

[949] "West Moundville," *Wisconsin State Register* (Madison), Friday 5 January 1940, p. 3, col. 5. Also, "Moundville," *Portage Daily Register* (Wisconsin), Thursday 18 January 1940, p. 12, col. 1.
[950] Vera Lois Thornton Banks obituary, Pflanz Mantey Mendrala Funeral Home in Portage (pmmfh.com/obits2017/aaobitBanksVera.html). Excerpts on Vera's memorial #178,413,831 by TRISH (findagrave.com) plus a genealogical postscript.
[951] Charles R. Thornton WW2 draft card, Westfield, Wisconsin, local board #1, 16 February 1942; "US WWII Draft Cards Young Men, 1940–1947" > Wisconsin > Stemo–Vaness > Thompson–Thorson > images 1225–26 of 1944 (ancestry.com). Wilma Heames was registrar.
[952] "Obituaries…Charles Thornton," *Wisconsin State Journal* (Madison), Sunday 12 May 1968, section 2, p 3, col. 2. Vera Lois Thornton Banks obituary, Pflanz Mantey Mendrala Funeral Home in Portage (pmmfh.com/obits2017/aaobitBanksVera.html). Excerpts on Vera's memorial #178,413,831 by TRISH (findagrave.com).
[953] Charles R. and Vera L. Thornton joint grave marker, Moundville, Marquette County, Wisconsin, image, memorial #178,413,831 by TRISH (findagrave.com).
[954] William P. Thornton household for son Charley R. age 7, 1910 US census, New Albany, Story County, Iowa, ED 195, sheet 7A, dwelling 155, family 156.
[955] Charles R. Thornton household for wife Thelma, 1930 US census, Nevada, Story County, Iowa, ED 22, sheet 15B, dwelling 368, family 339A.
[956] "Around Town," *Green Bay Press-Gazette* (Wisconsin), Tuesday 19 March 1940, p. 6, col. 2—twelve days prior to Charles and Thelma's divorce.
[957] Thomas Reinhart household for daughter Thelma Thornton, 1940 US census, Green Bay, Brown County, Wisconsin, ED 5-38, sheet 9B, dwelling 191.
[958] Genealogical postscript to Vera's obituary and memorial #178,413,831 by TRISH (findagrave.com).

(Carpenter) Banks. He was born 30 May 1923 in Wautoma, Waushara County, Wisconsin; died 14 October 1993 of cancer; and was buried Silver Lake Cemetery, Portage, Columbia County, Wisconsin.[959]

Vera's biological father, Merlin E. Jones, was born in Moundville Township 21 October 1892, the son of Levi and Cora Jones. He married first 4 August 1917 Verda Conger, who died 21 May 1918 after giving birth to Vera. He married second Gertrude Parrott 21 May 1921. He served in the army during World War I, returned to Endeavor and opened the E. E. Jones Garage and Service Station, where he was a Standard Oil dealer for 38 years. He also operated a funeral coach livery service, ambulance service, and school bus service in the area.[960]

In 1920 the Hume household included a Wisconsin-born baby Vera Jones (surname crossed out), a "ward" aged one year and eight months.[961] In 1930 ten-year-old Vera was listed as their daughter; they owned a "radio set."[962]

Charles and wife Vera lived in Endeavor, telephone Endeavor 4R13; he was self-employed. As of 16 February 1942, he was 5 feet 10 inches tall, weighted 164 pounds, and had blue eyes and gray hair.[963]

Evidently Vera was one to make her own way. At some point in the 1940s, she went to California and sold real estate. In the 1950s, returning to Wisconsin, she leased the White Diner in Endeavor, and in 1959 leased the dining and lunch counter facilities at the Oneida Hotel (evidently in Portage). At that time Charles reportedly worked for "a construction crew on the new I-system."[964]

In 1971 Vera Thornton of Portage was named as one of three children of Mr. and Mrs. Merlin Jones, the other two being Keith of Milwaukee and Kenneth of Bowling Green, Warren County, Kentucky.[965]

---

[959] "Obituaries . . . Allen Banks," *Portage Daily Register* (Wisconsin), Sunday 17 October 1993, p. 2A, col. 1.
[960] "Merlin E. Jones," *Portage Daily Register* (Wisconsin), Monday 22 December 1980, p. 4, col. 3.
[961] George W. Hume household for "ward" Vera, age 1 year 8 months, 1920 US census, Moundville Township, Marquette County, Wisconsin, ED 133, sheet 2A, dwelling 26, family 27.
[962] George Hume household, 1930 US census, Moundville Township, Marquette County, Wisconsin, ED 8, sheet 5B, dwelling/family 140.
[963] Charles R. Thornton WW2 draft card, Westfield, Wisconsin, local board #1, 16 February 1942; "US WWII Draft Cards Young Men, 1940–1947" > Wisconsin > Stemo–Vaness > Thompson–Thorson > images 1225–26 of 1944 (ancestry.com).
[964] "Mrs. Thornton Takes Over Dining Room at Oneida," *Portage Daily Register* (Wisconsin), Friday 30 October 1959, p. 12, cols. 1–3. She also had four children!
[965] "Endeavor couple marks 50 years," *Portage Daily Register* (Wisconsin), Tuesday 11 May 1971, p. 4, cols. 5–6.

She was a member of the Moundville Methodist Church and a life member of the Eastern Star. In Vera's early married life, she sold real estate for the Morgan Agency in West Covina, CA. She was a member of the Sherman Oaks California Woman's Club. Vera ran many restaurants including The White Diner, The Hilton in Endeavor, and The Hut in Nevada, IA, The Wauona Café, The Portage Hotel and The Oneida Hotel in Portage. Vera was a very good cook and made numerous pies daily at each restaurant she owned and operated. She was also a social worker for Columbia County, visiting families in need with their meal planning.

Vera's favorite pastime was watching basketball and NASCAR races on TV. She also enjoyed sewing, playing cards, Bingo and games on her IPad. She had a great memory right to the end of her life. Friends and family alike who had questions on almost anything related to a specific date, time or occasion, would say, "Ask Vera; she never forgets anything."[966]

---

[966] Vera Lois Thornton Banks obituary, Pflanz Mantey Mendrala Funeral Home in Portage (pmmfh.com/obits2017/aaobitBanksVera.html). Excerpts on Vera's memorial #178,413,831 by TRISH (findagrave.com).

Chapter 22
Third Generation

William Henry Smith–Rose Ruth Haines Family
parents at chapter 6

Clinton "spent most of his life in the vicinity of Pardeeville and Dalton in farming and construction work"

22. WILLIAM HENRY³ SMITH (*Alice² Scholes, Ann¹ Mills, Samuel^A*)
Birth: about 1866 in Wisconsin[967]
Death: reportedly 1936 in Wisconsin
Burial: reportedly at Pardeeville Cemetery, Columbia County, Wisconsin, at O.C.A. #092[968]
Spouse: **ROSE RUTH HAINES**, married in Burleson County, Texas, most likely 11 May 1891[969]
Spouse's parents: Robert M. and Abbie (Blaisdell) Haines
Spouse's birth: June 1861[970] in Wyocena, Columbia County, Wisconsin

---

[967] Joseph Smith household (in Samuel Ellis household) for son William age 14, 1880 US census, Moundville, Marquette County, Wisconsin, ED 223, p. 563C, dwelling 28, no family number.

[968] William Henry Smith grave marker, no image, Pardeeville Cemetery, Columbia County, Wisconsin, memorial #118,443,613 by Bob (findagrave.com). Death year not documented.

[969] For 11 May 1891: "Mrs. Smith Rites," *Wisconsin State Journal* (Madison), Wednesday 24 March 1948, p. 4, col. 2. Census entries also imply an 1891 marriage. For 1892: Andrew Mack Haines and Thomas Vanburen Haines, compilers, *Deacon Samuel Haines of Westbury, Wiltshire, England, and His Descendants in America, 1635–1901* (North Hampton, New Hampshire: privately printed, 1902), p. 196; "North America, Family Histories, 1500–2000" > H > Haines > Deacon Samuel Haines of Westbury… > image 211 of 419 (ancestry.com). Also, William Smith–Rose Haynes marriage index entry; "Texas, County Marriage Index, 1837–1977," p. 124, image 633, record 1544, FHL #956,566, DGS #4,539,361 (familysearch.org).

[970] Andrew Mack Haines and Thomas Vanburen Haines, compilers, *Deacon Samuel Haines of Westbury, Wiltshire, England, and His Descendants in America, 1635–1901* (North Hampton, New Hampshire: privately printed, 1902), p. 196; "North America, Family Histories, 1500–2000" > H > Haines > Deacon Samuel Haines of Westbury… > image 211 of 419 (ancestry.com).

Spouse's death: March 1948

Spouse's burial: 24 March 1948 at Pardeeville Cemetery, Columbia County, Wisconsin[971]

1900: William, wife Rose, and two children in Buffalo Township, Marquette County, Wisconsin. He was farming.[972]

1910: William, wife Rosa, and three children in Wyocena Township, Columbia County, Wisconsin, on Town Line Road.[973]

1920: William, wife Rose, and three children (all over 18) in Wyocena.[974]

1930: William and Rose in Wyocena.[975]

1940: Rose, age 78 and widowed, was living on "old age pension" and owned a $500 house in Pardeeville, Columbia County, Wisconsin, well below the statewide average in Wisconsin. She had completed five years of schooling.[976]

Children of William Henry[3] and Rose Ruth (Haines) Smith:

i. CLINTON WILLIAM[4] SMITH (*William H.[3] Smith, Alice[2] Scholes, Ann[1] Mills, Samuel[A]*) was born 6 June 1892 in Endeavor, Moundville

---

[971] "Mrs. Smith Rites," *Wisconsin State Journal* (Madison), Wednesday 24 March 1948, p. 4, col. 2.
[972] William Smith household, 1900 US census, Buffalo Township, Marquette County, Wisconsin, ED 91, sheet 7A, dwelling/family 118.
[973] William H. Smith household, 1910 US census, Wyocena, Columbia County, Wisconsin, ED 35, sheets 21A–B, dwelling 438, family 444.
[974] William H. Smith household, 1920 US census, Wyocena, Columbia County, Wisconsin, ED 18, sheet 14B, dwelling 348, family 354.
[975] William Smith household, 1930 US census, Wyocena, Columbia County, Wisconsin, ED 36, sheet 1A, dwelling/family 3.
[976] Rose Smith, 1940 US census, Pardeeville, Columbia County, Wisconsin, ED 11-22, sheet 3A, dwelling 57. Statewide figures from US Census Bureau, Census of Housing, Historical Census of Housing Tables, Median Home Values Unadjusted 1940 (https://www2.census.gov/programs-surveys/decennial/tables/time-series/coh-values/values-unadj.txt).

Township, Marquette County, Wisconsin[977]; died 23 February 1951 at Portage Hospital after two years with a heart ailment;[978] and was buried at Greenwood Cemetery, Kingston, Green Lake County, Wisconsin, with his wife.[979]

"He spent most of his life in the vicinity of Pardeeville and Dalton where he was engaged in farming and construction work. For the past two years he has been in poor health, spending weeks at a time in the hospital for treatment for a heart ailment."[980]

He married 21 August 1924 FLORENCE JENNIE TRIMBELL, daughter of Byron and Zaida (Leete) Trimbell. She was born 22 April 1905 in Rock Hill, Kingston Township, Green Lake County, Wisconsin; died suddenly and unexpectedly 26 January 1950, in Portage Hospital;[981] and was buried at Greenwood Cemetery.[982]

On 7 June 1937, "Clint" applied for a Social Security number; he was employed as a track laborer by the Chicago and Northwestern Railway.[983]

---

[977] Clinton William Smith, WW2 draft card, serial #U1373, Green Lake County Local Board, 27 April 1944; "US, World War II Draft Registration Cards, 1942" > Wisconsin > Smith–Smith > Popp–Sparacino > images 137–38 of 2075 (ancestry.com). For birth in Endeavor, Clint William Smith, Social Security Carrier Employee Registration; "US, Chicago and North Western Railroad Employment Records, 1935–1970" > CNW Social Security Applications > Sliptz–Smith > image 224 of 299 (ancestry.com). For birth in 1893: Andrew Mack Haines and Thomas Vanburen Haines, compilers, *Deacon Samuel Haines of Westbury, Wiltshire, England, and His Descendants in America, 1635–1901* (North Hampton, New Hampshire: privately printed, 1902), p. 196; "North America, Family Histories, 1500–2000" > H > Haines > Deacon Samuel Haines of Westbury… > image 211 of 419 (ancestry.com).

[978] "Obituary . . . Clinton William Smith," *Portage Daily Register* (Wisconsin), Wednesday 28 February 1951, p. 6, cols. 5–6.

[979] Clinton W. and Florence J. Smith, joint grave marker, image, Greenwood Cemetery, Kingston, Green Lake County, Wisconsin, memorials #76,915,692 and #76,915,693 respectively, by Steve Seim (findagrave.com).

[980] "Obituary . . . Clinton William Smith," *Portage Daily Register* (Wisconsin), Wednesday 28 February 1951, p. 6, cols. 5–6.

[981] "Obituary . . . Mrs. Clinton W. Smith," *Portage Daily Register* (Wisconsin), Thursday 2 February 1950, p. 6, col. 4.

[982] Clinton W. and Florence J. Smith, joint grave marker, image, Greenwood Cemetery, Kingston, Green Lake County, Wisconsin, memorials #76,915,692 and #76,915,693 respectively, by Steve Seim (findagrave.com).

[983] Clint William Smith, Social Security Carrier Employee Registration; "US, Chicago and North Western Railroad Employment Records, 1935–1970" > CNW Social Security Applications > Sliptz–Smith > image 224 of 299 (ancestry.com).

As of 27 April 1942, Clinton was six feet tall and weighed 185 pounds, with blue eyes and gray hair. He and Florence and his employer Gus Utke were in Dalton village, Green Lake County, Wisconsin.[984] Florence attended school at Rock Hill and Kingston in Green Lake County. "Her cheerful disposition endeared her to her many friends and her family, and she was known for her generosity and willingness to be of service whenever the opportunity offered. [She was a] faithful, staunch supporter of the Congregational Missionary Society of which she was an active member when her health permitted her to be there."[985]

ii. RALPH RAY[4] SMITH (*William H.[3] Smith, Alice[2] Scholes, Ann[1] Mills, Samuel[A]*) was born 21 October 1896 in Wyocena Township, Columbia County, Wisconsin; died 20 October 1977 in Green Lake County, Wisconsin; and was buried at Dartford Cemetery there. He married 2 May 1922 EVANGELINE LEGHORN,[986] the daughter of Irish-born James and Elizabeth (Williamson) Leghorn. Evangeline was born 16 March 1902 in Buffalo, Marquette County, Wisconsin,[987] and died 2 April 1974, "after suffering a heart attack while preparing to begin work at the election polls."[988] She was buried at Dartford Cemetery, Green Lake County.[989]

Ralph served in World War I from 7 February 1918 to 27 January 1919.[990] He completed eight years of schooling, Evangeline two years of high school.[991]

---

[984] Clinton William Smith, WW2 draft card, serial #U1373, Green Lake County Local Board, 27 April 1944; "US, World War II Draft Registration Cards, 1942" > Wisconsin > Smith–Smith > Popp–Sparacino > images 137–38 of 2075 (ancestry.com).

[985] "Obituary . . . Mrs. Clinton W. Smith, *Portage Daily Register* (Wisconsin), Thursday 2 February 1950, p. 6, col. 4.

[986] "Winnebagoland . . . Ralph R. Smith," *Oshkosh Northwestern* (Wisconsin), Friday 21 October 1977, p. 26, col. 1. For burial, Ralph and Evangeline Smith joint grave marker, image Dartford Cemetery, Green Lake County, Wisconsin, memorials #115,057,890 by Marshall Bruce, and #98,238,697 by Tombstoner & Family respectively (findagrave.com). Ralph's name and military service are on an adjacent military marker.

[987] Evangeline Leghorn index entry, "Wisconsin, Births and Christenings Index, 1801–1928," FHL #1,305,092, item 1, DGS #7,615,064 (familysearch.org).

[988] "Mrs. Smith," *Portage Daily Register* (Wisconsin), Wednesday 10 April 1974, p. 5, col. 3.

[989] Ralph and Evangeline Smith joint grave marker, image, Dartford Cemetery, Green Lake County, Wisconsin, memorials #115,057,890 by Marshall Bruce, and #98,238,697 by Tombstoner & Family respectively (findagrave.com).

[990] "Winnebagoland . . . Ralph R. Smith," *Oshkosh Northwestern* (Wisconsin), Friday 21 October 1977, p. 26, col. 1.

[991] Ralph R. Smith household, 1940 US census, Green Lake village, Green Lake County, Wisconsin, ED 24-9, sheet 4B–5A, dwelling 97.

In 1930 Ralph had a barber shop in Montello; they owned a radio set and rented their house for $15 a month.⁹⁹² In 1940 they owned their house in Green Lake, valued at $3,000. (The statewide average house value that year was $3232.) He was still barbering, and she had a retail bakery shop.⁹⁹³

As of 27 April 1942, he was 5 feet 11 inches tall and weighed 235 pounds, with gray eyes and brown hair.⁹⁹⁴ In 1968 Ralph and Evangeline, then residing in Princeton, attended a reunion of students who had attended the Endeavor Academy (story 3, p. 149 above).⁹⁹⁵

iii. BERNICE I.⁴ SMITH (*William H.³ Smith, Alice² Scholes, Ann¹ Mills, Samuel^A*) was born 27 July 1900 and died 29 July 1972 in Portage, Columbia County, Wisconsin, last residence Pardeeville there.⁹⁹⁶ She married 1924 PAUL FINGER,⁹⁹⁷ possibly the son of Minnie (-?-) (Finger) Beer.⁹⁹⁸ Paul was born 11 June 1899 in Germany;⁹⁹⁹ died 5 June 1974 in Wyocena, Columbia County, Wisconsin;¹⁰⁰⁰ and was buried with his wife at Pardeeville Cemetery, Columbia County.¹⁰⁰¹ He was at that time

---

⁹⁹² Ralph Smith household, 1930 US census, Montello, Marquette County, Wisconsin, ED 7, sheet 2B, dwelling 45, family 47.

⁹⁹³ Ralph R. Smith household, 1940 US census, Green Lake village, Green Lake County, Wisconsin, ED 24-9, sheet 4B–5A, dwelling 97. Statewide figures from US Census Bureau, Census of Housing, Historical Census of Housing Tables, Median Home Values Unadjusted 1940 (https://www2.census.gov/programs-surveys/decennial/tables/time-series/coh-values/values-unadj.txt).

⁹⁹⁴ Ralph Ray Smith WW2 draft card, 27 April 1942, Green Lake County Local Board, serial #U1011; "US, World War II Draft Registration Cards, 1942" > Wisconsin > Smith–Sobek > Popp–Sparacino > images 171–72 of 2120 (ancestry.com).

⁹⁹⁵ "Academy Grads Meet for School Reunion," *Portage Daily Register* (Wisconsin), Saturday 31 August 1968, p. 6, cols. 4–5. Presumably one or both had studied there, but the article did not identify former students by name.

⁹⁹⁶ Bernice Finger index entry, US Social Security Death Index. Exact death date: "Mrs. Paul Finger," *Wisconsin State Journal* (Madison), Monday 31 July 1972, p. 2, col. 1.

⁹⁹⁷ "Mrs. Paul Finger," *Wisconsin State Journal* (Madison), Monday 31 July 1972, p. 2, col. 1.

⁹⁹⁸ Peter Beer household for second wife Minnie age 32 and stepson Paul Finger age 10, all born Germany, 1910 US census, Milwaukee, Milwaukee County, Wisconsin, Ward 9, ED 83, sheet 4A, dwelling 41, family 56.

⁹⁹⁹ Bernice and Paul Finger joint grave marker, image, Pardeeville Cemetery, Pardeeville, Wisconsin; memorials #151,521,344 and #151,521,343 respectively, by David Moll (findagrave.com). The exact birth and death dates and places do not appear on the marker and are not sourced.

¹⁰⁰⁰ "Paul Finger," *Portage Daily Register* (Wisconsin), Thursday 6 June 1974, p. 5, col. 1.

¹⁰⁰¹ Paul and Bernice Finger, joint grave marker, image, Pardeeville Cemetery, Columbia County, Wisconsin, memorials #151,521,344 and #151,521,343, for Paul and Bernice, respectively, by David Moll (findagrave.com).

a retired farmer of Wyocena.[1002] Curiously, Paul has not been found in the 1920, 1930, or 1940 censuses.

In 1910 Paul was ten years old, the stepson of German-born machinist Peter Beer, living in Milwaukee. Peter's wife Minnie, three years into her second marriage, may well have been Paul's mother.[1003] In 1942 Mrs. Minnie Beer of 2229 North First Street in Milwaukee was the person would always know his address,[1004] even though he was living almost 100 miles away in Pardeeville.

1918: as of 12 September, Paul was tall, of medium build, with grey eyes and light brown hair. Aged 19, he lived at 2434 North Avenue in Milwaukee, and worked as a farmer for Chas. Evert at the Milwaukee County Farm in Wauwatosa.[1005]

1925, May: Paul and Bernice were living in Milwaukee and visiting in Pardeeville.[1006]

1931: the family moved to her parents' in Pardeeville.[1007]

1933, February 25: Paul was elected one of four delegates from the Wyocena and Pacific local to attend the Farmers Union convention to be held at Portage, where "much of advantage to the farmer in this time of depression may be learned."[1008]

1942, January 15: the Fingers were back in Milwaukee.[1009] That fall Paul was back in Pardeeville.[1010]

[1002] "Paul Finger," *Portage Daily Register* (Wisconsin), Thursday 6 June 1974, p. 5, col. 1.
[1003] Peter Beer household for second wife Minnie age 32 and stepson Paul Finger age 10, all born Germany, 1910 US census, Milwaukee, Milwaukee County, Wisconsin, Ward 9, ED 83, sheet 4A, dwelling 41, family 56.
[1004] Paul Finger WW2 draft card, 16 February 1942, Portage local board, serial #1121, order #10,895; "US, World War II Draft Cards, 1940–1947" > Wisconsin > DuQuayne–Genske > Filipowicz–Finn > images 981–82 of 1951 (ancestry.com).
[1005] Paul Finger WWI draft card, serial #5232, order #1353, Local Board, Division #4, Milwaukee, Wisconsin, 12 September 1918; "US, World War I Draft Registration Cards, 1917–1918" > Wisconsin > Milwaukee City > 04 > Draft Card F > image 106 of 410 (ancestry.com).
[1006] "Pardeeville," *Portage Daily Register* (Wisconsin), Thursday 21 May 1925, p. 4, col. 4.
[1007] "Pardeeville," *Portage Daily Register* (Wisconsin), Friday 17 July 1931, p. 6, col. 2.
[1008] "Wyocena-Pacific Farmers Union Business Meeting," *Portage Daily Register* (Wisconsin), Wednesday 1 March 1933, p. 4, col. 1. Wyocena and Pacific are adjacent townships just east of Portage, near the center of Columbia County.
[1009] "Pardeeville," *Portage Daily Register* (Wisconsin), Thursday 15 January 1942, p. 4, col. 2.
[1010] "For Sale" want ads, *Portage Daily Register* (Wisconsin), Wednesday 22 September 1943, p. 5, col. 1.

1942, February 16: Paul was 5 feet 9 inches tall, weighed 180, had blue eyes and brown hair, living in Pardeeville, Columbia County, Wisconsin.[1011]

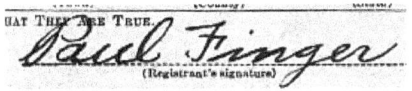

Bernice and Paul farmed "for many years" in Wyocena Township, Columbia County; she was a member of the United Methodist Church.[1012] Bernice cared for her unmarried aunt Mary I. Smith (Chapter 24) in the winter of 1954–55.[1013] In the middle 1940s and for at least the next ten years, Paul frequently advertised feeder pigs and white leghorn pullets for sale, and later some farm machinery, including dairy equipment and electric brooders.[1014]

In 1952 Bernice was one of several local people featured in a full-page newspaper advertisement for Siegler oil heaters, which were said to cook, provide hot water, and heat up to three rooms. "Although our Siegler heater is new," she said, "we are already convinced that it will do a fine job of heating our house including keeping the floors warm and it is very easy to keep its heavy porcelain finish spotlessly clean."[1015] In the fall of 1962 they took a vacation trip north to Sault St. Marie, "the new bridge," and the straits of Mackinac.[1016]

[1011] Paul Finger WW2 draft card, 16 February 1942, Portage local board, serial #1121, order #10,895; "US, World War II Draft Cards, 1940–1947" > Wisconsin > DuQuayne–Genske > Filipowicz–Finn > images 981–82 of 1951 (ancestry.com).
[1012] "Mrs. Paul Finger," *Wisconsin State Journal* (Madison), Monday 31 July 1972, p. 2, col. 1.
[1013] "Miss Mary I. Smith Dies at Hospital, Services Thursday," *Portage Daily Register* (Wisconsin), Wednesday 9 February 1955, p. 3, col. 2.
[1014] For example, *Portage Daily Register* (Wisconsin) classified advertisements: Wednesday 22 September 1943, p. 5, col. 1; Thursday 17 March 1955, p. 5, col. 4.
[1015] "What Your Neighbors Think of Their Siegler Heater," advertisement, *Portage Daily Register* (Wisconsin), Monday 20 October 1952, p. 8.
[1016] Mrs. Gordon Fuller, "Wyocena Area News," *Portage Daily Register* (Wisconsin), Friday 5 October 1962, p. 4, cols. 5–6.

Chapter 23

Third Generation

Eva Florence Smith–Richard Albert Beichl Family
parents at chapter 6

From selling hardware to selling real estate

23. EVA FLORENCE[3] **SMITH** (*Alice*[2] *Scholes, Ann*[1] *Mills, Samuel*[A])
Birth: July 1875 in Wisconsin[1017]
Death: 3 January 1962 in Beaver Dam, Dodge County, Wisconsin[1018]
Burial: as E. Florence Beichl, Section 10, Oakwood Cemetery, Beaver Dam, Dodge County[1019]
Spouse: **RICHARD ALBERT BEICHL** married second about September 1909[1020]
Spouse's parents: Edward and Teressia (-?-) Beichl
Spouse's birth: 19 October 1859 in Trenton, Dodge County, Wisconsin[1021]

[1017] E. Florence Smith grave marker (1875–1952), image, Oakwood Cemetery, Beaver Dam, Dodge County, Wisconsin, Section 10, memorial #8,352,239 by Cemetery Walker and Tara Bandekow (findagrave.com).[1017] Also, Florence Smith, servant, in Robert Reley household, 1900 US census, Beaver Dam, Dodge County, Wisconsin, ED 80, sheet 20A–B, dwelling 398, family 422.
[1018] Eva F. Beichl age 86, death index entry, certificate #507; "Wisconsin, Death Index, 1959–1997" > 1979–1997 > B > image 166 of 1941 (ancestry.com). Also, Mrs. Gordon Fuller, "Wyocena Area News," *Portage Daily Register* (Wisconsin), Friday 5 January 1962, p. 4, col. 5.
[1019] E. Florence Smith grave marker (1875–1952), image, Oakwood Cemetery, Beaver Dam, Dodge County, Wisconsin, Section 10, memorial #8,352,239 by Cemetery Walker and Tara Bandekow (findagrave.com).
[1020] Richard Beichl household for Florence age 35, married 7/12 years, 1910 US census, Beaver Dam, Dodge County, Wisconsin, Ward 8, ED 5, dwelling 144, family 145.
[1021] Edward Beichl household for son Richard age 20, 1880 US census, Trenton, Dodge County, Wisconsin, ED 26, p. 23 or 431C, dwelling 194, family 202.

Spouse's death: 12 February 1927, said to be 67 years, 3 months, 23 days[1022]
Spouse's burial: Section 10, Oakwood Cemetery, Beaver Dam, Dodge County, Wisconsin[1023]

Richard married first 20 January 1887 to Line Anna Hofferbert, who was born 12 August 1861 in Chambersburg, Franklin County, Pennsylvania; died 2 September 1900; and was buried at Oakwood Cemetery, Beaver Dam, Wisconsin, 5 September.[1024] Her parents were George and Barbara (-?-) Hofferbert.[1025] Their children, all born in Beaver Dam, Dodge County, Wisconsin, were: Theodor Eduard Beichl, born 16 February 1889, baptized 7 April;[1026] Johannes Nicolaus Alexander Beichl, born 9 January 1894, baptized 5 February;[1027] and Richard Keil Emerson Beichl, born in 16 October 1895, baptized 8? December.[1028]

[1022] Richard Albert Beichl death and burial, Beaver Dam Lutheran Church records p. 367, 1927, item 5; "US, Evangelical Lutheran Church in America Church Records, 1781–1969"> Congregational Records > Wisconsin > Beaver Dam > First > image 528 of 862 (ancestry.com).

[1023] Richard Albert Beichl grave marker, image, Oakwood Cemetery, Beaver Dam, Dodge County, Wisconsin, memorial #8,352,238 by Cemetery Walker and Tara Bandekow (findagrave.com).

[1024] Line Anna Hofferbert Beichl birth, marriage, death, and burial record, p. 337, 1900, item 12; Beaver Dam Lutheran Church death records p. 24, 1889, item 6; "US, Evangelical Lutheran Church in America Church Records, 1781–1969"> Congregational Records > Wisconsin > Beaver Dam > First > image 327 of 862 (ancestry.com).

[1025] Richard Albert Beichl–Line Anna Hofferbert marriage 20 January 1887, Beaver Dam Lutheran Church records, p. 230, Copulation 1887, item 1; "US, Evangelical Lutheran Church in America Church Records, 1781–1969"> Congregational Records > Wisconsin > Beaver Dam > First > image 273 of 862 (ancestry.com).

[1026] Theodor Eduard Beichl birth and baptism, Beaver Dam Lutheran Church death records p. 24, 1889, item 6; "US, Evangelical Lutheran Church in America Church Records, 1781–1969"> Congregational Records > Wisconsin > Beaver Dam > First > image 198 of 862 (ancestry.com).

[1027] Johannes Nicolaus Alexander Beichl birth and baptism, Beaver Dam Lutheran Church records p. 62, 1894 item 8; "US, Evangelical Lutheran Church in America Church Records, 1781–1969"> Congregational Records > Wisconsin > Beaver Dam > First > image 217 of 862 (ancestry.com).

[1028] Richard Keil Emerson Beichl birth and baptism, Beaver Dam Lutheran Church records p. 75, 1895 item 42; "US, Evangelical Lutheran Church in America Church Records, 1781–1969"> Congregational Records > Wisconsin > Beaver Dam > First > image 223 of 862 (ancestry.com).

Reportedly Richard Beichl and John Wollenburg were co-owners of a hardware store in Beaver Dam from 1885 to 1903.[1029] In 1900 and 1910 Richard was a hardware merchant who owned his own home; Lina died soon after the 1900 census.

In 1910 newlyweds Richard and Florence had been married about seven months and were residing at 212 Grove Street in Beaver Dam, a house Richard owned without a mortgage. The household included two teenage stepsons and Richard's brother Otto.[1030] In 1920 they were in the same house; Richard and son were both real estate agents.[1031] Florence completed eight years of schooling.[1032]

Florence in the years following Richard's death lived in Beaver Dam, Dodge County, Wisconsin:

1930: a widow at the 212 Grove Street house, valued at $6000; she had a radio set and three female lodgers—a widow, a school teacher, and a clerk in a stove factory.[1033]

1935–1940: a nurse in the household of Olga Pfeffer and son John, who worked as an auditor in the stove factory.[1034]

1945: visited sister Mary Smith (Chapter 24) at 402 East Pleasant in Portage.[1035]

[1029] *Daily Citizen* (Beaver Dam, Wisconsin), Wednesday 21 November 1990, p. 17, col. 2.
[1030] Richard A. Beichl household, 1900 US census, Beaver Dam, Dodge County, Wisconsin, Ward 4, ED 82, sheet 12B, dwelling 279, family 295. Similarly, 1910, Ward 8, ED 5, sheet 15A, dwelling 144, family 145.
[1031] Richard A. Beichl household, 1920 US census, Beaver Dam, Dodge County, Wisconsin, Ward 8, ED 32, sheet 22B, dwelling 555, family 568.
[1032] Olga Pfeffer household for nurse Florence Brickle [Beichl], 1940 US census, Beaver Dam, Dodge County, Wisconsin, Ward 9, ED 14-10, sheet 71, dwelling 162.
[1033] Florence Beichl household, 1930 US census, Beaver Dam, Dodge County, Wisconsin, Ward 8, ED 9, sheet 16A, dwelling 390, family 399.
[1034] Olga Pfeffer household for nurse Florence Brickle [Beichl], 1940 US census, Beaver Dam, Dodge County, Wisconsin, Ward 9, ED 14-10, sheet 71, dwelling 162.
[1035] "Local Brevities," *Portage Daily Register* (Wisconsin), Thursday 15 March 1945, p. 3, col. 2.

1948, June 19: attended the joint 40th marriage anniversary celebration for Mr. and Mrs. Harry Russell and Mr. and Mrs. Fred Russell (Chapter 33) of Endeavor.[1036]

1949: "Mrs. E. C. Taylor, Mrs. Florence Beichl and Mrs. Catherine Broitzman were hostesses for a meeting of Circle 3, W.S.C.S. [Women's Society of Christian Service]."[1037]

February 1951: Florence, of Beaver Dam, was among those "from away" who attended her nephew Clinton Smith's funeral in Dalton—about 30 miles (Chapter 22, child i).[1038]

November 1951: Mrs. Fred Russell (Lillian, Chapter 33) of Endeavor hosted cousins—sisters Florence Beichl of Beaver Dam and Miss Mary Smith (Chapter 24) of Portage—Thursday to Saturday. Among the guests for a Friday lunch were first cousins Mrs. Lida Hume (Chapter 18) and Mrs. Elmer Scholes (Chapter 34), and niece Miss Olive Heames (Chapter 27, child ii).[1039]

Memorial Day 1955: "Mr. and Mrs. Sam Scholes of Beloit and Mrs. Florence Beichl of Beaver Dam spent the holiday weekend with the former's sister, Mrs. Fred Russell" (Chapters 35 and 33).[1040]

10 August 1957: "Mrs. Florence Beichl of Beaver Dam, and Mrs. Ralph Smith (Chapter 22, child ii) of Green Lake, spent Saturday afternoon and were supper guests of Mrs. Fred Russell (Chapter 33). They also called on Mrs. Hattie Schwemerlein (Chapter 28) and Mrs. Frank Harrison."[1041]

[1036] "Two Couples Observe 40th Wedding Day," *Portage Daily Register & Democrat* (Wisconsin), Friday 25 June 1948, p. 6, cols. 3–5.
[1037] "Memories: 1939–1989…55 Years Ago 1949," *Beaver Dam Daily Citizen* (Wisconsin), Saturday 28 February 2004, p. 3, col. 2.
[1038] "Obituary: Clinton William Smith," *Portage Daily Register* (Wisconsin), Wednesday 28 February 1951, p. 6, cols. 5–7.
[1039] Mrs. Fred Russell, "Endeavor," *Portage Daily Register* (Wisconsin), Wednesday 14 November 1951, p. 8, cols. 1 and 2. Similarly, 15 November, p. 14, col. 2.
[1040] Mrs. Fred Russell, "Endeavor," *Portage Daily Register* (Wisconsin), Thursday 2 June 1955, p. 11, col. 1.
[1041] "Endeavor Locals," *Portage Daily Register* (Wisconsin), Thursday 15 August 1957, p. 8, col. 1.

11 September 1958: "Mrs. Florence Beichl, Beaver Dam, is spending a few days with her cousin, Mrs. Lillian Russell" (Chapter 33).[1042]

30 September 1960: "Mr. and Mrs. Robert Smith, Mr. and Mrs. Maurice Nelli and family and Mrs. Barry Ramsey and baby daughter, all of Beloit; also Mr. and Mrs. Paul Finger of Wyocena and Mrs. Florence Beichl of Beaver Dam, called on Mrs. Fred Russell Sunday afternoon" (Chapter 33).[1043]

April 1961: "Mrs. Florence Beichl of Beaver Dam is spending this week with her niece, Mr. and Mrs. Paul Finger" (Chapter 22, child iii).[1044]

October 1961: "Mr. and Mrs. Paul Finger [Chapter 22, child iii] drove to Beaver Dam Sunday to see her aunt, Mrs. Florence Beichl and then to Princeton to see her brother, Mr. and Mrs. Ralph Smith."[1045]

November 1961: "Mr. and Mrs. Paul Finger drove to Beaver Dam Sunday to call on her aunt, Mrs. Florence Beichl at the Lutheran hospital." Florence was "slightly improved, but she still remains in a critical condition."[1046] She died three days into the New Year.[1047]

[1042] Mrs. Gust Peterson, "Endeavor Area News," *Portage Daily Register* (Wisconsin), Thursday 11 September 1958, p. 12, col. 3.
[1043] Mrs. Clayton S. Mills, "Endeavor Area News," *Portage Daily Register* (Wisconsin), Friday 30 September 1960, p. 9, cols. 2–3.
[1044] Mrs. Gordon Fuller, "Wyocena Area News," *Portage Daily Register* (Wisconsin), Saturday 29 April 1961, p. 6, col. 3.
[1045] Mrs. Gordon Fuller, "Wyocena Area News," *Portage Daily Register* (Wisconsin), Saturday 7 October 1961, p. 6, col. 3.
[1046] Mrs. Gordon Fuller, "Wyocena Area News," *Portage Daily Register* (Wisconsin), Friday 1 December 1961, p. 4, col. 6.
[1047] Eva F. Beichl age 86, death index entry, certificate #507; "Wisconsin, Death Index, 1959–1997" > 1979–1997 > B > image 166 of 1941 (ancestry.com). Also, Mrs. Gordon Fuller, "Wyocena Area News," *Portage Daily Register* (Wisconsin), Friday 5 January 1962, p. 4, col. 5.

Chapter 24

Third Generation

Mary Irene Smith Family
<u>parents at Chapter 6</u>

"Farm laborer" and housekeeper

24. MARY IRENE³ SMITH (*Alice² Scholes, Ann¹ Mills, Samuel^A*)
Birth: 17 March 1877 in Wisconsin[1048]
Death: 8 February 1955 in Portage, Columbia County, Wisconsin, "after a long illness"
Burial: Moundville Cemetery, Marquette County, Wisconsin[1049]

Mary completed five years of schooling.[1050]

1910: both Mary and brother Robert were "farm laborers" in their mother's household.

1920: in her widowed mother's rented household, Mary was listed as a widow,[1051] perhaps a clerical error by the census enumerator.

1930: single and a "relative," she was keeping house at 805 De Witt Street in Portage for 73-year-old Charles W. Smith, a

---

[1048] For March 1877, Joseph Smith household for Mary I. age 23, 1900 US census, Moundville, Marquette County, Wisconsin, ED 93, sheet 1B, dwelling/family 14. Also, Scholes ledger book, 65, giving exact birth date and stating "single."
[1049] "Mary I. Smith," *Wisconsin State Journal* (Madison), Wednesday 9 February 1955, p. 4, col. 2. Also, "Miss Mary I. Smith Dies at Hospital[,] Services, Thursday," *Portage Daily Register* (Wisconsin), 9 February 1955, p. 3, col. 2.
[1050] Mary I. Smith, single, in Columbia County Home for the Poor, 1940 US census, Wyocena, Columbia County, Wisconsin, ED 11-38, sheet 6A, line 31.
[1051] Alice Smith household for daughter Mary I., widow, 1920 US census, Moundville Township, Marquette County, Wisconsin, ED 133, dwelling 5, family 6. To date no evidence has been found that this was other than a clerical error.

widowed Wisconsin-born commercial salesman in groceries and fruit.[1052] Charles W. was the oldest son of John S. and Electa (Condit) Smith, born 24 July 1857.[1053] Charles married Elizabeth E. (-?-) Smith about 1880 and they had five children, four of whom were living in 1900.[1054] How Charles was related to Mary has not been determined.

1931: When Charles's employer since 1904, Edward Dewey and Sons Wholesale Grocery, closed its line of business, he associated with the local John J. Welsh insurance agency.[1055] He died 23 April 1939.[1056]

1935: Mary was in Portage.

1940: Mary, age 63 and single, was a resident of the County Home for the Poor, at Wyocena, Columbia County.[1057]

1950s: in the Portage hospital October 1950 and again January 1954;[1058] and with a niece, Mrs. Paul Finger (Chapter 22, child iii), in December 1954 and January 1955.[1059]

[1052] Charles W. Smith household for "relative" Mary I. Smith, single, 1930 US census, Portage, Columbia County, Wisconsin, Ward 3, ED 26, sheet 83, dwelling 192, family 239, at 805 De Witt Street.

[1053] Jotham Halsey Condit, *Genealogical Record of the Condit Family: Descendants of John Conditt, a native of Great Britain, who settled in Newark, N.J., 1678 to 1885* (Newark, New Jersey: Ward & Tichenor, 1885), 367, entry #314; "North America, Family Histories, 1500–2000" > C > Cu > Genealogical record… > image 367 of 470 under "Philip, Fifth Grandson of John" (ancestry.com).

[1054] Charles W. Smith household for wife Elizabeth E. married 20 years, 1900 US census, Portage, Columbia County, Wisconsin, Ward 3, sheet 13B, dwelling 286, family 297 on Franklin Street (ancestry.com).

[1055] "Grocery Salesman Will Take Up Active Insurance Work," *Portage Register-Democrat* (Wisconsin), Friday 8 May 1931, p. 4, col. 3.

[1056] "Veteran Salesman, Charles W. Smith, Is Buried Today," *Portage Daily Register* (Wisconsin), Wednesday 26 April 1939, p. 1, col. 2.

[1057] Mary I. Smith, single, in Columbia County Home for the Poor, 1940 US census, Wyocena, Columbia County, Wisconsin, ED 11-38, sheet 6A, line 31.

[1058] "Hospital Admissions," *Portage Daily Register* (Wisconsin), Monday 16 October 1950, p. 3, col. 5. Similarly, "Hospital Releases," Monday 4 January 1954, p. 3, col. 8.

[1059] "Mary I. Smith," *Wisconsin State Journal* (Madison), Wednesday 9 February 1955, p. 4, col. 2. Also, "Miss Mary I. Smith Dies at Hospital[,] Services, Thursday," *Portage Daily Register* (Wisconsin), 9 February 1955, p. 3, col. 2.

Chapter 25

Third Generation

Robert Joseph Smith–Myrtle M. Page Family
parents at Chapter 6

Donald served as "12th Ward alderman and president of the [Madison] City Council in the 1960s"

25. Robert Joseph³ Smith (*Alice² Scholes, Ann¹ Mills, Samuel^A*)
Birth: 7 May 1892 in Wisconsin[1060]
Death: 25 August 1976 in Portage, Wisconsin
Burial: Moundville Cemetery[1061]
Spouse: **Myrtle M. Page**, married 13 January 1914 in Janesville[1062]
Spouse's parents: Charles and Elizabeth (Perkins) Page
Spouse's birth: 17 November 1895 in Endeavor
Spouse's death: 8 February 1984 in Clinton, Rock County, Wisconsin
Spouse's burial: Moundville Cemetery[1063]

Robert and Myrtle both completed eight years of education.[1064]

Robert J Smith
(signature or mark)

[1060] Robert Joseph Smith WWI draft card, 5 June 1917, Moundville local board, serial #523, order #26; "US, World War I Draft Registration Cards, 1917–1918" > Marquette County > ALL > draft card S > image 159 of 245 (ancestry.com). Also, Joseph Smith household for Robert J. age 8, 1900 US census, Moundville, Marquette County, Wisconsin, ED 93, sheet 1B, dwelling/family 14.
[1061] "Obituaries . . . Robert Smith," *Portage Daily Register* (Wisconsin), Wednesday 25 August 1976, p. 5, col. 1.
[1062] "Robert Smiths Have Anniversary Party," *Capital Times* (Madison, Wisconsin), Tuesday 15 January 1974, p. 7, col. 1.
[1063] "Myrtle M. Smith," *Portage Daily Register* (Wisconsin), Friday 10 February 1984, p. 16, col. 2.
[1064] Robert Smith household, 1940 US census, Beloit, Rock County, Wisconsin, Ward 6, ED 53-7, sheet 13A, dwelling 304.

1917 June 5: Robert claimed an exemption from the WWI draft "to work farm." He was tall, of medium build, with blue eyes and light brown hair.[1065]

1920: Robert was farming in Marquette County[1066]

1930: Out of farming, the family was living at 1701 Prairie Avenue in Beloit, Rock County, and owned a radio set. Robert was a gas engine mechanic.[1067]

1940: they were renting at 921 Milwaukee Road in Beloit for $25 a month; he was employed as a church janitor, earning $1080 during 1939.[1068]

1942 April 27: He was employed at "Fairbanks Morse" in Beloit. He weighed 175 pounds, stood 5 feet 11 inches tall, with blue eyes, brown hair, and a small scar on left arm.[1069]

1976: At his death he was a member of the 25-Year Club at Beloit's Fairbanks-Morris Foundry.[1070]

[1065] Robert Joseph Smith WWI draft card, 5 June 1917, Moundville local board, serial #523, order #26; US, World War I Draft Registration Cards, 1917–1918 > Marquette County > ALL > draft card S > image 159 of 245 (ancestry.com).
[1066] Robert J. Smith household, 1920 US census, Moundville Township, Marquette County, Wisconsin, ED 133, sheet 1A, dwelling 10, family 11.
[1067] Robert Smith household, 1930 US census, Beloit, Rock County, Wisconsin, Ward 4, ED 6, sheet 12A, dwelling 273, family 291.
[1068] Robert Smith household, 1940 US census, Beloit, Rock County, Wisconsin, Ward 6, ED 53-7, sheet 13A, dwelling 304.
[1069] Robert Joseph Smith WWII draft card, local board 3, Beloit, 27 April 1942; "US, World War II Draft Registration Cards, 1942" > Wisconsin > Smith–Sobek > Popp–Sparacino > images 291–92 of 2120 (ancestry.com).
[1070] "Obituaries . . . Robert Smith," *Portage Daily Register* (Wisconsin), Wednesday 25 August 1976, p. 5, col. 1. Beloit's 1960 city directory includes a listing and advertisement for "Fairbanks Morse & Co., Beloit Division," a manufacturer of hydraulic machinery, electric motors and generators, diesel engines, and the like—but no reference whatsoever for a Fairbanks-Morris Foundry (*Polk's Beloit [Rock County, Wis.] City Directory 1960*, p. 5 of manufacturers' department, image 62 of 530). Similarly, the Beloit Local History Digitization has many hits for Fairbanks Morse (uwdc.library.wisc.edu/collections/localhistories/beloitlochist) and none for Fairbanks Morris—perhaps a casual mispronunciation and occasional misprint for Fairbanks Morse?

Among the children of Robert and Myrtle, born in Wisconsin:

i. DONALD HARRISON[4] SMITH (*Robert J.[3] Smith, Alice[2] Scholes, Ann[1] Mills, Samuel[A]*) was born 10 October 1915 and died 21 January 1995 in a Wisconsin Dells nursing home. He married 23 November 1938 CHARLOTTE ANNIE THOMPSON,[1071] born 14 June 1917 in Manchester, Boone County, Illinois, and died 30 December 2000, the daughter of Edward and Edith (Farmer) Thompson.[1072]

He and Charlotte both completed four years of high school. In 1935 she was living in Capron, Boone County, Illinois. In 1940 they were renting an apartment at 622 Milwaukee in Janesville, Rock County, Wisconsin, for $25 a month. He was a salesman for a wholesale bakery; she was a retail clerk. He earned $1868 for 52 weeks in 1939, she earned $325 for 26 weeks.[1073]

As of 16 October 1940, he was 5 feet 11 inches tall and weighed 185 pounds; he had blue eyes and red hair, as well as a stiff forefinger on his right arm, a tattoo on his left arm, and a small scar over his right eye. He was working for the Colvin Baking Company (300 East Milwaukee), and living at 403 Pease Court in Janesville, with telephone number 4447W.[1074]

In the early 1950s Donald worked with the Rock County Sheriff's Department, and owned and operated retail grocery stores in Clinton and Janesville. The family moved to Madison in 1955 or 1956, where Dorothy worked 25 years in the state Department of Revenue, and Donald worked in retail sales for Oscar Mayer and American Family. "He was the 12th Ward alderman and president of the City Council in the 1960s and served as a Dane County supervisor in the late 1970s and early 1980s. He was a member of the Lakeview Lutheran Church."[1075]

[1071] "Obituaries . . . Smith, Donald H.," *Wisconsin State Journal* (Madison), 25 January 1995, p. 4D or 29, col. 5.
[1072] Charlotte Annie Thompson index entry, "US, Social Security Applications and Claims Index, 1936–2007" (ancestry.com).
[1073] Donald Smith household, 1940 US census, Janesville, Rock County, Wisconsin, Ward 4, ED 53-34, sheet 7B, dwelling 209.
[1074] Donald Harrison Smith WW2 draft card, serial #12, order #572, 16 October 1940, Janesville local board, "US WWII Draft Cards Young Men, 1940–1947" > Wisconsin > Schultz–Stemmler > Smith–Smith > images 1304–5 of 1930 (ancestry.com).
[1075] "Obituaries . . . Smith, Donald H.," *Wisconsin State Journal* (Madison), 25 January 1995, p. 4D or 29, col. 5. Also, Robert J. Smith household, 1920 US census, Moundville Township, Marquette County, Wisconsin, ED 133, sheet 1A, dwelling 10, family 11. For 1955 move to Madison, "Obituaries . . . Smith, Charlotte," *Wisconsin State Journal* (Madison), 31 January 2000, p. 17 or B5, col. 2.

ii. ELWYN[4] ROBERT "RED" SMITH (*Robert J.[3] Smith, Alice[2] Scholes, Ann[1] Mills, Samuel[A]*) was born 6 February 1920 in Moundville and died 10 July 2004.[1076] He married 4 August 1943 in Bremerton, Kitsap County, Washington, RUTH RACHEL ETTA SCHOVILLE. Their affidavits were made 29 July and 2 August.[1077] Reportedly she was born in Soldiers Grove, Crawford County, Wisconsin, 23 January 1927, the daughter of Lloyd and Maida (Bailey) Schoville; died 14 January 2016; and was buried at Floral Lawn Cemetery, South Beloit, Winnebago County, Illinois.[1078]

As of 1 July 1941, Elwyn was 6 feet 2 inches and weighed 175 pounds. He had hazel eyes, brown hair, and a tattoo on his right arm. He was a machinist employed by Warner(?) Electric Brake in South Beloit, Illinois (just over the state line).[1079] Soon thereafter he was stationed in Hawaii, as he served in the US Marine Corps from 29 December 1941 to 5 January 1945.[1080]

[1076] Elwyn Robert Smith index entry, "US, Social Security Applications and Claims, 1936–2007" (ancestry.com). Also, Robert Smith household for son Elwin age 10, 1930 US census, Beloit, Rock County, Wisconsin, Ward 4, ED 6, sheet 12A, dwelling 273, family 291.

[1077] Elwyn Robert Smith–Ruth Rachel Etta Schoville affidavits and marriage license #15908, 29 July 1942, Kitsap County, Washington; "Washington, County Marriages, 1855–2008" > Kitsap > Marriage applications 1943, vol. 23, #15501–16007 > image 506 of 624, DGS #4,255,796 (familysearch.org). Both resided in Beloit. Also, "Obituaries . . . Smith, Donald H.," *Wisconsin State Journal* (Madison), 25 January 1995, p. 4D or 29, col. 5.

[1078] Ruth R. Schoville Smith, no image of grave marker, Floral Lawn Cemetery, South Beloit, Winnebago County, Illinois, memorial #13,072,747 by william wisen, including obituary-style information but no source citations.

[1079] Elwyn Robert Smith, WW2 draft card, serial #S-14, order #S2354, Local Board 3, 1 July 1941; "US WWII Draft Cards Young Men, 1940–1947" > Wisconsin > Schultz–Stemmler > Smith–Smith > images 1855–56 of 1930 (ancestry.com).

[1080] Elwyn Smith entry, "US, Department of Veterans Affairs, BIRLS Death File, 1850–2010" (ancestry.com).

Chapter 26
Third Generation

Nettie A. Scholes–Thomas Clarence Moran Family
<u>parents at Chapter 7</u>

"In 1940 Allan was a union organizer in an iron foundry"

26. NETTIE A.³ **SCHOLES** (*Robert*² *Scholes, Ann*¹ *Mills, Samuel*ᴬ)
Birth: reportedly 21 October 1869 in Marathon County, Wisconsin (age 28 in probate 24 October 1898)[1081]
Death: 12 July 1952 in Wauwatosa, Milwaukee County, Wisconsin
Burial: Prairie Home Cemetery, Waukesha, Waukesha County, Wisconsin[1082]
Spouse: **THOMAS CLARENCE MORAN,** married 1 January 1895 in Marquette County, Wisconsin
Spouse's parents: Stephen and Mary (Calvey) Moran[1083]
Spouse's birth: 1862, reportedly 4 August in Columbia County, Wisconsin
Spouse's death: 1923, reportedly 14 July in Waukesha, Waukesha County, Wisconsin
Spouse's burial: Prairie Home Cemetery, Waukesha[1084]

Nettie completed eight years of school.[1085]

[1081] Robert Scholes probate, Marquette County, Wisconsin, Box 9, file 481; "Wisconsin, Wills and Probate Records, 1800–1987" > Marquette > Probate Records Box 7 File 420–Box 9 File 522 > image 1443 of 1775 (ancestry.com).
[1082] Nettie Scholes Moran grave marker, image, Prairie Home Cemetery, Waukesha, Waukesha County, Wisconsin, memorial #117,539,292 by KJS (findagrave.com).
[1083] Nettie A. Scholes–Thomas C. Moran marriage index entry, 1 January 1895, Marquette County, Wisconsin, citing "Wisconsin, County Marriages, 1836–1911," FHL #1,292,024, DGS #7,615,097, image 1883 (familysearch.org/ark:/61903/1:1:XRNY-SXN).
[1084] Thomas C. Moran grave marker, image, Prairie Home Cemetery, Waukesha, Waukesha County, Wisconsin, memorial #117,532,329 by KJS (findagrave.com).
[1085] Nettie Moran household, 1940 US census, Waukesha, Waukesha County, Wisconsin, Ward 6, ED 67-53, sheets 1A–B, dwelling 135.

1895: Around the time of their marriage, Thomas was an "engineer" at the "State Ind. School," where he also resided.[1086] This was the Wisconsin Industrial School for Boys, first founded in 1860 or 1861; in 1895 it housed 375 boys in several buildings on West College Avenue.[1087] Two of the buildings, now on the National Register of Historic Places, are still in use.[1088]

1896: Oldest son Allan born 28 February at 135 East Park Avenue in Waukesha, Waukesha County, Wisconsin.[1089]

1897: Thomas C. Moran and Fred M. Ploss were in the steam heating business at 534 Main in Waukesha; the Morans lived at 110 East Main.[1090] Neither family was present in 1899.

1900: Father Thomas worked as a steamfitter in Waukesha; they rented a house at 1 Millers Court.[1091]

1901: Ploss and Moran were at 534 West Main, now in the plumbing business. Morans lived at 123 East Park.[1092]

June 1903: Nettie and children visited the E. C. Moran family (Thomas's brother) in Portage.[1093] Ploss and Moran were absent from the 1903 city directory.

[1086] Thomas C. Moran entry, *Wright's Directory of Waukesha, 1895*, p. 90, image 44 of 185; also, p. 21, image 5 of 185 (ancestry.com).
[1087] For much more information, "Wisconsin Industrial School History" (linkstothepast.com/waukesha/scindboy.php).
[1088] Allume Architects, "Building of the Week—Wisconsin Industrial School for Boys 10/1/18" (http://allumearchitects.com/blog-post/building-week-%E2%80%93-wisconsin-industrial-school-boys-0).
[1089] "Obituary…Allan C. Moran," *Waukesha Daily Freeman* (Wisconsin), Wednesday 16 February 1966, p. 16, col. 3. Also, Thomas C. Moran household for son Allen, 1900 US census, Waukesha, Waukesha County, Wisconsin, Ward 6, ED 143, sheet 11A, dwelling 248, family 286.
[1090] Moran and Ploss entries, *Wright's Directory of Waukesha for 1897–98* (Milwaukee: A. G. Wright, 1897), pp. 109 and 117, images 54 and 58 of 98 (ancestry.com).
[1091] Thomas C. Moran household, 1900 US census, Waukesha, Waukesha County, Wisconsin, Ward 6, ED 143, sheet 11A, dwelling 248, family 286.
[1092] Moran and Ploss entries, *Wright's Directory of Waukesha for 1901–02* (Milwaukee: A. G. Wright, 1901), pp. 91 and 98, images 40 and 44 of 98 (ancestry.com).
[1093] "Tales of the Town," *Portage Daily Democrat* (Wisconsin), Monday 29 June 1903, p. 3, col. 1.

1906: Thomas's name was in bold type in "plumbing and heating," at the same business and residential addresses as 1901.[1094]

1909: Thomas was in plumbing, with no bold type, at the same addresses as 1901.[1095]

July 1909: "Thomas C. Moran, a brother of E. C. Moran of this city [Portage, Columbia County], has entered the state sanitarium at Wales, near Waukesha [Waukesha County], to be treated for tuberculosis."[1096]

1910: Thomas was a plumber with his own shop, and they owned their house without a mortgage at 123 East Park Avenue in Waukesha.[1097]

1911: Thomas was a plumber but with no separate business address; similarly in 1913, when son Allan was listed as a student.[1098]

1915: Thomas was a grocer at 534 West Main (no separate residential address given) the same location that he and Ploss had worked out of a decade or so earlier. Both Lelah and Allan were students.[1099]

1917: Same location, with Allan now a laborer.[1100]

[1094] Moran entry, *Wright's Directory of Waukesha for 1906–07* (Milwaukee: A. G. Wright, 1906), p. 120, image 63 of 121 (ancestry.com).
[1095] Moran entry, *Wright's Directory of Waukesha for 1909–10* (Milwaukee: A. G. Wright, 1909), p. 125, image 60 of 196 (ancestry.com).
[1096] "Brief News Notes of the City," *Portage Daily Register* (Wisconsin), Friday 9 July 1909, p. 3, col. 4.
[1097] Thomas C. Moran household, 1910 US census, Waukesha, Waukesha County, Wisconsin, Ward 6, ED 182, sheet 6A, dwelling 126, family 138.
[1098] Moran entry, *Wright's Directory of Waukesha for 1911–12* (Milwaukee: A. G. Wright, 1911), p. 127, image 64 of 139 (ancestry.com). Similarly, *1913–14*, p. 132, image 67 of 144.
[1099] Moran entry, *Wright's Directory of Waukesha for 1915–16* (Milwaukee: A. G. Wright, 1915), p. 146, image 74 of 125 (ancestry.com).
[1100] Moran entry, *Wright's Directory of Waukesha for 1917* (Milwaukee: A. G. Wright, 1917), p. 146, image 65 of 131 (ancestry.com).

1919: Same location, Thomas in bold type, Lelah a teacher, Allan "USA" (perhaps US Army in World War I).[1101]

1920: Thomas owned a different house at 396 Main Street, which doubled as a retail grocery.[1102]

1921: Thomas still worked at the grocery, same address, telephone 395-J. Also present were Nettie and Lelah (student).

1923: Same as 1921, except Lelah taught at Union School.[1103]

1925: Nettie, widowed since 1923, ran the grocery store at the same address.

1927 and 1929: Lelah was teaching at Union School.[1104]

1930: Nettie owned a $5000 house at 135 East Park Avenue in Waukesha. They owned a radio set, like most but not all of their near neighbors (as the enumerator traveled). Lelah was teaching in an "opportunity room." Brother Allen was a grocery salesman. His wife "Oliva" was enumerated in or near the household in a confusing manner.[1105]

1931: Lelah was teaching.

[1101] Moran entry, *Wright's Directory of Waukesha for 1919* (Milwaukee: A. G. Wright, 1919), p. 192, image 102 of 206 (ancestry.com).
[1102] Thomas Moran household, 1920 US census, Waukesha, Waukesha County, Wisconsin, Ward 6, ED 204, sheet 2B, dwelling 39, family 43.
[1103] Moran entry, *Wright's Directory of Waukesha for 1923* (Milwaukee: A. G. Wright, 1923), p. 224, image 119 of 242 (ancestry.com).
[1104] Thomas Moran entry, *Wright's Waukesha Directory 1921* (Milwaukee: Wright Directory Company, 1921), p. 225, image 118 of 238. Lelah was a student. Similarly, *1925*, pp. 184 and 349, images 100 and 182 of 237; Lelah was teaching at Union School. Similarly, *1927*, p. 246, image 127 of 285. Similarly, *1929*, p. 228, image 119 of 302.
[1105] Nettie Moran household, 1930 US census, Waukesha, Waukesha County, Wisconsin, Ward 6, ED 48, sheet 17A, dwelling 358, family 398. Olivia Moran, a "relative" age 38 and nine years married, but with no husband present, was next door at dwelling 357, family 397. She may perhaps have been renting a room, although the census has no such notation.

1934: Lelah was teaching at Union School. Allan and Olivia were there; he was a laborer.[1106]

March 1935: Nettie joined with several other children, grandchildren, and great-grandchildren for a party at Campbell's Hall in Endeavor, Marquette County, for her mother, Mrs. Caroline Ellison (Chapter 7), in honor of her 87th birthday.[1107]

1940: Nettie owned a $2500 house at 135 East Park Avenue in Waukesha, Waukesha County, Wisconsin.[1108] If the 1930 and 1940 census figures are reasonably accurate, the house lost half its value during the decade of the Great Depression. In 1940, the statewide average house value in Wisconsin was $3232.[1109]

December 1947: "Mrs. Thomas C. Moran" was "ill at her home" on Park Avenue in Waukesha, and daughter Lelah was visiting.[1110]

July 1950: Mrs. James Hollerup (Chapter 7, child v) and sister Mrs. Hattie Schwemerlein (Chapter 28) of Portage "left Monday to spend the week with Mrs. Hollerup's son Delmer and family and a sister, Mrs. Nettie Moran and other relatives in Waukesha."[1111]

December 1950: "Mrs. James Hollerup received word Thursday [30 November 1950] that her sister, Mrs. Nettie Moran of Waukesha, had fallen and broken her hip. Mrs. Moran will be remembered as Nettie Scholes."

[1106] *Wright's Waukesha Directory 1931*, p. 242, image 121 of 295. Similarly, *1934*, p. 233, image 115 of 288. Lelah was teaching at Barstow School; Allen C. (laborer) and wife Olivia were present as well.

[1107] "North Endeavor," *Portage Daily Register* (Wisconsin), Saturday 9 March 1935, p. 4, col. 5.

[1108] Nettie Moran household, 1940 US census, Waukesha, Waukesha County, Wisconsin, Ward 6, ED 67-53, sheets 1A–B, dwelling 135.

[1109] Statewide figures from US Census Bureau, Census of Housing, Historical Census of Housing Tables, Median Home Values Unadjusted 1940 (https://www2.census.gov/programs-surveys/decennial/tables/time-series/coh-values/values-unadj.txt).

[1110] "Personals," *Waukesha Daily Freeman* (Wisconsin), Thursday 18 December 1947, p. 5, col. 4.

[1111] Mrs. Fred Russell, "Endeavor," *Portage Daily Register* (Wisconsin), Wednesday 26 July 1950, p. 6, col. 5. Mrs. James Hollerup = Pearl Christi Ellison, half-sister of Hattie Schwemerlein.

March 1951: "Mr. and Mrs. Gust Peterson drove to Waukesha on Monday to visit Mrs. Peterson's aunt, Mrs. Nettie Moran, who is confined to the hospital with a broken hip."[1112]

Children of Nettie A.³ (Scholes) and Thomas C. Moran, all born in Wisconsin:

i. ALLAN CLARENCE⁴ MORAN (*Nettie³ Scholes, Robert² Scholes, Ann¹ Mills, Samuel^A*) was born 29 February 1896, at 135 East Park Avenue in Waukesha, Waukesha County, Wisconsin; died 15 February 1966 at the Veterans Administration hospital in Wood, Wood County, Wisconsin, last residence Milwaukee;[1113] and was buried at Prairie Home Cemetery, Waukesha.[1114] He married OLIVIA A. STEINMETZ 1920–21,[1115] the daughter of Theodore M. and Katherine (Schoenofen) Steinmetz. Olivia's parents were married in 1882 "at St. Lawrence." They had seven children.[1116] Olivia was born 1891, possibly 25 November in Wisconsin; died 1963, possibly 15 March in Wauwatosa, Milwaukee County, Wisconsin; and was buried at Prairie Home Cemetery, Waukesha, Waukesha County, Wisconsin.[1117]

In World War I, Allen was a private first class in Company E, 107th Engineers; they left Brest, France, on the S.S. *Haverford*, sailing 4 May 1919 and arriving in Philadelphia 18 May 1919.[1118]

The 1930 census taker may have been confused. Olivia and Allan were apparently living separately in adjacent houses, with Allan employed as

---

[1112] "Endeavor Locals," *Portage Daily Register* (Wisconsin), Thursday 15 March 1951, p. 10, col. 6.

[1113] "Obituary…Allan C. Moran," *Waukesha Daily Freeman* (Wisconsin), Wednesday 16 February 1966, p. 16, col. 3. Also, Thomas C. Moran household for son Allen, 1900 US census, Waukesha, Waukesha County, Wisconsin, Ward 6, ED 143, sheet 11A, dwelling 248, family 286.

[1114] Allan Clarence Moran grave marker, image, Prairie Home Cemetery, Waukesha, Wisconsin, memorial #117,539,245 by KJS (findagrave.com).

[1115] In 1930, Allan reported his first marriage ten years earlier, Olivia nine.

[1116] "Nonagenarian Celebrates 91st Birthday Wednesday," *Marshfield News-Herald* (Wisconsin), Thursday 15 February 1951, p. 7, cols. 2–3.

[1117] Olivia A. Moran grave marker, Prairie Home Cemetery, Waukesha, Wisconsin, image, memorial #117,539,300 by KJS (findagrave.com).

[1118] Allen C. Moran, #257684, "Passenger List of Organizations and Casuals Returning to the United States," sheet 6, 3rd class; "US Army Transport Service, Passenger Lists, 1910–1939" > Incoming > Haverford > 22 March 1919–1 August 1919 > image 599 of 733. (As of 20 June 2020, ancestry.com mislabeled this as Connecticut church abstracts.)

a grocery salesman in an apparent household headed by his mother Nettie.[1119]

In 1940 Allan was a union organizer in an iron foundry, living in his widowed mother's house at 135 East Park Avenue, which she owned and was valued at $2500.[1120] As of 27 April 1942 his employer was the International Brotherhood of Foundry Employees; it was headquartered in St. Louis; Allan's residence was in Waukesha. He was 5 feet 9 inches tall and weighed 135 pounds, with blue eyes, brown hair, and "webb toes" on both feet.[1121]

ii. LELA/LELAH N.[4] MORAN (*Nettie[3] Scholes, Robert[2] Scholes, Ann[1] Mills, Samuel[A]*) was born about April 1897 or possibly 1898;[1122] died reportedly 25 June 1962 in Wauwatosa, Milwaukee County, Wisconsin, and was buried at Valhalla Memorial Park, Milwaukee. She reportedly married 1944 as his second wife EDWARD PAUL DAHMS, son of Gustav Friedrich Ferdinand and Wilhelmina Louisa Augusta (Raddatz) Dahms.[1123] Edward was Milwaukee through and through: born there at 940 Greenfield Avenue 30 October 1893, died there 10 December 1974

[1119] All at 135 East Park Avenue: Nettie Moran household for daughter Lela and son Allan, 1930 US census, Waukesha, Waukesha County, Wisconsin, Ward 6, ED 48, sheet 17A, dwelling 358, family 398. On the preceding sheet Olivia is at 135 East Park Avenue but it's called dwelling 357, family 397, and she is described as a "relative" of the Klicko family at dwelling 356, family 396, sheet 16B. This looks more like a badly confused enumerator than a marital separation.

[1120] Nettie Moran household for son Allan, 1940 US census, Waukesha, Waukesha County, Wisconsin, Ward 6, ED 67-53, sheet 1A, dwelling 12. Also, statewide figures from US Census Bureau, Census of Housing, Historical Census of Housing Tables, Median Home Values Unadjusted 1940 (https://www2.census.gov/programs-surveys/decennial/tables/time-series/coh-values/values-unadj.txt).

[1121] Allen Clarence Moran WW2 draft card, Waukesha local board #1, 27 April 1942, serial #U3922; "US, World War II Draft Registration Cards, 1940–1947" > Monson–Moriarty > Marks–Popp > images 1291–92 of 2144 (ancestry.com).

[1122] Thomas C. Moran household for daughter Lela, 1900 US census, Waukesha, Waukesha County, Wisconsin, Ward 6, ED 143, sheet 11A, dwelling 248, family 286.

[1123] Edward Paul Dahms, no image of grave marker, Valhalla Memorial Park, Milwaukee, Milwaukee County, Wisconsin, memorial #120,477,928 by Leanne (findagrave.com). The information is unsourced.

in Milwaukee, and was buried at Valhalla Memorial Park there.[1124] Lelah completed five years of college. During the late 1920s and 1930s she taught in local schools (see mother Nettie's timeline above); in 1940 she was living with her widowed mother and brother, and working as a "counciling" (counseling?) teacher in the public schools. In the previous year she was paid $1800 for 36 weeks' work.[1125]

5 June 1917: Edward was medium tall and slender, with blue eyes and blonde hair. He was living at 478 16th Avenue, and worked as an assembler at the Milwaukee Works of International Harvester Company.[1126] In World War I he served in Company K of the 340th Infantry, being promoted from private to corporal about December 1917.[1127]

27 April 1942: he was 5 feet 7 inches tall, weighed 160 pounds, and had blue eyes and blonde hair still. He worked at the Milwaukee YMCA at 633 North 4th Street, and resided at 6831 Aetna Court in Wauwatosa.[1128]

Edward worked as a physical education instructor at the YMCA for 40 years (1918–1958). In 1953 he chaired the Wisconsin District AAU Gymnastic Committee.[1129] Fifteen years after his retirement he was still running a mile every day.[1130]

[1124] Edward Dahms, Milwaukee birth register 30 October 1893, #7816; "Milwaukee, Wisconsin, Births, 1839–1911" > 1893 > volumes 189–191 > image 663 of 726 (ancestry.com). Also, Edward Paul Dahms, no image of grave marker, Valhalla Memorial Park, Milwaukee, Milwaukee County, Wisconsin, memorial #120,477,928 by Leanne (findagrave.com). The information is unsourced.

[1125] Nettie Moran household for daughter Lelah age 42, 1940 US census, Waukesha, Waukesha County, Wisconsin, Ward 6, ED 67-53, dwelling 135.

[1126] Edward Paul Dahms WWI draft card, Milwaukee 23rd ward local board, 5 June 1917 serial #2861, order #61; "US, World War I Draft Registration Cards, 1917–1918" > Wisconsin > Milwaukee City > 11 > Draft Card D (ancestry.com).

[1127] "Wisconsin News Stated in Brief," *Stevens Point Journal* (Wisconsin), Wednesday 12 September 1917, p. 7, col. 1.

[1128] Edward Paul Dahms WWII draft card, local board 33 in Wauwatosa, 27 April 1942, serial #U2463, no order #; "US, World War II Draft Registration Cards, 1942" > Wisconsin > Dahlstrom–Danielson > Clore–Gould > images 124–25 of 2091 (ancestry.com).

[1129] "District AAU Gymnastic Tournament Set for March At La Crosse State," *La Crosse Tribune,* Monday 29 December 1952, p. 9, col. 1.

[1130] "Octogenarian Leads Milers," *Journal Times* (Racine, Wisconsin), Thursday 1 November 1973, p. 25, col. 3.

Edward reportedly married three times: first in 1921 to Nell Hunn (1895–1940); second in 1944 to Lelah (1898–1962); and third in 1970 to Anne M. Geyer (1904–2001), who outlived him.[1131]

iii. UNKNOWN CHILD[4] MORAN (*Nettie[3] Scholes, Robert[2] Scholes, Ann[1] Mills, Samuel[A]*) was born after the 1900 census and died before 1910.[1132]

[1131] Edward Paul Dahms, no image of grave marker, Valhalla Memorial Park, Milwaukee, Milwaukee County, Wisconsin, memorial #120,477,928 by Leanne (findagrave.com). The information is unsourced.
[1132] Thomas C. Moran household for wife Nettie (who had 2 children, 2 living in 1900, and 3 children, 2 living in 1910) 1910 US census, Waukesha, Waukesha County, Wisconsin, Ward 6, ED 182, sheet 6A, dwelling 126, family 138.

Chapter 27
Third Generation

Mary H. Scholes–William Robert Heames Family
<u>parents at Chapter 7</u>

1955 auction items include cattle, hogs, poultry, a 1937 Lafayette coupe, and "a team of good work horses"

27. **Mary H.³ Scholes** (*Robert² Scholes, Ann¹ Mills, Samuel⁴*)
Birth: October 1871,[1133] reportedly 22 October, in Moundville, Marquette County, Wisconsin[1134]
Death: 1948, reportedly 1 August
Burial: Moundville Cemetery, Marquette County, Wisconsin[1135]
Spouse: **William Robert Heames,** married 24 December 1890 in Portage, Columbia County, Wisconsin
Spouse's parents: George and Jane (Keen) Heames[1136]
Spouse's birth: July 1859 in New Jersey[1137]
Spouse's death: 7 February 1924 in Moundville[1138]

[1133] William Heames household for wife Mary, 1900 US census, Moundville, Marquette County, Wisconsin, ED 93, sheet 2B, dwelling/family 40. Also, Robert Scholes probate, Marquette County, Wisconsin, Box 9, file 481; "Wisconsin, Wills and Probate Records, 1800–1987" > Marquette > Probate Records Box 7 File 420–Box 9 File 522 > image 1443 of 1775 (ancestry.com).
[1134] Apparent transcribed obituary by gadgetlover2 gives exact date of birth without sourcing (ancestry.com/mediaui-viewer/tree/118507718/person/140177428089/media/0d6d2c5c-4573-4e64-8a76-88dfa2357c6c).
[1135] Mary and William Heames joint grave marker, image, Moundville Cemetery, Endeavor, Marquette County, Wisconsin, memorials #65,848,564 and #65,848,588 respectively, by Sue (findagrave.com).
[1136] Mary H. Scholes–William R. Heames marriage index entry, 24 December 1890, Portage, Columbia County, Wisconsin, citing "Wisconsin, County Marriages, 1836–1911," ref. #762, FHL #1,275,885, DGS #7,714,205, image 507 (familysearch.org).
[1137] William Heames household, 1900 US census, Moundville, Marquette County, Wisconsin, ED 93, sheet 2B, dwelling/family 40.
[1138] "Obituary…William Heams [Heames]," *Portage Daily Register* (Wisconsin), Friday 8 February 1924, p. 1, col. 6.

Spouse's burial: Moundville Cemetery, Marquette County, Wisconsin[1139]

Mary completed five years of schooling.[1140] At their marriage, Will was described as a "well-to-do farmer" of Moundville, and Mary as "well known in Portage, having spent the past year here."[1141]

Spring 1899: the family was living in Moundville Township, Marquette County.[1142]

1910: they had a mortgaged farm on West Moundville Road.[1143]

1919: they were "preparing their residence at Endeavor."[1144]

1922–23: William's ill health was noted in local newspapers; on 19 January 1923 the Modern Woodmen had a "bee" cutting wood for him (no doubt firewood).[1145]

1930: Widow Mary had three daughters at home. They owned the farm but no value was given; they did not own a radio set.[1146]

1940: Mary owned the farm, valued at $3000, on Cemetery Road in Endeavor. Daughter Wilma was a post-office clerk; Olive had no occupation.[1147]

[1139] Mary and William Heames joint grave marker, image, Moundville Cemetery, Endeavor, Marquette County, Wisconsin, memorials #65,848,564 and #65,848,588 respectively, by Sue (findagrave.com).

[1140] Mary Heames household, 1940 US census, Moundville, Marquette County, Wisconsin, ED 39-8, sheet 4A–B, dwelling 101.

[1141] "Home News," *Portage Democrat* (Wisconsin), Friday 26 December 1890, p. 3, col. 1.

[1142] Robert Scholes probate, Marquette County, Wisconsin, Box 9, file 481; "Wisconsin, Wills and Probate Records, 1800–1987" > Marquette > Probate Records Box 7 File 420–Box 9 File 522 > image 1457–58 of 1775 (ancestry.com).

[1143] William R. Heames household, 1910 US census, Moundville, Marquette County, Wisconsin, ED 149, sheet 5B, dwelling 117, family 119.

[1144] "Moundville," *Portage Daily Register* (Wisconsin), Thursday 22 May 1919, p. 6, col. 4.

[1145] "Moundville," *Portage Daily Register* (Wisconsin), Wednesday 23 January 1924, p. 2, col. 4.

[1146] Mary Heames household, 1930 US census, Moundville, Marquette County, Wisconsin, ED 8, sheet 4A, dwelling/family 102.

[1147] Mary Heames household, 1940 US census, Moundville, Marquette County, Wisconsin, ED 39-8, sheet 4A–B, dwelling 101.

Children of Mary H. (Scholes) and Will Heames, all born in Wisconsin:[1148]

i. GEORGE R.[4] HEAMES (*Mary H.[3] Scholes, Robert[2] Scholes, Ann[1] Mills, Samuel[A]*) was born 16 November 1891 in Moundville, Wisconsin[1149] and died 14 September 1918 in Brest, France. He was buried at Moundville Cemetery, Wisconsin[1150]

As of 5 June 1917, George was tall and slender, with brown eyes and brown hair.[1151] He appears to have enlisted 26 April 1918[1152] and departed for France in August.[1153] He was to serve as a "wagoner" in the Supply Company, 64th Infantry, 7th Division, in World War I, but died of pneumonia,[1154] apparently at Brest, France, shortly after his arrival.[1155] In the absence of antibiotics, and in the presence of a worldwide influenza pandemic, it is not surprising that during World

---

[1148] The children's spacing is unusual: five children in less than eight years, followed by a 13-year gap, then two more in two years.

[1149] George R. Heames, WWI draft card, Moundville Precinct, #6, 5 June 1917; "US, World War I Draft Registration Cards, 1917–1918" > Wisconsin > Marquette County > Draft Card H > image 58 of 162 (ancestry.com). Also, William Heames household for son George R., 1900 US census, Moundville, Marquette County, Wisconsin, ED 93, sheet 2B, dwelling/family 40.

[1150] George R. Heames grave marker, image, Moundville Cemetery, Wisconsin, memorial #103,178,127 by Joey (findagrave.com). For pneumonia, *Wisconsin's Gold Star List*, p. 86, Marquette County; "Wisconsin's Gold Star List" > image 87 of 225 (ancestry.com).

[1151] George R. Heames, WWI draft card, Moundville Precinct, #6, 5 June 1917; "US, World War I Draft Registration Cards, 1917–1918" > Wisconsin > Marquette County > Draft Card H > image 58 of 162 (ancestry.com).

[1152] George R. Heames, Application for Headstone, War Department, 30 May 1934; "US, Headstone Applications for Military Veterans, 1925–1963" > Healing–Henle > image 80 of 3794 (ancestry.com).

[1153] The typewritten US Army Transport Passenger Lists give varying dates and ships heading to France, all supposedly carrying George, but evidently he was en route before the end of August 1918.

[1154] "Casualties," *Appleton Crescent* (Wisconsin), Monday 14 October 1918, p. 3, col. 4. Also, W. M. Haulsee, compiler, *Soldiers of the Great War* (Washington, DC: Soldiers Record, 1920) 3:458; "American Soldiers of World War I" > Soldiers of the Great War Volume 3 > Wisconsin > Died of Disease > Wagoners > image 41 of 46 (ancestry.com).

[1155] George R. Heames, Application for Headstone, US War Department, 30 May 1934; "US, Headstone Applications for Military Veterans, 1925–1963" > Healing–Henle > image 80 of 3794 (ancestry.com).

War I, "disease caused more deaths in the American Army than did enemy action."[1156]

[signature: George L. Heames]
(Signature or mark)

ii. OLIVE HARRIET[4] HEAMES (*Mary H.[3] Scholes, Robert[2] Scholes, Ann[1] Mills, Samuel[A]*) was born 23 January 1893 in Moundville,[1157] died 22 August 1991 in Portage, Columbia County, Wisconsin; and was buried at Moundville Cemetery.[1158]

In the spring of 1907, Olive Heames and Roby Jones represented Moundville at the "annual spelling contest" at Montello.[1159] Olive left the family farm in 1923, moving to Endeavor, where she was a member of Trinity United Church of Christ.[1160] She completed eight years of schooling.[1161] In 1963 her home was near or next door to the Raymond Hopwoods.[1162]

That spring, "A lost Christmas dolly was retrieved through the co-operation of Party Line [evidently a radio program] . . . Children playing with the doll had left it on a car trunk. The doll had fallen off somewhere along Highway 51. Nathan Taylor, Portage, picked it up and his wife reported the find to WPDR [radio station]. The child's great-aunt, Olive Heames, a Party-Line fan, heard the announcement. The Taylors were contacted and Mrs. Taylor, that night, made a trip to Moundville where she was almost as welcome as Santa Claus had been."[1163]

[1156] *The United States World War I Centennial Commission*, "Diseases in World War I: Infectious Diseases" (worldwar1centennial.org/index.php/diseases-in-world-war-i.html).

[1157] William Heames household for daughter Olive, 1900 US census, Moundville, Marquette County, Wisconsin, ED 93, sheet 2B, dwelling/family 40.

[1158] "Death Notices...Heames, Olive Harriet," *Wisconsin State Journal* (Madison), Saturday 24 August 1991, p. 8, cols. 1–2.

[1159] "Moundville," *Portage Daily Register* (Wisconsin), Friday 24 May 1907, p. 4, col. 2.

[1160] "Death Notices...Heames, Olive Harriet," *Wisconsin State Journal* (Madison), Saturday 24 August 1991, p. 8, cols. 1–2.

[1161] Mary Heames household, 1940 US census, Endeavor, Marquette County, Wisconsin, ED 39-8, sheets 4A–B, dwelling 101.

[1162] "Endeavor Area News," *Portage Daily Register* (Wisconsin), Thursday 13 June 1963, section 2, p. 9, cols. 3–4.

[1163] Mrs. Clayton Mills, "Endeavor Area News," *Portage Daily Register* (Wisconsin), Friday 31 May 1963, p. 7, col. 7.

In 1964, at age 71, Olive was the oldest family member to attend the Heames Reunion, held at the old William and Mary Heames (Chapter 27) place, then occupied by Mr. and Mrs. Sheldon Peterson.[1164]

iii. EDWARD FRANCIS[4] HEAMES (*Mary H.[3] Scholes, Robert[2] Scholes, Ann[1] Mills, Samuel[A]*) was born 18 June 1894;[1165] died 26 December 1959 in Poway, San Diego County, California; and was buried at Moundville Cemetery.[1166] He married 31 May 1919[1167] GRACIA TOPPING, the daughter of James and Edith (Pattee) Topping. Gracia was born 24 November 1897 in Stockton, Portage County, Wisconsin; died 7 November 1988 in Portage, Columbia County, Wisconsin; and was buried with her husband. Gracia "grew up in Moundville Township; attended school there and later attended Stevens Point Normal School. She taught school until her marriage."[1168] The year before she taught in Buffalo.[1169]

As of 5 June 1917, Edward was farming with his father in Moundville Township, Marquette County, Wisconsin, and was described as tall, medium in size, with blue eyes, light brown hair, and no disability. He claimed an exemption to help his father farm, but the draft registrar wrote a stern clarification: "He [Edward] does not support his father."[1170]

- **1920:** they were renting and farming in Moundville Township.[1171]

[1164] "Heames Reunion in Moundville," *Portage Daily Register* (Wisconsin), Wednesday 17 June 1964, p. 5, col. 4.

[1165] For exact date, Edward F. Heames, WWI draft card, #293, #7, local board, Moundville, Marquette County, Wisconsin, 5 June 1917; "US, World War I Draft Registration Cards, 1917–1918" > Wisconsin > Marquette County > ALL > Draft Card H, image 57 of 162 (ancestry.com). Also, William Heames household for son Edward F., 1900 US census, Moundville, Marquette County, Wisconsin, ED 93, sheet 2B, dwelling/family 40.

[1166] Edward F. and Gracia Heames joint grave marker, image, Moundville Cemetery, Wisconsin, memorials #103,123,168 and #103,123,061, respectively, by Joey (findagrave.com).

[1167] "Two Graduate and Two Marry," *Portage Register-Democrat* (Wisconsin), Saturday 31 May 1919, p. 4, col. 4.

[1168] "Obituaries…Gracia Heames, *Portage Daily Register* (Wisconsin), Tuesday 8 November 1988, p. 11, cols. 1–2.

[1169] "Two Graduate and Two Marry," *Portage Register-Democrat* (Wisconsin), Saturday 31 May 1919, p. 4, col. 4.

[1170] Edward F. Heames, WWI draft card, #293, #7, local board, Moundville, Marquette County, Wisconsin, 5 June 1917; "US, World War I Draft Registration Cards, 1917–1918" > Wisconsin > Marquette County > ALL > Draft Card H, image 57 of 162 (ancestry.com).

[1171] Edward F. Heames household, 1920 US census, Moundville Township, Marquette County, Wisconsin, ED 133, sheet 1B, dwelling 20, family 21.

- **1930:** owned a house (no value given), farmed in Moundville, and were among the few owning a radio set.[1172]
- **1938:** attended a "Topping–Grover Reunion."
- **1940:** owned a $2000 house and were farming in Moundville. Gracia completed one year of college, Edward eight years of school.[1173]
- **Fall 1948:** Edward had his livestock and equipment auctioned off and put the 127-acre farm up for sale: "54 acres of work land and a complete set of farm buildings, including silo."[1174]
- **1958, 26 December:** Edward and Gracia "of Endeavor, Wisconsin" were visiting relatives in the as yet unincorporated town of Poway, San Diego County, California.[1175]
- **1959:** Now living in Poway at 14015 Sycamore Drive, Edward was "walking on an unlighted area on Midland Drive" there when he was killed by an oncoming car.[1176] The widowed Gracia moved in with her mother, Mrs. Edith Topping, in San Gabriel, Los Angeles County.[1177]
- **1960 & 1962:** Gracia M. Heames (Republican) and brother Jed L. Topping (did not name a preference) registered to vote from 223 East Broadway in Los Angeles, San Gabriel Precinct 43.[1178]
- **1966:** Edith died 20 February 1966.[1179]

[1172] Edward Heames household, 1930 US census, Moundville Township, Marquette County, Wisconsin, ED 8, sheet 7A, dwelling 210, no family number given.

[1173] Edward F. Heames household, 1940 US census, Moundville Township, Marquette County, Wisconsin, ED 39-8, sheet 6A, dwelling 136.

[1174] "Tri-County Insured Auction" advertisement, *Portage Daily Register* (Wisconsin), Tuesday 26 October 1948, p. 6, cols. 4–5.

[1175] B. E. Miller, "Poway Valley Patter," *Daily Times Advocate* (Escondido, California), Friday 26 December 1958, p. 6, col. 2. According to Gracia's 1988 obituary, they had moved there in 1956: "Obituaries…Gracia Heames, *Portage Daily Register* (Wisconsin), Tuesday 8 November 1988, p. 11, cols. 1–2.

[1176] "Poway Man Killed Crossing Street," *Daily Times Advocate* (Escondido, California), Saturday 26 December 1959, p. 1, col. 8.

[1177] B. E. Miller, "Poway," *Daily Times Advocate* (Escondido, California), Saturday 16 January 1960, p. 1, col. 8.

[1178] Mrs. Gracia M. Heames [*sic*] and Jed L. Topping, 1960 voter registrations, 223 East Broadway, San Gabriel Precinct 43; "California, Voter Registrations, 1900–1968" > Los Angeles County > 1960 > roll 144, image 268 of 730 (ancestry.com). Similarly, 1962 > Roll 165 > image 658 of 767. This was not a census: non-registrants such as mother Edith or Jed's wife Beth may have been present as well.

[1179] "Edith Topping," *Daily Times Advocate* (Escondido, California), Monday 21 February 1966, p. 8, col. 1.

- **1968:** Gracia visited Endeavor for a reunion of Christian Academy students there (see story #3, pp. 149–51).[1180]
- **Late 1950s–1982:** Gracia lived in California, eventually returning to Wisconsin. A member of the Moundville Methodist Church and the Ladies Aid, she was active in the Sunday School.[1181]

iv. JANE ELIZABETH[4] HEAMES (*Mary H.[3] Scholes, Robert[2] Scholes, Ann[1] Mills, Samuel[A]*) was born 6 February 1896,[1182] died 30 October 1980, and was buried at Moundville Cemetery, Wisconsin. She married 1920 in Endeavor GUST A. PETERSON.[1183] His parents may have both been born in Sweden.[1184] Gust was born 10 March 1890, Homestead Township, Florence County, Wisconsin;[1185] died 1970,[1186] reportedly 15 March;[1187] and was buried with his wife.

In the spring of 1916, Jane graduated from the Rural School Teachers Department at Stevens Point Normal School.[1188]

[1180] "Academy Grads Meet for School Reunion," *Portage Daily Register* (Wisconsin), Saturday 31 August 1968, p. 6, cols. 4–5.

[1181] "Obituaries…Gracia Heames, *Portage Daily Register* (Wisconsin), Tuesday 8 November 1988, p. 11, cols. 1–2.

[1182] "Jane E. Peterson," *Portage Daily Register* (Wisconsin), Friday 31 October 1980, p. 8, col. 1. Also, William Heames household for daughter Jane E., 1900 US census, Moundville, Marquette County, Wisconsin, ED 93, sheet 2B, dwelling/family 40.

[1183] "Jane E. Peterson," *Portage Daily Register* (Wisconsin), Friday 31 October 1980, p. 8, col. 1. They were to celebrate their 48th anniversary Sunday 22 June 1968: "Endeavor Area News," *Portage Daily Register,* Wednesday 19 June 1968, p. 6, col. 1.

[1184] George Lintner household for laborer Gust Peterson, 1920 US census, Douglas Township, Marquette County, Wisconsin, ED 129, sheet 5A, dwelling 77, family 79. Douglas is immediately west of Moundville Township. Gust's brother John died at age 85 in Manitoba, Canada, in late April or early May 1965, so born about 1880: "Endeavor Area News," *Portage Daily Register* (Wisconsin), Thursday 6 May 1965, p. 8, col. 8.

[1185] Gust A. and Jane E. Peterson, joint grave marker, Moundville Cemetery, Wisconsin, memorials #103,123,578 and #103,123,348 respectively, by Joey (findagrave.com).

[1186] "Jane E. Peterson," *Portage Daily Register* (Wisconsin), Friday 31 October 1980, p. 8, col. 1.

[1187] Gust A. Peterson index entry, certificate 3613, Wisconsin, Death Index, 1959–1977 (ancestry.com).

[1188] "The 22nd Annual Commencement of Stevens Point Normal School," *Gazette* (Stevens Point, Wisconsin), Wednesday 31 May 1916, pp. 3–4. The vast majority of graduates were women, divided into four departments: primary teachers, grammar grade teachers, home economics, and rural school teachers. Each graduate in the first three groups included the title of a project or paper on some aspect of education; the rural school teacher certificants did not.

As of 5 June 1917, Gust Peterson was medium in height and weight, with gray eyes and brown hair. He was single and farming for A.E. Baker in Moundville.[1189] In World War I he served as an Army private in Remount Squadron 314.[1190]

Remount squadrons cared for and moved horses to wherever they were needed. According to the operation report of 28 June 1919, over two years (1917–1919) the American Expeditionary Forces' Remount Service in France expanded from one officer and clerk to an organization of 493 officers and 14,598 enlisted men on duty 1 January 1919.

"During the life of the A.E.F., 243,360 animals were procured from the United States, France, England, and Spain. A fruitless search for animals extended in the summer of 1918 to Portugal and Morocco." Remount Squadron 314, the unit in which Gust served, "reported to the Army October 5, 1918, and was ordered to Autrecourt where an evacuating station was established. All animals received there were shipped back to S.O.S. Veterinary Hospital." Later, Remount Squadron 314 operated a depot in Coblenz.[1191]

1920: Gust was back home, single, and working for another farmer.

1930: He and Jane were farming in Moundville Township; they owned a radio set.[1192]

1940: They owned their home, valued at $1200, below the statewide average of $3232.[1193]

1944: Gust shifted from farming to selling to farmers. He became "involved in the John Deere business in Endeavor."[1194]

[1189] Gust Peterson WWI draft card, 5 June 1917, Moundville, Marquette County, Wisconsin, order #21; "US, World War I Draft Registration Cards, 1917–1918" > Wisconsin > Marquette County > Draft Card P > image 25 of 99 (ancestry.com).

[1190] "Gust Peterson," *Wisconsin State Journal* (Madison), Monday 16 March 1970, p. 34 or p. 2 section 2, col. 4. Also, Wisconsin Veterans Museum World War I Database (museum.dva.state.wi.us/WWIRoster).

[1191] *Operation Report of the Remount Service During WWI,* paragraphs 1, 192, and 239 (freepages.rootsweb.com/~gregkrenzelok/genealogy/veterinary%20corp%20in%20ww1/operationremountservicereportww1.html).

[1192] George Lintner household for laborer Gust Peterson, 1920 US census, Douglas Township, Marquette County, Wisconsin, ED 129, sheet 5A, dwelling 77, family 79. Similarly, Gust Peterson household, 1930, Moundville Township, ED 8, sheet 5B, dwelling/family 151.

[1193] Gust Peterson household, 1940 US census, Moundville Township, Marquette County, Wisconsin, ED 39-8, sheet 7B, dwelling 169. Statewide figures from US Census Bureau, Census of Housing, Historical Census of Housing Tables, Median Home Values Unadjusted 1940 (https://www2.census.gov/programs-surveys/decennial/tables/time-series/coh-values/values-unadj.txt).

[1194] "Obituaries . . . Sheldon W. Peterson," *Wisconsin State Journal* (Madison), Friday 8 April 2005, p. 15 or B5, cols. 5–6.

Jane was a member of Trinity United Church of Christ in Endeavor.[1195] She completed two years of college; Gust completed eight years of school.[1196]

v. HAZEL D.[4] HEAMES *(Mary H.[3] Scholes, Robert[2] Scholes, Ann[1] Mills, Samuel[A])* was born March 1899,[1197] died in 1969,[1198] and was buried at Westfield East Cemetery, Marquette County, Wisconsin.[1199] She married in Westfield 18 June 1921 ELMER EMIL POMPLIN, the son of Emil F. and Ida Amelia (Maik) Pomplun.[1200] Elmer was born 1899,[1201] died 5 January 1975 in Wautoma (last residence Westfield), and was buried with his wife.[1202]

Pomplins through the years:

1935: in Green Lake, Wisconsin.

1940: renting at 243 Spring Street in Westfield, Marquette County, Wisconsin. Elmer was a garage mechanic, and in the previous year he had earned $800 for 40 weeks' work. He completed 6 years of schooling, Hazel one year of high school.[1203]

1942: "Elmer Pomplin, who has been employed by Arnold Schauer, resigned and rented the Allie Borsack garage and took possession April 1," evidently in Westfield.[1204]

[1195] "Jane E. Peterson," *Portage Daily Register* (Wisconsin), Friday 31 October 1980, p. 8, col. 1.

[1196] Gust Peterson household, 1940 US census, Moundville Township, Marquette County, Wisconsin, ED 39-8, sheet 7B, dwelling 169.

[1197] William Heames household for daughter Hazel, 1900 US census, Moundville, Marquette County, Wisconsin, ED 93, sheet 2B, dwelling/family 40.

[1198] Elmer and Hazel (Heames) Pomplin, joint grave marker, image, East Westfield Cemetery, Wisconsin, memorials #79,454,195 and #79,454,196 respectively, by David Woody (findagrave.com).

[1199] Elmer and Hazel (Heames) Pomplin, joint grave marker, image, East Westfield Cemetery, Wisconsin, memorials #79,454,195 and #79,454,196 respectively, by David Woody (findagrave.com).

[1200] Emil and Ida Amelia Pomplun, joint grave marker, image, East Westfield Cemetery, Wisconsin, memorials #69,163,229 and 69,162,733 respectively, by L. Thompson (findagrave.com). Also, "Wed Half Century," *Capital Times* (Madison, Wisconsin), Wednesday 5 May 1948, p. 16, col. 2.

[1201] Elmer and Hazel (Heames) Pomplin, joint grave marker, image, East Westfield Cemetery, Wisconsin, memorials #79,454,195 and #79,454,196 respectively, by David Woody (findagrave.com).

[1202] "Obituaries . . . E. Pomplin," *Portage Daily Register* (Wisconsin), Tuesday 7 January 1975, p. 5, col. 4.

[1203] Elmer E. Pomplin household (Hazel D. informant), 1940 US census, Westfield, Marquette, Wisconsin, sheet 10A, dwelling 243.

[1204] "What Your Friends Are Doing in Central Wisconsin . . . Westfield," *Daily Tribune* (Wisconsin Rapids), Saturday 11 April 1942, p. 6, col. 6.

1951: "Burglars broke into Elmer Pomplin's Texaco filling station Sunday night. They stole several batteries and tires."[1205]

1962: "Mr. and Mrs. Elmer Pomplin, the Wilbur Pomplin family, and Mr. and Mrs. Hollis Bandt and children joined 46 members of the Heames family at a reunion at the Sheldon Peterson home at Endeavor, Sunday afternoon."[1206]

1963 December 7: Elmer retired after 21 years in the business world, "the last 8 being in the Standard Station formerly known as Clark's."[1207]

1969+: Elmer was by no means retired from everything. A widower, he married second as her second husband Lula E. (Van Alstine) Sanford, a retired schoolteacher who was born 29 December 1901 in Wisconsin Dells and died 30 July 1975 in Stevens Point, Portage County, Wisconsin.

Her first husband, Frank Sanford, had died in 1969. She taught school for more than 45 years.[1208]

1971: Elmer was crew foreman for a "Green Thumb" project renovating the village hall in Neshkoro, Marquette County, Wisconsin.[1209]

vi. HOPE LORRAINE[4] HEAMES (*Mary H.[3] Scholes, Robert[2] Scholes, Ann[1] Mills, Samuel[A]*) was born 26 June 1911 in Moundville, Marquette County, Wisconsin,[1210] died on Palm Sunday 1947, and was buried at Underhill Cemetery, Packwaukee, Marquette County, Wisconsin.[1211] She married 3 November 1934 JOHN ALBERT WILLIAMSON, the son of Leslie E. and Charlotte M. (Wilkins) Williamson.[1212] John was born

---

[1205] "Westfield," *Portage Daily Register*, Wednesday 19 September 1951, p. 11, col. 4.

[1206] Aloise Swader, "Westfield Area News," *Portage Daily Register* (Wisconsin), Wednesday 13 June 1962, p. 6, col. 4.

[1207] "Elmer Pomplin Has Decided to Retire," *Portage Daily Register*, Wednesday 11 December 1963, p. 10, col. 5.

[1208] "Mrs. Lula E. Pomplin," *Daily Northwestern* (Oshkosh, Wisconsin), Thursday 31 July 1975, p. 32, col. 2.

[1209] "Green Thumb Program Under Way in Neshkoro," *Portage Daily Register*, Friday 17 December 1971, p. 7, cols. 1–3.

[1210] "Obituary, Mrs. John Williamson," *Portage Daily Register* (Wisconsin), Thursday 10 April 1947, p. 4, col. 3. Also, William Heames household for daughter Hope L., age 9, 1920 US census, Moundville, Marquette County, Wisconsin, ED 133, sheet 5A, dwelling 93, family 95.

[1211] "Hope L. Mother 1911–1947" grave marker, image, Underhill Cemetery, Packwaukee, Wisconsin, memorial #104,519,819 by Barb Voss for Hope L. Heames Williamson (findagrave.com).

[1212] John Albert Williamson, US Social Security Applications and Claims Index, 1936–2007. Also, Leslie E. Williamson household, 1920 US census, Packwaukee Township, Marquette County, Wisconsin, ED 137, sheet 5B, dwelling/family 99.

6 December 1912, died 28 September 1998, and was buried in Underhill Cemetery, Packwaukee, Marquette County, Wisconsin.[1213] After a year of teacher training at Westfield, Hope taught four years at the Williams School.[1214] She completed four years of high school; John completed eight years of grade school. He was a farmer. In 1940 they rented for $4 a month.[1215]

vii. WILMA RAE[4] HEAMES (*Mary H.[3] Scholes, Robert[2] Scholes, Ann[1] Mills, Samuel[A]*) was born 5 August 1913 in Endeavor, Marquette County, Wisconsin;[1216] died 26 December 2005 in DeForest, Dane County, Wisconsin, the last of the siblings, and was buried at Moundville Cemetery, Endeavor, Marquette County.[1217] In 1940 Wilma, who completed four years of high school, was employed as a post office clerk.[1218]

She married first 9 February 1946 at Endeavor Congregational Church LAWRENCE MILO BUSKAGER,[1219] reportedly the son of Louis and Lucy (Rodderfeld) Buskager.[1220] He was born 3 October 1906 in Sun Prairie Township, Dane County, Wisconsin; died 13 September 1955 in Leeds Township, Columbia County; and was buried at Moundville Cemetery.[1221]

[1213] John A. Williamson grave marker, image, Underhill Cemetery, Packwaukee, Wisconsin, memorial #144,807,067 by McFarland (findagrave.com).
[1214] "Obituary, Mrs. John Williamson," *Portage Daily Register* (Wisconsin), Thursday 10 April 1947, p. 4, col. 3.
[1215] John A. Williamson household for wife Hope, 1940 US census, Packwaukee Township, Marquette County, Wisconsin, ED 39-14, sheet 8A, dwelling 169.
[1216] "Wilma R. Thayer," *Portage Daily Register* (Wisconsin), Thursday 29 December 2005, p. 17, col. 5. Also, William Heames household for daughter Wilma R., 1920 US census, Moundville, Marquette County, Wisconsin, ED 133, sheet 5A, dwelling 93, family 95.
[1217] "Thayer, Wilma R.," *Wisconsin State Journal* (Madison), Thursday 29 December 2005, p. 4, col. 4. The obituary mislocates Moundville Cemetery in Columbia County.
[1218] Mary Heames household for daughter Wilma, 1940 US census, Moundville, Marquette County, Wisconsin, ED 39-8, sheets 4A–B, dwelling 101.
[1219] "Wilma Heames Becomes Bride of Mr. Buskager," *Capital Times* (Madison, Wisconsin), Sunday 17 February 1946, p. 23, col. 7.
[1220] Unnamed Buskager born 3 October 1906 in Sun Prairie, Dane County, Wisconsin, parents named; "Wisconsin Births and Christenings, 1826–1926," record #64, item 2 p. 458, volumes 4–5, FHL #1,302,859, DGS #7,609,647 (familysearch.org). Original record not viewed.
[1221] "Obituary: Lawrence Milo Buskager," *Portage Daily Register* (Wisconsin), Monday 26 September 1955, p. 4, col. 3. Also, "Rural Poynette Man Takes Own Life at His Farm," *Portage Daily Register* (Wisconsin), Wednesday 14 September 1955, p. 1, col. 5.

Buskager's farm and estate auction list included cattle, hogs, poultry, crops, "a team of good work horses," much equipment, a 1937 Lafayette coupe, and most of all "a good 60 acre farm . . . all tillable and completely fenced with woven wire," north of North Leeds on Highway 22.[1222]

Wilma married second as his second wife 30 December 1956 in Poynette, Columbia County, Wisconsin, ERVIN ADRIAN THAYER.[1223] Ervin was reportedly the son of Charles Russell and Dora Adelia (Fry) Thayer.[1224] He was born 13 July 1900 in Fairfield, Sauk County, Wisconsin,[1225] died 25 January 1978 in Madison,[1226] and was buried at Fairfield Cemetery, Baraboo, Sauk County, Wisconsin.[1227] He had married first Mary Avis Moungey 18 February 1922 in Portage; the marriage evidently did not last; she died 25 September 1998 there.[1228] She was the daughter of John and Angeline (Gray) Moungey.[1229]

Wilma was a member of Sherman Avenue United Methodist Church, Royal Neighbors, and the Retired Senior Volunteer Program.[1230] In 1972 the Thayers moved from Leeds Center to 1734 Sheridan Street in Madison. He was at various points an employee of Grants and of Del

---

[1222] "Farm Loan Service Sale, Lawrence Buskager Estate" advertisement, Wednesday 21 September 1955, p. 6, cols. 1–2.

[1223] "Newlyweds Are Feted By Neighbors," *Portage Daily Register* (Wisconsin), Tuesday 8 January 1957, p. 3, col. 2. (Second marriage for both.) The Thayers were living separately in 1956 and presumably had for some time before that: "Repeat Vows Here Saturday," *Portage Daily Register* (Wisconsin), Tuesday 16 October 1956, p. 3, cols. 1–2. Ervin was in Poynette and Mary in Portage.

[1224] Erwin Adrian Thayer index entry, "Wisconsin Births and Christenings, 1826–1926," record #193, item 1 p. 240, FHL #1,305,586, DGS #7,616,058 (familysearch.org). Parents and dates listed unsourced, Ervin Thayer grave marker, Row 3S, Fairfield Cemetery, Baraboo, Wisconsin, image, memorial #41,190,968 by Marc Thayer, III, and Anthony Dahler (findagrave.com). Original record not viewed.

[1225] Ervin Adrian Thayer WWI draft card, Baraboo, Sauk County, Wisconsin, local board, 12 September 1918, serial #1298, order #A996; "US, World War I Draft Registration Cards, 1917–1918" > Wisconsin > Sauk County > Draft Card T > image 99 of 189 (ancestry.com).

[1226] "Thayer, Erwin A.," *Capital Times* (Madison, Wisconsin), Thursday 26 January 1978, p. 3, col. 3.

[1227] Ervin Thayer grave marker, Row 3S, Fairfield Cemetery, Baraboo, Wisconsin, image, memorial #41,490,968 by Marc Thayer, III, and Anthony Dahler (findagrave.com).

[1228] "Obituaries . . . Mary A. Thayer," *Portage Daily Register* (Wisconsin), Saturday 26 September 1998, p. 2, cols. 2–3.

[1229] "Additional Locals," *Portage Daily Register* (Wisconsin), Monday 13 May 1929, p. 4, col. 4.

[1230] "Thayer, Wilma R.," *Wisconsin State Journal* (Madison), Thursday 29 December 2005, p. 4, col. 4.

Monte Canning Company in Arlington, Columbia County, Wisconsin.[1231]

[1231] "Erwin Thayers move here from Leeds Center," *Capital Times* (Madison, Wisconsin), Thursday 17 August 1972, p. 20, col. 4. Also, "Thayer, Erwin A.," *Capital Times* (Madison, Wisconsin), Thursday 26 January 1978, p. 3, col. 3.

Chapter 28

Third Generation

Hattie C. Scholes–John Rodney Schwemerlein Family
parents at Chapter 7

In 1915, Mrs. Schwemerlein endorsed Doan's Kidney Pills in a newspaper advertisement.

---

28. HATTIE C.³ SCHOLES (*Robert² Scholes, Ann¹ Mills, Samuel*⁴)
Birth: May 1877 in Wisconsin, likely Marquette County[1232]
Death: 22 December 1957, Endeavor, Marquette County, Wisconsin[1233]
Burial: Hillcrest Cemetery, Endeavor, Wisconsin[1234]
Spouse: **RODNEY "J. RODDY" "JOHN C." SCHWEMERLEIN**, married 25 January 1899, Marquette County, Wisconsin
Spouse's parents: Conrad and Catherine (Marman) Schwemerline [Schwemerlein],[1235] both born in Germany[1236]
Spouse's birth: 12 March 1865 in "what is now Davis corners," Adams County, Wisconsin
Spouse's death: 17 March 1948

[1232] John C. Schwemerline [Schwemerlein] household, 1900 US census, Douglas Township, Marquette County, Wisconsin, ED 93, sheet 9B, dwelling/family 184. Also, Robert Scholes probate, Marquette County, Wisconsin, Box 9, file 481; "Wisconsin, Wills and Probate Records, 1800–1987" > Marquette > Probate Records Box 7 File 420–Box 9 File 522 > image 1443 of 1775 (ancestry.com).
[1233] "Mrs. Schwemerlein," *Wisconsin State Journal* (Madison), Monday 23 December 1957, p. 10, cols. 1–2.
[1234] Hattie C. and J. Roddy Schwemerlein joint grave marker, image, Hill Crest Cemetery, Endeavor, Marquette County, Wisconsin, memorials #103,096,947 and #208,225,557 respectively, by Janet Marie and Joey (findagrave.com). Many records and newspaper articles have "John C. Schwemerline."
[1235] Harriet C. Scholes–John C. Schwemerline [Schwemerlein] marriage index entry, 25 March 1899, Marquette County, Wisconsin; "Wisconsin Marriages, 1836–1930," FHL #1,292,025, DGS #7,615,078, image 302 (familysearch.org).
[1236] John C. Schwemerline [Schwemerlein] household, 1900 US census, Douglas Township, Marquette County, Wisconsin, ED 93, sheet 9B, dwelling/family 184.

Spouse's burial: Hillcrest Cemetery, Endeavor, Wisconsin[1237]

"At five years of age he moved with his parents to a farm near Briggsville. At the age of 19, he took up carpenter work in Briggsville," Douglas Township, Marquette County, Wisconsin.[1238]

In 1900 newlyweds John and Harriet were living in Douglas Township, next door to his apparent brother A. H. Schwemerline. John was a carpenter.[1239] Both John and Harriet had completed eight years of schooling.[1240]

In 1908 they were at Briggsville, Marquette County, where Hattie entertained her Sunday School class.[1241] That spring they bought a house on East Pleasant Street for $1200 and moved into Portage.[1242] In 1915, Mrs. Schwemerlein appeared in a local newspaper ad for Doan's Kidney Pills.[1243]

Hattie's husband at least occasionally used the name "Rodney" in the early 1920s. "Mrs. Mary Hames [Heames] visited her invalid brother-in-law Roddie Schwemerlein of Portage the first of last week."[1244] In the spring of 1926, "Mrs. Nettie Moran of Waukesha is a guest of her sister, Mrs. J. C. Schwemerlein, East Pleasant Street."[1245]

[1237] "Obituary…J. C. Schwemerlein," *Portage Daily Register,* Wednesday 24 March 1948, p. 5, cols. 5–6.
[1238] "Obituary…J. C. Schwemerlein," *Portage Daily Register,* Wednesday 24 March 1948, p. 5, cols. 5–6.
[1239] John C. Schwemerline [Schwemerlein] household, 1900 US census, Douglas Township, Marquette County, Wisconsin, ED 93, sheet 9B, dwelling/family 184.
[1240] John C. Schwemerlein household, 1940 US census, Portage, Columbia County, Wisconsin, Ward 2, ED 11-24, sheet 10A, dwelling 166.
[1241] "Briggsville," *Portage Daily Democrat* (Wisconsin), Friday 24 January 1908, p. 2, col. 2.
[1242] "Brief News Notes of the City," *Portage Daily Register* (Wisconsin), Thursday 19 March 1908, p. 2, col. 2.
[1243] Advertisement, *Portage Daily Register* (Wisconsin), Monday 25 January 1915, p. 4, col. 5.
[1244] "Moundville," *Portage Daily Register* (Wisconsin), Tuesday 10 June 1924, p. 4, col. 2.
[1245] "Local Happenings," *Portage Daily Register* (Wisconsin), Tuesday 13 April 1926, p. 3, col. 2.

In 1930 the Schwemerleins owned a radio set and a $4000 house at 324 East Pleasant Street in Portage; he was a house carpenter.[1246] They were in the same house in 1940 (valued at $3500, still a bit above the statewide average) and he showed no occupation.[1247] The preceding year he had his first stroke. "Since that time he has been unable to work. During the past year he became almost helpless." Among those attending the 1948 funeral were "Mr. and Mrs. William Crawford [Chapter 7, child iv], Milwaukee . . . Mrs. Lelah Dahms [Chapter 26, child ii], Wauwatosa, and Miss Mary Smith [Chapter 24] and Miss Marion Scholes [Chapter 32] of Portage."[1248]

Hattie survived a broken arm later that year. In 1949, she "spent several days . . . with her sister, Mrs. James Hollerup. They were Thursday dinner guests of Miss Olive Heames."[1249] The following summer, "Mrs. James Hollerup and sister, Mrs. Hattie Schwemerlein of Portage left Monday to spend the week with Mrs. Hollerup's son, Delmer [Delmar Krueger] and family and a sister, Mrs. Nettie Moran and other relatives in Waukesha."[1250]

Following Hattie's funeral, the Gust Petersons had luncheon guests: Mrs. and Mrs. Ed Dahms (Chapter 26, child ii), of Wauwatosa; Mrs. Myrtle Crawford (Chapter 7, child iv) and Mr. and Mrs. Alden [Alfred Anson] Moore (Chapter 7, child iv), Waukesha; Mr. and Mrs. Elmer Pomplin (Chapter 27, child v), Westfield; James Hollerup (Chapter 7, child v); and Miss Olive Heames (Chapter 27, child ii).[1251]

[1246] John C. Schwemerlein household, 1930 US census, Portage, Columbia County, Wisconsin, Ward 2, ED 25, sheet 7B, dwelling 159, family 171.
[1247] John C. Schwemerlein household, 1940 US census, Portage, Columbia County, Wisconsin, Ward 2, ED 11-24, sheet 10A, dwelling 166. Statewide figures from US Census Bureau, Census of Housing, Historical Census of Housing Tables, Median Home Values Unadjusted 1940 (https://www2.census.gov/programs-surveys/decennial/tables/time-series/coh-values/values-unadj.txt).
[1248] "Obituary…J. C. Schwemerlein," *Portage Daily Register* (Wisconsin), Wednesday 24 March 1948, p. 5, cols. 5–6.
[1249] "Endeavor Locals," *Portage Daily Register* (Wisconsin), Wednesday 17 August 1949, p. 5, col. 4.
[1250] Mrs. Fred Russell, "Endeavor," *Portage Daily Register* (Wisconsin), Wednesday 26 July 1950, p. 6, col. 5.
[1251] "Endeavor," *Portage Daily Register* (Wisconsin), Saturday 4 January 1958, p. 2, col. 4.

Hattie was survived by one half-sibling, "Myrtle, Mrs. William Crawford of Waukesha" AKA Myrtle May (Ellison) (Moore) Crawford 1889–1969 (Chapter 7, child iv).

Chapter 29

Third Generation

Eleanor "Nellie" Elizabeth Scholes Family
parents at Chapter 8

Librarian in three states: "always her delight to help a sincere student"

29. ELEANOR ELIZABETH "NELLIE"³ SCHOLES (*Samuel Mills² Scholes, Ann¹ Mills, Samuel¹ᴬ*)
Birth: 15 March 1878 in Marquette, Green Lake County, Wisconsin
Death: 24 August 1948 in Los Angeles County, California[1252]
Burial: Dartford Cemetery, Green Lake, Green Lake County, Wisconsin[1253]

Nellie obtained her library degree at the University of Wisconsin in 1907, and worked in libraries in Mosinee, Marinette, and Black Earth, Wisconsin, as well as Maywood, Illinois.[1254] As "state cataloguer" for the Wisconsin Library Commission, she organized libraries in many of the state's high schools and public libraries.[1255] Between 1914 and 1919 she

---

[1252] Samuel Scholes Family Record; Scholes ledger book, 30, in author's possession. Also, Nellie E. Scholes death index entry, 24 August 1948, "California Death Index, 1940–1997" (ancestry.com). Original not viewed.
[1253] Bonnie E. and Nellie E. Scholes, joint grave marker, image, Dartford Cemetery, Green Lake, Green Lake County, Wisconsin, memorials #90,858,159 and #90,858,166 respectively, by Janet Milburn (findagrave.com). Memorial erroneously lists Bonnie's birth year as 1892.
[1254] Nellie E. Scholes entries: *Seventh Biennial Report of the Free Library Commission of Wisconsin 1907–1908* (Madison: Democrat Printing, 1908), p. 43; "Alumni Notes," *Wisconsin Library Bulletin,* June 1909, 5:58; and "Summer School Notes," *Wisconsin Library Bulletin,* December 1910, 6:151.
[1255] Bonnie Scholes, "Nellie E. Scholes, Former Green Lake Woman, Died Last Month in California," undated newspaper clipping, probably fall 1948, probably from the *Green Lake County Reporter* (Wisconsin) based on typeface used; in author's possession, Scholes tub 2:48.

was the librarian at the State Normal School in Santa Barbara, California,[1256] and a "college librarian" in 1930.[1257]

Her brother recalled that Nellie had been "terribly ill when she was about twelve or fourteen. It was undoubtedly a burst appendix, but the village doctor called it indigestion. She was never quite well again, although she became a capable librarian in later years. She took up Christian Science—a fad among librarians then—and some sort of raw food cult. By 1926, she gave up and had surgery for gallstones. Then the old trouble and resulting adhesions were discovered."[1258]

On a return trip from California to Green Lake in 1924–25, Nellie "assisted in organizing the Green Lake Public Library, in the start of which she had a very real part when a few 'neighbors' formed a book club, which grew into a 'rental library,' then became, in truth the Green Lake Public Library. . . . Few of her friends knew that she had a joy in writing short stories and won a substantial prize from *Success Magazine* [founded 1897, still in publication as of 2020] for one of her unique portrayals of family life. Always it was her delight to help someone—especially a sincere student—to find the material he needed."[1259]

[1256] "Santa Barbara Libraries," *University of California History Digital Archives* (lib.berkeley.edu/uchistory/general_history/campuses/ucsb/library.html). Nellie E. Scholes entry, *Directory of Secondary and Normal Schools for the School Year 1915–1916* (Sacramento: California State Printing Office, 1916), p. 119. Similarly, *1919–1920*, p. 160. Also, *American Library Annual 1916–1917* (New York: R. R. Bowker, 1917), p. 436, with a brief description naming it the "State Normal School of Manual Arts and Home Economics."

[1257] Ellen L. Marbel household for Bonnie E. and Elinor Scholes, 1930 US census, Pasadena, Los Angeles County, California, ED 1224, sheet 4A, dwelling 92, family 98.

[1258] Samuel Ray Scholes, typescript 1960–1961, sometimes called "Pop's Peregrinations," in author's possession.

[1259] Bonnie Scholes, "Nellie E. Scholes, Former Green Lake Woman, Died Last Month in California," undated newspaper clipping, probably fall 1948, probably from the *Green Lake County Reporter* (Wisconsin) based on typeface used; Scholes tub 2:48, in author's possession.

Chapter 30

Third Generation

Bonnie Elizabeth Scholes
parents at Chapter 8

"I would not have missed it for five dollars"—*one response to Bonnie's 1922 talk on diet in rural Illinois*

30. **BONNIE ELIZABETH³ SCHOLES** (*Samuel Mills² Scholes, Ann¹ Mills, Samuel⁴*)
Birth: 12 June 1882 in Marquette, Green Lake County, Wisconsin[1260]
Death: Pasadena, Los Angeles County, 27 March 1957[1261]
Burial: Dartford Cemetery, Green Lake, Green Lake County, Wisconsin[1262]

In 1901–1902, Bonnie and her younger brother Samuel both attended Ripon College as freshmen.[1263] She graduated from the University of Wisconsin with a BS in 1912, having left school for a time so that her brother could continue.[1264] Over the next ten years she taught, wrote, added a degree, and taught in colleges and home extension programs around the country:

- the Woman's College of Alabama in Montgomery (1913)[1265]

[1260] Samuel Scholes Family Record, Scholes ledger book, 30, in author's possession.
[1261] Bonnie E. Scholes entry, "Necrology," *Wisconsin Alumnus* 58(15):35, 25 July 1957.
[1262] Bonnie E. and Nellie E. Scholes, joint grave marker, image, Dartford Cemetery, Green Lake, Green Lake County, Wisconsin, memorials #90,858,159 and #90,858,166 respectively, by Janet Milburn (findagrave.com). Memorial erroneously lists Bonnie's birth year as 1892.
[1263] *Catalogue, Ripon College, 1901–1902* (Ripon, Wisconsin: C. H. Ellsworth, 1901), p. 53.
[1264] Bonnie E. Scholes entry, "Necrology," *Wisconsin Alumnus* 58(15):35, 25 July 1957.
[1265] Advertisement, *Montgomery Advertiser* (Alabama), Sunday 14 July 1912, p. 27.

- University of Wisconsin (1914–15), including a class on "Principles of the Selection and Preparation of Food," which had a chemistry prerequisite[1266]
- "Chairman of Home Economics for Santa Barbara County" for the US Food Administration during World War I[1267]
- Columbia University (1919), where she earned a master's degree in education and practical arts[1268]
- Cornell University (1920)[1269]
- University of Illinois (1921–22)[1270]

In Marengo, McHenry County, Illinois, she spoke at the Home Bureau on "anti-acid and anti-constipation diets," which apparently was a hit: "Miss Scholes made the facts very plain. The audience of about forty were intensely interested from start to finish and a common expression after the meeting was, 'I would not have missed it for five dollars.'"[1271] With Harriet E. Philips, Bonnie wrote a University of Illinois extension circular published in May 1923 on how to run a "Baking Club" for teenagers who had already learned bread making.[1272]

In 1930 and 1940 Bonnie was teaching in public schools in Pasadena,[1273] and in 1940 she was president of the Wisconsin

---

[1266] *Bulletin of the University of Wisconsin College of Agriculture*, "Courses in Home Economics 1914–1915" (Madison: University of Wisconsin, June 1914), 3, 30.

[1267] USFA letterhead for Miss Bonnie E. Scholes; Mozley binder, item 51, in author's possession.

[1268] Bonnie Elizabeth Scholes entries, *Columbia University Bulletin of Information, Catalogue 1919–1920*, 31 July 1920, pp. 276, 284.

[1269] *Thirty-fourth Annual Report of the New York State College of Agriculture at Cornell University* (Utica: State Hospitals Press, 1922), 19.

[1270] *University of Illinois Annual Register 1921–1922* (Urbana: University of Illinois, February 1922), p. 358.

[1271] "Home Bureau Meets," *Marengo Republican-News* (Illinois), Thursday 13 April 1922, p. 1, col. 3.

[1272] Bonnie E. Scholes and Harriet M. Philips, *Baking Club Manual* (Urbana: University of Illinois Agricultural College and Experiment Station, May 1923). Five universities in less than nine years is an impressive record. It might be that she never sought or was offered an academic or extension position. But from a 21st-century viewpoint, she may not have received proper consideration for a permanent job.

[1273] Ellen L. Marbel household for Bonnie E. and Elinor Scholes, 1930 US census, Pasadena, Los Angeles County, California, ED 1224, sheet 4A, dwelling 92, family 98.

alumnae club for southern California.[1274] Along with sister Nellie and mother Harriet, they lived at 1147 North Catalina in Pasadena in 1940 and 1942.[1275] In 1951, 1953, and 1954, Bonnie was at 733 North Los Robles in Pasadena.[1276]

In 1951 she echoed her grandfather Thomas Mozley's 1846 letter to his brother Edward, when she encouraged an educated niece and nephew to try their fortunes farther west. California, she wrote, is "just full of Univs and colleges. Even the high schools are better than some eastern colleges."[1277]

She did not forget her roots. "On Sunday [29 May 1955], a family gathering was held at the Elmer Scholes (first cousin, Chapter 34) home in Moundville in honor of Miss Bonnie Scholes of Pasadena, California, who is visiting relatives here. A pot luck dinner was served at noon. About 40 were present."[1278]

[1274] Harriet Scholes household for Bonnie E., 1940 US census, Pasadena, Los Angeles County, California, ED 19-452, sheet 18B, dwelling 39. Also, "Alumnae Club Directory," *Wisconsin Alumnus* 42(1):96, November 1940.
[1275] Scholes family entries, *Thurston's Pasadena City Directory 1940* (Los Angeles: Los Angeles Directory Company, 1940), p. 587; also *1942*, p. 598.
[1276] Bonnie Scholes, *Thurston's Pasadena City Directory 1951* (Los Angeles: Los Angeles Directory Company, 1951), p. 636, image 315 of 494; similarly, *1953*, p. 624, image 320 of 403; *1954*, p. 597, image 318 of 717, and p. 178 (by street), image 488 of 717 (ancestry.com).
[1277] Bonnie Scholes letter to her nephew's wife Eloise (Bassett) Scholes, 5 July 1951, in author's possession.
[1278] Mrs. Fred Russell, "Endeavor," *Portage Daily Register* (Wisconsin), Thursday 2 June 1955, p. 11, col. 1.

Chapter 31
Third Generation

Samuel Ray Scholes–Lois E. Boren Family
parents at Chapter 8

On Avogadro's Number
(as Shakespeare's Prospero might write):

I once wrought wonders with my sorcery;
But, when I saw what Chemistry could do,
I broke my wand, forgot the secret words,
And threw my magic books into the sea.[1279]

---

31. SAMUEL RAY[3] **SCHOLES** (*Samuel Mills*[2] *Scholes, Ann*[1] *Mills, Samuel*[A])
Birth: 22 January 1884 in Marquette, Green Lake County, Wisconsin
Death: 16 August 1974 in North Hornell, Steuben County, New York
Burial: Alfred Rural Cemetery, New York
Spouse: **LOIS ELIZABETH BOREN** married 10 April 1914 in Pittsburgh[1280]
Spouse's parents: Addison and Bertha "Bertie" (Linhart) Boren
Spouse's birth: 23 June 1894 in Pittsburgh
Spouse's death: 9 July 1979 in Dansville, Livingston County, New York
Spouse's burial: Alfred Rural Cemetery, New York[1281]

[1279] S. R. Scholes, *Journal of Chemical Education* 42:126, March 1965. Copy in author's possession. Five additional stanzas note the chemical phenomenon that equal volumes of gases must contain equal numbers of molecules. That number is 6x10 to the 23rd power. The final stanza applied poetry to make the number more understandable:
"If all the lands in all the world were lawns
(No desert, mountain, forest or plowed ground),
Where grass blades grew, one hundred to the foot,
On each square foot ten thousand, all the Earth
Has room for two times ten to nineteenth power.
So, thirty thousand grassy worlds might raise
The blades to tie the Avogadro Number."
[1280] Samuel Scholes Family Record, Scholes ledger book, 30–31, in author's possession.
[1281] "Well Known Alfred Musician Dies at 85," *Alfred Sun* (New York), Thursday 12 July 1979, p. 3, cols. 1–4.

Probably to minimize confusion, he was called "Ray" and his father "Sam." In 1893, Sam took older sisters Nellie and Bonnie to the Chicago World's Fair; son Ray was deemed too young to go, but got even: "I read so much about the Fair and saw so many pictures that I knew almost as much about it as the attenders did."

After college, Ray spent three years coaching and teaching science in Wausau (Wisconsin) for $65 per month. "My football team saved its final game with the first forward pass ever seen in the Wisconsin Valley. I had spent six weeks at Chicago U., in 1907, and got some pointers from A. A. Stagg. That third year, my pay was $1000 and I could have stayed on [at Wausau]. But chemistry got into me, and I headed for Yale."[1282]

In 1917 he was 6 feet tall and slender, with gray eyes and black hair.[1283] Having graduated from Ripon College (1905 AB) and Yale University (1911 PhD), Ray met his future wife when he came to the University of Pittsburgh as a research fellow, and attended the Unitarian Church there.[1284]

Ray became a world authority in glass chemistry and author of the widely used text *Modern Glass Practice*.[1285] He worked in both industry and academia:

- 1913–20, chemist, H.C. Fry Glass Company, Rochester, Beaver County, Pennsylvania
- 1914–17, assistant director, Mellon Institute, University of Pittsburgh

---

[1282] Samuel Ray Scholes, typescript 1960–1961, sometimes called "Pop's Peregrinations," in author's possession. Also, *Who Was Who in America 1974–1976* (Chicago: Marquis Who's Who, 1976), 6:364.
[1283] Samuel Ray Scholes, WWI draft card, 12 September 1918, series #2471, order #a2260, Beaver County, Pennsylvania; "United States World War I Draft Registration Cards, 1917–1918" > Pennsylvania > Beaver County local board #2 > Maantidos–Z > image 2788 of 5071 (familysearch.org).
[1284] "Memories of Lois Boren Scholes," February 1977, typed transcript of tape recording, in Barbara White Miller et al., *The Chronicles of the Blacks, the Linharts, the Borens, 1754–1991* (privately printed, 1991), 277–79. Also, *Who Was Who in America 1974–1976* (Chicago: Marquis Who's Who, 1976) 6:364.
[1285] Samuel R. Scholes, *Modern Glass Practice*, revised edition (Chicago: Industrial Publications, 1946).

- 1918–20, chemistry professor, Geneva College, Beaver Falls, Pennsylvania
- 1920–21, superintendent, Utility Glass Works, Lonaconing, Maryland
- 1921–29, chemist, Federal Glass Company, Columbus, Franklin County, Ohio
- 1926–29, lecturer on glass technology, Ohio State University, Columbus
- 1929–31, technical director, Fostoria Glass Company, Moundsville, West Virginia
- 1932–46, glass technologist, New York State College of Ceramics, Alfred University, Alfred, New York
- 1946–48, college dean
- 1948–52, associate dean, and thereafter emeritus professor[1286]

In 1932 he was called to found and head the first glass science program in the United States at the New York State College of Ceramics at Alfred University, and was instrumental in standardizing the process of glassmaking. (The university's four-story ceramics library is named in his honor.) He also wrote hymns, a weekly local newspaper column, and poetry both serious and humorous.[1287] He dedicated *Modern Glass Practice*

> To that observant man, unknown, unsung,
> Who saw what countless men before had missed:
> The gleam, among the ashes of his fire,
> Of glass; who pondered long with knitted brows,
> And tried, and failed, and tried again, until
> He found how it was made from earth and fire.
> And to the heirs of his creative zeal,
> Who handed down from age to age the art
> Of glass; who tireless sought for better ways,
> Improving bit by bit their gift to men
> Of usefulness and beauty—that which is
> The eye of science, carrier of light.

[1286] *Who Was Who in America 1974–1976* (Chicago: Marquis Who's Who, 1976) 6:364.
[1287] "Dr. Scholes Dies at 90," *Alfred Sun* (New York), Thursday 22 August 1974, p. 1, cols. 1–2, and p. 3, cols. 3–5. Also, "1998 Samuel R. Scholes Lecture" program, and three-page typescript, "Biographical Data Concerning Samuel Ray Scholes," about 1947 (archival box 9, folder 1), both in author's possession.

In Grandview Heights (Columbus, Ohio), Ray served on the school board 1922–29, and in Alfred he chaired the Unitarian Universalist Church board for several years.[1288] As of 1962, mostly retired, he held five US patents, and had authored two books and 55 technical papers.[1289] He was the only grandchild of Thomas and Elizabeth Mozley who spent his life east of Wisconsin rather than west. Later in life he identified as a Republican, but the family story is that in 1932, with the Depression at full force, Lois and Ray cast their votes for socialist Norman Thomas.

Lois was an active organizer, teacher, and participant in music. She directed several church choirs over the years (around 1947, serving as vice-president of the National Association of Choir Directors), organized handbell ringing in the area, and founded and directed the annual Church Music Institute in Alfred from 1949 to 1969.[1290] Her hospitality was legendary. Her daughter recalled, "She said that the important thing was to have a good time, yourself, and then, usually, the guests would enjoy it too. That was one of her most successful recipes."[1291]

Children of Samuel Ray Scholes Sr.^{3} and Lois (Boren) Scholes:

The four children were good friends for life, helping each other in many ways over the years. But for reasons difficult to discern at this distance, politically they split right down the middle, with Sam Jr. and Ad conservative, Ann and Jim liberal. The three brothers shared a competitive interest in fine-tuning and racing Day Sailer sailboats, often traveling hundreds of miles to compete in regattas.

i. SAMUEL RAY^4 SCHOLES JR. (*Samuel R.^{3} Scholes Sr., Samuel Mills^2 Scholes, Ann^1 Mills, Samuel^A*) was born 5 June 1915 in Pittsburgh and

---

[1288] Samuel Ray Scholes, typescript 1960–1961, sometimes called "Pop's Peregrinations," in author's possession.
[1289] "Faculties of AU and Tech Honor Dr. Samuel Scholes," *Wellsville Daily Reporter* (New York), Wednesday 6 December 1961, p. 9, col. 1.
[1290] "Well Known Alfred Musician Dies at 85," *Alfred Sun*, Thursday 12 July 1979, p. 3, cols. 1–4. Also, "Memories of Lois Elizabeth Boren Scholes," tape recording of her reminiscences, February 1977, later transcribed and published in Barbara White Miller, *The Chronicles of The Blacks, The Linharts, The Borens, 1754–1991* (N.p.: privately printed, 1991), 272–86. Also, "Biographical Data Concerning Samuel Ray Scholes," late 1940s typescript, in author's possession, archival box 9, folder 1.
[1291] Ann Scholes Colvin, "Lois," undated typescript, late 1979, in author's possession. Ann gathered material for a biography of her mother but did not live to write it.

died 24 May 2012.[1292] He married DORIS EMILY HAHN/HANN, who was reportedly born 6 April 1915 in Bridgeton, Cumberland County, New Jersey, the daughter of Charles A. and Effie M. (Fogg) Hahn. She died 5 October 1993 after a lengthy illness.[1293]

As an Alfred University student in 1937, Doris managed display advertising for the student publication *Fiat Lux* and was secretary of the Theta Theta Chi sorority.[1294] She taught six years in New Jersey, and in 1956 she was teaching senior math at Alfred-Almond Central School.[1295] Long after graduation, in the 1950s, she began working at the university in admissions, ultimately retiring in 1980. She was described as having the best attitudes for admissions work—"warmth, friendliness, and unselfish helpfulness."[1296]

Sam earned a bachelor's degree in chemistry from Alfred University in 1937 and a PhD from Yale in 1940. He taught chemistry for the next 40 years at Alfred (1940–41), Tufts University (1941–46), and Alfred again (1946–80), where he chaired the chemistry department (1956–70).

"I never worked a day in my life," he told *Chemical and Engineering News* editor-in-chief Madeleine Jacobs in 2003. "I just went to school." Teaching did not seem like work to him. In his late 80s he gave Jacobs the impression "that, if asked, he'd be back in the classroom tomorrow." He was a sixty-year member of the American Chemical Society.

Outside of academia, he was a life member of the Alfred Fire Department, serving as chief for two years, and was elected Village Board trustee for seven consecutive terms. He was an avid golfer, bowler, and amateur radio operator and judge (Morse Code only, please).[1297] Sam lived independently in Alfred until the end of his life, active in the Union University Church, and golfing at Wellsville Country Club well into his nineties. An annual lecture at Alfred

---

[1292] Samuel R. Scholes index entry, US Social Security Death Index (1935–2014).
[1293] Doris Hahn Scholes, no image of grave marker, Alfred Rural Cemetery, Alfred, New York, memorial #201,658,700 by Zoe Tom (findagrave.com).
[1294] *Fiat Lux [1937]*, Alfred University 1936–37, p. 108; "US, School Yearbooks, 1900–1999" > New York > Village of Alfred > Alfred University > 1937 > image 121 of 191 (ancestry.com). Similarly, p. 132 with picture, image 147 of 191.
[1295] "Teacher Joins Alfred Faculty," *Democrat and Chronicle* (Rochester, New York), Wednesday 31 October 1956, p. 11, col. 1.
[1296] "Ten retiring AU staff members honored at trustees dinner," *Alfred Sun* (New York), 22 May 1980, p. 1.
[1297] "The Formula for Teaching Success," *Alfred Magazine* (Summer 2003), 12–13, reprinted from *Chemical and Engineering News*, 14 April. Also, "Our Honoree," biography for the Samuel R. Scholes, Jr. lectures, in author's possession.

University was established in his name in 1999.[1298] He observed his 90th birthday in 2005 with a family gathering and by climbing the steps up to the Davis Memorial Carillon at Alfred University.[1299]

Sam's generosity of spirit might not be obvious from his vita, but his youngest brother put it this way at Sam's funeral service:

> I am remembering a cold fall day in 1927, a Saturday. Sam was 12; I was 6. We were living in Grandview Heights, a suburb of Columbus, Ohio. Sam had a paper route, and delivered the *Columbus Dispatch*. He collected from his customers every Saturday. On that cold day he took me along on his route, me perched in front of him on the cross bar of his bicycle, shivering and uncomfortable but secure and happy. Mid-morning, he bought a package of chipped beef, which we shared the rest of the morning.
> Move ahead to the summer of 1940. Sam had just completed his PhD in chemistry at Yale University and was about to start teaching at Tufts University. I had just floundered through a miserable second year at Alfred University, making a complete hash of it. Sam thought I might do better if I got away from home and offered to pay my tuition, as a kind of payback for the help the family had given him in graduate school. I transferred that fall to Middlebury College. That move changed my life.
> Move ahead to July 2nd, 1942, a month after I graduated from Middlebury. Sam drove me to Fort Niagara, where I was to become a member of the Army of the United States, courtesy of the US government and the draft. Before I made the fateful step forward from civilian life to army life, Sam and I said our farewells. As we shook hands I felt a rolled-up something he was slipping to me. It was a $20 bill. You can't imagine how important that was at the time. I was flat broke . . . that 20 dollars was a Godsend. That was my big brother. For the next 70 years he

---

[1298] Samuel Scholes Jr. obituary, *Evening Tribune* (Hornell, New York), 27 May 2012.
[1299] Personal knowledge of author.

continued to be my big brother, generous and caring.[1300]

ii. LOIS ANN[4] SCHOLES (*Samuel R.[3] Scholes Sr., Samuel Mills[2] Scholes, Ann[1] Mills, Samuel[A]*) was born 25 June 1916 in Pittsburgh and died very suddenly November 1983 in Gaithersburg, Montgomery County, Maryland.[1301] She married 22 December 1947 in Alfred, New York, BURTON HOUSTON COLVIN.[1302] He was born 12 July 1916 in West Warwick, Kent County, Rhode Island, and died of prostate cancer 24 August 2001 in Maryland, the son of Asa Burton and Sara Elsie (Houston) Colvin.[1303]

At Alfred University, Ann was a member (along with brother Sam) of Eta Mu Alpha, a thirteen-year-old honorary scholastic fraternity "dedicated to the cause of furthering intellectual activity on the Alfred campus." She was assistant editor for "society" in the student publication *Fiat Lux*.[1304]

After graduating, Ann earned a master's degree in mathematics at Syracuse (1939), did further graduate work at the University of Wisconsin, and spent a year teaching high school in New York state. From 1941 to 1943 she worked at the Hawkeye Division of Eastman Kodak in Rochester, and from 1943 to 1945 taught in the USMAP program at Cornell University. In 1945–46 she was a substitute associate professor of mathematics at Alfred, and the following year a graduate assistant in mathematics at the University of Wisconsin.[1305]

An accomplished teacher at all levels, she had a special way with young children. After thorough preparation and curriculum development, she came to class with a verve and spontaneity which almost always sparked a like response from the class. Her quick wit and spontaneous humor could surprise teenagers and younger adults who did not

---

[1300] James B. Scholes at Sam Scholes Memorial Service, Alfred, New York, 16 June 2012; in author's possession, archival box 13, "Memorials."

[1301] "Scholes–Colvin Wedding," unlabeled newspaper clipping, probably *Alfred Sun*, late December 1947. Also, Ann Colvin index entry, US Social Security Death Index, 1934–2014.

[1302] Burton Houston Colvin funeral program, 13 October 2001, Unitarian Universalist Church of Rockville, Maryland; in author's possession, Scholes tub 4, file 71.

[1303] Burton Houston Colvin entry, *Who's Who in America, 55th edition, 2001* (New Providence, New Jersey: Marquis Who's Who, 2000).

[1304] *Fiat Lux [1937]*, Alfred University 1936–37, p. 61 including photo; "US, School Yearbooks, 1900–1999" > New York > Village of Alfred > Alfred University > 1937 > image 72 of 191 (ancestry.com). Similarly, p. 108 for society editor, image 121 of 191.

[1305] "Scholes–Colvin Wedding," unlabeled loose newspaper clipping, probably *Alfred Sun*, late December 1947.

expect levity from one of her age. Her interest in music came naturally. In the early 1980s she accepted her mother's collection of fine English hand bells, schooled herself to ring, took training in leading hand-bell ringers, and directed a bell choir in the church. Ann's was an eager, questing, enthusiastic, energetic spirit, emboldened by strong convictions and great perseverance.[1306]

Burt worked for the National Institute of Standards and Technology from 1972 to 1991, and was inducted into the institute's gallery posthumously in 2002.[1307] In his last year he wrote "biographical notes":

> My sister, brother and I were born during the strike-savaged depression years of 1912–1916, when our small Rhode Island town was being destroyed economically by the move of the textile mills to the south. . . .
>
> We were very poor, but fortunately had wonderful parents. My Mother was very handsome, smart and spirited. Before her marriage she had been a milliner and earned a widespread reputation for the dashing hats she designed. My Father was a delightful, loving parent, always supportive of us children. In school he had excelled in 'elocution' and often delighted us children by reciting some long dramatic poem he had mastered for some elocution contest.
>
> From early on my Mother impressed upon us that we must somehow get a college education to get out of our depressed town. And, in fact, by dint of hard work and help from many, we did all graduate from college. I was fortunate to be able to work my way through Brown University, graduating in 1938. After completing a fellowship year of graduate mathematics study at Brown, I went on to the University of Wisconsin to

---

[1306] Burton H. Colvin, typewritten biographical and reminiscent material about Ann, late 1983; in author's possession, Scholes box 13, memorials.

[1307] "The NIST Portrait Gallery of Distinguished Scientists, Engineers and Administrators honors NBS/NIST alumni for outstanding career contributions to the work of NBS/NIST. Portraits and biographies of those selected are displayed in the corridor of the NIST cafeteria at Gaithersburg, and in the Digital Portrait Gallery at NIST Gaithersburg and NIST Boulder sites" (nist.gov/system/files/documents/2019/10/07/portrait_gallery_program_brochure_2019.pdf); NIST > Office of the Director > Standards Alumni Association> NIST Portrait Gallery.

work towards a Ph.D. There I met (Lois) Ann Scholes, who was also studying graduate mathematics. We were married several years later.

After several wartime years on the faculty at Wisconsin and a brief stint in New York City with the Office of Scientific Research and Development, I accepted a job at the Boeing Company in Seattle, which had just established a research group in physical science and mathematics to prepare for the missile-satellite age. . . .

Ann was a lifelong Unitarian and introduced me to Unitarianism. She was very active in the religious education programs of the Seattle churches and later in the Rockville church. She was a wonderful wife, mother and companion until her unexpected death in 1983.

After some time at Boeing it became evident that a main strength of mine was my ability to recruit exceptionally good scientific researchers to work under my scientific and administrative leadership. After a few years of hard work we were able to assemble a "world class" group of exceptional research workers. . . .

While at Boeing I was allowed to take leave during a number of summers to allow me to work with the School Mathematics Study Group (SMSG), one of the largest and most influential of the efforts supported by the National Science Foundation (NSF) to improve the teaching of mathematics in the 1960s and 1970s.

The years at Boeing were very difficult but very satisfying professionally and I stayed on until the economic debacle of the early 1970s forced the dissolution of the Research Laboratories. . . . Although already 55 years old in 1972, I decided to go to Maryland and the National Bureau of Standards (NBS), now the National Institute of Standards and Technology (NIST). While at NBS I was afforded the opportunity to help establish and promote the National Physical Science Consortium, an effort to support Ph.D. studies in physical science and mathematics by minorities and women.

iii. ADDISON BOREN[4] SCHOLES (*Samuel R.[3] Scholes Sr., Samuel Mills[2] Scholes, Ann[1] Mills, Samuel[A]*) was born 8 October 1917, in Rochester, Beaver County, Pennsylvania, and died 28 March 2006 in Upper Saucon Township, Pennsylvania.[1308] He married 22 December 1939 in Alfred, Allegany County, New York, VIRGINIA MAY WOODRING/ROBINSON, the daughter of Millard H. and Gladys (Murray) Woodring.[1309] Virginia was born about 1918 (reportedly 2 November 1917) in Coudersport, Potter County, Pennsylvania; died after a long illness 10 July 2002 in Upper Saucon Township, Pennsylvania; and was buried at Alfred Rural Cemetery.[1310] Millard and Gladys's marriage did not last long; she and toddler Virginia were living with Gladys's father and stepmother in 1920.[1311] Gladys married second 6 June 1922 Lloyd W. Robinson, an instructor living in Andover. He was born about 1895 to C.A. and Louise (Watson) Robinson.[1312] Virginia and Addison both attended Alfred High School, and graduated from Alfred University early in 1939.[1313] In 1937 she

---

[1308] *The Morning Call*, 30 March 2006 (https://www.legacy.com/obituaries/mcall/obituary.aspx?n=addison-scholes&pid=17271116).
[1309] Millard H. Woodring–Gladys F. Murray marriage 14 June 1916, Wellsville, Allegany County, New York, #2792, p. 558; "New York County Marriages, 1847–1849 and 1907–1936" > Allegany >1908–1917 > image 306 of 309 (ancestry.com). Congregational minister Wm. H. Woodring (evidently the groom's father) officiated. Millard was clerk in a turbine plant, Gladys was a musician. As of 1920 Gladys and toddler Virginia were living in the household of Gladys's father Benjamin Murray at 42 Cummings Place in Wellsville: 1920 US census, ED 39, sheet 9B, dwelling 193, family 213. Millard was not found in that year. Gladys married second 6 June 1922 in Wellsville Lloyd W. Robinson: Allegany County, New York, #4719, p. 342; "New York County Marriages, 1847–1849 and 1907–1936" > Allegany >1824–1932 > image 172 of 492 (ancestry.com). Also, Lloyd W. Robinson household for "adopted" Virginia, 1930 US census, Alfred, Allegany County, New York, ED 1, sheet 6A, dwelling 131, family 163.
[1310] Virginia R. Scholes, no grave marker image, Alfred Rural Cemetery, Alfred, New York, lot 154, memorial #1,658,727 by Zoe Tom (findagrave.com). Also, "Virginia R. Scholes," *Morning Call* (Allentown), Friday 12 July 2002, p. 26 or B11, col. 1.
[1311] Benjamin Murray household, Wellsville, Allegany County, New York, 1920 US census, ED 39, sheet 9B, dwelling 193, family 213.
[1312] Gladys married second 6 June 1922 in Wellsville Lloyd W. Robinson: Allegany County, New York, #4719, p. 342; "New York County Marriages, 1847–1849 and 1907–1936" > Allegany >1824–1932 > image 172 of 492 (ancestry.com). Also, Lloyd W. Robinson household for "adopted" Virginia, 1930 US census, Alfred, Allegany County, New York, ED 1, sheet 6A, dwelling 131, family 163.
[1313] "Two Popular Alfred Young People United in Marriage at the Village Church Friday," *Alfred Sun* (New York), Thursday 28 December 1939, p. 1, col. 1.

was first violin in the college orchestra, and among the second altos in the women's glee club.[1314] After graduation Ad was employed by the National Lead Company (since 1971, NL Industries) as a research engineer.[1315]

Virginia completed Red Cross advanced first-aid training (33 hours total) in the fall of 1954 in Warren, Warren County, Pennsylvania.[1316] Five years later she was teaching boys' archery classes at the YMCA.[1317] In 1960 she played violin in the Warren Civic Orchestra.[1318]

Addison worked in research and development for almost his entire professional life. An inventor with more than 40 patents to his credit, he was an elected fellow of the American Ceramic Society.

He was employed at Sylvania Corporation in Massachusetts, then joined the Air Force Research Project at Alfred University, developing ceramic liners for the exhaust systems of jet fighter planes, then returned to Sylvania in Warren, Pennsylvania. For the next 25 years, he worked at Ball Corporation, Muncie, Indiana as director of development and led research and development teams. He was recognized in 1980 with the Award of Excellence for outstanding contribution to Ball Corporation.

He was a world authority on glass coatings. His invention of a process for coating glass has had application worldwide. He contributed a ceramic device which makes possible the atomic clock in satellites, essential to the Global Positioning System. In retirement, he was a valued consultant and was still an

---

[1314] *Fiat Lux [1937]*, Alfred University 1936–37, p. 117 including photo; "US, School Yearbooks, 1900–1999" > New York > Village of Alfred > Alfred University > 1937 > image 130 of 191 (ancestry.com). Similarly, glee club, p. 119 including photo, image 132 of 191.

[1315] "Two Popular Alfred Young People United in Marriage at the Village Church Friday," *Alfred Sun* (New York), Thursday 28 December 1939, p. 1, col. 1.

[1316] "County News in Brief," *Warren County Observer* (Pennsylvania), Thursday 11 November 1954, p. 4, col. 2.

[1317] "Boys' Archery Classes Begin at Y Thursday," *Warren Times Mirror* (Pennsylvania), Wednesday 21 October 1959, p. 18, col. 2.

[1318] "String Section," *Warren Times Mirror* (Pennsylvania), Tuesday 15 November 1960, p. 6, col. 1.

avid inventor. In recent months he had been devising a method for refurbishing florescent light bulbs.

He was an active musician, singing in and directing barbershop quartets. He was a certified harmony accuracy judge for barbershop music competitions. An avid amateur radio operator, he achieved the highest-level extra radio license and often served as a net manager for the American Relay Radio League. He was also an active sailor, competing nationwide in the Day Sailer class and serving one term as president of the Day Sailer Association. In later years, he cruised Lake Erie, single-handing a 27-foot sloop. He brought an intense energy and competitive spirit to racing, as he did to everything he was involved in. As an undergraduate at Alfred University, he was the smallest man on the football team at 140 pounds, but played like a tiger. He brought to the laboratory, to his community, to his family and to every endeavor intense commitment.[1319]

iv. JAMES BERT[4] SCHOLES (*Samuel R.[3] Scholes Sr., Samuel Mills[2] Scholes, Ann[1] Mills, Samuel[A]*) was born 16 February 1921 in Stamford, Fairfield County, Connecticut; died 16 November 2016 from complications of a fall in Livonia, Livingston County, New York; and was buried with his wife at Alfred Rural Cemetery.[1320] He married HARRIET ELOISE BASSETT, who was born 12 July 1920 in Winchendon, Massachusetts; died overnight 24/25 August 2011 at Teresa House in Geneseo, Livingston County, New York; and was buried at Alfred Rural Cemetery.[1321]

[1319] "Addison Scholes" (https://www.legacy.com/obituaries/mcall/obituary.aspx?n=addison-scholes&pid=17271116).
[1320] Personal knowledge of author.
[1321] Eloise Bassett Scholes grave marker, image, Alfred Rural Cemetery, Alfred, New York, memorial #75,725,286 by nmbo (findagrave.com).

Her parents were Leon B. and Rachel M. (Burdick) Bassett.[1322] The family lived in Massachusetts and in Milton, Rock County, Wisconsin. The Depression brought them back to Alfred, where Leon worked for his father; in 1932 he joined the University staff and in 1938 the Ceramic College staff, receiving an honorary degree of professional ceramic engineering in 1950. "His studies led to patents and successful processes in glaze refractories and abrasive technology."[1323]

Jim and Eloise met in the fall of 1932, when she turned him down for the Halloween party. Ten years later they were married. She worked as a ceramic artist, and later as an occupational therapy aide at Mountain Home Veterans Administration when they lived in Tennessee.[1324]

In the early 1960s they lived in a large Victorian house near the campus of the State University of New York at Geneseo, and she acted as "house mother" for eight young women there. They habitually locked all doors overnight, but one bitter February night, Eloise insisted that they not do so: "Someone might need to come in out of the cold!"

A few years later, no longer a house mother, she met some new Chinese students on the campus in the graduate library program, who were miserable with culture shock. Could they possibly live at the Scholes house? And yes, they could. At year's end, one of the girls wrote, "You are the best person I was ever met."

Many other lost souls and relatives could have said the same—even a few birds. One spring a family of nesting robins in their new house's eaves was broken up, with only one of the parents left to warm and feed all the babies. On Eloise's insistence, they went out and bought a supply of earthworms from a local bait shop to be placed, a few at a time, near the nest.[1325]

[1322] Commonwealth of Massachusetts Certificate of Birth 3:139, Harriet Eloise Bassett; in author's possession. A family story has it that a doting relative saw the new baby and exclaimed "Dear little Hattie!"—at which point the second given name came into play instead.

[1323] Leon Burdette Bassett death notice, *Sabbath Recorder* 195:15, 27 October 1973. Transcribed online at memorial #117,094,585 in Alfred Rural Cemetery, by Jon Saunders and Kris Evans (findagrave.com).

[1324] VA notification of personnel action, Mrs. Harriet B. Scholes, 1 August 1958; in author's possession, Scholes Box 5.

[1325] James B. Scholes memorial notes, 25 August 2011, in author's possession, Scholes box 13, "Memorials."

From Jim's 1992 autobiography for his Middlebury class's fiftieth reunion:

> Almost immediately after our [1942] graduation, Uncle Sam grabbed me and sent me off to become an army engineer, perhaps in a confusion of abbreviations, I having majored in English. I served as an engineer officer in odd assignments in North Africa (running a hotel [in Bizerte], messing about in Civil Affairs), Italy, and France (with the 266th Combat Engineers, where our division was "containing" the St. Nazaire pocket in a quiet part of the war).[1326]
>
> Post war I did graduate work in English, emerging at long last with a Ph.D. from the University of North Carolina and finding myself in the classroom pretty steadily thereafter, teaching in Kansas, Illinois, Tennessee, North Carolina, and finally at SUNY Geneseo, where I spent twenty-five years, the last six chairing the English Department (in a sad time of diminishing resources). Along the way I was named "teacher of the year" in 1964 and received the Chancellor's Award for Excellence in Teaching in 1976.
> Cornell University allowed me to be a "visiting fellow" in their China Program when I was awarded a Foreign Area Study Fellowship by the Ford Foundation in 1966. Two years later I was a Fulbright Lecturer in American Literature at the National Taiwan University.
> I retired in 1984, to have a go at theater, having served a long apprenticeship hamming it up in the classroom and having acted professionally in the summers for years. That has kept me just about as busy as I want to be. Highlights have been roles with the Playmakers Repertory Company in Chapel

---

[1326] James B. Scholes Military Record and Report of Separation, Certificate of Service 0-1110236, 1st Lieutenant, 266th Engineer Combat Battalion, active duty 3 February 1943–24 January 1946 (European Theater 13 April 1943–1 November 1945). In author's possession.

Hill, N.C. and in recent summers with the Hangar Theatre in Ithaca, N.Y., and in a number of Rochester-area theaters, where I have been consistently occupied.[1327]

His dramatic vehicles ranged from Chekhov's *The Cherry Orchard* to *On Golden Pond* to the occasional TV soap opera bit—and later in the Geriactors, a senior traveling troupe which he co-founded. "Friends, colleagues, and relatives cherish memories of his enthusiasm, his determination, his unfailing sense of humor, and his generosity with time, money, and spirit."[1328]

[1327] *Middlebury College Class of 1942 Fiftieth Reunion,* James B. Scholes autobiography (unpaginated, alphabetical by surname). Later awards: SUNY Geneseo Career Service Award, 17 May 1985. Also, Arts Leadership Award, Genesee Valley Council on the Arts, 1 October 2005; copies in author's possession.
[1328] James Bert Scholes (obituary), 21 November 2016 (https://embser.blogspot.com/2016/11/james-bert-scholes.html).

Chapter 32

Third Generation

Marion Edith Scholes Family
<u>parents at Chapter 9</u>

Nine cousins from Pomona to Philadelphia, but mostly Wisconsin

32. MARION EDITH³ SCHOLES (*William² Scholes, Ann¹ Mills, Samuel^A*)
Birth: about June 1890 in Wisconsin[1329]
Death: 13 March 1962 in Portage, Columbia County, Wisconsin, said to be 73 years old[1330]
Burial: Moundville Cemetery, Endeavor, Marquette County, Wisconsin[1331]

Her parents' only child, she did not marry. "Miss Scholes was a teacher in the Columbia County rural schools for many years until her aging parents required her help and loving care," likely in the 1910s and 1920s. She was active in the First Methodist Church of Portage, the Women's Christian Temperance Union, as well as a member of the Women's Society of Christian Service, the Pollyanna Club of the church, and the Portage Civic League.[1332]

A few years after father William's death in 1929, "Marion felt that she needed a little more income so she had the rooms upstairs fixed so that she could use it for a little apartment for herself and she rented the

---

[1329] William Scholes household, 1900 US census, Fort Winnebago, Columbia County, Wisconsin, ED 8, sheet 6A, dwelling 105, family 113.
[1330] "Marion Scholes," clipping dated 13 March 1962, datelined Portage; Stella Scholes collection, item 4, in author's possession. The obituary is also transcribed at Marion E. Scholes memorial #103,171,137 (see following note). The text says she was 73 years old; the clipping is dated (handwritten) 13 March 1962, implying birth 1889.
[1331] Marion E. Scholes 1889–1962 grave marker, image, Moundville Cemetery, Marquette Co., Wisconsin, memorial #103,171,137 for Marion Edith Scholes by Barb Voss (findagrave.com).
[1332] "Obituary…Marion Edith Scholes," *Portage Daily Register* (Wisconsin), Saturday 17 March 1962, p. 4, col. 8.

downstairs," about 1936 or 1937. "She continued renting the downstairs to various families until about 1958 or 1959 (I think). It seemed then to be getting hard to get renters."[1333]

As of 21 November 1945, "Miss Marion Scholes" was "assisting with the house work at the Norman Scholes home."[1334]

In 1954 the family donated a memorial window to the Moundville Methodist Church. Marion, custodian of the Scholes family Bible, gave an account of the pioneer couple, William and Ann. Two first cousins traveled farthest for the ceremony—Ruth Emma (Scholes) Redman of Pennsylvania and Samuel Ray Scholes of New York.[1335]

In 1962 she died "unexpectedly . . . at the home of Miss Collette Wright where she had served as a companion for many years."[1336]

Nine first cousins were listed as surviving her, five in Wisconsin and four "from away"; five on the Scholes side, four on the Dixon side:[1337]

From away:
Mrs. Ruth (Dixon) Jones, Pomona, Los Angeles County, California (Chapter 19)
Dr. S. Ray Scholes, Alfred, Allegany County, New York (Chapter 31)
Samuel E. Scholes, Buena Vista, Virginia (Chapter 35)
Mrs. Ruth Redman, Drexel Hill, Upper Darby Township, Pennsylvania (Chapter 37)

From Wisconsin:
Robert Smith, Beloit (Chapter 25)

[1333] Letter from "Aunt Ruth and Elizabeth" to Stella and Norman Scholes, "Feb. 16," well after 1962; Stella Scholes collection, item 18, in author's possession.
[1334] "Admit Church Members Sunday," *Portage Daily Register* (Wisconsin), Thursday 10 April 1947, p. 4, col. 7.
[1335] "Members of Scholes Family Dedicate Memorial Window," *Portage Daily Register* (Wisconsin), Tuesday 24 August 1954, p. 3, col. 1.
[1336] "Marion Scholes," clipping dated 13 March 1962, datelined Portage; Stella Scholes collection, item 4, in author's possession.
[1337] "Obituary…Marion Edith Scholes," *Portage Daily Register* (Wisconsin), Saturday 17 March 1962, p. 4, col. 8.

Mrs. Lillian Russell, Endeavor (Chapter 33)
Mrs. Sarah (Dixon) Wade, Endeavor (daughter of Mary Ellen Dixon's brother William, 1898–1989)
Mrs. Ethel (Dixon) Brooks, Delavan (daughter of Mary Ellen Dixon's brother Aaron, 1891–1972)
Mrs. Eunice (Dixon) Giese, Portage (daughter of Mary Ellen Dixon's brother William, 1910–1994)

Chapter 33

Third Generation

Lillian Estelle Scholes–Fred Gaylord Russell Family
parents at Chapter 10

Buttermaker, saw mill operator, materials inspector

33. LILLIAN ESTELLE³ SCHOLES (*George² Scholes, Ann¹ Mills, Samuel^A*)
Birth: 18 December 1885 in Marquette County, Wisconsin[1338]
Death: 19 January 1970 in Portage, Columbia County, Wisconsin, age 84[1339]
Burial: Moundville Cemetery, Endeavor, Marquette County, Wisconsin[1340]
Spouse: **FRED GAYLORD RUSSELL,** married 18 June 1908, the brother of Edith Eliza (Russell) (Bell) Boettcher (Chapter 15, child i)
Spouse's parents: Lorin and Caroline (Gaylord) Russell
Spouse's birth: 27 June 1885 in Moundville Township, Marquette County, Wisconsin
Spouse's death: 2 June 1951 in Portage, Columbia County, Wisconsin, after an extended illness (heart ailment) followed by a stroke[1341]
Spouse's burial: Moundville Cemetery, Endeavor, Marquette County, Wisconsin[1342]

[1338] George W. Scholes household for daughter Lillie E., 1900 US census, Moundville Township, Marquette County, Wisconsin, ED 93, sheet 2A, dwelling/family 38. For reportedly exact date and place, Lillian E. and Fred G. Russell, joint grave marker, image, memorials #69,931,107 and #69,931,101 respectively, by Oscar Sandstrom (findagrave.com).

[1339] Lillian E. Russell death index entry, "Wisconsin, Death Index, 1959–1997," certificate 237.

[1340] Lillian E. and Fred G. Russell, joint grave marker, image, memorials #69,931,107 and #69,931,101 respectively, by Oscar Sandstrom (findagrave.com).

[1341] "Obituary…Fred Gaylord Russell," *Portage Daily Register* (Wisconsin), Saturday 16 June 1951, p. 6, col. 4.

[1342] Lillian E. and Fred G. Russell, joint grave marker, image, memorials #69,931,107 and #69,931,101 respectively, by Oscar Sandstrom (findagrave.com).

Fred Russell "grew to manhood in Moundville where he helped on the home farm of his parents, and where he attended what is now known as the Pleasant View School. He then took a dairy course at the University of Wisconsin and occupied positions as buttermaker at Moundville, Portage, Montello, Ryan [Delaware County], Iowa, and other places."

Lillian and Fred spent the first eleven years of their married life on a farm in Moundville. In the fall of 1920 they moved to Endeavor where they remained. Fred and brother-in-law Samuel E. Scholes ran a feed and saw mill known as the Russell and Scholes mill during the 1920s. From about 1931 he was employed by the Wisconsin State Highway Commission as inspector of materials.[1343]

Fred completed seven years of schooling, Lillian two years of high school.[1344] In 1930 Fred was a miller and they owned a $2500 house on Academy Boulevard in Endeavor; they had no radio set.[1345] In 1940 they were renting a house on Prospect Avenue in Endeavor, Marquette County, for $5 a month. Lillian's widowed and aged father was with them there. Fred worked as an inspector for the state highway department, which in the previous year had paid him $600 for 26 weeks' work.[1346]

"During his illness he showed that uncomplaining spirit of courage, patience and fortitude which characterized his life . . . . He will be greatly missed by all who knew him." Among those attending his funeral were Edith Boettcher of Rochester, Minnesota (Chapter 15, child i); numerous Russells; Mr. and Mrs. Sam Scholes and daughter Verna (Chapter 35) and Mr. and Mrs. Robert Smith (Chapter 25) of Beloit; Miss Marion Scholes of Portage (Chapter 32); and Mr. and Mrs. Ray Sherwin of Sparta (Chapter 13, child i).[1347]

[1343] "Obituary…Fred Gaylord Russell," *Portage Daily Register* (Wisconsin), Saturday 16 June 1951, p. 6, col. 4.
[1344] Fred Russell household, 1940 US census, Endeavor, Marquette County, Wisconsin, ED 39-8, dwelling 55, sheet 2B.
[1345] Fred G. Russell household, 1930 US census, Moundville, Marquette County, Wisconsin, ED 8, sheet 1B, dwelling/family 34.
[1346] Fred Russell household, 1940 US census, Endeavor, Marquette County, Wisconsin, ED 39-8, dwelling 55, sheet 2B.
[1347] "Obituary…Fred Gaylord Russell," *Portage Daily Register* (Wisconsin), Saturday 16 June 1951, p. 6, col. 4.

Child of Lillian Estelle*³* and Fred Russell:

i. ELAYNE VENETTA/VENETA*⁴* RUSSELL (*Lillian³ Scholes* [by adoption], *George² Scholes, Ann¹ Mills, Samuel^A*) was born 28 November 1917 in Wisconsin; died 22 November 2010 at Wisconsin Dells, Columbia County, Wisconsin;[1348] and was buried at Hill Crest Cemetery, Endeavor, Marquette County, Wisconsin[1349] She was adopted: "Mr and Mrs Fred Russell recently took a little 6 weeks old baby girl from the Foundlings Home in Milwaukee. We sincerely hope she may grow up to be a comfort to them."[1350]

Elayne married 20 March 1936 RUDOLPH WALTER "RUDY" HINZE in Endeavor, Marquette County.[1351] The son of Herman and Sophie (Longfeldt) Hinze, he was born 11 February 1909 in Skokie, Cook County, Illinois; died 12 December 1994 in Portage, Columbia County, Wisconsin;[1352] and was buried at Hill Crest Cemetery.[1353] Rudy moved from Chicago to Marquette County in the early 1930s and evidently never left. In 1940 he was working as an egg candler in the poultry and egg business; in the previous year he earned $1090 for 52 weeks' work. They were renting a place on Park Street in Endeavor for $8 a month. Elayne completed four years of high school, Rudy eight years of school.[1354]

He worked at Dairyland Poultry in Endeavor and later at Bradebrush, Inc., in Westfield, Marquette County, until he retired in the late 1960s. "Mr. Hinze enjoyed to curl and to shoot pool. He also enjoyed

---

[1348] Elayne Hinze obituary abstract from *Beaver Dam Daily Citizen* (Wisconsin), 24 November 2010, no page or column number; "US, Obituary Collection, 1930–2018" (ancestry.com). Also, Fred Russell household for daughter "Elain" V., 1920 US census, Moundville, Marquette County, Wisconsin, ED 133, sheet 3B, dwelling 65, family 66.
[1349] Elayne V. and Rudolph W. Hinze, joint grave marker, Hill Crest Cemetery, Endeavor, Wisconsin, memorials #105,811,332 and #105,811,507 respectively, by Joey (findagrave.com).
[1350] "Elaine's Story" posted 29 August 2013 by M2043, transcribed from *Marquette County Epitome* (Endeavor, Wisconsin), 15 February 1918 (ancestry.com/mediaui-viewer/tree/80694282/person/76021397613/media/5399c845-98da-41f7-ae06-616fd9cf2eb6).
[1351] "Russell–Hinze," *Wisconsin State Journal* (Madison), Tuesday 31 March 1936, p. 14, cols. 6–8.
[1352] "Rudolph W. "Rudy" Hinze," *Portage Daily Register* (Wisconsin), Wednesday 14 December 1994, p. 5, col.1.
[1353] Elayne V. and Rudolph W. Hinze, joint grave marker, Hill Crest Cemetery, Endeavor, Wisconsin, memorial #105,811,332 and #105,811,507 respectively, by Joey (findagrave.com).
[1354] Rudy Henze [Hinze] household, 1940 US census, Moundville Township, Marquette County, Wisconsin, ED 39-8, sheet 3B, dwelling 67.

hunting and fishing and was a member of the Endeavor Lyons" [*sic*].[1355]

Elayne was working in the Post Office in 1975 when she was interviewed about life in Endeavor (population 328). "I've lived here all my life," she told a reporter. "It's a nice place to raise a family, but it's hard if you want to buy something because you usually can't get it right away." She had no desire to move to a larger community.[1356]

[1355] "Rudolph W. "Rudy" Hinze," *Portage Daily Register* (Wisconsin), Wednesday 14 December 1994, p. 5, col.1.
[1356] Mary Scoviak, "Endeavor: a nice place to live," *Portage Daily Register* (Wisconsin), Friday 18 April 1975, p. 3, cols. 2–4.

Table 2: Scholes and Russell, allied families

ANN MILLS & WILLIAM SCHOLES
Generation 1

MARY SCHOLES (1835–1910, Ch. 3) m. Bissell Sherwin	Generation 2, siblings	GEORGE SCHOLES (1857–1929, Ch. 10) m. Susanna Audis
FRANK R. SHERWIN (1858–1929, Ch. 13) m. Annie Henry	Generation 3, 1st cousins	LILLIAN E. SCHOLES (1885–1970, Ch. 33) **m. Fred G. Russell**
WILLIAM A. BELL (1888–1923, Ch.15, child 1) **m. Edith Eliza Russell**	Generation 4, 2nd cousins	ELAYNE V. RUSSELL (1917–2010, adopted, Ch. 33, child i) m. Rudolph Hinze

William Bell and Lillian Scholes were first cousins once removed (different generations). Their spouses, Edith and Fred, were siblings, children of Lorin and Caroline (Gaylord) Russell. By adoption, William and Elayne were second cousins in the Scholes line, sharing great-grandparents William and Ann Scholes. Edith Russell was Elayne's aunt; Fred Russell was William's uncle-in-law. Elayne was 2nd cousin once removed to William's 3 children in the Scholes line. But on the Russell side, William's 3 children and Elayne were all grandchildren of Lorin and Caroline Russell.

Note that relationships don't change just because one line has longer generations than another; William Bell and Elayne (Russell) Hinze barely overlap in time, but they remain related as second cousins—even though he died when she was six years old.

Chapter 34

Third Generation

Elmer Roy Scholes–Mary Elsie Rood Family
parents at Chapter 10

Glacier National Park to Florida

34. ELMER ROY^3 **SCHOLES** (*George*^{2} *Scholes, Ann Mills*^{1}*, Samuel*^{A})
Birth: 19 November 1891, Moundville, Wisconsin[1357]
Death: 18 November 1955 (age 63) "following an extended illness"[1358]
Burial: with his wife at Moundville Cemetery, Endeavor, Marquette County, Wisconsin[1359]
Spouse: 24 December 1913 in Buffalo Township, Marquette County, Wisconsin, **MARY ELSIE ROOD**
Spouse's parents: Albert W. and Louise (Pixley) Rood
Spouse's birth: 13 December 1893[1360]
Spouse's death: 15 November 1988 in Madison[1361]

[1357] Elmer R. Scholes, WWI draft card, Buffalo Precinct, Marquette County, Wisconsin, 5 June 1917; "US, World War I Draft Registration Cards, 1917–1919" > Wisconsin > Marquette County > Draft Card S > image 52 of 245 (ancestry.com). Also, George W. Scholes household for son Elmer R., 1900 US census, Moundville Township, Marquette County, Wisconsin, ED 93, sheet 2A, dwelling/family 38.
[1358] "Elmer Scholes Dies at Hospital; Services Monday," *Portage Daily Register* (Wisconsin), Friday 18 November 1955, p. 3, col. 3.
[1359] Elmer R. Scholes and Elsie R. Scholes joint grave marker, Moundville Cemetery, Endeavor, Wisconsin, image, memorials #79,121,360 and #79,121,513 by Barb Voss (findagrave.com). The memorial adds unsourced information to what is on the grave marker.
[1360] "Obituaries…Elsie Scholes," *Portage Daily Register* (Wisconsin), Thursday 17 November 1988, p. 7, col. 1. Also, Albert W. Rood household for daughter Mary, 1900 US census, Buffalo Township, Marquette County, Wisconsin, ED 91, sheet 2A, dwelling/family 26.
[1361] "Records…Deaths…Area," *Wisconsin State Journal* (Madison), Wednesday 16 November 1988, p. 3C, col. 4. Her findagrave.com memorial appears to be in error.

Spouse's burial: with her husband[1362]

On 5 June 1917, Elmer was of medium height and build, with blue eyes and brown hair, a self-employed farmer with wife and children. He claimed exemption from the draft on account of his having a family to support.[1363] He completed two years of high school, Elsie completed eight years of school.[1364]

1920: Elmer B. [R.] was renting a farm in Moundville.[1365]

1930: They were on River Road, where they owned the farm and a radio set.[1366]

1936: "The Y.W.C. gathered at the home of Mrs. Elsie Scholes, Thursday to entertain Mrs. Robey [Maltby] and Mrs. Lois Harvey [Chapter 19, children ii and vi] before their return to California."[1367]

1940: Their River Road house was valued at $800, about a quarter of the $3232 Wisconsin statewide average that year.[1368]

Among the children of Elmer³ and Mary (Rood) Scholes:

[1362] Elmer R. Scholes and Elsie R. Scholes joint grave marker, Moundville Cemetery, Endeavor, Wisconsin, image, memorials #79,121,360 and #79,121,513 by Barb Voss (findagrave.com). The memorial adds unsourced information to what is on the grave marker.

[1363] Elmer R. Scholes, WWI draft card, Buffalo Precinct, Marquette County, Wisconsin, 5 June 1917; "US, World War I Draft Registration Cards, 1917–1919" > Wisconsin > Marquette County > Draft Card S > image 52 of 245 (ancestry.com).

[1364] Elmer R. Scholes household, 1940 US census, Moundville Township, Marquette County, Wisconsin, ED 39-8, sheet 5A, dwelling 120.

[1365] Elmer B. [R.] Scholes household, 1920 US census, Moundville Township, Marquette County, Wisconsin, ED 133, sheet 5A, dwelling 100, family 102.

[1366] Elmer R. Scholes household, 1930 US census, Moundville Township, Marquette County, Wisconsin, ED 8, sheet 4A, dwelling/family 110.

[1367] "Moundville," *Portage Daily Register* (Wisconsin), Thursday 30 July 1936, p. 5, col. 6.

[1368] Elmer R. Scholes household, 1940 US census, Moundville Township, Marquette County, Wisconsin, ED 39-8, sheet 5A, dwelling 120. Statewide figures from US Census Bureau, Census of Housing, Historical Census of Housing Tables, Median Home Values Unadjusted 1940 (https://www2.census.gov/programs-surveys/decennial/tables/time-series/coh-values/values-unadj.txt).

i. MARJORIE E.⁴ SCHOLES (*Elmer³ Scholes, George² Scholes, Ann¹ Mills, Samuel^A*) was born 1915 (reportedly 29 April in Wisconsin), died 2013 (reportedly 16 May in Westfield, Marquette County),[1369] and was buried with her husband in Westfield East Cemetery.[1370] She married JOHN DUDLEY GRAY 26 January 1935 in Briggsville, Marquette County.[1371] The son of Frank David and Gladys J. (Warren) Gray,[1372] he was born 14 April 1915 in Oxford, Marquette County, Wisconsin,[1373] and died 8 June 1982[1374] at Westfield in the same county.

Marjorie graduated from Portage High School in 1933, part of the largest graduating class to date.[1375] In 1940, John and Marjorie were renting a house for $10 a month in Douglas, Marquette County, Wisconsin. He completed one year of high school, and was working as an attendant at a gasoline filling station.[1376] When he registered for the draft that fall, he was unemployed, 5 feet 6 inches tall, and 160 pounds, with blue eyes and brown hair.[1377]

Later he farmed in Newton Township, Marquette County, and worked at the Baraboo Ammunition Plant in Sauk County. He was a member of Faith United Methodist Church in Westfield.[1378]

[1369] Marjorie E. Gray obituary, transcribed from *Daily Register* (Portage, Wisconsin), Friday 17 May 2013 (genealogybank.com).

[1370] Marjorie E. Gray joint grave marker, Westfield East Cemetery, Westfield, Marquette County, Wisconsin, image, memorial #79,453,678 for Marjorie E. Scholes Gray by David Woody (findagrave.com). The memorial adds unsourced information to what is on the grave marker.

[1371] "Briggsville," *Wisconsin State Register* (Portage), Friday 1 February 1935, p. 5, col. 3. Rev. F. W. Heberlein officiated.

[1372] John D. Gray joint grave marker, Westfield East Cemetery, Westfield, Wisconsin, image, memorial #79,453,677 for John Dudley Gray by David Woody (findagrave.com). The memorial adds unsourced information to what is on the grave marker.

[1373] John Dudley Gray WW2 draft card, 16 October 1940, Westfield Local Board, serial #427, order #293; "US WWII Draft Cards Young Men, 1940–1947" > Wisconsin > Genskow–Harwell > Grassl–Greco > images 1308–9 of 1969 (ancestry.com).

[1374] Marjorie E. Gray obituary, transcribed from *Daily Register* (Portage, Wisconsin), Friday 17 May 2013 (genealogybank.com).

[1375] "1933 Graduates of Portage High School," *Daily Register* (Portage, Wisconsin) Saturday 10 June 1933, p. 4, full page.

[1376] John Gray household, 1940 US census, Douglas, Marquette County, Wisconsin, ED 39-3, sheet 6B, dwelling 124.

[1377] John Dudley Gray WW2 draft card, 16 October 1940, Westfield Local Board, serial #427, order #293; "US WWII Draft Cards Young Men, 1940–1947" > Wisconsin > Genskow–Harwell > Grassl–Greco > images 1308–9 of 1969 (ancestry.com).

[1378] "John D. Gray," *Portage Daily Register* (Wisconsin), Wednesday 9 June 1982, p.13, col. 1.

ii. DOROTHY/DORTHEY M.[4] SCHOLES (*Elmer*[3] *Scholes, George*[2] *Scholes, Ann*[1] *Mills, Samuel*[A]) was born 25 August 1916 in Marquette County, Wisconsin; died 25 August 1999 in Bonita Springs, Florida; and was buried with her second husband at Plot 139, Pacific Cemetery, Portage, Columbia County, Wisconsin.[1379]

In June 1926 nineteen-year-old DARWIN ALFRED MARKHARDT of Hampden Township, Columbia County, obtained a license to marry Marvel Jones of Poynette, Columbia County.[1380] The son of Oscar and Sena (Ylvisaker) Markhardt, he was born 13 December 1906 in Columbus, Columbia County, Wisconsin, baptized 28 July 1907 in DeForest, Dane County there,[1381] died 5 April 1949, and was buried at Hampden Cemetery, Columbia County.[1382]

Darwin and Marvel did marry: the following November, "Mrs. and Mrs. Darwin Markhardt of Portage spent Thanksgiving with her parents Mr. and Mrs. B. Jones."[1383] The couple was still socializing in 1931,[1384] but the marriage apparently did not last.

On 25 January 1935, Dorothy's sister Marjorie Scholes married John Gray. Darwin Markhardt was best man and Dorothy was her sister's attendant.[1385] Ten months later Darwin Markhardt (of Portage) and Dorothy Scholes (of Endeavor) were licensed to marry,[1386] and did so

---

[1379] William J. and Dorthey Murray joint grave marker, Pacific Cemetery, Plot 139, Portage, Columbia County, Wisconsin, image, memorials #80,839,385 and #80,839,384 respectively by Kim (findagrave.com). The memorials add unsourced information to what is on the grave marker.
[1380] "Local Happenings," *Portage Daily Register* (Wisconsin), Monday 7 June 1926, p. 3, col. 1.
[1381] Darwin Alfred Markhardt birth and baptism #16 of 1907, Spring Prairie Lutheran Church; "US, Evangelical Lutheran Church in America Church Records, 1781–1969 > Congregational Records > Wisconsin > DeForest > Spring Prairie Lutheran Church > image 16 of 681 (ancestry.com). Witnesses were Mrs. Henry Brown, Ida Olsen, John Ylvisaker, and Lewis Aruble.
[1382] "Darwin Markhardt," *Portage Daily Register* (Wisconsin), Monday 18 April 1949, p. 3, col. 1.
[1383] "Arlington" local notes, *Portage Daily Register* (Wisconsin), Thursday 2 December 1926, p. 3, col. 3
[1384] For instance, "Hampden" local notes, *Portage Daily Register* (Wisconsin), 21 November 1931, p. 4, col. 7.
[1385] "Briggsville," *Wisconsin State Register* (Portage), Friday 1 February 1935, p. 5, col. 3.
[1386] "License Applications," *Portage Daily Register* (Wisconsin), Saturday 16 November 1935, p. 1, col. 2.

19 November 1935 at Trail Creek, near Glacier Park, Montana.[1387] Dorothy had completed four years of high school; Darwin completed eight years of schooling.[1388]

In 1935, they lived near Glacier National Park, possibly on Trail Creek Road.[1389] In 1940 Darwin was a truck driver working on highway construction; they were back in Moundville, living with her parents and family. (He had earned $500 for 26 weeks' work during 1939.) "Outside of living in Montana a year and a half he spent most of the time farming near Arlington, Columbia County, Wisconsin." At the time of Darwin's death from "a very brief and sudden illness" in 1949, he was living near Westfield, Marquette County.[1390]

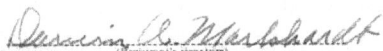

Dorothy married second May 1950 WILLIAM JAMES MURRAY,[1391] son of Charles W. and Mary (Meyers?) Murray. William was born 21 September 1906 in Gregory, Gregory County, South Dakota,[1392] and died after a brief illness 12 April 1972 in Naples, Collier County, Florida,

---

[1387] Elmer R. Scoles [Scholes] household for daughter Dorothy and son-in-law Darwin Markhardt, 1940 US census, Moundville, Marquette County, Wisconsin, ED 39-8, sheet 6A, dwelling 120. For marriage date, "Darwin Markhardt," *Portage Daily Register* (Wisconsin), Monday 18 April 1949, p. 3, col. 1.

[1388] Elmer R. Scoles [Scholes] household for daughter Dorothy and son-in-law Darwin Markhardt, 1940 US census, Moundville, Marquette County, Wisconsin, ED 39-8, sheet 6A, dwelling 120.

[1389] Elmer R. Scoles [Scholes] household for daughter Dorothy and son-in-law Dominic Markhardt, 1940 US census, Moundville, Marquette County, Wisconsin, ED 39-8, sheet 6A, dwelling 120.

[1390] "Darwin Markhardt," *Portage Daily Register* (Wisconsin), Monday 18 April 1949, p. 3, col. 1.

[1391] Mrs. Vern Hume, "East Moundville," *Portage Daily Register* (Wisconsin), Friday 19 May 1950, p. 8, col. 1.: "Mrs. Dorothy Markhardt and William Murray of the town of Pacific were married at DuBuque [*sic*] and enjoyed a week's honeymoon before returning Sunday to spend Mother's Day with Mrs. Markhardt's parents the Elmer Scholes." So they may have married about 6 May.

[1392] William James Murray WW2 draft card, 16 October 1940, serial #3121, order #1819, local board, Portage, Wisconsin; "US, World War II Draft Cards Young Men, 1940–1947" > McTavish–Novasic > Murray–Myers > images 42–43 of 1978 (ancestry.com). For mother's given name, Charles W. Murry household for wife Mary (married 9 years), 1910 US census, Randall Precinct, Gregory County, South Dakota, ED 22, sheet 8B, dwelling 156, family 159. For possible surname, Maria Meyers birth record, 26 October 1882 in Milwaukee to James and Cornelia (Picher) Meyers; "Milwaukee, Wisconsin, Births, 1839–1911" > 1882–1883 > 33–34 > image 65 of 507 (ancestry.com).

and was buried with his wife Dorothy. As of 16 October 1940, William was 5 feet 10 inches tall, weighed 160 pounds, and had blue eyes and brown hair.[1393]

He served as chairman of Pacific Township, Columbia County, Wisconsin, for 20 years, and worked for the state conservation department.[1394]

Wm. J. Murray.
(Registrant's signature)

In 1963 Dorothy reportedly moved from Portage to Bonita Springs, Lee County, Florida. For ten years there she worked as a sales clerk for Eckerd Drugs.[1395] William's obituary has him wintering at "Bamboo Mobile Village" near Naples, Collier County, Florida, and summering in Portage.[1396]

iii. MILDRED ILENE[4] SCHOLES (*Elmer[3] Scholes, George[2] Scholes, Ann[1] Mills, Samuel[A]*) was born 25 September 1920,[1397] and died 16 March 2015 at Wyocena, Columbia County. She married 3 October 1942 at Moundville MERLIN B. WILCOX, son of Alfred and Isobel (Barry) Wilcox. Merlin was born 13 June 1917 in Portage, and died there 19

[1393] William James Murray WW2 draft card, 16 October 1940, serial #3121, order #1819, local board, Portage, Wisconsin; "US, World War II Draft Cards Young Men, 1940–1947" > McTavish–Novasic > Murray–Myers > images 42–43 of 1978 (ancestry.com).

[1394] William J. and Dorthey Murray joint grave marker, Pacific Cemetery, Plot 139, Portage, Columbia County, Wisconsin, image, memorials #80,839,385 and #80,839,384 respectively by Kim (findagrave.com). The memorials add unsourced information to what is on the grave marker. Also, "William Murray," *Portage Daily Register* (Wisconsin), 14 April 1972, p. 5, col. 4. His Florida obituary stated that he was "retired from the conservation in Wisconsin": "William James Murray," *News-Press* (Fort Myers, Florida), Thursday 13 April 1972, p. 2, col. 4.

[1395] "Dorthey [*sic*] Murray," *Portage Daily Register* (Wisconsin), Wednesday 18 August 1999, p. 2, col. 2.

[1396] "William J. Murray," *Naples Daily News* (Florida), Thursday 13 April 1972, p. 16, col. 6.

[1397] "Mildred I. Wilcox," *Portage Daily Register* (Wisconsin) on-line, 16 March 2015 (https://www.wiscnews.com/portagedailyregister/news/local/obituaries/mildred-i-wilcox/article_53dbaa0c-f825-5f6f-b914-6f1fcba62cc2.html).

February 1981. A retired farmer,[1398] he was buried at North Marcellon Cemetery.[1399]

"They farmed together for many years on the family farm while raising three children . . . . Mildred also worked in Portage at the A&W Root Beer Stand and AMPI" (Associated Milk Producers Incorporated).[1400] In 1962 Merlin was using contour strip-cropping and observed better erosion control and crop production as a result. As of 1975 the family's 255-acre dairy and beef operation had been in the Wilcox name since 1855.[1401]

[1398] "Mildred Scholes, Merlin B. Wilcox Wed at Endeavor," *Wisconsin State Journal* (Madison), Sunday 4 October 1942, p. 22, col. 6. (Curiously her 2015 obituary gives April.) Also, "Merlin B. Wilcox," *Portage Daily Register* (Wisconsin), Thursday 19 February 1981, p. 4, col. 4.

[1399] Merlin Barry and Mildred I. (Scholes) Wilcox, joint grave marker, image, North Marcellon Cemetery, Marcellon, Columbia County, Wisconsin, memorials #29,359,232 and #71,450,696 respectively, by Gleem (findagrave.com).

[1400] "Mildred I. Wilcox," *Portage Daily Register* (Wisconsin) on-line, 16 March 2015 (https://www.wiscnews.com/portagedailyregister/news/local/obituaries/mildred-i-wilcox/article_53dbaa0c-f825-5f6f-b914-6f1fcba62cc2.html).

[1401] Warren Fitzgerald, "Soil Conservation News," *Portage Daily Register* (Wisconsin), Tuesday 3 April 1962, p. 5, col. 6. Also, Jack Kelly, "Landowners are honored for conservation work," *Portage Daily Register* (Wisconsin), Wednesday 7 May 1975, p. 3, cols. 3–4.

Chapter 35
Third Generation

Samuel Eugene Scholes–Edna Peake Family
parents at Chapter 10

Commencement message during World War II:
"Every man is your brother, even the German and the Jap"

35. SAMUEL EUGENE³ SCHOLES (*George² Scholes, Ann¹ Mills, Samuel⁴*)
Birth: 3 August 1895 in Wisconsin[1402]
Death: 6 July 1983 at the Veterans Home in King, Waupaca County, Wisconsin[1403]
Burial: Moundville Cemetery, Endeavor, Marquette County, Wisconsin[1404]
Spouse: **EDNA MAE PEAKE,** married 23 October 1920 in Moundville Township, Marquette County, Wisconsin
Spouse's parents: Joseph and Lulu (Loveland) Peake
Spouse's birth: 6 October 1900 in Endeavor, Marquette County
Spouse's death: 24 March 1989 in Waupaca Hospital
Spouse's burial: Moundville Cemetery[1405]

Edna was a graduate of Endeavor Academy and "a successful teacher in the schools of Marquette county the past two years."[1406] She

---

[1402] Samuel Eugene Scholes, WWI draft card, serial #172, order #29, Moundville Precinct local board, 5 June 1917; "US, World War I Draft Registration Cards, 1917–1918" > Wisconsin > Marquette County > Draft Card S > images 53–54 of 245 (ancestry.com). Also, George W. Scholes household for son Samuel E., 1900 US census, Moundville Township, Marquette County, Wisconsin, ED 93, sheet 2A, dwelling/family 38.
[1403] Samuel Scholes, US Department of Veterans Affairs BIRLS Death File, 1850–2010 (ancestry.com).
[1404] Edna M. and Samuel E. Scholes, joint grave marker, Moundville Cemetery, Endeavor, Wisconsin, image, memorials # 102,556,312 and #102,556,219 respectively, by Joey (findagrave.com).
[1405] "Edna Mae Scholes," *Portage Daily Register* (Wisconsin), Friday 26 May 1989, p. 5, col. 1.
[1406] "Scholes–Peake," clipping from unidentified newspaper, October 1920, Stella Scholes collection, item #3, in author's possession.

was teaching in Westfield in the spring of 1920.[1407] She completed four years of high school, Samuel two.[1408]

1917: As of 5 June, Samuel was tall and slender, with blue eyes and brown hair.[1409] He enlisted for World War I 20 September 1917, served in the 331st Field Artillery in France, and was released 19 February 1919.[1410]

Sam E. Scholes

1920: Samuel was described as "one of Moundville's most prosperous young farmers."[1411]

1935: Samuel and Edna were in Columbia County, Wisconsin.

1940–41: renting at $12 a month on Commercial Street, in Brandon, Fond du Lac County, Wisconsin, where Samuel was a butcher in the local locker plant.[1412]

1943: living at 1029 Harrison Avenue in Beloit, Rock County, Wisconsin, with brother Eldred (in the US Navy). Samuel was a machinist at F-M & Company.[1413]

[1407] "Moundville," *Portage Daily Register* (Wisconsin), Monday 12 April 1920, p. 5, col. 1.
[1408] Samuel Scholer [Scholes] household, 1940 US census, Brandon, Fond Du Lac County, Wisconsin, ED 20-4, sheet 5A, dwelling 108.
[1409] Samuel Eugene Scholes, WWI draft card, serial #172, order #29, Moundville Precinct local board, 5 June 1917; "US, World War I Draft Registration Cards, 1917–1918" > Wisconsin > Marquette County > Draft Card S > images 53–54 of 245 (ancestry.com).
[1410] Samuel Scholes, US Department of Veterans Affairs BIRLS Death File, 1850-2010 (ancestry.com). Also, for specific unit, "Scholes, Samuel E.," *Wisconsin State Journal*, Friday 8 July 1983, section 3, p. 7, col. 3.
[1411] "Scholes–Peake," clipping from unidentified newspaper, October 1920, Stella Scholes collection, item #3, in author's possession.
[1412] Samuel Scholer [Scholes] household, 1940 US census, Brandon, Fond Du Lac County, Wisconsin, ED 20-4, sheet 5A, dwelling 108. Also, "Portage," Thursday 23 January 1941, p. 14, col. 5.
[1413] Scholes entries, *Polk's Beloit (Rock County, Wis.) City Directory 1943* (Milwaukee: R.L. Polk & Company), p. 206, image 102 of 206 (ancestry.com).

1962: when Marion Edith Scholes died, her cousin Samuel E. Scholes was living in Buena Vista, Virginia.[1414]

1965: Samuel and Edna traveled from South Beloit, Winnebago County, Illinois, to visit relatives in Kansas.[1415] At some point prior to his 1969 retirement and return to Moundville, Samuel was employed at Fairbanks Diesel in Beloit. He was a member of the American Legion post at King and the Douglas Bible Church.[1416]

1982: Samuel and Edna moved into the Wisconsin Veterans Home.[1417]

Among the children of Samuel E.³ and Edna (Peake) Scholes:

i. JEAN ARDIS⁴ SCHOLES (*Samuel E.³ Scholes, George² Scholes, Ann¹ Mills, Samuel^A*) was born 10 August 1921, died 23 February 2015 in New Braunfels, Cowal County, Texas;[1418] and was buried at Tucker Swamp Baptist Church Cemetery, Southampton County, Virginia.[1419] She married September 1943 WALTER HOLTER KISSINGER,[1420] the son of George M. and Elizabeth (Weaver) Kissinger, who was born about

---

[1414] "Obituary," Marion Edith Scholes, *Portage Daily Register,* Saturday 17 March 1962, p. 4, col. 8. Buena Vista is an independent city surrounded by Rockbridge County, Virginia.

[1415] Jacq Woolsey and Marj Walle, "Our Town," *Salina Journal* (Kansas), Tuesday 7 September 1965, p. 6, col. 1.

[1416] "Scholes, Samuel E.," *Wisconsin State Journal*, Friday 8 July 1983, section 3, p. 7, col. 3.

[1417] "Edna Mae Scholes," *Portage Daily Register* (Wisconsin), Friday 26 May 1989, p. 5, col. 1.

[1418] "Ardis S. Kissinger," obituary transcribed from *New Braunfels Herald-Zeitung* (Texas), Thursday 26 February 2015. Also, Samuel E. Scholes household for daughter Ardis, 1930 US census, Moundville, Marquette County, Wisconsin, ED 8, sheet 3A–B, dwelling/family 85.

[1419] Ardis S. Kissinger grave marker, Tuckers Swamp Baptist Church Cemetery, Southampton County, Virginia; memorial #201,159,883 by Martha Fontaine Byrum (findagrave.com).

[1420] "Miss Jean Scholes Becomes the Bride of Virginia Pastor," *Portage Daily Register* (Wisconsin), Saturday 4 September 1943, p. 3, col. 3. The date of marriage is not given.

1918,[1421] and died 12 April 1977 in Newport News (independent city), Virginia.[1422]

Jean graduated from nursing school at Methodist Hospital in Madison, Wisconsin, 11 May 1942. In the midst of World War II, Rev. Edwin Moll's commencement address urged the newly-minted nurses to minister to their enemies as well as to their allies or friends: "Every man is your brother, even the German and the Jap, because we were all created by God."[1423]

Walter grew up in Williamsport, Lycoming County, Pennsylvania. A graduate of Moody Bible Institute in Chicago, he also studied at the Baptist Bible Seminary in Johnson City, Broome County, New York.[1424] Prior to retiring to the Burdette neighborhood in Franklin (independent city), Virginia, William was pastor at several Virginia churches:

- Tucker's Swamp in Zuni;
- Vesuvius, Stuarts Draft, and Natural Bridge;
- Calvary in Radford;
- Beaver Dam in Roanoke; and
- Fourth Street in Portsmouth.[1425]

ii. GEORGE STANLEY[4] SCHOLES (*Samuel Eugene[3] Scholes, George[2] Scholes, Ann[1] Mills, Samuel[A]*) was born 6 June 1926 in Endeavor, Marquette County, Wisconsin; died 17 September 2016 in Lancaster, Lancaster County, Pennsylvania;[1426] and was buried at Moundville Cemetery, Marquette County, Wisconsin.[1427] He married as her second husband 11 June 1955 JEANNE ANNA (ASHMEAD) BOGGS.[1428] She was the daughter of Fred R. and Helen G. (Schutt) Ashmead, born about

---

[1421] William Holter Kissinger, 12 April 1977 death certificate #77-013680 Virginia; DGS #100,937,995, image 182 of 502. Wife Ardis was informant.
[1422] "Rev. Kissinger," *Daily Press* (Newport News, Virginia), Wednesday 13 April 1977, p. 5, col. 5 (age at death 59).
[1423] "18 Nurses Receive Hospital Diplomas," *Capital Times* (Madison, Wisconsin), Tuesday 12 May 1942, p. 9, col. 4.
[1424] "Miss Jean Scholes Becomes the Bride of Virginia Pastor," *Portage Daily Register* (Wisconsin), Saturday 4 September 1943, p. 3, col. 3.
[1425] "Area Deaths and Funerals . . . Rev. Kissinger," *Daily Press* (Newport News, Virginia), Wednesday 13 April 1977, p. 5, col. 5.
[1426] "George S. Scholes 6/6/1926–9/17/2016," *LNP Lancaster Online*, September 2016, p. 11, cols. 3–4. Also, Samuel E. Scholes household for son George, 1930 US census, Moundville, Marquette County, Wisconsin, ED 8, sheet 3A–B, dwelling/family 85.
[1427] Jeanne A. and George S. Scholes, joint grave marker, Moundville Cemetery, Marquette County, Wisconsin, image, memorials #202,304,581 and #170,229,146 respectively, by Jami Hayes and Donna Butler Scheaffer (findagrave.com).
[1428] "Jeanne Scholes, audit coordinator," *Lancaster New Era* (Pennsylvania), Tuesday 19 August 1997, p. 15, cols. 3–4.

1922, died 18 August 1977 (age 75), and was buried with her husband.[1429]

George graduated from high school in Brandon, Fond du Lac County, Wisconsin. In World War II, he joined the U.S. Navy's V12 program after high school, and graduated with the rank of ensign from the Midshipman's School at Northwestern University in Evanston, Illinois. After training in ordnance at the Washington Gun Factory and Jacksonville Naval Air Station, he was assigned to ACORN52 in Guam; his unit occupied the Japanese Naval Base at Truk Atoll in the Pacific. In 1948 he graduated from the University of Wisconsin with a degree in electrical engineering.

He worked 32 years for RCA as design engineer, sales manager for power tubes, and marketing manager for semiconductors.[1430] In 1973 he took charge of industrial marketing in the Power Transistor Department.[1431] Then he worked twelve years for Siemens Corporation in Iselin, Middlesex County, New Jersey, as director of marketing for discrete semiconductors.

He was survived by "long-time companion and fiancee" Norma Thomas.[1432] He visited all 50 US states and all 10 Canadian provinces, as well as Mexico, Iceland, Belgium, England, Germany, Australia, Japan, Truk, Guam, New Guinea, Tahiti, St. Thomas, Nassau, St. Croix, Jamaica, Grand Cayman, Barbados, Margarita Island, and Bermuda.

Jeanne's mother Helen was "a pioneer women's bowling champion of Lancaster County." [1433]

Jeanne married first 13 July 1946 Bruce A. Boggs Jr.; they separated 20 April 1951 and were divorced 7 March 1952.[1434] In later years she worked as an audit coordinator for Opinion Research Corporation in

---

[1429] Jeanne A. and George S. Scholes, joint grave marker, Moundville Cemetery, Marquette County, Wisconsin, image, memorials #202,304,581 and #170,229,146 respectively, by Jami Hayes and Donna Butler Scheaffer (findagrave.com).

[1430] "George S. Scholes 6/6/1926–9/17/2016," *LNP Lancaster Online*, 20 September 2016, p. 11, cols. 3–4.

[1431] Val E. Vallery, "Business Whirl," *Courier-News* (Bridgewater, New Jersey), Tuesday 6 March 1973, p. D6, col. 1.

[1432] "George S. Scholes 6/6/1926–9/17/2016," *LNP Lancaster Online*, 20 September 2016, p. 11, cols. 3–4.

[1433] Fred R. Ashmead household for wife Helen G. and daughter Jeanne A. age 18, 1940 US census, Lancaster, Lancaster County, Pennsylvania, ED 36-95, sheet 3A, dwelling 58. Also, "Mrs. Fred R. Ashmead Jr.," *Philadelphia Inquirer*, Saturday 27 March 1971, p. 20, col. 4.

[1434] "Miss Ashmead, Bruce A. Boggs Wed Saturday," *Sunday News* (Lancaster, Pennsylvania), Sunday 14 July 1946, p. 3, cols. 3–4. Also, "Man Wed 36 Years Given Divorce," *Lancaster New Era* (Pennsylvania), Friday 7 March 1952, p. 24, col. 3. They had separated 10 April 1951.

Princeton, New Jersey. A member of Highland Presbyterian Church in Lancaster, she was also very active with the American Red Cross.[1435]

[1435] "Jeanne Scholes, audit coordinator," *Lancaster New Era* (Pennsylvania), Tuesday 19 August 1997, p. 15, cols. 3–4.

Chapter 36

Third Generation

Robert Henry Scholes–Pearl Alida Edwards Family
parents at Chapter 11

Electrical engineering and several marriages

36. ROBERT HENRY³ SCHOLES *(James² Scholes, Ann¹ Mills, Samuel^A)*
Born: 22 September 1891, Moundville, Marquette County, Wisconsin
Died: 13 November 1934 of heart ailment at parents' home[1436]
Burial: Moundville Cemetery, Endeavor, Marquette County, Wisconsin[1437]
Spouse: **PEARL ALIDA EDWARDS,** married 24 December 1913[1438]
Spouse's parents: Thomas O. and Minnie (Benkelman) Edwards[1439]

[1436] "Chicago Man Dies at Home of His Parents," *Portage Daily Register* (Wisconsin), Monday 19 November 1934, p. 4, col. 1. Also, letter from Bonnie Margaret Jacobs to Stella Scholes, 10 October 1991, citing Columbia County, Wisconsin, marriage record 13-117-260; Stella Scholes collection, item 19, in author's possession.

[1437] Robert Henry Scholes grave marker, no image, Moundville Cemetery, Endeavor, Marquette County, Wisconsin, memorial #39,027,978 by Anita Smith (findagrave.com).

[1438] "Chicago Man Dies at Home of His Parents," *Portage Daily Register* (Wisconsin), Monday 19 November 1934, p. 4, col. 1. Also, letter from Bonnie Margaret Jacobs to Stella Scholes, 10 October 1991, citing Columbia County, Wisconsin, marriage record 13-117-260; Stella Scholes collection, item #19, in author's possession.

[1439] "Obituaries . . . Rites Set Saturday . . . Thomas O. Edwards, 93, Retired Carpenter, Dies," *Capital Times* (Madison, Wisconsin), Friday 5 April 1963, p. 28, col. 1; clipping, Stella Scholes collection, item #4, in author's possession. Thomas, a retired carpenter, was born in Caledonia Township and lived in the Madison area for 60 years. Also, copy of family photo, "Minnie Benkelman and Thomas Edwards and daughters Pearl and Hazel," Stella Scholes collection, item #12 (verso), in author's possession. Also, marriage certificate for Thomas and Minnie, married in Lewiston, Columbia County. Rev. L. B. Webb officiated; Stella Scholes collection, item #21 (verso), in author's possession.

Spouse's birth: 24 August 1893 in Wisconsin (either Baraboo, Sauk County, or in Portage, Columbia County)[1440]
Spouse's death: 8 September 1967 in rural Madison, Dane County [1441]
Spouse's burial: Moundville Cemetery, Endeavor, Marquette County, Wisconsin[1442]

Pearl's mother Minnie (Benkelman) Edwards reportedly died 25 February 1901 of consumption, leaving daughters Pearl and Hazel, aged 8 and 6. Minnie's sister Cora reportedly died of cancer 18 June 1904. Father Thomas evidently remarried, as a Mrs. Thomas Edwards was in the family group attending Cora's funeral.[1443]

After their marriage, Robert and Pearl resided in Portage, Kilbourne, Mineral Point, and Madison, where he completed the electrical engineering course at the University of Wisconsin. He then worked for Sargent & Lundy (a power generation and transmission firm) for seven years and for Byllsby's Engineering Company, both in Chicago. He moved his church membership from Moundville to Ravenswood Methodist Church in the city.[1444] Later on, for many years Pearl was employed by the Wisconsin Telephone Company.[1445]

[1440] "Rural Madison Woman Dies;" unidentified newspaper clipping dated 8 September 1967, Stella Scholes collection, item #7, in author's possession. Also, "Supplemental report of given name of child" for Pearl Alida Edwards, giving parents' names and her birth date; Stella Scholes collection, item #21, in author's possession. It may be that she was born in Baraboo, but the parents had to swear to her name in Columbia County later.
[1441] "Mrs. Schulenberg," *Wisconsin State Journal* (Madison), Sunday 10 September 1967, section 2, p. 4, col. 3.
[1442] "Rural Madison Woman Dies;" unidentified newspaper clipping dated 8 September 1967, Stella Scholes collection, item 7, in author's possession. Also, Pearl Alida (Edwards) [Scholes] Schulenberg, grave marker, no image, Moundville Cemetery, Endeavor, Marquette County, Wisconsin, memorial #39,027,859 by Anita Smith (findagrave.com).
[1443] Letter from Bonnie Margaret Jacobs to Stella Scholes, 10 October 1991; Stella Scholes collection, item #19, in author's possession. Bonnie mentioned "my book" and her researching the Benkelmans back to the 1500s as well as the family's emigration from Germany 1849–1853.
[1444] "Chicago Man Dies at Home of His Parents," *Portage Daily Register* (Wisconsin), Monday 19 November 1934, p. 4, col. 1.
[1445] "Mrs. Schulenberg," *Wisconsin State Journal* (Madison), Sunday 10 September 1967, section 2, p. 4, col. 3.

Robert Henry Scholt...
(Signature or mark)

Following Robert's untimely death, Pearl evidently married second William H. Schulenberg of Oregon, Dane County, Wisconsin, reportedly on 6 January 1938.[1446] The date has not been documented, but it's plausible: (1) when she sang in a Christmas cantata in Madison that December, she was called Pearl Schulenberg, and (2) in January 1942 William H. Schulenberg transferred to Pearl A. Schulenberg his title to four lots in Waubesa Beach on the southwest edge of Madison.[1447] William died in Madison 3 March 1942.[1448] After her death in 1967, Pearl's estate was filed in court as amounting to $22,000,[1449] roughly equivalent to at least $131,000 in 2019.[1450]

In 1940 Pearl's father Thomas Edwards was reportedly a widower, living in a $3000 house in Dunn Township, Dane County.[1451] He married fourth 15 August 1941, when he was in Oregon, Dane County, Alice L. Carr of Chicago—licensed 8 August in Madison.[1452] It did not last: although they had both been lonely, they were not lonely enough: "Mrs. Edwards, 67, told the judge that she and Edwards, 72, had known each other years ago and met again last summer. Both felt lonely, she said, and so they wed Aug. 15." Her husband, however, insisted on retaining

---

[1446] Pearl Alida Edwards Schulenberg, no grave marker image, memorial #39,027,859 by Anita Smith (findagrave.com), stating without documentation that they married 6 January 1938.

[1447] "Trousdale Methodist," *Capital Times* (Madison, Wisconsin), Sunday 18 December 1938, p. 21, col. 1. Also, "Madison Records…Real Estate Transfers," *Wisconsin State Journal* (Madison), Friday 30 January 1942, p. 13, col. 1.

[1448] "W. H. Schulenberg Dies at Hospital," *Capital Times* (Madison, Wisconsin), Tuesday 3 March 1942, p. 2, col. 8.

[1449] "Probate Court," *Capital Times* (Madison, Wisconsin), Tuesday 19 September 1967, p. 2, col. 1.

[1450] "Measuring Worth" (measuringworth.com/calculators/uscompare/relativevalue.php).

[1451] Thomas D. Edwardo [Thomas O. Edwards], 1940 US census, Dunn Township, Dane County, Wisconsin, ED 13-25, sheet 2A, dwelling 23. His house was valued at slightly less than the Wisconsin average of $3232: statewide house value figures from US Census Bureau, Census of Housing, Historical Census of Housing Tables, Median Home Values Unadjusted 1940 (https://www2.census.gov/programs-surveys/decennial/tables/time-series/coh-values/values-unadj.txt).

[1452] "Marriage Licenses," *Capital Times* (Madison, Wisconsin), Friday 8 August 1941, p. 18, col. 6. The date 15 August 1941 is written following Thomas's 1938 marriage in a hand-crafted family tree, with no name, place, or source citation.

his female housekeeper after the wedding, despite Alice's protests. She was granted a divorce 19 December 1941, four months and four days after the marriage.[1453]

[1453] "Hoppman Gives Divorces to Three," *Capital Times* (Madison, Wisconsin), Saturday 20 December 1941, p. 3, col. 4. Also, "Housekeeper 'Breaks Up' Marriage," *Wisconsin State Journal* (Madison), Saturday 20 December 1941, p. 3, col. 5.

Children of Robert and Pearl Alida (Edwards) Scholes:

i. ORETTA ETHLYN[4] SCHOLES (*Robert[3] Scholes, James[2] Scholes, Ann[1] Mills, Samuel[A]*) was born 24 April 1915 in Chicago, died 6 December 1994 in Madison, Dane County, Wisconsin,[1454] and was buried at Roselawn Memorial Park, Monona, there.[1455] She married three times: first ARTHUR J. PEDERSON (or JEN ARTHUR PEDERSEN), second DONALD SMITH, and third ELTON CRUGER
Oretta reportedly "sang with the Art Van Dam band in Chicago during the big band era."[1456] (This claim may refer to jazz accordionist Art Van Damme, "one of the biggest stars of the 1950s with a 15-minute radio and TV program, a noted role in the NBC orchestra, and many miscellaneous recordings.")[1457] In later years she worked as a telephone operator for Madison General Hospital and Bell Telephone.[1458]
In 1935 she and Arthur were both in Chicago. They married 19 November 1937 in Cook County, Illinois.[1459] He was born in Chicago 17 May 1917, the son of Oluf and Anna (Winther) Pederson, and died 28 August 2000 in Marshfield, Wood County, Wisconsin[1460] In 1940 they were renting at $20 a month; she had completed four years of high school, Arthur two.[1461] That year they bought a lot in Waubesa Beach near Madison, Dane County, Wisconsin.[1462] In 1941 they were living at RD (Rural Delivery), Oregon, Dane County, Wisconsin.[1463]

[1454] "Oretta E. Cruger," *Wisconsin State Journal,* Wednesday 7 December 1994, p. 16, col. 1.
[1455] Oretta E. Cruger grave marker, Section F, Roselawn Memorial Park, Monona, Wisconsin, image, memorial #71,171,005 by M. Marolis (findagrave.com).
[1456] "Oretta E. Cruger," *Wisconsin State Journal,* Wednesday 7 December 1994, p. 16, col. 1.
[1457] National Association of Music Merchants (namm.org/library/oral-history/art-van-damme).
[1458] "Oretta E. Cruger," *Wisconsin State Journal,* Wednesday 7 December 1994, p. 16, col. 1.
[1459] Oretta E. Scholes–Arthur J. Pederson marriage index entry, #15,567,672, 19 November 1937, Cook County, Illinois; "Cook County, Illinois, Marriage Index, 1930–1960" (ancestry.com).
[1460] "Deaths . . . Arthur J. Pedersen," *Kenosha News* (Wisconsin), Wednesday 30 August 2000, p. C2, col. 2.
[1461] Arthur Pederson household, 1940 US census, Dunn Township, Dane County, Wisconsin, ED 13-25, sheet 1B, dwelling 20.
[1462] "Records: Real Estate Transfers," *Wisconsin State Journal* (Madison), Sunday 29 September 1940, p. 3, col. 4. A. J. Healy and wife sold to Arthur J. Pederson and wife lot 8, block 3, Waubesa Beach, Town of Dunn.
[1463] "Arth J" and Oretta Pedersen, *Wright's Madison City Directory 1941* (Milwaukee: Wright Directory Company, 1941), p. 416, image 201 of 458 (ancestry.com).

He was a "stereotyper" for a local newspaper. They were still married as of 7 August 1942, when he was planning to join the Army Air Force,[1464] but evidently by late 1945 they had parted ways. Arthur wound up in the Army Air Force until December 1945, as a communications sergeant in the 24th Artillery Division in the Pacific. He married second 29 December 1945 Viola Adelsen at St. Mary's Lutheran Church in Kenosha. He worked for American Motors as a layout inspector for many years, and from 1946 to 1960 he ran a TV and radio sales and repair business. A member of St. Mary's Lutheran Church, he played mandolin; enjoyed building and repairing violins, photography, woodworking, camping, horticulture, golf, and Green Bay Packers football games.[1465]

Oretta married second after 7 August 1942 DONALD SMITH. Little is known of him other than that he was born about 1914 and the divorce was granted 16 October 1948 in Madison, Wisconsin, for "cruel and inhuman treatment"[1466]

Oretta married third ELTON CHARLES CRUGER (marriage license 6 April 1951 in Madison).[1467] The son of Henry Jefferson and Anna (Sickles) Cruger,[1468] Elton was born 23 August 1908 in Waterloo, Jefferson County, Wisconsin; died 3 January 1971 in Madison;[1469] and was buried at Roselawn Memorial Park, Monona, Dane County, Wisconsin.[1470]

At her third marriage, Oretta was living on "Route 4," and Elton was at 2702 Union Street in Madison.[1471] Earlier, when Elton was 16 years old and living in Minneapolis, his mother had attempted to revive long-standing claims that the family was entitled to New York City

---

[1464] "Arthur Pederson, Times Employe, Joins Air Force," *Capital Times* (Madison, Wisconsin), Friday 7 August 1942, p. 5, col. 3.
[1465] "Deaths . . . Arthur J. Pedersen," *Kenosha News* (Wisconsin), Wednesday 30 August 2000, p. C2, col. 2.
[1466] "Divorces Granted," *Wisconsin State Journal* (Madison), Saturday 16 October 1948, p. 2, col. 6. She was of Waubesa Beach; he was at 2138 Sommers Avenue. Also, "Circuit Court," *Capital Times* (Madison, Wisconsin), Saturday 16 October 1948, p. 10, col. 6. Donald was age 34.
[1467] "Daily Records . . . Marriage Licenses," *Capital Times* (Madison, Wisconsin), Friday 6 April 1951, p. 22, col. 6.
[1468] "Third Minneapolitan Seeks share in Trinity Millions: Mrs. H. J. Cruger Asserts Great Great Aunt Originally Owned Land," *Minneapolis Star* (Minnesota), Wednesday 28 January 1925, p. 4, cols. 2–4.
[1469] "Elton C. Cruger Dies At Age 62," *Capital Times* (Madison, Wisconsin), Monday 4 January 1971, p. 19, col. 2.
[1470] Elton C. Cruger military grave marker, image, Roselawn Memorial Park, Monona, Dane County, Wisconsin, memorial #5,141,407 by robert cruger (findagrave.com).
[1471] "Daily Records . . . Marriage Licenses," *Capital Times* (Madison, Wisconsin), Friday 6 April 1951, p. 22, col. 6.

real estate first owned and farmed by a Dutch ancestor who had settled there in the 1660s.[1472]

As of 16 October 1940, Elton was 5 feet 8 inches tall and weighed 147 pounds, with brown eyes and hair.[1473] In World War II, he was a sergeant, 327 Base Unit AAF (Army Air Force?).[1474] He was "a member of Bashford Methodist Church, the Wisconsin Campers' Association, and the Amalgamated Meatcutters and Butcher Workmen, Local 538."[1475]

ii. NORMAN FREDERICK*4* SCHOLES (*Robert3 Scholes, James2 Scholes, Ann1 Mills, SamuelA*) was born 6 July 1919[1476] in Mineral Point, Iowa County, Wisconsin, and died 25 March 2010 in Monona, Dane County. He married 23 June 1943 in Briggsville, Marquette County, STELLA MAE LARSON.[1477] The daughter of Lewis and Emma (North) Larson, she was born 23 June 1925 in Beloit, Rock County, and died 3 May 2010 in Monona.[1478]

Norman and Stella were both of Endeavor, Marquette County.[1479] As of 16 October 1940 he was 5 feet 7 inches tall and weighed 140 pounds, with blue eyes and brown hair. His grandmother Emma Scholes would always know his address; his phone number in

---

[1472] "Third Minneapolitan Seeks share in Trinity Millions: Mrs. H. J. Cruger Asserts Great Great Aunt Originally Owned Land," *Minneapolis Star* (Minnesota), Wednesday 28 January 1925, p. 4, cols. 2–4.

[1473] Elton Charles Cruger WW2 draft card, serial #H579, order #0588, 16 October 1940, Local Board 2, Dane County, Wisconsin; "US WWII Draft Cards Young Men, 1940–1947" > Wisconsin > Chsney–Duquaine > Cross–Crusan > images 1794–95 of 1963 (ancestry.com).

[1474] Elton Charles Cruger grave marker, image, Roselawn Memorial Park, Monona, Dane County, Wisconsin, memorial #5,141,407 by Robert cruger (findagrave.com).

[1475] "Elton C. Cruger Dies at Age 62," *Capital Times* (Madison, Wisconsin), Monday 4 January 1971, p. 19, col. 2.

[1476] "Scholes Fete 63rd Anniversary," *Capital Times* (Madison, Wisconsin), Saturday–Sunday 15–16 July 2006, p. C4, col. 4.

[1477] "Obituaries . . . Norman F. Scholes," *Portage Daily Register* (Wisconsin), Monday 29 March 2010, p. 12, col. 5. Also, Norman F. and Stella M. Scholes, joint grave marker, image, Moundville Cemetery, Endeavor, Wisconsin, memorials #52,031,194 and #52,013,440 respectively, by Kathy (Weller) Medick (findagrave.com).

[1478] "Obituaries . . . Scholes, Stella M.," *Wisconsin State Journal* (Madison), Wednesday 5 May 2010, p. 6, col. 3.

[1479] "Larson–Scholes," *Capital Times* (Madison, Wisconsin), Friday 14 May 1943, p. 12, col. 7.

Endeavor was "1 long 1 short on 2."[1480]

On 22 September 1944 Norman oversaw the sale of cattle, draft horses, poultry, and equipment at "the place formerly known as the 'James Scholes Farm,' located about 7 miles N.E. of Portage and about 6 miles S.E. of Endeavor on the River Road, and about 3 miles E. of Corning Station and Rudy Pfuehler's Corners E. of U.S. Hwy. 51," in Fort Winnebago Township.[1481] Soon thereafter the 146-acre farm itself was advertised for rent.[1482]

By the following spring Norman was in training at the Great Lakes Naval Station near Chicago.[1483] In November he was reportedly assigned to the Philippines "and is likely on the way now."[1484] By late March 1946 he was released from the Navy as a seaman second class.[1485] That fall he and Stella sold property to his mother Pearl A. Schulenberg in Lot 8, Block 3, Waubesa Beach second addition, in Madison, Dane County.[1486]

In 1958 and 1959 Norman was a laborer for Zien Sheet Metal (possibly a plumbing business), and the family lived at 2817 South 67th Street in Milwaukee.[1487] He retired in 1982; in later years his hobbies included visiting old train depots, wood-crafting, and history.[1488]

"While raising her family, [Stella] also cared for several newborn foster children until permanent homes could be found for them. Over the years, she enjoyed many crafts, and most recently, she enjoyed new

---

[1480] Norman F. Scholes WW2 draft card, serial #169, order #45, 16 October 1940, Local Board 1, Westfield; "US WWII Draft Cards Young Men, 1940–1947 > Wisconsin > Rising–Schultz > Schoenbeck–Scholz > images 1501–2 of 1953 (ancestry.com).

[1481] Auction Notice, *Portage Daily Register* (Wisconsin), Friday 8 September 1944, p. 8, cols. 3–4.

[1482] Classified Ads, "For Rent," *Portage Daily Register* (Wisconsin), Wednesday 11 October 1944, p. 8, col. 2.

[1483] "East Moundville," *Portage Daily Register* (Wisconsin), Wednesday 21 March 1945, p. 8, col. 8.

[1484] "East Moundville Personals," *Portage Daily Register* (Wisconsin), Wednesday 21 November 1945, p. 4, cols. 7–8.

[1485] "Local, Area Men Released by Navy," *Capital Times* (Madison, Wisconsin), Saturday 30 March 1946, p. 3, col. 6.

[1486] "Madison Records . . . Real Estate Transfers," *Capital Times* (Madison, Wisconsin), Saturday 21 September 1946, p. 7, col. 3.

[1487] Norman F. and Stella Scholes entry, *Wright's Milwaukee City Directory 1959* (Milwaukee: Wright Directory Company, 1959), p. 1238, image 205 of 654. Similarly, *1959*, p. 1185, image 23 of 446 (ancestry.com). They were absent in 1956. Directories for 1957 and 1960 are incomplete at Ancestry.com.

[1488] "Obituaries . . . Norman F. Scholes," *Portage Daily Register* (Wisconsin), Monday 29 March 2010, p. 12, col. 5.

computer technology."[1489] In 1967 they were in Stoughton, Dane County.[1490] The couple spent 1982–2002 in Florida, then returning to Portage, Columbia County, Wisconsin.[1491] They were buried together at Moundville Cemetery, Endeavor, Marquette County.[1492]

[1489] "Obituaries . . . Scholes, Stella M.," *Wisconsin State Journal* (Madison), Wednesday 5 May 2010, p. 6, col. 3.
[1490] "Mrs. Schulenberg," *Wisconsin State Journal* (Madison), Sunday 10 September 1967, sec. 2, p. 4, col. 3.
[1491] "Obituaries . . . Scholes, Stella M.," *Wisconsin State Journal* (Madison), Wednesday 5 May 2010, p. 6, col. 3. Florida address from Family Tree, Horace D. Hume of Mendota, Illinois, handwritten, unsourced; Stella Scholes collection, item #8, in author's possession.
[1492] Norman F. and Stella M. Scholes, joint grave marker, image, Moundville Cemetery, Endeavor, Wisconsin, memorials #52,031,194 and #52,013,440 respectively, by Kathy (Weller) Medick (findagrave.com).

Chapter 37

Third Generation

Ruth Emma Scholes–Leo Robleske–George Redman Family
parents at Chapter 11

Three draft horses and a McCormick Deering tractor

37. RUTH EMMA³ SCHOLES (*James² Scholes, Ann¹ Mills, Samuel ᴬ*)
Birth: 18 August 1897 in Moundville Township, Marquette County, Wisconsin
Death: 19 May 1995 in Drexel Hill, Delaware County, Pennsylvania
Burial: with her first husband at Moundville Cemetery, Moundville Township, Marquette County, Wisconsin[1493]
Spouse #1: **LEO E. ROBLESKE** married July 1938[1494]
Spouse #1's parents: father Antone Wrobleski[1495]
Spouse #1's birth: 12 February 1903 in Albion, Dane County, Wisconsin[1496]

[1493] "Ruth E. Redman," *Portage Daily Register* (Wisconsin), Tuesday 30 May 1995, p. 5, cols. 1–2. The obituary is confused about the surname Wills. For dates and funeral card of Ruth E. Redman, Stella Scholes collection #10, in author's possession. Also, Leo E. Robleske and Ruth E. Redman joint marker, image, Moundville Cemetery, Endeavor, Marquette County, Wisconsin, memorials #102,778,753 and #102,778,293 respectively by Joey (findagrave.com).
[1494] "Here's Marriage License List in Nearby Counties," *Capital Times* (Madison, Wisconsin), Sunday 31 July 1938, p. 2, col. 2. Also, but likely mistaken, the obituary from unnamed newspaper gives June 1938 for marriage, Leo E. Robleske and Ruth E. Redman joint marker, image, Moundville Cemetery, Endeavor, Marquette County, Wisconsin, memorials #102,778,753 and #102,778,293 respectively by Joey (findagrave.com).
[1495] Obituary from unnamed newspaper, Leo E. Robleske and Ruth E. Redman joint marker, image, Moundville Cemetery, Endeavor, Marquette County, Wisconsin, memorials #102,778,753 and #102,778,293 respectively by Joey (findagrave.com).
[1496] Leo Robleske household, 1940 US census, Fort Winnebago Township, ED 11-10, sheet 4B, dwelling 83.

Spouse #1's death: 27 July 1941 in Fort Winnebago, Columbia County, Wisconsin[1497]

Spouse #1's burial: Moundville Cemetery, Endeavor, Marquette County, Wisconsin[1498]

Spouse #2: **GEORGE MANN REDMAN** married 12 April 1944 in Portage, Columbia County, Wisconsin, as his second wife[1499]

Spouse #2's parents: Henry and Elizabeth (Mann) Redman

Spouse #2's birth: 3 December 1878 in Philadelphia

Spouse #2's death: of heart disease, 24 December 1948 in Drexel Hill, Upper Darby Township, Delaware County, Pennsylvania[1500]

Spouse #2's burial: with his first family at Arlington Cemetery, Drexel Hill, Pennsylvania[1501]

Ruth attended the Moundville School. A member of the Moundville Methodist Church, she played the piano there for many years.[1502] In June 1916 she was one of nineteen graduates from Portage High School.[1503] She went on to study at Lawrence College[1504] and in 1921 graduated with a BA degree.[1505] The following year "Ruth Scholes" was one of six faculty members at Sidell Township High School in Vermilion

---

[1497] *Wisconsin State Journal* (Madison), Monday 28 July 1941, p. 15, col. 8.

[1498] Leo E. Robleske and Ruth E. Redman joint marker, image, Moundville Cemetery, Endeavor, Marquette County, Wisconsin, memorials #102,778,753 and #102,778,293 respectively by Joey (findagrave.com).

[1499] "Marriage Licenses," for Ruth E. Robleske of the Town of Fort Winnebago and George M. Redman of the Town of Upper Darby, Pennsylvania, *Portage Daily Register* (Wisconsin), Tuesday 11 April 1944, p. 3, col. 3. Similarly, "M. E. Parsonage Is Scene of Wedding," Thursday 13 April 1944, p. 3, col. 4. Also, "Ruth E. Redman," *Portage Daily Register* (Wisconsin), Tuesday 30 May 1995, p. 5, cols. 1–2. The obituary is confused about the surname Wills.

[1500] George Redman death certificate #106,485, Delaware County, Pennsylvania, 24 December 1948; "Pennsylvania, Death Certificates, 1906–1967" > 1948 > 104701–107500 > image 2724 of 4153 (ancestry.com).

[1501] Redman family marker, image, Grove Plot, Arlington Cemetery, Drexel Hill, Delaware County, Pennsylvania, George and Gertrude Redman memorials #134,910,722 and #134,910,723 respectively by Tony and Cindy Lloyd (findagrave.com).

[1502] "Ruth E. Redman," *Portage Daily Register* (Wisconsin), Tuesday 30 May 1995, p. 5, cols. 1–2.

[1503] "Commencement at the Portage High School," *Portage Daily Dispatch* (Wisconsin), Friday 16 June 1916, p. 1 (entire). The class motto: "Give to the world the best you have and the best will come back to you."

[1504] "Moundville," *Portage Daily Register* (Wisconsin), Monday 12 April 1920, p. 5, col. 1.

[1505] Ruth Emma Scholes, *Seventy-Second Annual Catalogue of Lawrence College, 1921–1922*, p. 205.

County, Illinois, a few miles southeast of Champaign-Urbana. She was teaching chemistry, physiology, and zoology.[1506] In the fall of 1929, "Ruth E. Scholes of Portage, Wisconsin," was teaching home economics in Prophetstown, Whiteside County, Illinois, where she was one of five members of the high-school faculty.[1507]

In 1940 husband Leo was farming. After several years of working for others, he bought "the Jacobson farm" in January 1940, prior to their marriage.[1508] The home was valued at $7000, more than double the Wisconsin average that year. Leo had completed seven years of schooling, Ruth six years of college.[1509]

How the widow Ruth of Wisconsin met widower George Redman of Upper Darby, Pennsylvania, remains a mystery. They were married 12 April 1944 with a minimum of fuss at the Methodist parsonage in Portage. First cousin Marion Scholes and sister-in-law Mrs. Pearl Schulenberg witnessed; Rev. Paul B. White officiated. George was the son of Harry and Elizabeth (Mann) Redman, both born in Philadelphia. The couple soon left for Philadelphia "where they will make their home."[1510] George had married first Gertrude Cromwell, who was born 15 September 1881 to J. M. and Eva (Ainsworth) Cromwell, and died 25 December 1942 of pulmonary thrombosis.[1511]

[1506] Ruth Scholes entry, Superintendent of Public Instruction, *Illinois School Directory 1922–1923*, Circular 166, p. 125.

[1507] "Prophetstown Briefs," *Sterling Daily Gazette* (Illinois), Thursday 9 May 1929, p. 12, col. 2. Also, "High School to Graduate Many," *Dispatch* (Moline, Illinois), Monday 24 March 1930, p. 14, col. 7.

[1508] Obituary from unnamed newspaper, Leo E. Robleske and Ruth E. Redman joint marker, image, Moundville Cemetery, Endeavor, Marquette County, Wisconsin, memorials #102,778,753 and #102,778,293 respectively by Joey (findagrave.com).

[1509] Leo Robleske household, 1940 US census, Fort Winnebago Township, Columbia County, Wisconsin, ED 11-10, sheet 4B, dwelling 83. Also, statewide figures from US Census Bureau, Census of Housing, Historical Census of Housing Tables, Median Home Values Unadjusted 1940 (https://www2.census.gov/programs-surveys/decennial/tables/time-series/coh-values/values-unadj.txt).

[1510] "M. E. Parsonage is Scene of Wedding," *Portage Daily Register* (Wisconsin), Thursday 13 April 1944, p. 3, col. 4.

[1511] Gertrude Cromwell Redman death certificate #107872, 25 December 1942, Drexel Hill, Delaware County, Pennsylvania; "Pennsylvania Death Certificates, 1906–1967" > 1942 > 106951–109650 (ancestry.com).

In 1940 George was working as a courthouse clerk. He had completed eight years of schooling; they were renting at 317 Edmonds Avenue in Drexel Hill, Delaware County, Pennsylvania, for $27 a month.[1512]

On 21 September 1944 Ruth had an auctioneer sell the farm animals and machinery from the place her first husband had purchased five years earlier—including a dozen cattle, three draft horses, six brood sows, 125 white leghorn hens, a De Laval Electric cream separator (set up for 110 volt alternating current), 8 tons of alfalfa and timothy hay, a McCormick Deering tractor model 10-20 "on steel, rubber on front," and "many other items too numerous to mention." The farm's location was carefully described:

> The 'Art Jacobson Farm' located ¼ of a mile east of the Port Hope Fox River Bridge, about ½ miles from County Trunk Highway F, about 2 ½ miles east of Rudy Pfuehler's Corners off from US Highway 51 to the east and thru Corning Station, about 8 miles northeast of Portage, about 6 miles southeast of Endeavor on the 'River Road.'

The seller's name was given in large type: "Mrs. Ruth Redman, owner (formerly Ruth Scholes)."[1513]

Ruth lived in Pennsylvania but visited Wisconsin friends and relations about every other year through at least 1962.[1514] In September 1958, "Mrs. Lillian Russell [Chapter 33], and Mrs. Elsie Scholes [Chapter 34] entertained for dinner on Wednesday at the home of Mrs. Russell in honor of a cousin, Mrs. George Redman of Drexel Hill, Penn. The guests were all cousins of the honoree. They included: Mrs. Lida Hume [Chapter 18], Mrs. Lois Hume [Chapter 21], Miss Olive Heames [Chapter 27, child ii], and Mrs. Gust Peterson [Chapter 27, child iv], . . . and Miss Marion

---

[1512] George M. Redman household, 1940 US census, Upper Darby Township, Delaware County, Pennsylvania, ED 23-207, sheet 13A, dwelling 246.
[1513] "Farm Service Way Auction Sale," advertisement, *Portage Daily Register* (Wisconsin), Monday 18 September 1944, p. 4, col. 7.
[1514] Various local notes for Ruth Redman in Portage newspapers 1949, 1950, 1952, 1954, 1956, 1962 at newspapers.com.

Scholes [Chapter 32], Portage."[1515] Ruth retired from Delaware County Memorial Hospital (in Pennsylvania) after 19 years as a dietitian.[1516]

[1515] Mrs. Gust Peterson, "Endeavor Area News," *Portage Daily Register* (Wisconsin), Thursday 11 September 1958, p. 12, col. 2. In this group, Marion and Lillian were first cousins to Ruth; Lida, Lois, and Elsie were first cousins by marriage; and Olive and Jane (Mrs. Gust Peterson) were first cousins once removed (a generation younger).
[1516] "Ruth E. Redman," *Portage Daily Register* (Wisconsin), Tuesday 30 May 1995, p. 5, cols. 1–2. The obituary makes confusing and mysterious use of the surname Wills.

Index

Note: Information items in the tables and footnotes are not indexed. Names are indexed under their surnames. Places (towns, counties, etc.) are indexed under state/province or nation. Titles such as "Dr." or "President" or "Rev." are not used in alphabetizing.

A

Adelberg
    Mrs. Clarence (-?-), 33
    Mr. & Mrs. Clarence, 151
Adelsen, Viola, 284
Adoption, 35, 109, 155, 180-181, 261
Ainsworth, Eva (Cromwell), 291
Alzo, Lisa, 2
American Relay Radio League, 250
American Society of Agricultural Engineers, 171
Anderson
    Albert, 143
    Maybelle (Ostrander), 143
    Myrtle Grace (Luger) (Hume), 143
Arizona
    Phoenix, 139
    Pima County, 143
    Tucson, 143
Arnsdorf
    Henry M., 100
    Margaret Matilda (Sherwin), 100
    Mary B. (Stuiber), 100
Arthur, Evan (1875 auction), 18
Ashmead
    Fred R., 276
    Helen G. (Schutt), 276

Jeanne Anna (Boggs) (Scholes), 276
At sea, 100
Auctions, 18-19, 66, 220, 226, 286, 292
Audiss
    Ann (Codling), 65
    Susanna Rebecca (Scholes), 22, 46, 65-67
    William, 46, 65-67
Austin
    Ethel Esther (Sherwin) (Schrieber), 91-93
    George, 92
    Laura (-?-), 92
    Lawrence B., 92
Avogadro's Number, 239
Ayers, Isabella (Orton), 83

B

Bad weather, 57
Bagley, Anna (Jenkins), 173
Bailey, Maida (Schoville), 204
Bain, Mrs. George, 135
Baker
    Ada M., 151
    A. E., 222
Bandt, Mr. & Mrs. Hollis, 224
Bankruptcy, 127, 128
Banks
    Allie, 182-183
    Alvin/Allen, 182
    Elizabeth (Carpenter), 182-183
    Vera Lois (Jones/Hume) (Thornton), 182
Baptists, 276
Barron, Mr. & Mrs. Harvey, 151
Barry, Isobel (Wilcox), 270
Bartels, Wilhelm, 15
Bassett

Harriet Eloise (Scholes), 250, 251
Leon B., 251
Rachel M. (Burdick), 251
Beer, Peter, 190
Beichl
Edward, 193
Eva Florence (Smith), 44, 63, 193, 194, 196, 197
Johannes Nicolaus Alexander, 194
Otto, 195
Richard Albert, 44, 193-195
Richard Keil Emerson, 194
Teressia (-?-), 193
Theodor Eduard, 194
Bell
Amy Jeannette (Evans), 62, 106, 108, 109
Edith Eliza (Russell) (Rhodes) (Boettcher), 33, 106-108, 145, 259
"Evangline," 115
Flora Ann (Sherwin), 27, 62, 75, 105
John James, 27, 75, 105
William, 115
William Albert, 106

Benkelman
Cora, 280
Hazel, 280
Minnie (Edwards), 279, 280
Benner, Joan, 2
Bennet (early settlers), 14
Bennett
Claire Watson Bennett, 158
Lois Margaret (Jones) (Harvey), 158, 159
Mildred Hazel (Jones), 159
Ruth (Watson), 158
William Carey, 158
Bentley, Roger G., 2
Berry
Buel, 111

    D. C. (1875 auction), 19
    Elizabeth M. (Rodger), 3, 114, 115
    Judson Stiles, 32, 111, 112
    Lydia A. (-?-), 111
    Margaret Alice "Maggie" (Hume), 32, 38, 111-114, 117, 118
    Margaret (Gale), 113-116
    Mildred Eliza (Blake) (Blaiklock), 112, 113, 117, 120
    Mrs. J. S., 151
    Robert Buell, 112, 113, 115-118
    Willis Harold, 114

"Berry Patch Addition," 118, 119
Bible Church, 275
Birkholz, Mary Ann (Krueger), 51
Bizerte, 252
Blackmon, Sarah (Mozley), 58
Blaiklock
    Edward Musgrave, 121
    Mildred Eliza (Berry) (Blake), 121
Blaisdell, Abbie (Haines), 185
Blake
    Carlotta Rosetta (Judd), 120
    Howard Judd, 120
    Louis, 120
    Mildred Eliza (Berry) (Blaiklock), 121
Bleeg, John P., 116
Boettcher
    Edith Eliza (Russell) (Bell) (Rhodes), 33, 106-108, 145, 259, 260
    Henry, 107-108
Boggs
    Bruce A. Jr., 277
    Jeanne Anna (Ashmead) (Scholes), 276
Bohan
    Anna C. (Rogers), 167
    Dorothy Louise (Greenwood) (Jasper) (Hume), 167
    William P., 167
Bohlig

      Charlotte (Sherwin), 97, 98, 101, 102
      John, 102
      John Ellsworth, 97, 98, 101, 102
      Mary (Dufner/Tofner), 102

Boren
      Addison, 239
      Bertha "Bertie" (Linhart), 239
      Lois Elizabeth (Scholes) 59, 239

Borsack, Allie, 224

Broitzman, Catherine, 196

Brookns, W. (1875 auction), 19

Brooks, Ethel (Dixon), 257

Brown, Susan Drusilla (Young), 73

Burdick, Rachel (Bassett), 251

Burrington, Edith (Sherwin) (Johnson), 85, 89
      Herbert J., 85, 91
      Nettie L. (Ranney), 91
      Wallace D., 91

Businesses, 2, 6
      American Institute of Banking, 121
      American Motors, 284
      American Pipe and Steel, 177
      Associated Milk Producers Incorporated, 271
      Badger Ordnance, 159
      Ball Corporation, Muncie, Indiana, 249
      Baraboo Ammunition Plant, 267
      Boeing Company (Seattle), 247
      Bradebrush, Inc., in Westfield, Wisconsin, 261
      Bremner Granite, 159
      Byllsby's Engineering Company (Chicago), 280
      California Tank & Manufacturing Corporation, 178
      Chicago and Northwestern Railway, 187
      Colvin Baking Company, 203
      CompuDyne, 143
      Dairyland Poultry in Endeavor, Wisconsin, 261
      Delaware County (Pennsylvania) Memorial Hospital, 293
      Durant Manufacturing, 51
      Edward Dewey and Sons Wholesale Grocery, 200

Eckerd Drugs, 270
E. E. Jones Garage and Service Station, 183
Elgin, Joliet, and Eastern Railroad, 116
Endeavor Bank, 70
Endeavor State Bank, 134
Equipment Manufacturers Institute, 171
Everbrite Electric Signs (Greenfield, Wisconsin), 143
Fairbanks Diesel (Beloit, Wisconsin), 275
Fairbanks-Morris Foundry or Fairbanks Morse & Company (Beloit, Wisconsin), 141, 202
Farmers' Mutual Fire Insurance Company, 70
Farmers and Merchants Bank (Tomah, Wisconsin), 89
Federal Glass Company, Columbus, Ohio, 241
Federal Reserve Bank of Cleveland, 121
Field Enterprises (World Book Encyclopedia), 117
Fostoria Glass Company, Moundsville, West Virginia, 241
General Indicator (Pardeeville, Wisconsin), 143
Goodyear Tire and Rubber, 132
Graham Rock Company, 165
Halsey-Stuart, 120
Eastman Kodak, Rochester, New York, 245
H. C. Fry Glass Company, Rochester, Pennsylvania, 240
Hume-Love Company, 170
International Harvester Company, 212
Kress Monument Company, 89
John J. Welsh insurance agency 200
La Crosse School of Music, 96
Lincoln National Insurance Company, 137
Maltby Monument Company (Los Angeles, California), 154
Marcellon Town Mutual Fire Insurance Company, 71
McKinney-Beveridge Automotive Company, 112
Milwaukee Railroad, 84
Monument Dealers Association (California), 154
National Bureau of Standards, 247
National Lead Company, 249
Northern Pacific Railroad, 103
Northern States Power Company, 113, 117

Opinion Research Corporation, Princeton, New Jersey, 277-278
Pomona Chamber of Commerce, 157
Pomona Granite Company, 155, 157, 161
Portage Novelty Boat and Storage Company, 35
Portage Plastics, 159
RCA, 277
Remington Arms UMC Company (Hoboken, Hudson County, New Jersey), 93
Rochester Dairy Co-op (Minnesota), 108
Sargent & Lundy, 280
Siemens Corporation, 277
Sioux Falls National Bank, 120
Sylvania Corporation, 249
US Electric Manufacturing Company, 159
US Water Company, 159
Utility Glass Works, Lonaconing, Maryland, 241
Warner(?) Electric Brake, 204
Washington Loan & Trust Company, 121
Weyenburg Shoe Manufacturing (Portage, Wisconsin), 127
Wisconsin Telephone Company, 280
Zien Sheet Metal (Milwaukee), 286

Buskager
Lawrence Milo, 225
Louis, 225
Lucy (Rodderfeld), 225
Wilma Rae (Heames), 217, 225

C

Cadman (early settlers), 14
California 32, 139, 163, 183, 221, 266
Alhambra, 151, 177
Bell (City), 149, 152-156, 159, 161, 166
Carmichael, 154
City of Industry, 176
Compton, 177
Encinitas, 102

Fort Macarthur San Pedro, 161
Hacienda Heights, 176
Hemet, 154
Huntington Park, 131, 158, 160
Inglewood, 152-154
Lakewood, 176
Long Beach, 177, 178
Los Angeles, 150, 153, 158, 159, 176, 233
Los Angeles County, 131, 149, 153, 154, 175, 177, 233
Maywood, Los Angeles County, 160
Mendocino County, 176
Monrovia, 175
Monrovia Township, 177
Monterey Park, 165, 174, 177
Norwalk, 177
Pasadena, 56, 59, 165, 176, 235, 237
Pomona, 155, 157, 256
Poway, San Diego County, 219, 220
Redlands, 157
Riverside, 151, 161
Riverside County, 154, 161, 162
Sacramento County, 154
San Bernardino County, 160
San Diego, 99-101
San Diego County, 102
San Gabriel, 220
Santa Ana, 177
Santa Barbara, 152, 234
Temple, 151
Temple City, 165
Ukiah, 176
West Covina, 184
Whittier, 178
Calvey, Mary (Moran), 205
Camp Fire, 101
Camp Robinson, 62
Canada, Ontario, 75
Cape Colony, South Africa, 43

Capetown, South Africa, 43
Carpenter
    Betsey (Naylor), 77
    Elizabeth (Banks), 182-183
Carr, Alice L. (Edwards), 281, 282
Carson
    Lizzie Sarah (Sawyer), 163
    Noah D., 163
Causes of Death
    Cancer, 183
    Carbon monoxide poisoning, 139, 140
    Carcinoma of stomach/stomach cancer, 86, 90
    Car crash, 51, 123, 127, 159, 173, 220
    Chronic diarrhea, 11, 17
    Consumption, 280
    Diphtheria, 74, 78, 79, 81, 157
    Heart ailment, 279
    Heart disease, 290
    Heart attack, 188
    "Heart trouble" and ill health, 96, 187
    "Infection," 172
    Influenza, 107
    Internal hemorrhage following operation, 55
    "Kidney trouble," 105
    Pneumonia, 69, 107, 217
    Prostate cancer, 245
    Pulmonary thrombosis, 291
    Stroke, 83, 259
    "Typhoid fever," 172
    Uremia and cystitis, 75-76
Cemeteries
    Alfred Rural Cemetery, Alfred, New York, 239, 250
    Arlington Cemetery, Drexel Hill, Pennsylvania, 290
    Beaver Lodge Cemetery, Ekalaka, Montana, 74, 78, 82
    Blakesburg Cemetery, Blakesburg, Iowa, 120
    Custer County Cemetery, Miles City, Montana, 81, 84
    Dartford Cemetery, Green Lake, Wisconsin, 55, 188, 233
    Douglas Cemetery, Marquette County, Wisconsin, 49

Eastern Montana State Veterans Cemetery, Miles City, Montana, 84
Fairfield Cemetery, Baraboo, Wisconsin, 226
Floral Lawn Cemetery, South Beloit, Illinois, 141, 204
Forest Home Cemetery, Milwaukee, Wisconsin, 129
Freeze Cemetery, Freeze, Latah County, Idaho, 173-174
Graceland Cemetery, Howard, South Dakota, 111, 112, 114, 115
Graceland Cemetery, Racine, Wisconsin, 167
Grand Meadow Cemetery, Mower County, Minnesota, 91
Greenwood Cemetery, Kingston, Wisconsin, 187
Greenwood Cemetery, Lincoln County, Wisconsin, 143
Hampden Cemetery, Columbia County, Wisconsin, 268
Hill Crest Cemetery, Endeavor, Wisconsin, 138, 229, 261
Lakeview Cemetery, Adams County, Wisconsin, 108
Mentor Cemetery, Humbird, Clark County, Wisconsin, 78
Moundville Cemetery, Endeavor, Marquette County, Wisconsin, 29, 30, 33, 41, 44-46, 49, 61, 65, 66, 69, 70, 106, 123-126, 128, 131, 133, 135, 136, 142-144, 149, 158, 159, 163, 164, 172, 179, 182, 201, 215-218, 221, 225, 255, 259, 265, 266, 273, 276, 277, 279, 280, 286, 289, 290
North Marcellon Cemetery, Columbia County, Wisconsin, 271
Oak Grove Cemetery, Tomah, Wisconsin, 92
Oakwood Cemetery, Beaver Dam, Wisconsin, 193, 194
Olivewood Cemetery, Riverside, California, 160, 162
Pacific Cemetery, Portage, Wisconsin, 268-270
Pardeeville Cemetery, Columbia County, Wisconsin, 185, 186, 189
Prairie Home Cemetery, Waukesha, Wisconsin, 205, 210
Restland Cemetery, Mendota, Illinois, 167
Riverside Cemetery, Charles City, Floyd County, Iowa, 90
Roselawn Memorial Park, Monona, Wisconsin, 143, 283, 284
Silver Lake Cemetery, Portage, Wisconsin, 126, 183
St. Mary's Cemetery, Alexis, Illinois. 167-168
Traer Cemetery, Traer, Decatur County, Kansas, 172
Tucker Swamp Baptist Church Cemetery, Southampton County, Virginia, 275

Underhill Cemetery, Packwaukee, Wisconsin, 225
Valhalla Memorial Park, Milwaukee, Wisconsin, 211, 212
Vicksburg National Cemetery, Mississippi, 11, 18
Vineland Cemetery, Clarkston, Washington, 173
Westfield East Cemetery, Wisconsin, 223, 267
Woodlawn (Woodland?) Cemetery, Sparta, Monroe County, Wisconsin, 27, 73, 78, 79, 81, 85-87, 95, 96, 99, 105-107
Woodlawn Cemetery, Sioux Falls, Minnehaha County, South Dakota, 121

Chapman (early settler), 14

Chesley
Alice (Naylor) (Hutton), 77
Anna, 76
Charlotte (Sovereign), 75
Cora, 76
Ella, 76
Emeline Ursula (Sabin) (Newhart) (Ridgway) (See), 76-77
Etta, 76
George, 75
Israel Benjamin, 74-78
Jennie Thressa (Young) (Sherwin), 27, 73-76, 78
Marietta (Pauley)(Porter), 76
Mrs. Marshall, 78

Chicago, see Illinois

Christian Science, 234

Christopherson
Annie C. (-?-), 139
Carl, 139
Gladys Anna Elizabeth (Peterson), 141
Grace Edna (Hume), 139, 140, 146
Henry George, 139-141

Civil War, 17, 30, 37, 47
Bounties, 17
Second Battle of Fair Oaks, 17, 25-27

Cleary, Emilia/Amelia, 109

Cocker (early settlers), 14

Cockroft

Peter, 42
Zillah (Smith), 41
Codling, Ann (Audiss), 65
Colleges, Universities, Preparatory Schools
Alfred University, New York, 241, 243-245, 249, 251
Ball State University (predecessor institution), Muncie, Indiana, 116
Baptist Bible Seminary, Johnson City, New York, 276
Brown University, 246
Central State Teachers College, at Stevens Point, Portage County, Wisconsin, 181
Christian Endeavor Academy (Moundville, Wisconsin), 2, 115, 128, 135, 138, 140, 142, 145, 168, 189, 221, 273
Columbia University, 236
Cornell University, 236, 245, 252
Geneva College, Beaver Falls, Pennsylvania, 241
La Crosse Business College, Wisconsin, 97
Lawrence College, 290
Mellon Institute, University of Pittsburgh, 240
Middlebury College, Vermont, 244, 252
Midshipman's School, Northwestern University, Evanston, Illinois, 277
Milwaukee Normal, 140
Moody Bible Institute, Chicago, 276
New York State College of Ceramics, Alfred, 241
Northern State Teachers College at Marquette, Michigan, 142
Northland College, Ashland, Wisconsin, 146
Nursing school, Methodist Hospital, Madison, Dane County, Wisconsin, 276
Ohio State University, Columbus, Ohio, 241
Ripon College, Ripon, Wisconsin, 235, 240
State Teachers College at Eau Claire, Wisconsin, 101
State Teachers College at Ellendale, North Dakota, 101
State Teachers College at Valley City, North Dakota, 97, 101
State University of New York at Geneseo, 251
Stevens Point Normal School, 128, 219, 221

St. Mary's of the Woods College, Terre Haute, Indiana, 168
Story's Business College (Portage, Wisconsin), 126
Syracuse University, 245
Tufts University, 243, 244
University of Illinois, 236
University of North Carolina, 252
University of Pittsburgh, 240
University of Wisconsin, 233, 235, 236, 245-247, 259, 277, 280
Woman's College of Alabama in Montgomery, 235
Yale University, 240, 243, 244

Colorado
Arapahoe County, 89
Burdett, 158
Denver, 175
Grand Junction, 172, 176
Littleton, 89
Mesa County, 172, 176
Washington County, 158

Colvin
Asa Burton, 245
Burton Houston, 245
Lois Ann (Scholes), 1, 3
Sara Elsie (Houston), 245

Condit, Electa (Smith), 200
Conger, Vera, 183
Congregational Church/United Church of Christ, 2, 99, 138, 145, 188, 218, 223, 225
Connecticut, 93
Stamford, Fairfield County, 250
Coon (early settlers), 14
Corrigan
Ethel Louise (Jones), 160
Grace (Courtis), 160
James C., 160
County Home for the Poor (Wyocena, Columbia County, Wisconsin), 200

Courtis, Grace (Corrigan), 160
Crawford
    Mr. & Mrs. William, 231
    Myrtle M. (Ellison) (Moore), 50, 231
    William, 50
Creag, G. (1875 auction), 18
Cromwell
    Eva (Ainsworth), 291
    Gertrude (Redman), 291
    J. M., 291
Crossman, Allie, 99
Cruger
    Anna (Sickles), 284
    Elton Charles, 283, 284
    Henry Jefferson, 284
    Oretta Ethlyn (Scholes) (Pederson/Pedersen) (Smith), 283, 284

D

Dahlstrom, Mr. & Mrs. Gaylord, 151
Dahms
    Anne M. (Geyer), 213
    Edward Paul, 211
    Gustav Friedrich Ferdinand, 211
    Lelah (Moran), 3, 207-209, 211, 213, 231
    Mr. & Mrs. Ed Dahms, 231
    Nell (Hunn), 213
    Wilhelmina Louisa Augusta (Raddatz), 211
Dakota, 33
Day Sailor Association, 242, 250
Delaware, 15
DeMott
    Esther (-?-), 179
    Isaac, 179
    Lois (Hume), 32, 179

Denmark, 52
    Söngebäk, 51
Dewsnap, Annis Jane, 35, 53
    Arden, 35
    Caroline "Carrie" (Eager), 30, 35
    Enoch Charles, 35, 53
    Freeman "Frank" Ellison, 35, 53
    Geraldine, 35
    Grace E. (Smith) (Hall), 35
    Mary, 35
    Sheldon, 35
    Vernon Charles, 53
Divorce, 50, 51(?), 97, 107, 108(?), 182, 277, 282, 284
Dixon
    Aaron, 62, 257
    Ethel (Brooks), 257
    Eunice (Giese), 257
    Favil, 61
    Mary Ellen (Scholes), 21, 61, 62, 63, 257
    May (Watson), 156
    Mr. and Mrs. Eph. Dixon, 62
    Mrs. Mae, 151
    Ruth May (Jones), 156, 256
    Sarah Ann (Fish?), 61
    Sarah (Wade), 257
    Thomas W., 137
    William, 62, 63, 156, 257
Dufner/Tofner, Mary (Bohlig), 102

E

Eager, Ann (-?-), 30
    Caroline "Carrie" (Dewsnap), 30, 35
    Edward, 35
    James, 30
    Sarah Ann (Hume), 30-32

Ebert, Robert, 151
Edwards
    Alice L. (Carr), 281
    Minnie (Benkelman), 279
    Pearl Alida (Scholes) (Schulenberg), 71, 279, 281, 291
    Thomas O., 279, 281
Ellis, Walter M., 146
Ellison
    Alice (Houlker), 47
    Annie Jane, 47
    Annis Jane (Dewsnap), 35, 53
    Caroline (Parks) (Scholes), 20, 46-49, 209
    Christopher, 46, 47, 49, 52
    (early settlers), 14
    Martin G., 47
    Mary Elizabeth (Powell), 47, 52
    Mary (Smith), 123, 125
    Myrtle May (Moore) (Crawford), 49, 50, 232
    Pearl Christi (Krueger) (Hollerup), 48, 50-52
    Priscilla (Walters), 46, 52
Emert
    Freeda Jane (Hume), 176
    Lily (Sharp), 176
    R. West, 176
Endorsements of Products, 229
    Doane's Kidney Pills, 229, 230
    Siegler Oil Heater, 191
England (place), 1, 13, 26, 33, 42, 46, 149
    Chiswick, Borough of Honslow, London, 121
    Glyade (??), 30
    Lancashire, 5, 6, 23, 29, 37, 41, 45, 47
    Lincolnshire, 66
    Liverpool, 12
    Manchester, 61
    Moorhey, 6
    Oldham, 5, 9, 11, 13
    Oldham, St. Mary's, 9
    Oldham, St. Peter's, 5, 9, 11, 20, 21, 23, 25 29, 37, 41, 45

    Prestwich, 9, 11, 12
    Salford, 47
    Sheepwashes, 6
    Sugar Meadow, 6
England (surname)
    Jay, 56
    Julia Anna, 56, 58
    Ruth, 56
Etkington, Maebelle (Slater), 142
Evans
    Amy Jeanette (Bell), 62, 106, 108, 109
    Carrie (Wagner), 109
    Chester "Chet," 109
    Emilia/Amelia (Cleary), 109
    George W., 108
    Harley James Jr., 108, 109
    Louis, 109
    Sarah J. Shalkop/Schellkopf, 108
Evert, Chas., 190

F

Falkland Islands, 82
Falkner
    C. W., 19
    (early settlers), 14
Farmer, Edith (Thompson), 203
Farming Close-ups; *see also* **Auctions**
    Scholes, George 66
    Scholes, Robert, 18
    Scholes, William (the emigrant), 11-12, 16, 18
    Sherwin, Ira, 27
    Wilcox, Merlin B., 271
Faulkner, Ann (Jones), 149
Fay, George W., 30
Finger

        Bernice (Smith), 189, 197, 200
        Minnie (-?-) (Beer), 189
        Paul, 189, 197
Fish
        Sarah Ann (Dixon), 61
        Thomas, 62
Fletcher, Corinna (Harvey), 158
Florida, 125, 139, 268-270, 287
        Bonita Springs, 268, 270
        Collier County, 269, 270
        Coral Gables, 132
        Dade County, 132
        Hillsborough County, 132
        Miami, 132
        Naples (including Bamboo Mobile Village), 269, 270
        Palma Cela Park, 132
        Tampa, 121, 132
Fogg, Effie M., 243
Ford Foundation, 252
Fort Niagara, 244
Foundlings Home, Milwaukee, 261
France, 252
        Brest, 210, 217
Fredrick
        Amelia (Leverenz?), 136
        Julius, 136
        William H. J., 136
Frisch, Mr. and Mrs. Ernest, 135
Fry, Dora Adelia (Thayer), 226

G

Gale
        Annie (Hughes), 116

  Clarence L., 116
  Margaret (Berry), 113-116
Gaubatz, Meta (Maas), 136
Gaylord, Caroline L. (Russell), 107, 259
Genealogical claims, 284
Geriactors, 253
Germany, 155, 189, 229
  Bremen, 130
Geyer, Anne M. (Dahms), 213
Giese, Ethel (Dixon), 257
Grand Canyon, 59
Gray
  Angeline (Moungey), 227
  Frank David, 267
  Gladys J. (Warren), 267
  John Dudley, 267
Greanes (Scholes), Elizabeth (supposed sister of William the emigrant), 12
Great Plains, 27
Green Lake Public Library (Wisconsin)**,** 234
Greenwood
  C. H. "Bill," 168
  Dorothy Louise (Bohan) (Jasper) (Hume), 167
Grey, James, 9
Guam, 277
Guatemala, 157

H

Hahn/Hann,
  Charles A., 243
  Doris Emily (Scholes), 3, 243
  Effie M. (Fogg), 243
Haines
  Abbie (Blaisdell), 185
  Robert M., 185

Rose Ruth (Smith), 43, 185
Hale, Mary Elizabeth (Franklin), 167
Hall, Grace E. (Smith) (Dewsnap), 35
Hamley (1875 auction), 18
Hampton, Jessica, 162
Hansen
    Agnes Otilie "Tillie" (Potts), 87, 88
    Oluf, 87
    Theoline (Torkelson), 87
Hansom, Charles, 135
Harlan
    James Franklin, 167
    Mary Elizabeth (Hale), 167
    Minnie Luvenia (Hume), 165, 167, 170
Harrison, Mrs. Frank, 196
Harvey
    Corinna (Fletcher), 158
    David Marvin, 158, 159
    John H., 158
    Lois Margaret (Jones) (Bennett), 154, 158, 159, 266
    Mrs. Marvin, 150
Hastert, Dennis, 171
Hawaii, 204
Heames
    Edward Francis, 219
    George R., 215, 217
    Gracia (Topping), 219-221
    Hazel D., 146, 223
    Hope Lorraine (Williamson), 224, 225
    Jane Elizabeth (Peterson), 221
    Jane (Keen), 146, 215
    Mary Elizabeth (Scholes), 47, 49, 215, 217, 219, 230
    Olive Harriet, 196, 217, 218 ("Party Line" doll rescue), 219, 231, 292
    William Robert, 49, 215, 217, 219
    Wilma Rae (Buskager) (Thayer), 217, 225, 226
Heames reunion, 219, 224
Hemstock, Maude (Taylor), 99

Henderson, Sarah, 15
Henry
    A. N., 93
    Annie (Sherwin), 27, 85
    Esther (Sprit), 85
    George, 85
Hill
    (early settlers), 14
    Mrs. Ira H., 98
Hinze
    Elayne Venetta (Russell), 261
    Herman, 261
    Rudolph Walter "Rudy," 196, 261
    Sophie, 261
Hofferbert
    Barbara (-?-), 194
    George, 194
    Line Anna (Beichl), 194
Hollerup
    Delmer 209
    James 48, 51, 52, 231
    Mrs. James, 209, 210, 231
    Pearl Christi (Ellison) (Krueger), 48, 50-52
Holmes, A., 47
Hopewood/Hopwood
    (early settlers), 14
    Elijah, 138
    Raymond Ira, 138, 139, 146, 218
    Velma E./Beulah (Hume), 138
Horatio Alger, 6
Horton, W. H., 35
Houlker, Alice (Ellison), 47
House values, 52, 62, 67, 88, 90, 99, 101, 107, 109, 113, 115, 117, 124, 127, 130, 134, 144, 151, 153, 156, 157, 159, 161, 166, 170, 186, 189, 195, 207-209, 217, 220, 222, 230, 260, 266, 281, 291
Houston, Sara Elsie (Colvin), 245

Hull
    Caroline (Brewster), 69
    Emma Maria (Scholes), 22, 69
    Henry, 69

Hume
    Alice Sarah (Smith), 32, 123
    Anna/Mary, 31
    Ann/Margaret (Walker), 29, 171
    Baby boy, 125
    Clarence, 168, 172
    Dorothy Louise (Bohan) (Greenwood) (Jasper), 167
    (early settlers), 14
    Edna Alice, 125
    Elda Mary (Quaden), 129, 145
    Elizabeth E. "Beth" (Topping) (Jones), 127
    Elizabeth (Moran), 126
    Eliza May "Lida" or Alida (Sutcliff), 32, 133, 135, 292
    Essie S. (Frederick), 136, 146
    Esther Lydia (Jenkins) (Smith) (Walton), 172-176
    Frank Roland, 129, 131
    George (1914-1989), 30, 165, 175-177
    George Walker (1874-1952), 30, 32, 176, 179
    Gerald, 181
    Glendon Ellison, 128, 131, 150, 151
    Grace Edna (Christopherson), 139, 146
    Horace Delbert, 2, 135, 165-172
    James, 15, 16, 29
    James Samuel, 32, 163, 165, 166, 169, 171
    Lila Edith (Shaw), 144
    Lloyd E., 136, 146
    Lois (DeMott), 32, 292
    Lydia Alberta "Birdie" (Sawyer) (Jones), 32, 151, 163, 165, 166
    Margaret Alice "Maggie" (Berry), 32, 38, 111, 112
    Martha Elizabeth Sarah Ann (Voertman), 34
    Martha (Russell), 32
    Merl George, 144, 150
    Minnie Luvenia (Harlan), 165, 167, 170

       Mr. and Mrs. Horace, 135
       Mr. and Mrs. Lloyd, 135
       Mr. and Mrs. Will, 151
       Mrs. Ann Hume, 151
       Mrs. James, 151
       Mrs. John, 135
       Myrtle Grace (Anderson) (Luger), 143
       Olive Mae (Slater) (Nordness), 142, 143
       Robert Isaac, 125-127, 145(?)
       Robert Walker, 17, 20, 29-32, 112
       Robert Walker Jr., 32, 39, 123, 130
       Ruth Florence (Kunow), 129
       Sarah Ann (Eager), 30, 31
       Sarah Ann Janet "Nettie" (Jones), 32, 149, 152, 166
       Sarah Ann (Scholes), 1, 6, 14, 15, 18-20, 29, 30
       Sarah "Sally" Lyle (Rood), 167
       Velma E./Beulah (Hopwood), 138, 146
       Verna Mildred "Lina" (Maas), 137
       Verne William "Vern," 142, 146
       William, 39
       William Scholes, 2, 13, 14, 133, 135, 146
Hume reunion, 128, 171
Hunn
       Nell (Dahms), 213
Hutton
       Alice (Naylor) (Chesley), 77

I

Idaho, 167, 173-175
       Benewah County, 175
       Fernwood, 175
       Latah County, 167, 173-175
       Lewiston, 173
       Moscow, 167, 174
       Potlatch, 174, 175

Winchester grade, "2 miles west of Potlatch," 173
Illinois, 47, 154, 252
Alexis, 168
Boone County, 203
Camp Grant, 153
Capron, 203
Champaign-Urbana, 291
Chicago, 63, 116, 120, 141, 151, 171, 261, 281, 283
Cook County, 283
Galena, 13
Great Lakes Naval Training Station, 286
Kankakee County, 92
Lake County, 141
La Salle County, 2, 135, 166, 167, 170, 171
Manchester, 203
Marengo, 236
Maywood, 233
McHenry County, 236
Mendota, 2, 135, 166, 167, 170, 171
Momence, 92
Peoria County, 93
Prophetstown, Whiteside County, 291
Sangamon County, 146
Sidell Township, Vermilion County, 291
Skokie, 261
South Beloit, Winnebago County, 204, 275
Springfield, 146
Vermilion County, 291
Waukegan, 141
Whiteside County, 291
Winnebago County, 93, 204

Illnesses
Arthritis, 80
Asthma, 107
Broken arm, 231
Broken hip, 210
Carder's cough, 5
Double pneumonia, 168

　　　　Indigestion/burst appendix, 234
　　　　Stroke, 83, 165, 231, 259
　　　　Tuberculosis, 207
Indiana, 125
　　　　Allen County, 137
　　　　Fort Wayne, 137
　　　　Gary, 115-116
　　　　Lake County, 115-116
　　　　South Bend, 131, 132
　　　　St. Joseph County, 131, 132
Ingraham, Mrs. Wendell, 135
Inventions and patents, 170, 171, 242, 249, 251
Iowa, 89, 120
　　　　Bremer, 133
　　　　Butler County, 133
　　　　Charles City, 85, 86, 90, 91
　　　　Decorah, 98
　　　　Delaware County, 260
　　　　Floyd County, 38, 85-87, 90, 91
　　　　Fremont Township, 133
　　　　Leland, 83
　　　　Nevada, 182, 184
　　　　Rockford, 38, 86, 87, 91
　　　　Ryan, 260
　　　　Sac County, 182
　　　　Story County, 182
　　　　Winnebago County, 83
Ireland, 86
Italy, 252

J

Jacobson, Mr. & Mrs. Arthur, 135
Jasper
　　　　Dorothy Louise (Bohan) (Greenwood) (Hume), 167
　　　　Edmund, 168

Jenkins
    Anna (Bagley), 173
    Esther Lydia (Hume) (Smith) (Walton), 172-176
    Grant, 173
    Oscar McKinley, 173
Jergens, Frederika, 34-35
Johnson
    (supposed nephew by marriage of William Scholes the emigrant), 12
    Edith Mary (Sherwin) (Burrington), 85, 89
    Engebret, 90
    Olena (Olson), 90
    William O., 90
Jones
    Adalene (McGowan), 154
    Almon, 38
    Amanda (Sherwin), 24, 26
    Ann (Faulkner), 149
    Arthur M., 150
    Beatrice Lewis (White), 162
    Cora (-?-), 183
    David F., 95
    Elizabeth E. "Beth" (Topping) (Hume), 127
    Emogene (Moran), 126
    Ethel Louise (Corrigan), 160
    Eva, 151
    Everett Henry, 155-157, 161
    George Walker, 160
    Georgia W. Jones, 162
    Harlan Edmund, 151, 160
    Harriet M. (Manley) (Sherwin), 27, 95, 98 99, 101, 103
    Henry Eden, 32, 39, 149, 151, 152, 166
    Hume McKinley, 2, 146, 154
    Keith, 183
    Kenneth, 183
    Levi, 183
    Lois Margaret (Harvey) (Bennett), 158, 159
    Lydia Alberta "Birdie" (Sawyer) (Hume), 32, 151, 163

      Marvel (Markhardt), 268
      Merlin E., 181, 183
      Merrill Robert, 157
      Mildred Hazel (Bennett), 159
      Mr. and Mrs. B., 268
      Oscar McKinley, 2
      Pearl Eliza, 152
      Robey Isabel (Maltby), 58-59, 152-154, 159, 218, 266
      Ruth May (Dixon), 156, 256
      Sarah Ann Jane "Nettie" (Hume), 32, 149, 150, 152, 165-166
      Thomas, 24, 26, 149
      Verda Conger, 181
      Walter F., 128, 150
      Willard, 150
Jones/Hume , Vera Lois (Thornton) (Banks), 180-183
Judd, Carlotta Rosetta, 120

K

Kaiser, Frank H., 151
Kansas, 252, 275
      Atwood, 174
      Ottawa, 58
      Rawlins County, 174
      Shawnee County, 112
      Topeka, 112
Keen/Keene
      (early settlers), 14
      Jane (Heames), 146, 215
Kentucky, 183
      Bowling Green, 183
      Warren County, 183
Kissinger
      Elizabeth (Weaver), 275
      George M., 275

Jean Ardis (Scholes), 275
Walter Holter, 275
Kreager
Florence (Sherwin) (Munro) (Lamb), 82, 83
Fred, 83
Lee Vern, 82-84
Nancy (Stanhope), 83
Kress
Adolph (Mr. and Mrs.), 89
Agnes Otilie "Tillie" (Potts) (Sherwin), 87, 89
Frederick R., 89
Krueger
Delmar, 231
Elmer Frank, 51
Frank Ferdinand, 51
Mary Ann (Birkholz), 51
Pearl Christi (Ellison) (Hollerup), 48, 50-52
Kunow
Caroline (Schirmer), 129
Hugo Charles, 129
Ruth Florence (Hume), 129

L

Labor organizations
AFSCME, 176
Amalgamated Meatcutters and Butcher Workmen, 285
Farmers Union, 190
Farmers Union, West Orchard Mesa ch., Local 23, 175
Lamb
Florence Anora "Flossie" (Sherwin) (Munro) (Kreager), 27, 62, 75, 80-82
Robert Ray, 82
Land and property transactions (including homesteads), 15, 16, 24, 26, 30, 56, 62, 79, 80, 82, 98, 118-119 ("Berry Patch Addition"), 281, 286

Larson
    Emma (North), 285
    Lewis, 285
    Stella Mae (Scholes), 1, 285
    Theoline (Torkelson) (Hansen), 87, 88
    Thomas, 88
Leete, Zaida (Trimbell), 187
Leghorn
    Elizabeth (Williamson), 188
    Evangeline (Smith), 188, 189
    James, 188
Leithold, Fred, 96
Lerum, Darlene, 2
Letters (excerpts)
    1849, William Scholes in Wisconsin to Oldham
    1951, Nellie Scholes in California to N.Y. nephew, 237
Leverentz?, Amelia (Fredrick), 136
Lindstrom
    Conrad, 141
    Jennie, 141
Linhart, Bertha "Bertie" (Boren), 239
Longfeldt, Sophie (Hinze), 261
Lottery, 6
Love, James E. "Ed," 170, 171
Loveland, Lulu (Peake), 273
Luger
    Freimund, 143
    Myrtle Grace (Anderson) (Hume), 143
Lunden, Miles J., 84
Lutheran, 203, 284

M

Maas
    Anita, 137
    Edward, 136
    Harold, 137
    Meta (Gaubatz), 136
    Raymond, 137
    Verna Mildred "Lina" (Hume), 136
Maik, Ida Amelia (Pomplin), 223
Maltby/Maltbey, A. (1875 auction), 19
    Caroline Adelia (Spicer), 153
    Elisha B., 151, 153
    Laura, 151
    Mr. & Mrs. Ray, 151
    Mrs. W. E., 150
    Robey Isabel (Jones), 58-59, 152-154, 159, 218, 266
    Willis Elisha, 151, 152, 154, 166
Manley
    Charlotte (Sawyer), 95, 98
    Harriet M. (Sherwin) (Jones), 27, 95, 98, 99, 101, 103
    Jackson, 95
Mann, Elizabeth (Redman), 290
Markhardt
    Darwin Alfred, 268
    Dorothy/Dorothey (Scholes) (Murray), 268, 269
    Marvel (Jones), 268
    Oscar, 268
    Sena (Ylvisaker), 268
Marman, Catherine (Schwemerlein), 229
Marquette County, see Wisconsin
Marriage Day, 56
Martin, Mrs. Elizabeth Townley, 53
Maryland
    Baltimore, 131
    Gaithersburg, 245
    Lonaconing, 241
    Montgomery County, 245
    Rockville, 247

Massachusetts, 251
    Winchendon, 250
McCray, Mary (Munro), 82
McGaw
    James, 89
    Lorraine (Potts), 89
McGowan
    Adalene (Jones)(adopted), 154, 155
    Elizabeth W. (Vroman), 155
    Frank A., 155
McKanny, J. (1875 auction), 19
McKinley, William, 2
Methodists, 34, 46, 62, 70, 115, 128, 135, 136, 140, 143, 144, 149, 151, 152, 158, 160, 184, 191, 221, 227, 255, 256, 267, 280, 285, 290, 291
Mexico, 157
Meyers(?), Mary, 269
Michigan, 151
    Antrim County, 93
    Central Lake Village, 93
    Chippewa County, 142
    Clinton, 93
    Lenawee County, 51
    Sanilac County, 163
    Sault Ste. Marie, 142
Migrations, 26, 27, 62, 66
Miller, Mr. and Mrs. Ed, 151
Mills
    Alice (daughter of Samuel and Alice Mills), 10
    Alice (Stocks), 9, 11-12
    Ann (Scholes), 1, 9, 11, 14, 18, 20, 24, 26,56
    Hannah, 10
    John, 9
    Joseph, 10
    Maria, 10
    Sally, 9
    Samuel (husband of Alice Stocks), 9, 11

Samuel (of Bow Street, Oldham, brother-in-law of William Scholes) 9
Sophia, 10
Milwaukee, see Wisconsin
Ministers, see Occupations
Minnesota, 76
    Alexandria, 151
    Arthur, Traverse County, 83
    Austin, Mower County, 91
    Big Stone County, 57
    Claremont, Dodge County, 77
    Fillmore County, 91
    Freeport, 102
    Grand Valley, 92
    Minneapolis, 101, 284
    Mower County, 86, 89, 92, 93
    Olmstead County, 107, 108
    Ortonville, 57
    Rochester, 107, 108, 260
    Stearns County, 102
Mississippi River, 53
Mississippi, Vicksburg, 11, 17, 26, 153
Missouri
    Jefferson Barracks, 153
    St. Louis, 52
Modern Glass Practice, 240, 241
Modern Woodman, 216
Moll, Rev. Edwin, 276 ("Every man is your brother, even the German and the Jap")
Montana, 27, 97
    Baker, 76, 78, 82-84
    Billings, 83
    Carter County, 75, 77, 79, 82
    Custer County, 81, 83
    Dawson County, 76
    Ekalaka, 77, 79, 80, 82
    Fallon County, 76, 78, 82-84
    Flathead County, 97

Forsyth, 82
Glacier National Park, 269
Glendive, 76
Kalispell, 97
Miles City, 83
Rosebud County, 82-84
Trail Creek, 269

Moore
Alden/Alfred Anson, 49, 50, 231
Betsy M. (-?-), 50
Myrtle M. (Ellison) (Crawford), 50
William H., 50

Moran
Allan Clarence, 206, 210, 211
Edward C., 126, 207
Elizabeth (Hume), 126
Emogene (Jones) Moran, 126, 127
Lelah (Dahms), 3, 207-209, 211, 213, 231
Mary (Calvey), 205
Nettie A. (Scholes), 47, 48, 63, 205, 209, 210, 230, 231
Olivia A. (Steinmetz), 208, 210, 211
Stephen, 205
Thomas Clarence, 49, 205
Unknown child, 213

Morehouse, Mrs. B., 151

Moungey
Angeline (Gray), 227
John, 227
Mary Avis (Thayer), 226

Mountford
(early settlers), 14
Bertha (Shaw), 144

Mozley
Elizabeth (Van Natta), 55, 242
Harriet Newell (Scholes), 21, 38, 55, 56, 62
Julia Anna (England), 56
Thomas, 55, 237, 242
William, 57

Munro
    Colin, 79, 82
    Florence Anora "Flossie" (Sherwin) (Lamb) (Kreager), 27, 62, 75, 80-82
    Mary (McCray), 82
    Rodic/Roderick, 82
Murison, Mr. & Mrs. Wallace, 151
Murner
    Florence Lucinda (Riffe), 131
    Gideon Wallace, 131
    Lois Joan, 131
Murray
    Charles W., 269
    Dorothy/Dorthey (Scholes) (Markhardt), 269
    Mary (Meyers?) Murray, 269
    William James, 269

N

National Institute of Standards and Technology, 246
National Register of Historic Places, 206
National Taiwan University, 252
Naturalization, 39, 43, 51, 82
Naylor
    Alice (Hutton) (Chesley), 77
    Betsey (Carpenter), 77
    John, 77
    Mrs. Nellie, 174
Nebraska
    Saline County, 62
Nelli, Mr. & Mrs. Maurice, 197
Newhart
    Emeline Ursula (Sabin) (Ridgway) (Chesley) (See), 76-77
    Robert Elwood, 77
New Jersey, 12, 94, 215
    Bridgeton, 243

Cumberland County, 243
Hoboken, 93, 117
Hudson County, 93
Iselin, Middlesex County, 277
Princeton, 277-278
West Hoboken, 94
New York, 12, 24-26, 50
Alfred, 2, 241, 245, 248, 251, 256
Dansville, 239
Genesee County [now Wyoming County], 23
Geneseo, 250
Ithaca, 253
Johnson City, Broome County, 276
Livonia, 250
Livingston County, 239
New York City, 93, 247, 284
North Hornell, 239
Rochester, 253
Steuben County, 239
Tompkins County, 111
Town of Warsaw, 23
Nixon, grandmother, 53
Nordness
Eugene H. "Curley," 143
Mrs. Obert (-?-), 143
Obert, 143
Olive Mae (Hume) (Slater), 143
North Africa, 252
North Carolina, 252
Chapel Hill, 253
North Dakota, 101, 168
Barlow, 103
Barnes County, 97
Beach, 75, 79, 80
Bellfield, 164
Benson County, 103
Billings County, 75, 79, 80
Bismarck, 98

Bowman, 169, 172
Braddock, 101
Burleigh County, 98
Carson, 104
Cass County, 101
Churchs Ferry, 101
Corwin Township, Stutsman County, 102
Denhoff, 104
Driscoll, 103
Dunn Center, 104
Eddy County, 101
Emmons County, 97, 101
Fargo, 101
Golden Valley County, 75, 80, 103
Golva, 103
Hazen, 104
Hume, 164
Hume Township, 176
Leeds, 103, 104
Linton, 7, 101
Mercer County, 103
Minnewaukan, 103, 104
Montpelier, 97, 101, 103, 104
Oberon, 103, 104
Paradise, 103
Pingree, 104
Ramsey County, 101
Scranton, 164
Sheyenne, 101
Sioux County, 103
Solen, 103, 104
Stanton, 103, 104
Stutsman County, 97, 101-103
Timmer, 104
Valley City, 97
Werner, 103
Wing, 104
Woodworth, 104

Ypsilanti, 103, 104
North, Emma (Larson), 285

O

Occupations
    Agricultural equipment manufacture, 170
    Alumnae club president, S. California, University of Wisconsin, 236
    Ambulance service, 183
    Assembler, 212
    Author of University of Illinois extension circular on running a "baking club," 236
    Automobile garage, 170
    Automobile sales, 112
    Auto service/mechanic, 112, 116, 117
    Bakery shop, 189
    Bank cashier, 130
    Bank clerk, 93
    Banker, 120, 121
    Bank examiner, 120
    Barber, 79, 128, 189
    Basketball coach, 103
    Blacksmith, 33, 42, 51, 58
    Boarding house operator, 132
    Bond sales, 120
    Bookkeeper, 125
    Bowling, 176
    Butcher, 274
    Buttermaker, 260
    Cannery, 227
    Carpenter, 50, 230, 231
    Ceramic artist, 251
    Chairman of Home Economics for Santa Barbara County (WWI), 236
    Chairman, Pacific Township, Columbia County, Wisconsin, 270

Chemist (drop forge), 144
Chemistry professor, 243
Child nurse, 50
Church janitor, 202
Church musician and organizer, 242
City council member (Madison, Wisconsin), 203
Clerk, 130, 144
Coal mining, 30
College admissions, 243
College dean, 241
College librarian, 234
Commercial salesman in groceries and fruit, 200
Construction crew, 183, 187
Cotton carder, 5, 6, 11
County clerk, 58
County supervisor (Dane County, Wisconsin), 203
Courthouse clerk, 292
Creamery, 33
Dairy and beef farming, 271
Department store sales, 142
Department store stock clerk, 142
Dining and lunch counter facilities, etc., 183, 184
Director of development, glass company, 249
Doctor, 140
Drug store sales clerk, 270
Egg candler, 261
Election clerk, 156
Electrical engineer, 277, 280
Electrical welder, 177
Electrician, 159
Engineer (railroad locomotive), 116
Engineer (Wisconsin Industrial School for Boys), 206
Engraver, 136
Executive, 101
Farmer, 18, 29, 30, 46, 62, 74, 75, 87, 90, 91, 107, 109, 124, 126, 128, 137, 139, 143, 150, 155, 159, 168, 180, 186, 187, 190, 219, 222, 225, 266, 267, 271, 274, 291
Farm laborer, 42, 43, 66, 70, 80, 84, 199

Feed and saw mill, 260
Financier, 120
Fireman (on a steam donkey engine in a logging camp), 175
Football coach, 240
Funeral coach livery service, 183
Garage mechanic, 223
Garage repair man, 140
Garage superintendent, 113
Gas engine mechanic, 201
Gas filling station, 267
Glass chemist and professor, 240
Grocer, 207, 208
Grower of "small fruit and vegetables," 97
Hardware merchant, 195
Head and stamp department, foreman, 93
Helper, Farmers Produce Company, 91
Hoist man (rock and gravel company), 165
Horsewoman, 168
Hospital aide, 115
Hospital dietitian, 293
House carpenter, 50, 96
Housekeeper, 66, 199
Hybrid Pioneer seed corn dealer, 128
Hydraulic engineer, 165
Inspector of materials, Wisconsin State Highway Commission, 260
Insurance salesman, 137
Inventor, 249, 251
Laborer, 50, 67, 77, 108, 177, 208, 286
Layout inspector, auto factory, 284
Librarian, 152, 233
Librarian, State Normal School, Santa Barbara, California, 234
Local newspaper, 155
Logger, 175
Machine shop foreman, 94
Machine shop trouble man, 94

Machinist, 51, 204, 274
Maid in rest home, 175
Mail carrier, 86, 87
Marketing manager, 277
Mathematician, 245
Mathematics curriculum design, 247
Mechanic, 113, 137
Mechanic, boat yard, 141
Midwife, 24
Milk Producers worker, 271
Miller, 96, 98, 260
Milliner, 246
Minister, 46, 55, 56, 66, 85
Monument maker, 151, 166
Motor winder (in factory), 159
Munition factory, 93
Musician, 249
Music teacher, 99, 140
Newspaper stereotyper, 284
Nurse, 26, 36, 39, 195, 276
Occupational therapy aide, 251
Office, state department of revenue (Wisconsin), 203
Office worker, machine shop, 141
Oil salesman, 90
Oil truck driver, 90
Old age pension, 186
"Philatelist in finance," 101
Photographer, 34
Pianist, 168
Policeman, 90
Postmaster, 164
Post Office clerk, 225
Plumber, 143
Plumbing and heating, 207
President, tank & manufacturing corp., 178
Product buyer, 182
Radio equipment manager, 101
Railroad, 84

Railroad telegrapher, 97, 101
Real estate appraiser, 89
Real estate sales, 183, 184, 195
Research engineer, 249
Retail clerk
Retoucher, 99
Root beer stand worker, 271
Rubber shop worker, 131
Sales and repair of TVs and radios, 284
Salesman, 124, 153, 161
Sales manager for power tubes, 277
Salesman, American Family, 203
Salesman, John Deere, 223
Salesman, Oscar Mayer, 203
Salesman, wholesale bakery, 203
School board member, 242
School bus service, 183
School principal, 97, 103
Secretary, 143
Secretary, music school, 96
Servant, 75
Service manager, tire company, 132
Sheep raiser, 82
Shoe factory worker, 127
Singer, 283
Social services, 143
Social worker, 184
Standard Oil dealer, 183
State cataloguer, Wisconsin Library Commission, 233
State conservation department, Wisconsin, 270
Station agent and telegraph operator, 103
Stationary engineer, 165
Steamfitter, 206
Steam heating, 206
Stenographer (insurance agency), 130, 161 (bankruptcy court)
Stone cutter, 155
Stove factory employee, 195

Superintendent, 177
Superintendent, American Woodworking Company (Montello), 143
Supervisor of inspection, farm equipment, 94
Tax assessor, 180
Teacher, 97, 101, 106, 109, 112, 113, 115, 116, 120, 137, 140, 144, 181, 208, 212, 219, 224, 225, 236, 240, 243, 245, 255, 273, 291
Teacher of the year, 252
Teamster, 77
Telephone office, 88
Telephone operator, 182, 283
Theater, 252-253
Track laborer, 187
Truck driver, highway construction, 269
Unemployed, 50
Union organizer, 211
USA (US Army?), 208
Wagon maker, 58
World travel, 277
YMCA physical education instructor, 212

Ohio, 2, 42, 125
Akron, 129, 131
Brimfield Township, 129
Cincinnati, 12
Cleveland, 94, 120, 121
Columbus, 242
Cuyahoga County, 94, 120, 121
Franklin County, 241
Grandview Heights, Columbus, 242, 244
Holmes County, 74
Knox Township, 74
Mansfield, 121
Portage County, 128, 129
Ravenna, 128
Richland County, 121
Summit County, 129

Oldham, see Lancashire

Olson
  Marie E. (Smith), 174
  Olena (Johnson), 90
Oregon, 115, 175
  Marion County, 120
  Salem, 120
Orton
  Irma L. (Kreager), 83
  Isabella (Ayers), 83
  William, 83
Ostrander, Maybelle, 143
Otto, Sheryl, 2

P

Pacific Branch of the National Home, Sawtelle, Los Angeles County, California, 153
Pacific Ocean, 27
Page
  Charles, 201
  Elizabeth (Perkins), 201
  Myrtle M. (Smith), 44, 201
Parker, Mary (See), 77
Parks
  Abigail (Welch?), 45
  Caroline (Scholes) (Ellison), 20, 45-49
  William [Caroline's brother], 47
  William Norman, 45
Parrott, Gertrude (Jones), 183
Pattee, Edith (Topping), 127
Pauley
  Ira, 76
  Lavina (-?-), 76
  Marietta (Chesley), 76
Peake
  Edna (Scholes), 67, 146, 273

    Joseph, 273
    Lulu (Loveland0, 273
Pederson/Pedersen
    Anna (Winthur), 283
    Arthur J., 283
    Oluf, 283
    Oretta Ethlyn (Scholes) (Smith) (Cruger), 283
Pennsylvania, 77
    Beaver Falls, 241
    Coudersport, 248
    Drexel Hill, Delaware County, 289, 292
    Drexel Hill, Upper Darby Township, 256, 290
    Lancaster, Lancaster County, 276, 278
    Philadelphia, 210, 290, 291
    Pittsburgh, 239, 242, 245
    Potter County, 245
    Rochester, Beaver County, 240, 248
    Upper Darby, 291
    Upper Saucon Township, 248
    Warren, Warren County, 249
    Williamsport, Lycoming County, 276
Pensions, 18, 26, 31, 47
Perkins, Elizabeth (Page), 201
Peterson
    Anna (-?-), 141
    Gladys Anna Elizabeth (Christopherson), 141
    Gottfried, 141
    Gust A., 221-223, 231, 292
    Mr. & Mrs. Sheldon, 219, 224
Philippines, 286
Phillips, Harriet E., 236
Pixley, Louise (Rood), 265
Ploss, Fred M., 206
Politics, 2, 31, 33, 58, 171, 242
Pomplin
    Elmer Emil, 223, 224
    Emil F., 223
    Ida Amelia (Maik), 223

       Lula E. (Van Alstine) (Sanford), 224
       Mr. & Mrs. Elmer Pomplin, 231
       Wilbur, 224
Porter
       Marietta (Pauley), 76
       William, 76
Potatoes, 12
Potters' Emigration Society, 2, 6, 9, 12, 14
Potts
       Agnes Otilie "Tillie" (Sherwin) (Kress), 87, 89
       Hassen Louis, 88
       Lorraine (McGaw), 89
Powell
       (early settlers), 14
       Alexander, 52
       Blanch (-?-)
       Glendon, 52
       Hannah (Stokes), 52
       John, 52
       Mary Elizabeth (Ellison), 48, 50-52
Presbyterians, 179, 278
Prestwich, see Lancashire
Probates, 42-43, 47, 281

Q

Quaden
       Alma (-?-), 129
       Bernhard, 129
       Elda Mary (Hume), 129
       Fred Charles, 129
       John, 130
       Ollie, 130
Quinn, Hanna Mountford, 53

R

Raddatz, Wilhelmina Louisa Augusta (Dahms), 211
Radio set (present or absent) as of 1930, 52, 67, 70, 90, 94, 101, 107, 109, 117, 120, 130, 134, 137, 139, 140, 144, 150, 153, 155, 156, 159, 161, 165, 170, 175, 189, 195, 201, 208, 216, 220, 222, 231, 260, 266
Ramsey, Mrs. Barry, 197
Ranney, Nettie L. (Burrington), 91
Real estate, see Land and Property
Redman
      Elizabeth (Mann), 290, 291
      George Mann, 71, 290, 291
      Henry "Harry," 290, 291
      Ruth Emma (Robleske) (Scholes), 3, 71, 256, 292
Reid
      Earl, 135
      Harold, 135
      John, 62
      Leon, 135
      Margaret, 62
      Mr. and Mrs. Ernest, 135
Reinhart
      Angeline (-?-), 182
      Thelma, 182
      Thomas, 182
Remount Squadron, 222
Rhode Island, 246
      West Warwick, Kent County, 245
Rhodes
      Edith Eliza (Russell) (Bell) (Boettcher), 33, 106-108
      Harry Colfax, 107
Riden, Mary (Sutcliff), 133
Ridgway
      Emeline Ursula (Sabin) (Newhart) (Chesley) (See), 76-77
      George, 77

Riffe, Florence Lucinda (Murner), 131
Riverside Park (Portage), 35
Robinson
    C. A., 248
    Louise (Watson), 248
    Lloyd W., 248
Robleske
    Antone Robleske/Wrobleski, 289
    Leo E., 71, 289
    Ruth Emma (Scholes) (Redman), 3, 71, 256
Rodderfeld, Wilma Rae (Buskager), 217, 225
Rodger
    David, 114
    Elizabeth M. (Berry), 114, 115, 145
    Lucy (Burwell), 114
Rogers, Anna C. (Bohan), 167
Rood
    Albert W., 265
    Louise (Pixley), 265
    Mary Elsie (Scholes), 67, 154, 159, 265, 266
    Morris, 167
    Sarah "Sally" Lyle (Hume), 167
    Susanna (-?-), 167
Russell, 260, 263
    Caroline L. (Gaylord), 106, 259
    Clayton, 33, 150
    Dorothey, 33
    Edith Eliza (Bell) (Rhodes) (Boettcher), 33, 106-108, 145, 259
    Elayne Venetta (Hinze), 261, 262
    Fred Gaylord, 67, 107, 196, 259, 261
    Harland, 33
    Henry Lyman, 32, 33
    James, 33
    Lillian Estelle (Scholes), 67, 196, 197, 257, 259, 261, 292
    Lorin J. Russell, 106-107, 259
    Martha (Hume), 32, 33
    Mr. & Mrs. Clayton, 151

Roberta, 33, 151
Wayne, 33, 150, 151
William E., 62

S

Sabin, Emeline Ursula (Newhart) (Ridgway) (Chesley), 76-77
Sanford
    Frank, 224
    Lula E. (Van Alstine) (Pomplin), 224
Sawyer
    Charlotte (Manley), 95
    Lizzie Sarah (Carson), 163
    Lydia Albert "Birdie" (Hume) (Jones), 32, 151, 163
Schauer, Arnold, 224
Schirmer, Caroline (Kunow), 129
Schoenofen, Katherine (Steinmetz), 210
Scholes, 7, 14, 263
    Addison Boren, 248
    Alice (Smith), 6, 15, 18-21, 39, 41-43
    Ann (Colvin), 1, 3
    Ann (Mills) (emigrant), 1, 9, 11, 14, 18, 20, 24, 26, 37, 256
    Bonnie Elizabeth, 1, 3, 58-59, 235-237
    Caroline Cornelia (Parks) (Ellison), 20, 45-49
    Church window (1954), 15
    Doris Emily (Hahn), 3, 243
    Dorothy/Dorthey M. (Markhardt) (Murray), 268, 269
    Edna (Peake), 67, 146, 273, 275
    Eldred, 274
    Eleanor "Nellie," 1, 57-59, 233, 237
    Elizabeth "Betty," 6, 15, 19, 20, 21, 26, 37-39, 43, 63, 86
    Ellen (Tetlow) (supposed sister of William the emigrant), 12
    Elmer Roy, 39, 67, 196, 237, 265
    Emma Maria (Hull), 22, 69, 71, 134, 285
    George Walker, 18-20, 22, 38, 46, 62, 65-67, 87

George Stanley, 276
Hannah Ellen, 21
Harriet C. "Hattie" (Schwemerlein), 47, 49, 196, 209, 229
Harriet Eloise (Bassett), 250, 251
Harriet Newell (Mozley), 21, 38, 55-59, 62, 152, 237
James Bert, 1, 250-253
James Mills (youngest son of emigrants William and Ann), 14, 18-20, 22, 62, 69-71, 87, 134, 150
James (supposed brother of William the emigrant), 12
Jean Ardis (Kissinger), 275
Jeanne Anna (Ashmead) (Boggs), 276
John (supposed brother of William the emigrant), 12
Laura Anna, 59
Lillian Estelle (Russell), 67, 196, 197, 257, 259
Lois Elizabeth (Boren), 59, 239, 240, 242
Maria, 6, 21
Marion Edith, 63, 87, 135, 231, 255, 260, 275, 291-293
Marjorie E. (Gray), 267, 268
Mary Elizabeth (Heames), 47, 49, 215, 217
Mary Ellen (Dixon), 21, 62, 63
Mary Elsie (Rood), 67, 154, 159, 266, 292
Mary H. (Heames), 215
Mary (Sherwin), 6, 15, 19, 20, 23, 24, 25, 26, 27, 39
Mildred Ilene (Wilcox), 270
Nettie A. (Moran), 47, 48, 63, 205, 209
Norman, 1, 256
Pearl Alida (Edwards) (Schulenberg), 71, 279-281, 283, 291
Oretta Ethlyn (Pederson/Pedersen) (Smith) (Cruger), 283
Robert (son of William and Ann), 6, 14, 18-21, 45-47, 63, 66
Robert Henry (son of James, grandson of William and Ann), 39, 71, 279-281, 283
Ruth Emma (Robleske) (Redman), 3, 71, 256, 289-292
Samuel Eugene, 62, 196, 256, 260, 273, 275
Samuel Mills (son of William and Ann), 14, 18, 19, 38, 55, 56
Samuel Ray, 2, 59, 234, 235, 239, 240, 256

Samuel Ray Jr., 242-245
Sarah Ann (Hume), 1, 6, 14, 15, 18-20, 29, 30
Stella (Larson), 1, 285-287
Susanna Rebecca (Audiss), 22, 46, 65-67
Unknown child, 63
Verna, 260
Virginia May (Woodring/Robinson), 248
William (son of William and Ann), 14, 18-21, 39, 61, 63
William (the emigrant), 1, 3, 5, 9, 11, 12, 14-20, 26, 37, 43, 153, 256

Schooling, years completed, 50, 52, 80, 83, 89, 93, 101, 107, 109, 116, 120, 124, 127, 130, 134, 137, 138, 141, 144, 151, 152, 155, 156, 159, 161, 166, 170, 176, 180, 186, 188, 195, 199, 201, 203, 206, 218, 220, 223, 225, 230, 260, 261, 266, 267, 269, 274, 283, 291, 292

Schoville
Lloyd, 204
Maida (Bailey), 204
Ruth Rachel Etta (Smith), 204

Schrieber
Ethel Esther (Sherwin) (Austin), 91-93
William Henry, 93

Schulenberg
Pearl Alida (Edwards) (Scholes), 71, 279-281, 283, 286, 291
William H., 281

Schwemerlein, 51
A. H., 230
Catherine (Marman), 229
Conrad, 229
Harriet C. "Hattie" (Scholes), 47, 49, 196, 209, 229-232
Rodney/J. Roddy/John C., 49, 229

Scotland, 86
Linlithgowshire, 29

See
Emeline Ursula (Sabin) (Newhart) (Ridgway), 77
James, 77
Mary (Parker), 77

William H., 77
Shalkop/Schellkopf, Sarah J. (Evans), 108
Sharp, Lily (Emert), 176
Shaw
    Bertha (Mountford), 144
    (early settlers), 14
    Joseph W., 144
    Lila Edith (Hume), 144
Sheep, 20
Sherwin, 62
    Agnes Otilie "Tillie" (Potts) (Kress), 87-89
    Amanda (Jones), 24, 26
    Annie (Henry), 27, 87
    Bissell, cover, 15-17, 20, 23-27
    Bissell Sr., 24-26
    Charles Truman, 27, 73, 74, 78, 106
    Charlotte May (Bohlig), 98, 101-103
    Edith Mary (Johnson) (Burrington), 85, 89
    Elbridge James, 75, 80-81
    Ethel Esther (Austin) (Schrieber), 91-93
    Eustice, 81
    Experience (Whitney), 23
    Flora Ann (Bell), 105
    Florence Anora "Flossie" (Munro) (Lamb) (Kreager), 27, 62, 75, 80-82
    Francis Roderick "Frank," 27, 38, 62, 85
    George Herbert, 24, 26, 28
    Harriet M. (Manley) (Jones), 2, 27, 95, 98, 99, 101, 103
    Herbert M., 97, 98, 101
    Ira Truman, 27, 75, 78-81
    Jane "Jennie" Thressa (Young) (Chesley), 27, 73-76, 78, 80
    Herbert Manley, 99, 103
    Lottie Mazie (Taylor), 27, 96, 98
    Margaret Matilda (Arnsdorf), 3, 100, 103
    Mary (Scholes), 6, 15, 19, 23-27, 39, 74, 106
    Myrtle "Mirty" T., 78
    Ray Forest, 63, 87, 88, 93, 135, 260

    Unknown child, 81
    Wayland, 79
    William Orlando, 26, 27, 39, 62, 63, 95, 96, 99, 135, 151
Ships
    Marmion, 12
    Themistocles, 117
Sickles, Anna (Cruger), 284
Siegler oil heater, 191
Signatures (as written)
    Austin, Lawrence B., 92
    Berry, Robert B., 116
    Bohlig, John Ellsworth, 104
    Ellison, Caroline C., 48
    Finger, Paul 191
    Heames, George R., 218
    Hume, James, 165
    Hume, Lloyd E., 138
    Hume, V. W., 142
    Kreager, Vern, 84
    Maltby, Willis Elisha, 153
    Markhardt, Darwin A., 269
    Moran, A. C., 211
    Murray, Wm. E., 270
    Quaden, Fred Chas., 130
    Scholes, Ann, 12
    Scholes, Elizabeth, 39
    Scholes, George W., 67
    Scholes, James M., 71
    Scholes, Jean Anna (Ashmead) (Boggs), 276
    Scholes, Robert, 46
    Scholes, Robert Henry, 281
    Scholes, Sam E., 274
    Sherwin, Ira T., 79
    Sherwin, Harriet M., 97
    Sherwin, Mary, 26, 27
    Smith, Alice, 43
    Smith, Robert J., 201
Sisk, Mattie Cardlie (Smith), 173

Skinner
    (early settlers), 14
    Enoch, 53
Slater
    Maebelle (Etkington), 142
    Olive Mae (Hume) (Nordness), 142, 143
    Thomas E., 142
Smith
    Alice Sarah (Hume), 32, 123
    Alice (Scholes), 6, 15, 18-21, 38, 42, 43
    Bernice I. (Finger), 189
    Betty, 42
    Charles W., 199, 200
    Charlotte Annie (Thompson), 203
    Clinton William, 63, 186-188, 196
    Donald, 283
    Donald Harrison Smith, 201, 203
    Electa (Condit), 200
    Elizabeth E. (-?-), 200
    Ella/Eva Florance, 42, 44
    Elwyn Robert "Red" Smith 204
    Esther Lydia (Hume) (Jenkins) (Walton), 172-176
    Evangeline (Leghorn), 188, 189
    Florence Eva (Beichl), 44, 63, 193
    George Walter, 173
    Grace E. (Hall) (Dewsnap), 35
    Henry, 41, 42
    Isaac, 123
    James, 42
    Jane, 42
    John S., 200
    Joseph Cockcroft., 18, 21, 38, 41-43
    Joseph [Jr.?], 42
    Marie E. (Olson), 173
    Martha, 42
    Mattie Cardlie (Sisk), 173
    Mary (Ellison) [Mrs. Isaac], 123, 125
    Mary Irene, 42-44, 191, 199, 200, 231

Myrtle M. (Page), 44
Oretta Ethlyn (Scholes) (Pederson/Pedersen) (Cruger), 283
Oritis Elmer "Ready," 173-175
Ralph Ray, 188, 189, 196, 197
Robert Joseph, 42-44, 197, 199, 201, 202, 256, 260
Rose Ruth (Haines), 43, 185, 186
Ruth Rachel Etta (Schoville), 204
William, 42, 63
William Henry, 43, 63, 185, 186
Zillah (Cockroft), 41

South Dakota, 32, 131, 269
Clear Lake, 76
Clinton County, 112
Clinton Township, Miner County, 115
Davison County, 111
Deuel County, 76
Fedora, Miner County, 112
Gregory, Gregory County, 269
Hutchinson County, 131
Lake County, 114
Roswell, Miner County, 114, 115
Sioux Falls, Minnehaha County, 111, 112, 114-118, 120, 150
Watertown, Codington County, 76

Sovereign, Charlotte (Chesley), 75
Spicer, Caroline Adelia (Maltby), 153
Sprit, Esther (Henry), 85
Stagg, A. A., 240
Stallard
Ethel Fern, 78, 79
Henry Wallace, 78
Ida May (Stiles), 78
Stanton (early settlers), 14
Steinmetz
Katherine (Schoenofen), 210
Olivia A. (Moran), 210
Theodore, 210

Stewart, Mr. & Mrs. Lloyd, 151
Stiles, Ida May (Stallard), 78
Stocks, Alice (Mills), 9, 11-12
Stockwell, Orin, 81
Stokes, Hannah (Powell), 52
Stories: 57, 119, 145, 169
Stratton
    Albert, 75, 80
    William G., 171
Strong, Lt. Colonel, 25, 27
Stuiber, Mary B., 100
Success Magazine, 234
Sutcliff(e)
    (early settlers), 14
    Edward, 133
    Eliza May "Lida" (Hume), 32, 133
    Mary (Riden), 133
Swannell, Fred, 135
Sweden, 52, 221
Swiss German 155

T

Table 1: Scholes-Ellison families, 54
Table 2: Scholes and Russell, allied families, 263
Taylor
    Emma F. (-?-), 96, 98, 99
    Lottie Mazie (Sherwin), 27, 96
    Maude (Hemstock), 99
    Mrs. E. C., 196
    Nathan, 218
    Vine E., 96, 98
Telephone lines, 164
Tennessee, 16, 251
    Chattanooga, 30

Tetlow, Ellen (supposed sister of William Scholes the emigrant), 12
Texas
    Amarillo, 82
    Burleson County, 185
    New Braunfels, Cowal County, 275
    Potter County, 82
Thackeray, Dr. Robert, 140
Thayer
    Charles Russell, 226
    Dora Adelia (Fry), 226
    Mary Avis (Moungey), 226
    Wilma Rae (Heames) (Buskager) 217, 225, 226
Thomas
    Norma, 277
    Norman, 242
    Ruby (Walton), 174
Thompson
    Charlotte Annie (Smith), 203
    Edith (Farmer), 203
    Edward, 203
Thornton
    Charles Roscoe, 182
    Mamie B. (-?-), 182
    Thelma (Reinhart), 182
    Vera Lois (Jones/Hume) (Banks), 182, 183
    William P., 182
Topping
    Edith (Pattee) Topping, 127, 219-221
    Elizabeth E. "Beth" (Jones) (Hume), 127, 145
    Gracia (Heames), 219-221
    James, 127, 219
    Jed L., 220
    Mr. and Mrs. Harland, 135
Topping-Grover reunion, 220
Torkelson, Theoline (Hansen) (Larson), 87, 88
Trimbell
    Byron, 187

Florence Jennie (Smith), 187
Zaida (Leete), 187
Truk Atoll, 277
Turner
Fred Sr., 151
Mrs. Fredrick Jr., 151
Tuttle, Lawrence, 135
Twigg/Twiggs, Thomas, 13, 14

U

Unitarian Universalists, 240, 242, 247
Utah, 152
Utke, Gus, 188

V

Van Alstine, Lula E. (Sanford) (Pomplin), 224
Van Damme, Art, 283
Van Natta, Elizabeth (Mozley), 56
Veterans Administration Hospital, 210
Virginia
Buena Vista, 256, 275
Fair Oaks, 24-26
Franklin (independent city), 276
Newport News (independent city), 276
Petersburg, 17
Portsmouth, 276
Radford, 276
Roanoke, 276
Zuni, 276
Voertman
Alma, 135
Arthur L., 34, 135, 151
Martha Elizabeth Sarah Ann (Hume), 34

Voss, Barbara, 2
Voter Registration, 151, 153, 154, 156, 162, 166, 220
Vroman, Elizabeth W. (McGowan), 155

W

Wade
    (early settlers), 14
    Lois M., 2
    Sarah (Dixon), 257
Wagner, Carrie (Evans), 109
Walker, Ann/Margaret (Hume), 29, 171
Walters, Priscilla (Ellison), 46, 52
Walton
    Esther Lydia (Hume) (Jenkins) (Smith), 172-176
    Hilbert Eugene, 174-176
    Oscar Hilbert, 174
    Ruby (Thomas), 174
War of 1812 land warrant, 15
Warren, Gladys J. (Gray), 167
Washington, 150, 169
    Asotin County, 173
    Bremerton, 204
    Clarkston, 173
    Colfax, 176
    Everett, 156
    Garfield, 165, 167, 170
    Garfield County, 173
    King County, 102
    Kitsap County, 204
    Peola, 173
    Pomeroy, 173
    Rosalie, 171
    Seattle, 247
    Snohomish County, 156
    Spokane, Spokane County, 120

Tacoma, 102
Vancouver Barracks, 100, 101
Whitman County, 167, 176
Watson
(early settlers), 14
Grace Fay (Walton), 174
Louise (Robinson0, 248
May (Dixon), 156
Ruth (Bennett), 158
Weaver, Elizabeth (Kissinger), 275
Welch (?), Abigail, 45
Wells (early settlers), 14
West Virginia, Moundsville, 241
White
Beatrice Lewis (Jones), 162
Harry J., 162
Louise (-?-), 162
Whitney, Experience (Sherwin), 23
Whitson, Selena, 151
Wilcox
Alfred, 270
Isobel (Berry), 270
Mildred Ilene (Scholes), 270
Wilkins, Charlotte M. (Williamson), 225
Williams, Mrs. G. R., 62
Williamson
Charlotte M. (Wilkins), 225
Elizabeth (Leghorn), 188
John Albert, 225
Leslie E., 225
Winthur, Anna (Pedersen), 283
Wisconsin, 1-3, 5-7, 9, 11-14, 16, 20-27, 30-34, 37-39, 41, 42, 44-53, 55-58, 61-63, 65-67, 69, 70, 73-79, 81, 85-89, 91, 92, 94-96, 98-100, 102, 105-109, 111, 114, 115, 120, 123, 125, 127-131, 134-145, 149, 151, 152, 154, 156-160, 163, 164, 166, 171, 172, 176, 181-183, 185-191, 193, 195, 199-201, 203-211, 215-222, 224-227, 229-233, 239, 241, 251, 255-257, 259-261, 265, 267-270, 273, 274, 276, 277, 280, 281, 283-285, 287, 291

Adams County, 108, 109, 229
Adrian Township, Monroe County, 27, 85
Albion, Dane County, 289
Arlington, 227, 269
Baraboo, 129, 136, 142
Beaver Dam, 62, 63, 193, 195, 196
Beloit, Rock County, 141, 197, 202, 256, 260, 274, 285
Black Earth, 233
Black River Falls, 78, 79, 81, 96
Brandon, Fond du Lac County, 274, 277
Briggsville, Marquette County, 47, 109, 127, 136, 230, 267, 285
Brooklyn, 51
Buffalo, 22, 107, 188
Buffalo Township, Marquette County, 42, 69, 70, 124, 139, 186, 265
Caledonia Township, Columbia County, 129
Cashton, 87-88
Clark County, 78
Clinton, 201, 203
Columbia County, 21, 30, 34, 45, 57, 62, 63, 73, 85, 95, 105, 115, 126-129, 134, 138, 142-145, 152, 156, 185, 186, 188, 199, 205, 218, 226, 227, 259, 261, 270, 274, 290
Columbus, Columbia County, 268
Crawford County, 204
Cudahy, 144
Dalton, 62, 187, 188, 196
Dane County, 91, 135, 142, 143, 225, 226, 268, 281, 283, 286
Dartford, 38
Davis Corners, 229
DeForest, 225, 268
Delavan, 257
Dividing Ridge, 38
Dodge County, 62, 63
Douglas, Marquette County, 267
Dunn Township, Dane County, 281
Eau Claire, Eau Claire County, 100

Elkhorn, 46
Endeavor, 22, 30, 33, 39, 46, 49, 52, 53, 66, 67, 69, 124, 129, 131, 136, 137, 139, 144, 155, 158, 164, 166, 183, 186-187, 196, 201, 209, 216, 217, 221, 224, 225, 229, 257, 260, 261, 273, 276, 285
Fairfield, 226
Florence County, 221
Fond du Lac County, 274, 277
Fort Winnebago, 27, 57, 62, 70, 73, 105, 152, 156, 290
Fox River, 14
Green Bay, 182
Greenfield Township, Monroe County, 95, 106
Green Lake, 223
Green Lake County, 21, 51, 56, 58, 62, 187-189, 196
Hales Corners, 131
Homestead Township, Florence County, 221
Humbird, 78
Iowa County, 63, 285
Irving Township, Jackson County, 75
Jackson County, 75, 76, 78, 79, 81, 96
Jackson Township, Adams County, 109
Janesville, 201, 203
Jefferson County, 32, 123, 182
Kenosha, 284
Kilbourne, 280
King, Waupaca County, 273
Kingston, 62, 187
La Crosse, 87, 93, 96,
La Crosse County, 96, 98
La Grange Township, Monroe County, 106
Lake Mills, 182
Leeds Center, 227
Leeds Township, Columbia County, 226
Leon Township, Monroe County, 88
Lincoln County, 143
Madison, 135, 137, 143, 151, 158, 203, 226, 227, 265, 280, 283, 284
Marathon County, 48, 205

Marcellon, 70, 151
Marcellon Township, Columbia County, 42
Marinette, 233
Marquette County, 14, 20-23, 25, 32, 34, 41, 42, 46, 47, 49-51, 65, 69, 107, 108, 111, 114, 123, 127, 129, 136, 138, 142, 144, 149, 154, 157-160, 179, 181, 183, 188, 202, 229, 230, 259, 261, 265, 267, 268, 273, 285
Marquette (village), 21, 56, 233, 235, 239
Moundville, Marquette County, 2, 16, 20-22, 30, 31, 33, 34, 37, 41, 45-50, 52, 55, 65, 69, 70, 107, 114, 124-126, 134, 144, 149, 154, 157, 159, 160, 164, 204, 215, 217, 219, 222, 224, 260, 269, 275, 279
Moundville Township, Marquette County, 133, 138, 139, 143, 154, 158, 181, 183, 219, 220, 237, 259, 265, 273, 289
Marshfield, Wood County, 283
Merrittville (Merritt's Landing) (later Endeavor), 66, 145
Milton, 251
Milwaukee, 13, 30, 33, 50-52, 94, 127, 135-137, 142, 151, 183, 190, 210, 211, 231
Milwaukee County, 49, 50, 94, 131, 137, 138, 144
Milwaukee County Farm, 190
Mineral Point, 63, 280, 285
Monona, Dane County, 285
Monroe County, 16, 20, 23-27, 63, 73, 74, 78, 81, 85-89, 92, 95, 98, 99, 102, 105-108, 135, 151
Montello, 49, 189, 260
Mosinee, 233
Neenah, 151
Neshkoro, 224
New Haven Township, Adams County, 108, 109
New Richmond, 91
Newton Township, Marquette County, 267
Oregon, Dane County, 281, 283
Oshkosh, 21, 55
Oxford, 51, 108, 109, 135, 267
Packwaukee, 20, 23, 25
Packwaukee Township, Marquette County, 136
Pardeeville, 63, 186, 187, 189-191

Plainfield, 151
Portage, 21, 30, 31, 33, 34, 37, 39, 44, 53, 61-63, 66, 67, 115, 125-127, 134, 135, 138, 142-145, 151, 164, 171, 181, 187, 189, 195, 199-201, 207, 209, 215, 216, 218, 219, 226, 230, 231, 255, 259-261, 270, 280, 287, 290, 291
Portage County, 139, 219
Port Hope, 14, 30, 57
Poynette, 33, 134
Prairie du Chien, 53
Prairie du Sac, 33, 151
Princeton, 51, 189
Racine, 105, 140
Racine County, 105
Randolph, 62
Ridgeville Township, Monroe County, 24, 26, 27, 86, 105, 106, 108
Ripon, 56
Rock County, 141, 201, 203, 251
Rock County Sheriff's Department, 203
Rock Hill, 187
Rockland, 87
Sauk County, 129, 136, 142, 226, 267
Shorewood Village, 137
Soldiers Grove, 204
Sparta, 20, 23, 25-27, 37, 39, 62, 63, 73, 74, 78, 81, 85-88, 95, 98, 99, 102, 107, 135, 151, 260
Spring Prairie, 105
St. Croix County, 91
Stevens Point, 115, 224
Stockton, 127, 219
Stoughton, 142, 287
Sun Prairie, 91, 225-226
Tomah, 89, 92, 105
Tomahawk, 143
Trenton, 193
Tunnel City, 62-63, 105
Walworth County, 46, 105
Waterloo, Jefferson County, 284

Waubesa Beach, 281, 283, 286
Waukesha, 47, 49, 50, 63, 129, 131, 205, 206, 208, 209, 230-232
Waukesha County, 47, 50, 63, 129, 131, 205, 206, 208, 209
Waupaca, 23
Wausau, 240
Waushara County, 183
Wautoma, 183, 223
Wauwatosa, 49, 190, 205, 210, 211, 231
Watertown, 32, 123, 127
West Allis, 50, 94, 137
Westfield, 140, 145, 155, 223, 224, 231, 261, 267, 269, 274
Whitefish Bay, 138
Winnebago County, 21, 55
Wisconsin Dells, 109, 203, 224, 261
Wisconsin Rapids, 182
Wood, 210
Wyocena, 142, 144, 185, 186, 188-191, 200, 270

Wisconsin General Hospital, 50
Wisconsin River, 53
Wisconsin State Highway Commission, 260
Wisconsin Veterans Home, 275
Wollenburg, John, 195
Women's Christian Temperance Union (WCTU), 255
Woodring
    Gladys (Murray), 248
    Millard H., 248
    Virginia May, 248
World War I, 51, 82, 84, 93, 100, 126, 137, 153, 183, 188, 202, 210, 212, 217-219, 222 (see also "remount squadron"), 274
World War II, 91, 143, 161, 204, 252, 273, 274, 277, 284, 285
Wright, Collette, 256

Y

Ylvisaker, Sena (Markhardt), 268
Young
      Jane "Jennie" Thressa (Sherwin) (Chesley), 27, 73-76, 78
      John, 73
      Susan Drusilla (Brown), 73

Z

Zielsdorf family, 80

#

www.ingramcontent.com/pod-product-compliance
Lightning Source LLC
Chambersburg PA
CBHW071649160426
43195CB00012B/1400